ADVANCES IN INDUSTRIAL AND LABOR RELATIONS

Volume 7 • 1996

ADVANCES IN INDUSTRIAL AND LABOR RELATIONS

Editors: DAVID LEWIN
Anderson Graduate School of Management
University of California, Los Angeles (UCLA)

BRUCE E. KAUFMAN
W.T. Beebe Institute of Personnel and Employment
Relations and Department of Economics
Georgia State University

DONNA SOCKELL
School of Management and Labor Relations
Rutgers University

VOLUME 7 • 1996

 JAI PRESS INC.

Greenwich, Connecticut ·   *London, England*

CONTENTS

LIST OF CONTRIBUTORS

Robert S. Atkin

Joseph M. Katz Graduate School of
Business
University of Pittsburgh

Chang-Ruey Ay

Institute of Business Administration
National Chung Cheng University

Karen E. Boroff

W. Paul Stillman School of Busineess
Seton Hall University

John T. Delaney

College of Business Administration
University of Iowa

Morley Gunderson

Centre for Industrial Relations
University of Toronto

Derek C. Jones

Department of Economics
Hamilton College

Bruce E. Kaufman

W.T. Beebe Institute of Personnel and
Employment Relations and
Department of Economics
Georgia State University

Morris M. Kleiner

Humphrey Institute and Industrial
Relations Center
University of Minnesota

David Lewin

Anderson Graduate School of
Management
University of California, Los Angeles
(UCLA)

Marick F. Masters

Joseph M. Katz Graduate School of
Business
University of Pittsburgh

Motohiro Morishima   Faculty of Policy Management
                                         Keio University

Anil Verma   Centre for Industrial Relations
                                         Univeristy of Toronto

David Weil   School of Management
                                         Boston University

SERIES EDITORS' INTRODUCTION

Volume 7 of *Advances in Industrial and Labor Relations* (AILR) contains selected papers which were originally presented to the fourth Bargaining Group Conference at the University of Toronto in October 1994 and other papers which were received by the editors of AILR through the regular manuscript submission process. Readers should note that all of these papers were subjected to AILR's double-blind refereeing process.

For the Bargaining Group Conference papers, Professor Morley Gunderson and Anil Verma of the University of Toronto serve as AILR guest editors. They have also written their own introductory paper which identifies the key themes from the Toronto conference, offers a framework for the analysis of the evolution of industrial relations systems across national borders, and provides a summary and integration of the conference papers within these themes and analytical framework. We are grateful to Gunderson and Verma for their contributions to AILR in these respects and as well for hosting the Fourth Bargaining Group Conference.

As to the other papers appearing in Volume 7 of AILR, these are briefly summarized as follows. First, Marick F. Masters and Robert S. Atkin examine the financial power (as reflected in standard accounting measures) of 11 major public sector unions operating at the federal, state, and local government levels in the United States. Their focus is on how the financial power of these unions changed as their membership growth rates declined during the 1980s. The authors' data sources include financial reports filed under the Labor-Management Reporting and Disclosure (Landrum-Griffin) Act of 1959 and reports on union membership and collective agreement coverage filed with the U.S. Office of Personnel Management.

Advances in Industrial and Labor Relations, Volume 7, pages ix-xii.
Copyright © 1996 by JAI Press Inc.
All rights of reproduction in any form reserved.
ISBN: 1-55938-925-7

Three findings from this paper are especially notable: (1) the financial power of public sector unions appears to be less than that of private sector unions; (2) there is a significant free-rider problem, as evidenced by the large number of public sector employees who are represented by unions and covered by collective agreements, but who do not pay union dues; and (3) in spite of these problems and the slower growth of public sector unions than in the two prior decades, these unions' financial circumstances improved rather than deteriorated during the 1980s. These are important findings since, in the United States as elsewhere, it is in the public sector that unions have recently been most prominent and have increased/sustained their memberships. Whether the public sector unions studied by Masters and Atkin will be able to maintain their financial strength with even slower future membership growth rates or absolute declines in membership remains to be determined, however. Stated differently, it is unclear whether the findings from Masters and Atkin's study will be replicated if and as public sector unions in the United States move deeper into stages of membership stabilization/decline.

Next, John T. Delaney examines the extent to which human resource (HR) innovations affect organizational outcomes and the extent to which these effects differ between union and nonunion settings. His analysis is based on an extensive survey of executives from 495 U.S. business units of U.S.-based corporate enterprises. While the response rate to the survey was only a little over 6%, the respondents were generally representative of large publicly-held U.S. business units.

Ten HR innovations were analyzed: (1) flexible job designs, (2) employee involvement, (3) profit sharing, (4) grievance procedures, (5) information sharing, (6) attitudes, (7) flexible scheduling, (8) day-care programs, (9) paternity leave programs, and (10) employee counseling. Two organizational outcomes were measured, namely, employee turnover and employee support for change (with such support generally being regarded as necessary for managerial flexibility to enhance organizational performance).

Among the key empirical findings are the following: HR innovations generally have positive effects on organizational outcomes; these positive effects prevail in a variety of settings—unionized and nonunion business units, large and small organizations, and high- and low-wage industries; the positive organizational effects of HR innovations are stronger in unionized than in nonunion settings.

These results suggest that innovative HR practices can have positive organizational impacts, specifically reduced employee turnover and increased employee support for change and flexibility, across a wide variety of workplace settings and diverse work groups. Such innovations are especially important in enabling managers and workers to cope with the pressures emanating from increased global competition (including competition of the type described later in this volume by Gunderson and Verma). And since the positive effects of the HR innovations were larger/stronger in unionized than in nonunion settings, such practices should not be regarded as union-like substitutes or as emanating primarily from management desires to avoid/reduce employee unionization.

Both analogous to and different from Delaney, David Weil argues that unions can enhance the implementation and enforcement of a wide range of macro-level labor policies, thereby facilitating achievement of the objectives of these policies. Unions do so by reducing the costs and enhancing the benefits of enforcement and complaints. Thus, unions can amortize the fixed cost of carrying forth a complaint over a larger number of employees and can protect complainants from reprisals for making complaints. Further, unions can internalize the collective benefits that may occur to the full workforce. In contrast, individuals may be reluctant to complain for fear of reprisal and because they may bear most of the costs of complaint filing, while the benefits may be spread over the larger workforce.

Weil documents how unions have enhanced implementation and enforcement of a wide range of policy initiatives: overtime regulations under the Fair Labor Standards Act (FLSA), inspections and enforcement of workplace health and safety under the Occupational Safety and Health Act (OSHA) and the Mine Safety and Health Act (MSHA), advance notification requirements under the Worker Adjustment and Retraining Notification Act (WARN), workers' compensation claims, and the receipt of unemployment insurance. The evidence with respect to pension plans is more mixed, with unions reducing the likelihood of having liberal vesting requirements and unfunded pension liabilities, but not having much impact on the investment decisions and portfolios of pension funds. With respect to comparable worth initiatives, unions tend to diminish their impact on reducing the male-female pay gap because of their opposition to lowering the pay of men as part of that process.

Overall, Weil argues that unions have been important in enhancing the effectiveness of national labor policy initiatives in the United States. Therefore, he contends, the decline of unionization in the United States has created a labor policy "enforcement gap," not just a worker "representation gap." Weil then offers recommendations for overcoming the enforcement gap: enhancing the enforcement capabilities of regulatory agencies, including by having them simultaneously enforce the various policies under their respective jurisdictions; enhancing individual rights in enforcement through heightened educational efforts, information dissemination, and guarantees against reprisals; and possible creation of employee councils at the workplace.

Readers of AILR may care to speculate whether these recommendations for enhanced enforcement of macro-level labor policies are akin to recent micro-level policies of employee involvement and participation adopted by business enterprises in that both sets of initiatives have a certain "substitution for unionism" underpinning. However, Delaney and perhaps Masters and Atkin as well would likely caution us that unionism per se is not inconsistent with and can even enhance the "enforcement" of both micro-level employee participation initiatives and macro-level labor policies.

With this volume, Professor Bruce Kaufman of Georgia State University joins David Lewin and Donna Sockell as an editor of AILR. The editors are also pleased to announce a new publication arrangement involving AILR between JAI Press, publishers of the series, and the Executive Board of the Industrial Relations Research Association (IRRA). Beginning in 1996, a joint AILR-IRRA call for papers on selected topics will be issued annually. These topics will form the basis for sessions to be held at the IRRA's annual meeting and for AILR refereeing of papers submitted competitively for these sessions. Papers accepted through this process will then be presented at the annual IRRA meeting and subsequently published in AILR. In 1996, the topics which provided the basis for the first AILR-IRRA call for papers were "New Forms of Work Organization: Impacts on Enterprises and Employees," and "Labor Organization in New Contexts: Innovation in Organizing, Bargaining and Representation." In addition to papers solicited through this jointly-sponsored competition with the IRRA, AILR will continue to publish on a regular basis high quality papers on all aspects of industrial relations. Submissions may be sent to the Editors of AILR at any time to any of the addresses listed below.

David Lewin
The John Anderson Graduate School of Management
110 Westwood Plaza, Suite A423
Box 951481
Los Angeles, CA 90095-1481

Bruce E. Kaufman
Georgia State University
University Plaza
Atlanta, GA 30303-3083

Donna Sockell
School of Management and Labor Relations
Rutgers University
New Brunswick, NJ 08903

WORKER PROTECTION IN THE NEW GLOBAL ECONOMY:
THE PAST AS PROLOGUE

Morley Gunderson and Anil Verma

ABSTRACT

A framework is provided to analyze changes in the employment relationship that occurred over the period since 1980, with particular emphasis on employee representation in the new global economy. That framework emphasizes the importance of the previous equilibrium in the industrial relations system, the causes of its dissolution, and the forces giving rise to a new equilibrium. The various papers from the Fourth Bargaining Group Conference hosted by the Centre for Industrial Relations at the Conference hosted by the Centre for Industrial Relations at the University of Toronto, and that appear in this issue, are then summarized and integrated into that framework. Those papers dealt with various aspects of employee representations in the new global economy: the economic rationale for the Wagner Act; using grievances to test the exit-voice hypothesis; the impact of alternative forms of employee representation on economic growth; the importance of successor unions in the evolution of industrial relations in former communist countries; and the evolution of white-collar HRM practices in Japans.

Advances in Industrial and Labor Relations, Volume 7, pages 1-13.

The context for business and, by extension, for employment relations, changed markedly during the 1970s and even more dramatically during the 1980s and 1990s. Although not everyone agrees about the present or future impacts of these changes on industrial relations systems, there appears to be general agreement that many of the rules by which labor and management played in the post-World War II period to 1970 came undone during the post-1970 period. To some, these changes represent a throwback to the early part of the twentieth century in which management played the dominant role in employment relations. While there may be some truth in the suggestion that globalization has strengthened management's hand in the employment relationship, the inference that the clock has merely been turned back in time is too simplistic to explain the complex behavior of "actors" in the industrial relations system since 1970. Employee representation through conventional forms of industrial unions may have declined as the main form of employee "voice"; however, other forms of voice and employee involvement have emerged to take up part of the vacuum.

The changing nature of the employment relationship in the new global economy was the focus of the Fourth Bargaining Group Conference, hosted by the Centre for Industrial Relations at the University of Toronto October 14-15, 1994. Dating back to 1978, the Bargaining Group is an informal network of researchers interested in collective bargaining and workplace conflict resolution. Although the Bargaining Group did not sponsor its own events until later, it contributed to the 1980 Nijenrode Conference in the Netherlands and the 1983 and 1987 Arden House Conferences sponsored by Columbia University.[1] Since then, the Bargaining Group has held a conference every two years: at Purdue University in 1988, Cornell University in 1990, the University of California, Berkeley, in 1992, the University of Toronto in 1994, and the University of Minnesota in 1996.[2]

At the 1994 conference in Toronto, a wide range of papers were presented on various aspects of the employment relationship and collective bargaining in the new global economy. While some of those papers have since been published elsewhere, several of them have been revised for publication in this volume of *Advances in Industrial and Labor Relations (AILR)*. These conference papers highlight key themes related to worker representation in the new global economy, especially concerns with current models of the employment relationship (Kaufman; Lewin and Boroff; Kleiner and Ay) and the adaptability of existing models during the transition of industrial relation systems in different countries (Jones; Morishima).

The purpose of this introductory paper is to contribute to our understanding of the evolution of current and evolving industrial relations systems in two ways. First, it presents a framework to analyze the changes in employment relations in the 1980-1996 period. Second, the papers from the Toronto conference that appear in this volume are summarized and integrated into this framework. The role for theory and research is to develop a better understanding of the previous "equilibrium" in the industrial relations system, the causes of its dissolution, and the forces that may be moving us toward a new one. Each of the papers included in this volume contributes to our developing knowledge base about the evolution of industrial relations systems.

CONCEPTUAL FRAMEWORK

One way to understand the evolution of industrial relations systems is to view the process as the attainment of an equilibrium among different stakeholder interests following shocks to the systems. In simple systems, new equilibria can be achieved over a relatively short period of time. However, as systems become larger in size and more complex in nature, as is the case with industrial relations systems, it can take decades for a new system to emerge (Erickson and Kuruvilla 1994).

The landmark study, *Industrialism and Industrial Man* (Kerr, Harbison, Dunlop, and Myers 1964), mapped the development of early transitions in industrial relations systems directly following industrialization. Within the U. S. industrial relations system, after many short-lived mini-equilibria during 1900-1935, a more stable equilibrium emerged in the 1940-1960 period. This evolution has been best described by Dunlop (1993) in his industrial relations system concept but also by others under such labels as the "New Deal" system, Fordist industrial relations, the Wagner Model, and "job control" unionism (Kaufman 1992).

The industrial relations system described by Dunlop is one in which key stakeholders—labor, management, and government—develop procedures and substantive work rules within broader environmental and ideological contexts. In a recently reprinted edition of the 1958 book, Dunlop provides further examples of how U.S. labor and management were able to develop new "rules" to respond to changing market conditions and technology (Dunlop 1993, pp. 32-41). In essence, the argument is that the actors can respond within the existing system to changing contextual conditions. Thus, from this perspective, the existing system is sufficiently flexible and adaptable to changing environmental factors.

With the publication of *The Transformation of American Industrial Relations* (Kochan, Katz, and McKersie 1986), many observers came to agree that the old industrial relations sytem equilibrium had changed irrevocably. Causes of the transformation included globalization, freer trade, industrial restructuring, deregulation, and the privatization of government services and enterprises. It was asserted that the loss of a "shared ideology" between management and labor led to the decline of the collective bargaining system, which resulted in the transformation of industrial relations. Although the transformation thesis remains subject to debate (see, for example, Lewin 1987), there are clear indications that the old system has been sufficiently altered to warrant a search for a new equilibrium with new roles for and expectations of the actors in the system.

The old order involved a system of worker voice and protection based largely on collective bargaining and legislative regulations in a variety of areas: labor standards, worker rights and anti-discrimination in employment, health and safety, workers' compensation, unemployment insurance, and other labor policies. The labor standards protection involved regulation in a variety of areas including minimum pay, holidays, hours of work, overtime pay, and termination.

In the old order, unions could take "wages out of competition" as a result of and to further increase their power in bargaining. In the new order, unions are finding it harder to do so because the business enterprise is often located in another country or continent. Employers have gained increased bargaining power because they can shift (or threaten to shift) production to other jurisdictions or countries. And, even if a particular employer cannot do so, a labor union may be in a situation in which, through bargaining, it risks putting that employer out of business because of greater competition elsewhere. The old adage was that it is necessary to organize up to the level of the product market in which the firm operates. In the old order, that usually meant organizing as much of the domestic industry as possible to reduce nonunion competition from within the industry. In the new order, this requires organizing an industry on a global scale, but international unionism has seldom achieved this level of organization or developed the coordination among nations required to bring it about.

Industrial restructuring in modern developed nations has commonly meant movement away from manufacturing and toward the more polarized service sector, with low-end personal services on the one hand and high-end business and professional services associated with the information economy on the other hand. Concomitantly, this has meant movement away from traditionally unionized sectors and toward nonunion sectors in both lower-end and higher-end services.

Deregulation has also taken its toll on union membership and representation. The previously regulated firms could often simply pass labor cost increases on to consumers in the form of rate and/or price increases. They were protected from nonunion competition by regulations that prevented or inhibited new entry into the industry. With deregulation, nonunion competitors can more easily enter the industry and compete for customers. Since the demand for labor is derived from the demand for the firm's products or services, such increased competition in the product market translates into increased pressure for cost cutting via wage and employment reductions.

Employers and unions are not the only actors who are constrained by the economic environment of the new global economy, however. Governments are under increased pressure to constrain costs because of pressures to reduce budgetary deficits. This translates into either expenditure reductions or tax increases or both. Expenditure reductions imply restraints on public sector wages and employment since labor costs are an especially large component of the total cost of providing public services. Tax increases, which went unchallenged for decades, increasingly appear to be politically unacceptable to the citizenry. Furthermore, such increases can lead to capital flight and plant relocations into jurisdictions or countries with low(er) taxes. This threat of the mobility of financial and physical capital can also put pressure on governments to reduce costly regulatory and legislative initiatives that may otherwise be favorable to labor. In such an environment then, different jurisdictions and countries compete for business investment by reducing taxes and regulatory and legislative costs.

To some, this is characterized as "social dumping" or a "race to the bottom" or "harmonization to the lowest common denominator." To others, it is normal competition simply applied to the political arena, constraining governments to be more sensitive to the cost consequences of their actions. Whatever the label, the outcome is invariably more pressure on governments to restrain their own labor costs and to reduce costly legislative and regulatory interventions in the area of labor protection.

SUMMARY AND INTEGRATION OF THE PAPERS

As indicated above, the following papers can be organized according to certain themes related to worker representation in the new global economy. These are concerns with the current models of the employment relationship, and issues pertaining to the adaptability of the existing models during the transition of industrial relations systems in different countries.

Kaufman and the Economic Rationale for the Wagner Act

While many scholars have argued that the legislative foundation of the U.S. system of labor relations, namely the Wagner Act and its successor the Taft-Hartley Act, has contributed to the decline of U.S. unionism during the 1970-1996 period (Freeman and Medoff 1984; Weiler 1990) and is thus outdated, Bruce E. Kaufman informs and reminds us that support for employee unionism and collective bargaining was, at best, a secondary rationale for this legislation. Based on analysis of literature dealing with the economic rationale for the Wagner Act, the stated rationale in the act itself as articulated at that time by Sen. Wagner and other officials, and examination of the literature on the impact of unions and collective bargaining in light of the rationale for the Act, Kaufman reaches four main conclusions:

1. The economic rationale for the Wagner Act was first and foremost to promote macroeconomic recovery from the depression of 1929-1933 by encouraging unions and collective bargaining. Legislative support for these institutions was aimed at reversing the downward spiral of wages and prices, augmenting purchasing power by redistributing income from capital to labor, and ultimately developing and sustaining higher levels of aggregate demand.

2. While at that time there may have been some merit to the original rationale for the Wagner Act, even then it was a distinctly "second best" approach to

promoting economic recovery and likely did not facilitate the ultimate recovery.

3. In the post-World War II period, a strong consensus developed that monetary and fiscal policies are more effective macroeconomic enhancement and stabilization tools than "labor" policies.

4. At present, the conditions that inspired the original Wagner Act (i.e., high joblessness and especially declining real wages) have re-emerged as serious concerns.

These conclusions appear to be reinforced by the continued rise of global economic competition. That is, such competition further undermines—renders ineffectual—the idea of the Wagner Act as a macroeconomic stabilization device for the United States, even if one were to grant that this idea appeared relatively well suited to an era in which the United States dominated world markets. For labor unions, enhanced global competition requires the organization of workers on an international scale if labor is to be taken out of competition. This is even less likely to occur in the near future than in the recent past—in part and only in part because the Wagner Act model is widely regarded as inhibiting change and as serving only relatively narrowly-defined union interests.

Lewin and Boroff: The Exit-Voice Hypothesis

David Lewin and Karen E. Boroff argue that Hirschman's exit-voice hypothesis implies that, when employees perceive themselves to be in a deteriorating employment relationship, they are more likely to file a grievance (as a form of voice) the greater their degree of loyalty to the firm and the greater their perception that such voice will improve the employment relationship. The expected positive relationship between loyalty to the organization and the use of grievances occurs because employees with a high degree of loyalty to the organization will try to use voice to improve the employment relationship, especially if they perceive that such efforts may be effective. Also following Hirschman, Lewin and Boroff argue that the exit-voice framework implies that employees are more likely to intend to quit the firm (as a form of exit) the lower their degree of loyalty to the organization and the lower they rate the effectiveness of their grievance (i.e., voice) procedure.

The authors test these implications of the exit-voice framework on two data sets. One was derived from a 1991 survey of unionized employees in a U.S.-based multinational telecommunications firm. The survey yielded 3,160 responses (a response rate of 39%) of which the researchers utilized 1,300 who perceived themselves to have experienced unfair treatment by management. Restriction of the analysis to this group, something not done by previous researchers, was based on Hirschman's proposition that exit-voice mechanisms will be used or activated by persons who find themselves in a "deteriorated state" (rather than by employees as a whole).[3] The second data set was based on a 1987 survey of nonunion employees in a large U.S.-based multinational firm that specializes in overnight mail and freight delivery. The survey yielded 579 respondents (a response rate of 43%) of which the researchers utilized 400 who perceived themselves to have experienced unfair treatment by management. The voice mechanism in this case (firm) was a formal, multi-step, nonunion employee complaint procedure.

Lewin and Boroff's empirical analysis did not confirm the expected positive relationship between loyalty and the use of voice through grievances or complaints, after controlling for the impact of other determinants of voice. Rather, in both data sets a statistically significant negative relationship was found, indicating that more loyal employees are less likely to file a grievance or a complaint even when they perceive themselves to have been unfairly treated and are in a deteriorating employment relationship. As Lewin and Boroff put it, these employees primarily appear to "suffer in silence." Further, the authors' empirical analysis did not confirm the expected positive relationship between employee perceptions of the effectiveness or quality of the grievance/complaint procedure and usage of the procedure.

The analysis also unexpectedly found that employees who expected to quit the firm were more likely to file written complaints; that is, there was a positive rather than a negative relationship between (intent to) exit and (the use of) voice. However, Lewin and Boroff's analysis confirmed the expected relationship that more loyal employees were less likely to quit, as were employees who perceived the grievance and complaint procedures to be effective or of high quality.

To the extent that these results are generalizable, they suggest that, by the late 1980s and early 1990s in the United States, employee voice (in the form of grievances or complaints) was not an alternative to exit (intent to quit), either in union or nonunion settings (as Hirschman proposed in 1970). Rather, employee loyalty to the organization decreases the likelihood of using voice mechanisms, such as grievance and complaint procedures. These findings have potentially important implications for employee protection in the new global economy. By the late 1980s and early 1990s in the United States, the adverse economic conditions and high uncertainty facing many workers were such that they likely would be reluctant to exercise their exit (quit) option. Instead, and in such circumstances, they could be expected to utilize such forms of voice as grievances or complaints to improve their work situations. But the opposite seems to have occurred; employees who were unlikely to quit were also unlikely to use voice or, in other words, to "suffer in silence." Somewhat more optomistically, Lewin and Boroff's research may be interpreted to suggest that employer strategies to enhance employee loyalty and commitment to the organization may be well placed in the sense that these initiatives may reduce both grievances/complaints and quits.

Kleiner and Ay: Employee Representation and Economic Growth

Morris M. Kleiner and Chang-Ruey Ay provide a theoretical and empirical analysis of the impact of alternative forms of employee representation on economic performance among OECD countries. The forms of employee representation they studied include (1) unionization, (2) voluntary joint consultation, and (3) statutory, mandatory representation. Since the latter two categories can coexist with unionization, the effect of various combinations of these forms of representation with different degrees of unionization are also examined by the authors.Aggregate production functions for countries are estimated with different measures of "output" and different measures of the forms of employee representation. The dependent variables or output measures are productivity per worker, productivity growth per hour, and investment per worker.

Their empirical results suggest that productivity growth and investment tends to be higher in countries such as Japan, with relatively low levels of unionization but strong forms of voluntary joint consultation. In contrast, productivity growth and investment tends to be lower in countries such as the United States, with low levels of unionization, weak forms of voluntary joint consultation, and adversarial labor relations. Productivity growth and investment also were not relatively higher in countries with mandated works councils and high levels of unionization. In essence, non-adversarial, voluntary joint consultation seemed most conducive to high productivity growth and investment among the worker representation arrangements studied in this paper.

The authors caution, however, that it is difficult to disentangle the effect of different forms of employee representation on productivity and investment using national level studies. Further, they emphasize that the effects of the alternative forms of representation were small. As such, the appropriateness of particular forms of employee representation in nations could be based on such factors as the extent to which they promote industrial democracy and employee satisfaction as well as on the extent to which they affect productivity and investment. Indeed, and from the perspective of global economic competition and other key forces influencing modern economies and societies, it may be posited that, whatever particular forms they take, mechanisms for employee representation that focus on enhancing workers' role in democratizing the workplace—a cooperative orientation—may be better suited to business enterprises than mechanisms that aim to shift economic returns from capital to labor—an adversarial orientation.

Jones: Successor Unions and the Evolution of IR in Former Communist Countries

Derek C. Jones deals with the transition to new industrial relations systems in the former communist countries of Czechoslovakia, Estonia, Bulgaria, and Russia. His paper focuses on the question of whether successor unions established under the former regime are capable of adapting to the new, more market-oriented environment that prevails in each of these countries.

The analysis is based on surveys sent to union leaders in the four countries over the 1991-1994 period. The results generally confirm that successor unions are capable of adapting to the new environment in spite of the dramatic changes that are occurring. Signs of such adaptation include decentralization of union structures, increased emphasis on job-related concerns, greater variability in the profiles and compensation of union leaders, severing of the connection between membership in the Communist Party and political beliefs, and greater democracy within successor unions. Employee participation in workplace issues, however, remains low in the post-communist era to date. Nevertheless, successor unions that have emerged out of the former communist unions have larger memberships than the newer unions without formal ties to the past.

Although all four of these Eastern European countries are undergoing dramatic changes in their industrial relations system, no single new system seems to be emerging. Instead, notable differences prevail among these countries, especially with respect to the power and privileges granted to former union officials and members of the Communist Party. Whether such differences will decline over time in an increasingly global context, as might be inferred from the dominant thesis in the aforementioned *Industrialism and Industrial Man,* or whether they will persist and perhaps even widen, remains an empirical question of key interest to students of international/comparative industrial relations.

Morishima: Evolution of White-Collar HRM in Japan

Motohiro Morishima analyzes how human resource management (HRM) practices in the white-collar sector of Japan are evolving in the new economic order. The changes are occurring in response to four interrelated environmental pressures: lagging productivity, an aging workforce, slow growth and greater competition, and changing managerial values. Particular attention is paid to the extent to which HRM practices are deviating from the traditional model with its twin characteristics of "life-time" employment and pay based on skill acquisition, usually related to seniority and experience.

The analysis is based on survey responses from 1,618 top HRM managers or their delegates (a response rate of 43%) as well as on qualitative interviews and selected case evidence. Cluster analysis indicates that three HRM practices now prevail for white-collar workers in Japan:

1. The *traditional* HRM model retains both long-term employment and seniority-based appraisal and reward.
2. The *competitive appraisal* model retains long-term employment, but replaces seniority-based appraisal and reward with competitive performance-based appraisal and individualized rewards and career paths.
3. The *transformed* HRM model replaces both long-term employment and seniority-based appraisal and reward, respectively, with employment externalization (e.g., part-timers, temporary workers and limited-term contracts) and with competitive performance-based appraisal and individualized rewards and career paths.

In essence, while the traditional model is "alive and well" for certain white-collar workers in Japan, two new HRM models are also emerging, with individualized performance-based appraisal and reward characterizing both of the new models and employment externalization characterizing one of them. The traditional system is most likely to be retained in Japanese firms that are unionized and in which management values employee well-being over profits. In contrast, the new HRM systems are likely to be adapted by Japanese organizations with high labor costs (due to aging workforces and high proportions of administrative employees) and which are experiencing financial or productivity declines.

The global competitive perspective presented in this introductory paper, which implies further weakening in the financial performance of Japanese firms compared to firms located/ headquartered elsewhere, strongly suggests that over time the traditional HRM system in Japan will be further eroded and perhaps supplanted by the competitive appraisal and transformed HRM systems. Whether one or the other of these latter two systems will come to dominate Japanese industry and workplace arrangements remains an important and intriguing empirical question.

IMPLICATIONS FOR WORKER REPRESENTATION AND PROTECTION

The papers from the Toronto Bargaining Group Conference which appear in this volume investigate various aspects of worker representation and protection in industrial relations systems that are evolving under a new global economic order. The search for a new paradigm or equilibrium requires studies that identify areas in which current systems are variously effective and ineffective and that identify how these systems performs in situations in which external shocks can be clearly identified. Each of the aforementioned papers contributes to one or the other of these objectives.

To illustrate, Kaufman argues that the original macroeconomic rationale for the Wagner Act is outdated, just as others have concluded that the adversarial framework for labor relations and collective bargaining contained in the act is unsuited to contemporary employment relationships in U.S. enterprises. Given today's (and tomorrow's) global competition, the macroeconomic and employee representation rationales underlying the Wagner (and Taft-Hartley) Act(s) need to be rethought. Unfortunately, and as Kaufman also points out, the recent recommendations of the U.S. Commission on the Future of Worker-Management Relations (1994) fail to deal with the original macroeconomic foundations of the law. Nevertheless, it is conceivable that fundamental rethinking of these as well as the labor relations foundations of the Wagner/Taft-Hartley Acts could serve to reshape the law better to serve modern economic and labor relations purposes, including supporting employer-initiated employee involvement and participation programs.

Given the economic uncertainty facing workers in a globally-dominated economic environment, they are unlikely to want voluntarily to leave their jobs (i.e., exit). Lewin and Boroff found that even among employees who believe that they have been unfairly treated by their employees, and contrary to received exit-voice theory, employee loyalty to the firm was negatively related to the exercise of voice through such forms as grievance and complaint filing. Instead, the dominant response of employees to perceived workplace injustice apparently is to "suffer in silence." Yet, more loyal employees are also less likely than others to intend to leave (exit) the firm—a finding which is consistent with exit-voice theory. These findings may be taken to suggest that employer strategies to enhance employee loyalty and commitment to the organization, including through team-based work and variable pay initiatives, may be well placed in the sense that they have the potential to reduce the incidence of grievances/complaints, quits, and suffering in silence.

Kleiner and Ay's analysis points to shortcomings of the U. S. adversarial model of labor relations in enhancing the productivity growth and investment necessary for competitive survival in the global economy. They also highlight similar shortcomings in the models of high unionization with mandatory representation via works councils. The best productivity and investment performance came from models, such as that in Japan, featuring low unionization and high voluntary consultation. To the extent that the evolution of industrial relations systems tends to be in the direction of the Japanese model, improved productivity and investment performance may result therefrom.

These effects are likely to be relatively small, however, and in addition may fade through time if we follow Morishima's analysis of the evolution of Japanese HRM practices. Morishima finds that, even though the traditional HRM system is currently "alive and well" in certain white-collar sectors in Japan, it is being overtaken by both competitive appraisal and transformed HRM systems. These new systems involve less employment stability for subsets of the Japanese workforce as well as more internally competitive performance assessment systems that are less tied to seniority than in the traditional Japanese employment system.

The ability of certain institutional features of existing industrial relations systems to adapt to new environmental forces is especially highlighted in the paper by Jones. He finds that successor unions established under communism have in general been able to adapt successfully in a number of countries undergoing the transition to market-based economies. But he also finds that workers represented by these unions are only marginally involved in the employee participation and involvement initiatives undertaken by the managements of newly market-oriented business enterprises in these formerly communist countries.

Change is the common thread across all of these studies. In certain circumstances, some of the existing institutional arrangements have been able to adapt and survive major environmental change (e.g., successor unions in communist countries and traditional HRM practices in Japan). Invariably, however, survival of institutional arrangements required change and adaptation. In other circumstances, gaps or vacuums have been created as, for example, in the enforcement of employment rights legislation, the effective implementation of innovative HRM practices, and the use of voice as voluntary exit declines. In still other circumstances, the changes that have negative effects on some parts of the industrial relations system also have positive effects on other parts. For example, the decline of unions, especially adversarially-oriented unions, may have beneficial effects on productivity and investment, while employer efforts to enhance employee loyalty and commitment may reduce both employee turnover and grievances/complaints.

Studies of the type that were presented at the Toronto Bargaining Group Conference and which appear in this volume help us to better understand the old industrial relations system, the strengths and weaknesses of new workplace arrangements, and the possibilities for and limitations on the emergence of a new industrial relations system equilibrium or paradigm. Insights drawn from these papers are particularly useful to understand the changes that are occurring in industrial relations sytems worldwide, how actors in industrial relations sytems may adapt to the changes, and especially the gaps and problems that are likely to be associated with institutional responses to such changes.

NOTES

1. Publications that emerged from these conferences include Lewin and Feuille (1983) and Lewin and Strauss (1988).

2. Publications that emerged from the Purdue and Cornell conferences include Chelius and Dworkin (1990) and Katz (1991).

3. Note that Hirschman (1970) focused on the "deteriorated state" of customers in their relationship to the firm, whereas Lewin and Boroff focus on the "deteriorated state" of employees in their relationship to the firm.

REFERENCES

Chelius, J., and J. Dworkin. Eds. 1990. *Reflections on the Transformation of Industrial Relations.* Metuchen, NJ: Scarecrow Press.

Dunlop, J. 1993. *Industrial Relations Systems.* New York: Holt, Rinehart and Winston.

Erickson, C.L., and S. Kuruvilla. 1994. "Critical Junctures in the Transformation of Industrial Relation Systems: A Comparative Study." Paper presented to the Fourth Bargaining Group Conference, Industrial Relation Centre, University of Toronto, October 14.

Freeman, R. B., and J. L. Medoff. 1984. *What Do Unions Do?* New York: Basic Books.

Hirschman, A. O. 1970. *Exit, Voice and Loyalty.* Cambridge, MA: Harvard University Press.

Katz, H. C. Ed. 1991. *The Future of Industrial Relations.* Ithaca, NY: ILR Press.

Kaufman, B. E. 1992. *The Origins and Evolution of the Field of Industrial Relations.* Ithaca, NY: ILR Press.

Kerr, C., F. A. Harbison, J. T. Dunlop, and C. A. Myers. 1964. *Industrialism and Industrial Man.* New York: Oxford University Press.

Kochan, T. A., H. C. Katz, and R. B. McKersie. 1986. *The Transformation of American Industrial Relations.* New York: Basic Books, 1986.

Lewin, D. 1987. "Industrial Relations as a Strategic Variable." Pp. 1-41 in *Human Resources and the Performance of the Firm*, edited by M. M. Kleiner, R. N. Block, M. Roomkin, and S. W. Salsburg. Madison, WI: Industrial Relations Research Association.

Lewin, D., and P. Feuille. 1983. "Behavioral Research in Industrial Relations." *Industrial and Labor Relations Review*. 36 (April): 341-360.

Lewin, D., and G. Strauss. 1988. "Behavioral Studies in Industrial Relations: Symposium Introduction." *Industrial Relations* 27 (Winter): 1-6.

U.S. Commission on the Future of Worker-Management Relations. 1994. *Fact Finding Report*. Washington, DC: U.S. Department of Labor and U.S. Department of Commerce.

Weiler, P. 1990. *Governing the Workplace*. Cambridge, MA: Harvard University Press.

WHY THE WAGNER ACT?
REESTABLISHING CONTACT WITH ITS ORIGINAL PURPOSE

Bruce E. Kaufman

ABSTRACT

Despite hundreds of articles and books on the National Labor Relations (Wagner) Act, a great diversity of opinion remains concerning the reasons for its enactment in 1935 and the Act's fundamental purpose. This paper reexamines both issues. It is concluded that the primary genesis of the Wagner Act was the economic calamity of the Great Depression, that the Act was first and foremost a macroeconomic recovery measure, and that its central purpose was to stop the process of deflation and promote economic recovery through the twin means of ending destructive competition through stabilization of the wage-price structure and stimulating aggregate demand by increasing consumer purchasing power through a redistribution of income from capital to labor. This interpretation sheds light on numerous issues of both an historical and policy nature.

Advances in Industrial and Labor Relations, Volume 7, pages 15-68.
Copyright © 1996 by JAI Press Inc.
All rights of reproduction in any form reserved.
ISBN: 1-55938-925-7

Ten years after enactment of the National Labor Relations (Wagner) Act, Leon Keyserling, legislative assistant to Senator Robert F. Wagner in the mid-1930s and chief draftsman of the act, wrote an article titled, "Why the Wagner Act?" The opening paragraphs are as germane today as when he wrote them. His article begins thus:

> Another look at the circumstances which gave rise to the National Labor Relations Act is timely for reasons that transcend the celebration of the Act's decennial. For today the Act is under review in the form of amendatory proposals, some of which may be worthy and others of which would effectuate repeal....It is true that justification of the aims of the Act, and even demonstration that it has worked reasonably well toward their fulfillment, do not alone prove that the Act should not be changed or that supplementary legislation may not be necessary. The Act may have been either too broad or too narrow in its original design. Nonetheless, the current public bewilderment about the Act's purposes makes delineation the first step toward re-evaluation. It may be most helpful to raise and pursue a single question: "Why was the Wagner Act passed?" A direct answer to this question may provide assuagement to much of the concern about what should be done with the Act today (Keyserling 1945, p. 5).

A half century after Keyserling wrote these words, the nation finds itself in the midst of renewed controversy over the Wagner Act. Illustrative is the appointment by President Bill Clinton in 1993 of the Commission on the Future of Worker-Management Relations (Dunlop Commission) and the ongoing debate over its recommendations for labor law reform. As the commission's *Fact Finding Report* (1994, p. 63) notes, "Since enactment of the National Labor Relations (Wagner) Act in 1935, the declared policy of the United States had been 'to encourage and protect collective bargaining.'" To determine whether this policy statement continues to serve the national interest, the commission held 11 regional hearings and heard testimony from 134 witnesses.

Reminiscent of the Senate hearings on the Wagner Act in the spring of 1935, the Commission heard a welter of sharply contrasting opinions. On one side were proponents of the act who advocated strengthening its provisions in order to restore a level playing field in labor-management relations, provide democracy in the workplace, and better protect workers rights, while on the other were critics who desired to weaken or eliminate parts of the act due to their conviction that it's principal effect is to foster labor monopoly and the economic inefficiency and lack of employee choice that monopoly entails. This divergence in opinion is reflected, in turn, in the academic literature, both with respect to labor policy in general and the Wagner Act in particular (e.g., Troy 1990; Weiler 1990).

As Keyserling argued 50 years ago, these debates are unnecessarily contentious and confused because the disputants often talk past each other with regard to the underlying rationale for unions in general and the Wagner Act in particular. To avoid this problem, the most fruitful place to begin a debate of the Wagner Act is an evaluation of three related questions: first, what is the basic purpose of the act? Second, to what degree does the act continue to fulfill this purpose? And third, does accomplishing this purpose still advance the public welfare? Although knowing the answer to the first of these questions (i.e., the original purpose of the act) is clearly not the sole desideratum for determining its social and economic efficacy or the direction for reform of its various provisions, it is surely necessary to have some consensus on this matter if progress is to be made on answering the other two questions.

What, then, is the answer to "why the Wagner Act?" Keyserling (1945, pp. 7-8) states his view thus:

> On June 7, 1933, Senator Wagner opened the debate on the National Industrial Recovery Bill [NIRA], which contained Section 7(a) the immediate forebear of the Wagner Act. The Senator immediately set this bill squarely in the context of America's long efforts to achieve the dual ends of economic justice and economic stability.....Never once in a long series of explanations of his proposal [the NLRA] did Senator Wagner deviate from the theme that it was aimed primarily toward greater economic stability through better economic balance.

These remarks by the person closest to Wagner in the drafting process leave little doubt as to either the origins or ultimate purpose of the National Labor Relations Act and Section 7(a) of the NIRA before it. The Wagner Act and Section 7(a), he says, were part of a coordinated macroeconomic program intended to combat the Depression through two related means: stabilization of the wage-price structure and promotion of consumer purchasing power. In particular, the evils against which these measures were directed included destructive competition and deficient aggregate demand and the downward spiral of wages, prices, employment, and labor standards that they bring about. The root of these evils, according to Wagner, lay in an imbalance in bargaining power between workers and firms in a market economy and the uncoordinated nature of economic decision making by households and firms—factors that lead to inadequate growth in wages relative to profits, dynamic instability in wages and prices during recessions and depressions, and boom and bust cycles in production and employment. The instruments by which these evils were to be eliminated included industrial self-regulation through trade associations, minimum wage and maximum hour provisions, expanded collective bargaining, establishment of unemployment and old age insurance funds, and counter-cyclical public works programs.

These measures found their first comprehensive expression in the National Industrial Recovery Act—a coordinated but hastily assembled and not entirely well thought out mix of most of the above mentioned stabilization tools administered through a loose form of tripartite "planning." After two years of experience with the NIRA, Wagner realized that it was in certain respects fatally flawed. Even before it was declared unconstitutional in June 1935, Wagner set to work on legislation to remedy these defects. One of these legislative remedies was the National Labor Relations Act, followed by the Social Security Act and Fair Labor Standards Act. Although each act was addressed toward a particular aspect of labor policy which, when viewed in terms of their specific legislative provisions, appear to have only a tangential relation to macroeconomic themes of stabilization and recovery, they were in fact motivated to a significant degree by Wagner's desire to reconstruct from the failed experiment of the NIRA an improved, more effective macroeconomic program to lift the country out of depression (Byrne 1951. On the macroeconomic origins of the Social Security Act and Fair Labor Standards Act, see Graebner 1980 and Linder 1990).

Although this interpretation is not one often emphasized, or in a number of cases even acknowledged, in the literatures of labor law, labor history, and industrial relations, the evidence for it in the historical record is quite strong. To develop this evidence, I examine Sen. Wagner's legislative record and speeches in the Senate from 1927-1935, provide numerous quotations from congressional testimony and the popular press of that era, and examine the language of the NIRA and NLRA to infer the drafters intent as to their purposes. The paper then concludes with a consideration of the implications of this analysis for the current debate on the Wagner Act and its reform.

THE PURPOSE OF THE WAGNER ACT

The literature on the Wagner Act spans hundreds of articles, chapters, and full-length books. A considerable diversity of opinion exists among these writers as to the principal purpose of the act. At least 12 different points of view can be found. These include:

- promotion of industrial democracy (Summers 1979),
- protection of workers rights to collective bargain (Mikva 1986),
- legislation to help organized labor cartelize labor markets (Posner 1984),
- promotion of higher wages to fuel consumer purchasing power (Mitchell 1986),
- containment of working class militancy and maintenance of capitalist hegemony (Finegold and Skocpol 1984),
- a response to the strike wave of 1933-1934 (Goldfield 1989),
- stabilization of markets (Gordon 1994),
- promotion of tripartite economic planning and a corporatist state (Tomlins 1985),
- building a cooperative social democracy (Barenberg 1993)
- establish labor's countervailing power to achieve balance in wage determination (Kochan, Katz, and McKersie 1986),
- promoting unions as a vehicle to enhance the status of individual workers (Millspaugh 1988), and
- promotion of political reform by an elite of progressive liberals (Plotke 1996).

The genesis of the Wagner Act is admittedly a product of numerous complex forces and reflects multiple concerns and motivations on the part of its supporters.

For these reasons, each of the rationales for the act identified above to one degree or another captures part of the reality of what it sought to accomplish. From my perspective, however, no study yet published has succeeded in zeroing in upon and succinctly summarizing the fundamental core purpose of the act as seen by the senator whose name it bears and many (though certainly not all) of the people who supported the legislation at the time of its passage in 1935. And what was this core purpose? Stated in a sentence, it was to serve as part of an overall economic program aimed at ending the Great Depression and promoting sustained recovery and growth through the twin instruments of stabilization of the wage-price structure and promotion of consumer purchasing power.

The remainder of this paper is devoted to development of this thesis. The argument is not claimed to be an entirely new one, as a number of previous writers on the act have noted that a major rationale for its passage was to restore puchasing power and stabilize markets (e.g., Bernstein 1950; Casebeer, 1987; Gordon, 1994; Hogler 1993; Marshall, 1992; Mitchell, 1986; Tomlins, 1985; Vittoz, 1987; Weiler, 1990). These studies, however, either do not give the macroeconomic rationale the centrality it deserves and/or do not adequately explicate the manner and mechanisms by which the Wagner Act was to accomplish its macroeconomic purpose. Of greater distress, a number of academic writers on unions and labor policy appear not to recognize at all the act's macroeconomic rationale (e.g., Freeman and Medoff 1984, Goldfield, 1989; Gross, 1985; Hirsch and Addison 1986; Posner, 1984).

To proceed, in the next section I take a four-pronged approach: first, to examine the rationale for the Wagner Act as stated in the "Findings and Policy" section (Section 1) of the act itself; second, to examine the rationale for the act as stated by Sen. Wagner; third, to do the same as stated by Wagner's legislative assistant, Keyserling; and fourth, to examine statements made about the purpose of the act by noted authorities in their testimony before Congress at the time the bill was being considered for adoption.

Findings and Policy

Section 1 of the National Labor Relations Act describes the purpose and rationale for the legislation. It contains four paragraphs (reprinted in National Labor Relations Board, *Legislative History of the National Labor Relations Act*, 1985; hereafter, NLRB).

Paragraph 1 states: "The denial by employers of the right of employees to organize and the refusal by employers to accept the procedure of collective bargaining lead to strikes and other forms of industrial strife or unrest, which have the intent or the necessary effect of burdening or obstructing commerce...."

Paragraph 2 states: "The inequality of bargaining power between employees who do not possess full freedom of association or actual liberty of contract, and employers who are organized in the corporate or other forms of ownership association substantially burdens and affects the flow of commerce, and tends to aggravate recurrent business depressions, by depressing wage rates and the purchasing power of wage earners in industry and by preventing the stabilization of competitive wage rates and working conditions within and between industries."

Paragraph 3 largely restates the arguments of the previous two paragraphs.

Paragraph 4 ends Section 1 with a statement of policy: "It is hereby declared the policy of the United States to eliminate the causes of certain substantial obstructions to the free flow of commerce and to mitigate and eliminate these obstructions when they have occurred by encouraging the practice and procedure of collective bargaining and by protecting the exercise by workers of full freedom of association, self-organization, and designation of representatives of their own choosing, for the purpose of negotiating the terms and conditions of their employment or other mutual aid or protection."

As I read these paragraphs, the drafters of the act (largely Sen. Wagner and his legislative aid, lawyer/economist Keyserling) rest the justification of the act upon two pillars—that the promotion and protection of collective bargaining will (a) reduce strikes and other forms of conflict that have the effect of interfering with production and trade and (b) will reduce or eliminate labor's inequality of bargaining power which, in turn, will stabilize wage rates and working conditions at competitive levels and promote economic recovery by expanding the income share and purchasing power of households.

Taken at face value, the language in Section 1 clearly suggests some of the interpretations of the act cited above have misconstrued its justification and intended purpose. While Section 1 emphasizes that it is national policy to promote collective bargaining and protect workers rights of self-organization, the stated purpose of doing so is not because of their intrinsic value per se, nor for the benefits of democracy in industry, but rather because of their instrumental value in attaining another valued goal—a full employment macroeconomy. This is clearly indicated by the fact that one and only one theme is cited in all four paragraphs of Section 1—that the purpose of the act is to restore prosperity by removing obstacles to a "free flow of commerce."

Statements by Wagner

Sen. Wagner's legislative aid, Keyserling, was largely responsible for the actual drafting of the act, though with close personal oversight and guidance from the senator. Keyserling later acknowledged that the substantive positions enunciated in Section 1 in justification of the act were expressly written with the Supreme Court in mind (Casebeer 1987). Earlier pieces of protective labor legislation (e.g., minimum wage laws) had been declared unconstitutional by the Supreme Court on the grounds that they violated the Constitution's protection of liberty of contract and exceeded the grant of power given to the Federal government under the commerce clause. In writing Section 1, Wagner and Keyserling attempted to surmount these legal hurdles through a joint attack on both principles—that freedom of contract promotes coercion, not liberty, when one party to the wage bargain (labor) is much weaker than the other and that the outcomes of such a bargain (strikes and low wages) seriously obstruct interstate commerce. Obviously, then, danger exists in inferring the drafters' ultimate purpose from a literal reading of Section 1, as the macroeconomic theme contained therein may itself have served a largely instrumental purpose—that is, to help win approval of the act by the Supreme Court.

To assemble additional evidence on the purpose of the NLRA, it is helpful to examine in more detail the rationale advanced by Sen. Wagner and Dr. Keyserling for the act, as contained in their speeches and writings. Wagner is considered first, given the universal acknowledgment of his central role in conceiving the legislation and his unstinting efforts to see it enacted into law.

Sen. Wagner spoke often and at length on the purposes of the proposed labor relations bill, the most important of which are reprinted in the legislative history of the act (NLRB 1985). A reading of these reveals several salient facts.

First, Wagner always made clear that the direct antecedent of the NLRA was the National Industrial Recovery Act, passed in 1933 as the centerpiece of the Roosevelt administration's anti-depression policy. When introducing the bill to the Senate on February 21, 1935, Wagner started his remarks with these introductory thoughts: (NLRB 1985, p. 1311)

> The recovery program [NIRA] has sought to bestow upon the business man and the worker a new freedom to grapple with the great economic challenges of our times. We have released the business man from the undiscriminating enforcement of the antitrust laws, which had been subjecting him to the attacks of the price cutters and wage reducers—the pirates of industry. In order to deal out the equal treatment upon which a just democratic society must rest, we at the same time guaranteed the freedom of action of the worker. In fact, the now famous Section 7(a), by stating that employees should be allowed to cooperate among themselves if they desired to do so, merely restated the principles that Congress has avowed for half a century.

Second, after linking the broad purpose of his proposed labor relations bill to the NIRA, Wagner goes on to note that its specific provisions are concerned with one particular part of the NIRA—Section 7(a). Thus, Wagner continues his remarks quoted above, saying (p. 1311):

> Congress is familiar with the events of the past two years. While industry's freedom of action has been encouraged until the trade association movement has blanketed the country, employees attempting in good faith to exercise their liberties under Section 7(a) have met with repeated rebuffs....While there is a different code for each trade, there is only one section 7(a), and no definite law written by Congress can mean something different in each industry. These difficulties are reducing section 7(a) to a sham and a delusion.

Third, in this address Wagner then cites two negative consequences that result from the "sham and delusion" to which Section 7(a) was reduced. The first is the growth of strikes; the second and more important is the adverse trend in real wages and purchasing power. He states (p. 1312):

> The break-down of section 7(a) brings results equally disastrous to industry and labor. Last summer it led to a procession of bloody and costly strikes, which in some cases swelled almost to the magnitude of national emergencies....There has been a second and even more serious consequence of the break-down of section 7(a). When employees are denied the freedom to act in concert even when they desire to do so, they cannot exercise a restraining influence upon the wayward members of their own group, and they cannot participate in our national endeavor to coordinate production and purchasing power. The consequences are already visible in the widening gap between wages and profits. If the consequences are allowed to produce their full harvest, the whole country will suffer from a new economic decline.

Though citing the adverse trends in wages and purchasing power as being the most deleterious consequences of the violations of Section 7(a), Wagner in this address does not go into further detail. In subsequent testimony to the Senate Committee on Education and Labor on March 11, 1935, he did greatly expand on the economic theory and importance of the proposed act (see NLRB 1985; pp. 1408-1432). The first section of his remarks are titled, "Legal Background of the Bill," and largely deals with the evolution of the antitrust laws and their application to concerted activities by business and labor. He then proceeds to the "Economic Background of the Bill" in the second section. He states:

> I am not pleading for any special group. It is well recognized today that the failure to spread adequate purchasing power among the vast masses of the consuming public disrupts the continuity of business operations and causes everyone to suffer. The piling up of excess capital reserves and plant capacities is a dead weight upon the whole economic structure....between 1922 and 1929 the development of productive capacities was four times as rapid as the rise in real wages. An unbalanced economy, fraught with certain disaster to every interest, was implicit in these undeniable developments. And in 1929 the disaster came....Finally, about two years ago, we set forth upon a new program, openly and completely reversing our earlier policies. Industrial cooperation was given sanction in order to limit the evils of destructive competition. Employees were guaranteed protection in their cooperative efforts, in order that they might help the Government to insure a sufficient flow of purchasing power through adequate wages. At the present time, there is controversy as to whether industrial cooperation is a wise policy....Still less open to question is the proposition that workers also should be allowed to cooperate fully. If...full freedom of association and self-organization among workers was desirable even when the antitrust laws were a policy, if not an actuality, how much more necessary this freedom is today, when the antitrust laws have been in part suspended. The government policy of fixing minimum wages and maximum hours is not a definitive solution. It is merely the foundation upon which can be built the mutual endeavors of a revived industry and a rehabilitated labor. This process of economic self-rule must fail unless every group is equally well represented. In order that the strong may not take advantage of the weak, every group must be equally strong.

Several features of his remarks in this section of the testimony are noteworthy. It is clear from the discussion in this section, for example, that in Wagner's view the proposed National Labor Relations Act was a direct descendant of the

NIRA and, in particular, was promulgated in order to provide the legal and administrative mechanism for the enforcement of labor's Section 7(a) rights. Wagner also clearly states that the purpose of the NIRA was to promote economic recovery and, more importantly, that the fundamental motivation for including Section 7(a) was also macroeconomic in nature—to use collective bargaining to end the deflationary process of wage and price reduction and, in the long run, to redistribute income from capital to labor, thereby augmenting household income, purchasing power, and aggregate demand. While Wagner made repeated references to various noneconomic benefits to be derived from adoption of the act (e.g., protection of fundamental workplace rights, democracy in industry), it is clear, not only in this section of his remarks but throughout the entire presentation, that the macroeconomic goals of stabilization and recovery are of foremost importance.

Keyserling

This perspective is supported by Keyserling who worked closely with Wagner in the drafting of both the NIRA and NLRA. Keyserling's viewpoint on the macroeconomic origin and purpose of the NLRA is clearly stated in the quotation cited in the introduction of this paper that came from an article written by him in 1945. Later in life, Keyserling amplified on the origins of the Wagner Act in a lengthy personal interview (Casebeer 1987). He states (pp. 297-298):

> The background to the Wagner Act of 1935 is contained in the history of the National Industrial Recovery Act. The National Industrial Recovery Act, which was one of the first measures of the New Deal, was originally an embodiment of the so-called Swope Plan...the original Swope Plan was merely a plan for the suspension of the antitrust laws so that business could more effectively cooperate in the determination of business policies, especially price policies, but also substitute avowed cooperation for alleged conflict.

He goes on to say (p. 309):

> If you read Senator Wagner's speeches from the time of the passage of the National Industrial Recovery Act in 1933 until the introduction of the Wagner Act, and certainly long before it became law, he was always making speeches on the Senate floor criticizing the National Industrial Recovery Act Boards on the ground that the wage and price provisions were terrible, that we were going to run into more recessions and trouble because of the failure of wages to keep up with profits and so forth. These speeches were the very basis of the thinking that the Wagner Act was intended to redress some of that, and if that was a real factor in the burdening of commerce, then it should enter into the preamble.

Testimony of Others

Evidence on the purpose of the Wagner Act can also be gleaned from an examination of the testimony of the numerous persons who testified on its behalf before the relevant Senate and House of Representatives committees. Although a diversity of viewpoints about specific features of the bill were advanced, as well as a variety of different justifications for the act itself, the macroeconomic theme of stabilization and recovery is a consistent theme in the remarks of the great majority of witnesses. Illustrative is the remarks of Harry Millis, professor of Economics at the University of Chicago, long-time labor arbitrator, and a member-to-be of the NLRB (also see testimony by persons such as Lloyd Garrison and Edwin Smith). He states in justification of the act (NLRB 1985, pp. 1553-1556):

> First. That the great majority of wage-earners are employed under such conditions that they must act in concert with reference to wage scales, hours, and working conditions if they are to have a reasonably effective voice as to the terms on which they shall work. Without organization there is in most modern industry unequal bargaining power....
>
> Second. The average employer....has been under the necessity of reducing costs because of the money saving, chiseling practices of his less socially minded competitors.... Informed labor leaders and observers recognize that most employers wish to do what is fair but that competition frequently prevents them....Nowadays we hear relatively less of equalizing bargaining power....my first point, and more of the need for standardization and control, of placing all firms in a market on pretty much the same plane of labor costs.
>
> Third. That a measure of control of wages is necessary if the needed relationship between consuming power and production is to be maintained and general instability checked....More recently a new doctrine has been invoked....I refer of course to the doctrine of high wages and mass purchasing power which has played an important role in this country in recent years and which underlies so much of the "new deal." The doctrine is that wages must be made high and kept high to provide the mass purchasing power required to maintain a market outlet for goods produced.
>
> Fourth. That if and when collective bargaining is definitely freed from undue militancy, as can be when wise management and good labor leadership are brought into cooperation, special problems connected with collective bargaining clear up and there are opportunities for gain to all parties....Many employers have found that they can conduct their business more satisfactorily on a union than a nonunion basis.

THE GENESIS OF THE WAGNER ACT

The statements and testimony provided above clearly attest to the importance attached to the twin goals of macroeconomic stability and recovery as motivations for passage of the NLRA. While issues of industrial democracy, protection of collective bargaining rights, reduction of industrial conflict, and other such objectives clearly played a role in the passage of the Wagner Act, none centered in the discussions and debates over the Wagner Act as much as did these macroeconomic themes. The reason for the transcendent attention given to economic stability and recovery would seem to be apparent from the time and context within which the debate over the Wagner Act took place. The year 1935 was, after all, mid-way through the greatest economic disaster in the nation's history—the Great Depression. Surprisingly, however, the macroeconomic genesis of the Wagner Act occurred well before the onset of the Great Depression. What I shall seek to show in this section are two things: first, that Sen. Wagner, as well as a like-minded group of progressive-liberal reformers, had by the mid to late 1920s already come to regard unemployment and macroeconomic instability as major evils and, second, that they had also formulated a relatively coherent, coordinated economic program to solve this problem. The Depression, therefore, did not give birth to the *ideas* that underlay the Wagner Act; what it did do is provide economic conditions that made these ideas both attractive and politically possible.

The Development of Wagner's Progressive Thought

The National Labor Relations Act was named after its chief sponsor, Robert Wagner, in recognition of the senator's unparalleled role in its conception, drafting, and enactment. More than most pieces of legislation, therefore, the origins and purpose of the NLRA are to be found in the economic and social philosophy of one man. But Wagner's thoughts and principles on these matters did not take form isolated from the broader society in which he grew up and the people he interacted with as lawyer, state senator, state supreme court judge, and finally U.S. senator. To understand Wagner's unswerving devotion to the cause of economic growth and security, one must first understand the context in which he grew up and the people and ideas that he came into contact with.

Wagner, as well as many other New Dealers, were products of the Progressive Era. Dating from the turn of the twentieth century to the beginning of the World War I, this period in American history was a time of reform and social consciousness. In many respects, it was the seed bed for ideas and movements that reappeared in later periods of political liberalism, such as the New Deal, Fair Deal, New Frontier, and Great Society. Although the Progressive Era saw numerous reform movements, some of which worked at cross-purposes, three themes stand out (Fusfield 1956). One was concern for what FDR was later to call the "forgotten man," which is to say the great mass of people of humble origins and circumstances at the base of the socio-economic pyramid; the second was suspicion of monopoly and vested interests in both the business and political spheres; and the third was a predisposition to solve these problems through various forms of state intervention, be it in the form of legislated protection of rights, regulation through administrative bodies, or legal prohibition.

Wagner grew up as a teenager and young adult in this milieu and imbibed its principles. He also experienced firsthand the suffering and indignities of poverty. Wagner states in this regard (Bryne 1951, pp. 7-8):

> Someone who merely reads of the suffering in the newspapers is likely to forget it as soon as the headlines carry a new story. But my own life has been a hard struggle. My father was a laborer and my mother was a working woman....I have known the bitterness which comes even at the temporary prospect of being denied opportunities for self development.

He goes on to say:

My own experience placed me in contact with others who were broken by unbearable burdens who were caught and lost in the intricacies of a great industrial machine for which they were not responsible and which had no sense of responsibility toward them. Many of these people had fine, useful qualities and were deserving of a better fate. The evils of mass poverty are indelibly imprinted upon my mind. Thus, I am unwilling to discontinue the fight for social betterment at the first favorable turn of the tide. I want to push on to victory and I know that it is a long unremitting push.

A galvanizing event in Wagner's early professional life as a New York State Senator was the fire at the Triangle Shirtwaist Company which killed over 100 people on March 25, 1911. He was appointed a member of a legislative commission to investigate the fire, as well as the broader question of employment conditions in the state of New York, and in his three years on the commission developed a vivid first-hand knowledge of the full range of industrial evils affecting the common worker. Based on the commission's investigations, Wagner and co-chairman Al Smith introduced more than 60 bills in the legislature to improve employment conditions. Commenting on Wagner and Smith's experiences with the commission, Francis Perkins (1946, p. 17), an adviser to the group and later U.S. Secretary of Labor for FDR, said, "They got a firsthand look at industrial and labor conditions, and from that they never recovered. They became firm and unshakable sponsors of political and legislative measures designed to overcome conditions unfavorable to human life."

Of the conditions unfavorable to human life, Wagner picked out insecurity of employment as the most pernicious. Speaking on the subject of employment, he states in this regard (Huthmacher 1968, p. 77), "If we deny our people that right [the right to work], we have denied them everything. If we fail them in preserving that right, we have failed them in everything." He then demonstrates his progressive principles by making the right to work a direct responsibility of government stating: "This is the psychological moment to give legal recognition to the principle that it is part of the essential function of government to provide regularity of employment." And, finally, he argues that government's protection of the right to work is important not only to promote social progress but also, "if the standard of living is to be maintained and advanced, and the production of our efficient methods given an outlet in profitable consumption." He goes on to describe government intervention (p. 83) as "the new economics of social control."

Wagner was the most articulate and forceful spokesman in the U.S. Congress for progressive legislation to improve employment conditions. He was not the only person either in Congress or the broader society, however, to focus on these matters and, in particular, the evils of unemployment and economic instability. Though the progressive-liberal reform movement was a distinct minority group in the 1920s (a period aptly referred to at the time as a "return to normalcy"), it nevertheless drew support and recognition from a number of prominent, highly visible persons and organizations.

One group, for example, was the institutional economists who dominated the field of labor research. Led by John R. Commons, they made unemployment their number one issue in the 1920s. Commons (1921, p. 4) labeled the business cycle as "the greatest of all the labor problems" for the insecurity of employment it breeds and the corrosive effect such insecurity has on employee well-being, loyalty and commitment to the employer, and labor-management relations. The house organ of the institutional school, the *American Labor Legislation Review*, featured a steady stream of articles throughout the 1920s (including several by Wagner) on solutions to unemployment and instability, including unemployment insurance, public works programs, government-funded labor exchanges, improved labor market statistics, and collective bargaining.

A second group was engineers affiliated with the scientific management movement and, most particularly, the Taylor Society and the American Society of Mechanical Engineers (Layton 1971). Although originally focused on shop-level production methods, after the inflationary boom associated with World War I and the subsequent plunge into depression in 1920-1921, proponents of scientific management came to see that it was necessary to tame the business cycle and eliminate unemployment if substantial progress was to be made in promoting efficiency and reducing waste. The person foremost in this movement was Secretary of Commerce Herbert Hoover. Hoover lobbied President Warren G. Harding in 1921 to establish a "President's Commission on Unemployment" and then chaired the group. Their report included a wide range of recommendations that were part of the progressive-liberal agenda, including a more complete collection of labor market and general business statistics, creation of a public works bureau, a program of counter-cyclical public works spending at the federal, state, and local levels, a system of unemployment insurance, and the control of credit expansion by the Federal Reserve Bank.

Hoover was also a strong supporter of protecting the right to bargain collectively (see Hoover 1952, p. 101) and became one of the nation's leading exponents of what became known in the 1920s as the "doctrine of high wages." The doctrine of high wages originated with Henry Ford and his decision to boost wages to $5 a day on the theory that with higher income people would buy more cars, and the increase in volume would result in lower unit cost, lower prices, and greater profits. High wages thus were seen as good for business. Hoover described the doctrine thus in a speech in 1926 (p. 108):

> It is not so many years ago that the employer considered it was in his interest to use the opportunities of unemployment and immigration to lower wages irrespective of other considerations....But we are a long way on the road to new conceptions. The very essence of great production is high wages and low prices, because it depends upon a widening range of consumption only to be obtained from the purchasing power of high real wages and increasing standards of living.

Hoover's other major policy interest was promotion of industrial cooperation through trade associations. Though he was a staunch foe of monopoly, he nevertheless thought that trade associations could play a beneficial role in improving the coordination of production and consumption through data collection, research, planning of capacity expansions, and elimination of unfair or unethical selling practices.

A third group was progressive businessmen (Fraser 1991; Gordon 1994). Examples include Edward Filene, Henry Kendall, Henry Dennison, and Gerard Swope. They realized, similar to Commons, that the new methods of personnel management and welfare capitalism being introduced in the 1920s among leading firms could only be effective if companies could promise employees some measure of employment security (Jacoby 1985; Slichter 1929). Management publications of that era carried numerous articles on methods companies could use to stabilize production and employment, such as producing for inventory and company-sponsored unemployment insurance. They also realized, however, that such efforts were of only modest utility unless stability was brought to the national economy. They thus became spokesmen for the doctrine of high wages, market stabilization through trade associations, and counter-cyclical public works spending.

Finally, a fourth group that made economic stabilization part of its agenda in the 1920s was organized labor. In its search for a strategy to combat the open shop campaign of anti-union employers in the 1920s, organized labor took on two causes as its own. One was to preach the economic virtues and benefits of labor-management cooperation; the second was wrap union involvement in the governance of industry in the politically appealing flag of industrial democracy. To entice employers to recognize and bargain with unions, the American Federation of Labor (AFL) pledged itself ready to work with companies in a partnership to boost production and eliminate inefficiency (McKelvey 1952). A focus on production naturally led to consideration of unemployment and cyclical booms and busts, while industrial democracy led to proposals for joint regulation of markets by labor and management, as organized in trade unions and trade associations. This credo was formalized in a document issued by the AFL Executive Council in 1923 titled, "Industry's Manifest Destiny." Its theme was that industry had become sufficiently complex and interdependent that greater coordination of production and consumption was necessary to maintain full employment and that this coordination was best accomplished by joint cooperation and consultation between the two major stakeholders of industry—labor and management (Farr 1959). Wed to the doctrine of voluntarism, most of organized labor (Sydney Hillman and John L. Lewis being notable exceptions) wanted to keep government's involvement in industry stabilization at a minimum, reflected in the AFL's opposition throughout the 1920s to legislation on minimum wages (except for women and children), maximum hours, and unemployment insurance.

Wagner's Pre-New Deal Legislative Agenda

Robert Wagner was elected to the Senate as a Democrat from the state of New York and took his seat in March 1927. One year later (March 5, 1928), he made his maiden speech before the Senate in support of a bill he had introduced the previous month. Of considerable relevance for the thesis of this paper is the subject of the speech—the growth in national unemployment—and the purpose of his bill—to direct the Department of Labor to make a periodic estimate of the number of people unemployed.

Although this bill is separated from the National Labor Relations Act by seven years and all the events that transpired in between, it nevertheless is a carbon copy of the NLRA in one vital respect. If one looks only at the specific provisions of both bills (i.e., improved labor market statistics, defining unfair labor practices and creation of a labor board), there is little macroeconomic content in them. When one looks at their broader purpose, however, the twin goals of economic stabilization and recovery stand out like a beacon. This broader purpose is stated in Section 1of the NLRA and in the first sentence of the unemployment statistics bill. This sentence reads:

> Whereas it is essential to the intelligent conduct of private and public business enterprises, to the proper timing for the inauguration of public works by the Federal Government, and the encouragement of similar undertakings by the States, to the formulation of sound economic policy, and it is prerequisite to the provision of relief against the hardship of unemployment and to the ultimate solution of the unemployment that accurate and all-inclusive statistics of employment and unemployment be had at frequent intervals; and Whereas it is apparent that the United States is now suffering from a decided growth in unemployment, and no nationwide statistics of unemployment in the United States are anywhere available: *Resolved,....*

Wagner's concern with stabilization and recovery was soon evidenced again when in April 1928 he introduced another three bills (Schwarz 1970, chap. 2). The bills were a package of economic measures: creation of a nation wide system of public employment offices, establishment of a several billion dollar fund to be used for public works expenditures during periods of recession, and expansion of the federal government's collection of economic statistics. Wagner's biographer (Huthmacher 1968, pp. 61-62) says of these measures:

> The principles involved in the "Three Bills"....were by no means original with Wagner....President Harding's 1921 conference on unemployment, presided over by Commerce Secretary Herbert Hoover, devoted ten consecutive pages of its report to the need for collecting more adequate statistics concerning the extent and character of joblessness....Interest in the idea of employment exchanges was also anything but new in 1928....Since 1917 every Congress had seen the introduction of a bill, formulated by the American Association of Labor Legislation, providing for a federal-state system of employment services....Nor was the idea of using governmental expenditures to stabilize the economy—so often regarded as an innovation of the New Deal or of Lord Keynes—of such recent origin. President Harding's conference endorsed public works as a countercyclical measure, and in ensuing years such organizations as the American Association for Labor Legislation, the International Labor Office, and the National Unemployment League sought to institutionalize the procedure through statute....Wagner's first package of antidepression proposals, then, was based on concepts that had been familiar to economists and reformers for some time past. But never had these measures been introduced in the national legislature in conjunction with one another as

part of a concerted, rounded attack on the problems of cyclical and technological unemployment.

Not only was Wagner's legislative approach to fighting unemployment unique, so too was his grasp of the underlying economic process behind unemployment. In this regard, he was thoroughly Keynesian in perspective and remarkably ahead of his time. In a speech to the Senate in 1929, for example, he states (U.S. Congress 1929-1930, p. 2101):

> Unemployment starts a vicious circle from which it is difficult to escape. Men fired in one plant invariably means more men fired in another plant. Men without jobs have no purchasing power and it is that power which makes the wheels of industry go around and brings the farmers' products to market....When I plead for measures calculated to prevent unemployment I plead for the welfare of every business man in the country.

He then justifies government intervention to reduce unemployment in these terms (U.S. Congress, 1927-1928, p. 8171):

> I am asked why should the Government interfere in this economic problem? My answer is threefold: First, the government was created for this very purpose, to solve problems cooperatively which we can not solve individually. Secondly, because unemployment holds out a threat to the security of every American home and to the peace and safety of the entire American people; and lastly, because the problem is such that no business man could solve it if he would, and he has not the necessary motive to solve it if he could.

Wagner goes on to further justify government involvement by noting the difference between the private cost of unemployment to the business man and the social cost to the nation, and how this divergence represents a form of market failure that can only be resolved by collective action (U.S. 1929-1930, p. 8171):

> Only on a national scale and from a national viewpoint does it become both desirable and economical to solve this problem. Let me tell you why. A manufacturer I know had 1,400 men in his employ. Business slackened: he discharged 500 and let them shift for themselves. That may be sound economy for that one manufacturer....But can America likewise release those 500 or 5,000,000 of wage earners who are similarly discharged by manufacturers throughout the land?...Must not those idle and their families be fed and clothed and sheltered? Is it desirable for Americans to destroy their standard of living and uproot their essential faith in the fairness and future of America? Is it fair to the rest of the working men and women of this country to compel them to compete with men who, because of prolonged unemployment, are ready to work at any price?

His concern about the economic and social costs of unemployment led Wagner in December 1930 to introduce yet another bill aimed at promoting stabilization and recovery. This time the object was to establish a joint federal-state program of unemployment insurance. Written with the assistance of John Andrews (a Wisconsin institutional labor economist) of the American Association for Labor Legislation, Wagner's bill enjoyed considerable support but was again opposed by Hoover and thus did not gain legislative enactment (Schwarz 1970). Wagner tabled the measure for the next several years, thinking that other legislative measures introduced during the early New Deal years were more pressing. Only in 1935 did unemployment insurance become a reality as part of the Social Security Act.

The one other pre-Depression activity of the senator that bears directly on the origins and purpose of the NLRA is his participation in 1928 in an on-the-spot investigation of economic conditions in the bituminous coal industry. Along with four other senators, Wagner spent several weeks in West Virginia, Pennsylvania, and Ohio touring coal facilities and visiting with employers and workers. Even the Republican members of the group were shocked at the substandard living conditions of the workers and the heavy-handed tactics used by the coal operators. Wagner remarked (Huthmacher 1968, p. 64), "Had I not seen it myself, I would not have believed that in the United States there were large areas where civil government was supplanted by a system that can only be compared with ancient feudalism."

Important weapons in the operators' arsenal of control devices were the labor injunction and yellow dog contract (a requirement that as a condition of employment the worker foreswear joining a union). On his tour, he heard numerous examples of how these measures had been abused and came back to Washington with renewed determination to eliminate them. Wagner was thus a strong supporter of the Norris-LaGuardia bill, which made both practices unenforceable in federal court, and worked diligently for its ultimate passage in 1932.

Wagner was well known as a friend of labor and clearly valued unions as instruments of social justice. His support for legislation such as the Norris-LaGuardia Act and later the NLRA is readily explainable on this basis. But even in the pre-Depression period, it is clear that the *primary* interest Wagner had in collective bargaining was for its potential role in promoting macroeconomic stability and growth. This assertion is readily documented by examination of his keynote address titled, "The New Responsibilities of Organized Labor," delivered in early 1929 to the annual convention of the New York Federation of Labor (reprinted in U.S. Congress 1928-29, pp. 235-237). After welcoming remarks in the first paragraph, Wagner gets to his main thesis in the second paragraph, saying:

> The time has come for labor to contribute to the framing of economic policy and to assume responsibility with the employer for its successful application....Necessarily the whole present relationship of organized labor to industry must change. Instead of a tug of war we shall have a joint venture, instead of conflict we shall have cooperation.

He goes on to say:

> I see only two major obstacles to its realization [the joint venture of organized labor and industry]. The first is the labor injunction,....the other is a state of mind.
> Many are guilty of the habit of thought that the wage earner has no stake or interest in business and is not concerned with efficiency or prosperity....Our thinking on the subject, I believe, would become clearer if we no longer spoke of wages as costs. As soon as costs are mentioned the efficiency expert jumps to the conclusion that he has to bear downward. But wages must not be kept down. The true highway to prosperity is along the road of high wages.

Wagner then moves from the subject of high wages to that of unemployment. On this he says:

> Let me call your attention to our gravest industrial problem, the malady of unemployment. No other business problem is more urgent or more important....

Finally, Wagner concludes his speech with a discussion of what organized labor can do to resolve these problems. He says:

> Here, then, is the task for organized labor. It can prod the government into action. It may attempt some remedy itself.... Longer hours and lower wages do not cure unemployment: on the contrary, they aggravate it....Organized labor must resist them with all the power in its command. It should insist that wage earners be given enough buying power to purchase the products of their efficiency....This can be accomplished by cooperative understanding with a well-organized, well-disciplined, far visioned labor movement.

We see here also many similarities with the position Wagner was to adopt six years later in the NLRA. In his spoken remarks to these labor leaders in 1929 and to the Senate in 1935 during debate of the NLRA, no question can exist about the issue of most concern to him. He says it over and over—eliminating unemployment and restoring prosperity. In this task he also articulates a specific vision for organized labor—to maintain high wages and reasonable hours of work, to work jointly with business at the firm level to promote productive efficiency, and to participate with business at the industry level in the formulation and implementation of economic policies to maintain stable production and expanding employment. As we shall see, Wagner remained remarkably true to this vision as political and economic events caused many a twist and turn on the road to the NLRA.

THE HOOVER PRESIDENCY

The hallmark of the progressive-liberal reformers of the 1920s was their commitment to a form of "controlled competition" in which social control mechanisms were used to promote efficiency, stability and social justice. Although this group represented a distinct minority in the national polity during most of the 1920s, the door to power and influence opened modestly with the election of Herbert Hoover as President in 1928.

Hoover is often type-cast as an arch conservative wed to the doctrine of laissez faire. The truth is considerably different (Arnold 1982; Hawley 1987). Shortly after the stock market crash in October 1929, for example, Hoover initiated a three part stabilization program. The first part was maintenance of wages, accomplished by calling business leaders to Washington in late 1929 and securing from them a commitment to avoid wage cuts. The second prong of his program was to use presidential persuasion to gain accelerated expenditures on construction and capital investments by all levels of government and major firms in the private sector, such as railroads and utilities. The third prong was to encourage the Federal Reserve to use monetary policy to bring about lower interest rates and easily available credit.

All three parts of Hoover's stabilization program were implemented during the first year of the Depression and seemed to enjoy success—the decline of gross national product over the first year of the 1929 downturn was only half of that registered in the first year of the preceding 1920-1921 downturn. The majority opinion in 1930 was that Hoover had demonstrated highly competent management of the crisis (Barber 1985).

Beginning in the fall of 1931 and extending to March 1933, the economy took a further nose dive, and so too did Hoover's popularity. Part of the problem was that Hoover misread the direction of economic change. He believed that the bottom of the cycle would be reached in the spring-summer of 1931 and recovery would then commence. Not only was his credibility hurt when the reverse occurred, his confidence on this matter had caused him to oppose congressional calls for expanded expenditures for public works and unemployment relief, such as from Sen. Wagner.

Also working against Hoover was a shift in public perception. Through most of his career Hoover had a reputation as a humanitarian, an activist administrator, and an astute manager of the economy. Beginning in late 1930, however, people began to see a different Hoover—one who was uncaring toward the needy and destitute, who resisted new ideas and programs for dealing with the Depression, and who had no constructive economic program of his own.

One cause of this shift was Hoover's commitment to voluntarism and fiscal rectitude. As described earlier, Hoover's conception of an activist government had strict limits. He favored government programs and activities that in a noncoercive way made it possible for the private economy to function more efficiently and effectively, but he strongly opposed more interventionist activities that sought to regulate or control private business. Likewise, while he favored accelerated spending for public works, he opposed spending for its own sake (pump priming) as a wasteful use of resources. Thus, in 1929 and 1930 when the crisis began he had a number of policy arrows in his quiver that he could use to attack the Depression (e.g., persuading business leaders to avoid wage cuts). When these failed to stem the economic decline, he was faced with either abandoning his principles in favor of more drastic policies or staying true to his beliefs even if this meant vetoing legislation that had widespread support in Congress and among the public. He often chose the latter course of action, which soon gave him a reputation for "do nothingness."

Although Hoover was unwilling to compromise on voluntarism, growing portions of the business community were. U.S. Steel's decision to cut wages in fall 1931 was a watershed event, for it signaled the beginning of the end for 1920s-style welfare capitalism. Increasingly desperate to halt the unraveling of their business affairs, growing numbers of corporate leaders began to consider recovery proposals that earlier would have been considered far too radical, such as the

Swope Plan and the National Economic Council put forward by the U.S. Chamber of Commerce (see Farr 1959). The Swope Plan, proposed in 1931 by Gerard Swope, president of General Electric Co., called for all firms with 50 or more employees to join trade associations which would be given authority to stabilize production and prices, subject to oversight of the Federal Trade Commission. Hoover opposed these plans, however, calling the Swope Plan (Hoover 1952, p. 334) "the most gigantic proposal of monopoly ever made in history." Lacking any alternative to a "more of the same" policy, and saddled with a growing perception of callousness, Hoover went down to resounding defeat in the presidential election of 1932.

THE ROOSEVELT PRESIDENCY

During the Hoover presidency Sen. Wagner came to be regarded by many as the body's leading economic thinker and, according to contemporaries, put forward the most comprehensive, well-articulated approach to economic stabilization of anyone (Byrne 1951). It was not Wagner who was elected president, however, but Franklin Roosevelt.

When Roosevelt assumed the presidency in March 1933, the nation seemed to be sliding toward the edge of the abyss. He was thus immediately confronted with the practical issue of what to do to turn the economy toward recovery. But unlike Wagner, Roosevelt did not come into office with a well-articulated program. What he did have was a general philosophy, certain fundamental precepts, a willingness to experiment, and a keen sense for the politically doable (Perkins 1946). These together produced the major parts of the New Deal, including the Wagner Act.

Roosevelt's philosophy was in a number of fundamental respects similar to Wagner's, despite their different socioeconomic backgrounds (Roosevelt's family was part of the well-to-do landed gentry of upstate New York; Wagner's grew up in a poor immigrant working class family in New York City). Roosevelt's social and economic philosophy, like Wagner's, had its roots in the pre-World War I Progressive era (Fusfeld 1956). The theme of the movement was to promote the interests of the common man through political and economic reform, and it emphasized that concentration of economic power was the major reason for the failure of American society to live up to its full potential. Thus, Roosevelt was not anti-business, but sought only to prevent the abuses of monopoly and special privilege. Earlier in his career, he spoke favorably of Secretary of Commerce Hoover's efforts to promote trade associations as a means of accomplishing greater coordination and efficiency in production. He also spoke in favor of protecting the Collective Bargaining rights of workers (as did Hoover) and, as state senator and later governor of New York, Roosevelt took an active role in working for enactment of protective labor legislation, such as minimum wages, unemployment insurance, and old age pensions.

Roosevelt was in certain ways more conservative than Hoover. During the 1932 campaign, for example, Roosevelt harshly criticized Hoover for not balancing the budget and promised, if elected, to do so—a promise he attempted to make good on by slashing federal government employees' salaries through the Economy in Government Act of 1933. When it came to government regulation of the private economy, however, Roosevelt was willing to go considerably beyond Hoover, for he saw it as the government's ultimate responsibility to provide for the common welfare. This was evidenced in his approach to devising a recovery program in 1933. Significant elements of it were a logical extension of Hoover's program, only Hoover had shrunk from fully applying it.

According to Roosevelt, the root cause of the Depression was a basic shortfall of demand relative to supply. He stated (Fusfeld 1956, p. 205) in a campaign speech at Ogelthorpe College in Atlanta, Georgia, in 1932:

> Our basic problem is not an insufficiency of capital. It is an insufficient distribution of buying power coupled with an oversufficient speculation in production. While wages rose in many of our industries, they did not rise proportionately to the reward to capital, and at the same time the purchasing power of other great groups of our population was permitted to shrink [a reference to shrinking farm incomes].

To deal with the problem, Roosevelt clearly desired, as did Hoover, to exhaust opportunities for private initiative and cooperative efforts. In his famous Commonwealth speech in 1932, for example, he states (reprinted in Zinn 1966):

> The government should assume the function of economic regulation only as a last resort, to be tried only when private initiative, inspired by high responsibility, with such assistance as government can give, has finally failed.

Going beyond Hoover's conception of voluntarism, however, Roosevelt further states:

> The responsible heads of finance and industry instead of acting each for himself, must work together to achieve the common end. They must, where necessary, sacrifice this or that private advantage; and in reciprocal self-denial must seek a general advantage. It is here that formal government—political government, if you choose, comes in. Whenever in the pursuit of this objective the lone wolf, the unethical competitor, the reckless promoter, the Ishmael or Insull whose hand is against every man's, declines to join in achieving an end recognized as being for the public welfare, and threatens to drag the industry back to a state of anarchy, the government may properly be asked to apply restraint.

Following this philosophy, Roosevelt launched the New Deal on taking office in March 1933. His clear goal was to stop the deflationary spiral of prices and wages, stabilize production and employment, restore purchasing power and consumer spending, and thus create an upward movement of output and jobs. To accomplish this, he favored monetary policy over fiscal policy (Fusfeld 1956; Greer 1958). Thus, his initial move was to cut government spending but encourage the Federal

Reserve to liberalize money and credit. Later in 1933, he took the United States off the gold standard, considered at the time as a move toward inflation. Expansionary monetary policy was regarded, however, as a necessary condition to facilitate recovery but not likely on its own to accomplish the needed boost to aggregate demand; something else was needed. One option was deficit spending, such as for the public works program advocated by Wagner, but Roosevelt was resistant to this option. Not having a good alternative, Roosevelt chose to wait.

THE NIRA

As has been recounted numerous times (e.g., Bernstein, 1950; Vittoz, 1987), Roosevelt's hand was forced by the Thirty-Hour Week bill introduced by Sen. Hugo Black (D-Al.) in December 1932 and passed by the Senate in early April 1933. The bill mandated that, with certain exceptions, all firms engaged in interstate commerce can employ workers no more than six hours per day, five days a week. The idea was that sharing the work would promote additional employment and purchasing power. Its major proponent was the American Federation of Labor and measure was considered a "labor bill." Business groups were strongly against it and flocked to Washington to lobby against it.

In search of a better option both from an economic and political point of view, the Roosevelt Administration's counter proposal was the National Industrial Recovery Act, enacted in June 1933 and hailed by Roosevelt as "probably....the most important and far reaching legislation ever enacted by the American Congress."

The NIRA contained three parts or "titles." Title I began with a statement of policy:

> A national emergency productive of widespread unemployment and disorganization of industry, which burdens interstate and foreign commerce, affects the public welfare, and undermines the standards of living of the American people, is hereby declared to exist. It is hereby declared to be the policy of Congress to remove obstructions to the free flow of interstate and foreign commerce...by promoting the organization of industry for the purpose of cooperative action among trade groups, to induce and maintain united action of labor and management under adequate governmental sanctions and supervision, to eliminate unfair competitive practices, to promote the fullest possible utilization of the present productive capacity of industries, to avoid undue restriction of production,....to increase the consumption of industrial and agricultural products by increasing purchasing power, to reduce and relive unemployment, to improve standards of labor, and otherwise rehabilitate industry and to conserve natural resources.

Section 3 of Title I spelled out the manner in which industrial self-regulation was to be accomplished. The principal mechanism was a "code of fair competition" that was to be drafted for each industry by representatives of companies working through trade associations. Once approved by the president, with input from consumers, labor, and other affected parties, the codes of fair competition had the force of law. The content of the codes was left open to industry with certain caveats. One caveat is contained in Section 3 which stipulated that the regulation of prices and selling practices contained in the codes were exempted from the antitrust laws as long as they did not foster monopoly or discriminate against specific firms, or groups of firms, in an industry.

Another caveat was contained in Section 7 of Title I. The most important part, Section 7(a), mandated:

> Every code of fair competition....shall contain the following conditions: (1) That employees shall have the right to organize and bargain collectively through representatives of their own choosing, and shall be free from the interference, restraint, or coercion of employers of labor, or their agents, in the designation of such representatives or in self- organization or in other concerted activities for the purpose of collective bargaining or other mutual aid or protection; (2) that no employee and no one seeking employment shall be required as a condition of employment to join any company union or to refrain from joining, organizing, or assisting a labor organization of his own choosing; and (3) that employers shall comply with the maximum hours of labor, minimum rates of pay, and other conditions of employment, approved or prescribed by the President.

Title II of the NIRA pertained to public works and construction projects. It provided for the expenditure of $3.3 billion on public works, such as highways, dams, government office buildings, and so on.

Title III contained miscellaneous provisions of modest substantive importance.

Purpose of the NIRA

At the signing ceremony for the NIRA, Roosevelt described its purposes at some length (Roosevelt's speech is reprinted in Lapp 1933). The bill's purposes were also discussed at length by Sen. Wagner in a speech given to the Senate upon official introduction of the legislation on June 7, 1933 (also reprinted in Lapp 1933). In summary:

*The NIRA was conceived as emergency legislation, was explicitly made temporary in nature (the NIRA was given a two-year lifespan, after which it was to expire unless extended by Congress), and was intended to stop the economic contraction then in full force. The most important historical antecedent of the NIRA was the regulatory agencies and market controls established by the Wilson Administration during World War I to spur defense production and to control the galloping inflation and labor unrest unleashed by the wartime economic boom. These controls were viewed by many as a successful experiment that illustrated the positive results to be gained from a program that substituted administrative regulation of markets and tripartite cooperation among business, labor, and government for unrestricted competition and a government policy of laissez faire toward the economy (Farr 1959; Tomlins 1985). It is thus not coincidence that Hugh Johnson, the man Roosevelt picked to head the National Recovery Administration (the administrative body charged with implementation of the NIRA), had earlier served as an administrator in the World War I controls program and was a vocal proponent for using such an approach to combat the Depression.

*The NIRA was first and foremost a piece of macroeconomic legislation, intended in the short run to stop the deflationary downward spiral of wages, prices, production, and employment and to promote purchasing power and recovery in the long run. The proponents of the act saw the Depression as resulting from two types of imbalances—an imbalance in the structure of prices in the economy and an imbalance in aggregate demand relative to aggregate supply.

The imbalance in prices was reflected in several developments—the faster growth in the return to capital relative to the return to labor in the 1920s, the decline of agricultural prices relative to industrial prices, the failure of product prices to fall as much in concentrated or "monopolistic" industries as in competitive industries, and the failure of repeated cuts in prices and wages to restore a balance between demand and supply in individual product and labor markets (Rosenof 1975). Title I of the NIRA (in conjunction with the Agricultural Adjustment Act passed earlier in the spring of 1933) was designed to solve these problems by changing the structure of relative prices and putting a floor under competition (Hacker 1934). Thus, it was intended that wages be raised relative to prices, that agricultural prices be raised relative to industrial prices, and that destructive competition be stopped by stabilizing prices and wages through the codes of fair competition. (Destructive competition as an economic process is defined and discussed in Clark 1923).

The second imbalance was between aggregate demand and aggregate supply. The proponents of the NIRA saw the Depression as due not only to distortions in relative prices but also due to inadequate purchasing power. The causes of inadequate purchasing power were thought to be numerous (Barber 1985): the faster growth of profits relative to wages (the relative price argument writ large), the inability of consumers, businesses, and government to maintain spending in the face of growing debt burdens brought on by deflation and restricted income flows, and inadequate foreign demand for American exports due to austerity measures imposed on the Axis governments by the Treaty of Versailles, political instability in several European countries, and "beggar thy neighbor" trade policies of various governments. Title II was intended to stimulate domestic spending by injecting several billions of dollars into the economy through public works.

*The NIRA was not a "labor" piece of legislation, nor was Sen. Wagner's involvement with and support of the NIRA primarily motivated by considerations related to support of unions and collective bargaining per se. Roosevelt, Francis Perkins (Roosevelt's Secretary of Labor), and Wagner were all advocates for improvements in labor conditions, but each favored legal enactment over collective bargaining as the principle means to achieve it. Thus, Roosevelt spoke often in his presidential campaign of the need to pass legislation to improve factory safety and eliminate child labor, but he rarely mentioned organized labor (Fusfeld 1956). Likewise, when Wagner was a senator in the New York state legislature in the 1910s he helped pass over 50 labor-related pieces of protective legislation, while in his early years in the U.S. Senate his principal focus was on gaining passage of his three bills on public works, employment exchanges, and improved labor market statistics. His only major legislative effort on behalf of organized labor prior to the NIRA was to secure passage of the Norris-LaGuardia Act. Perkins was also sympathetic toward unions and collective bargaining, but gave them little explicit role in the legislative program she pressed upon Roosevelt when she accepted his invitation to be Secretary of Labor (Bernstein 1950; Perkins 1946).

It is also noteworthy that organized labor gave Roosevelt only modest support in his campaign for the presidency (Sydney Hillman voted for Norman Thomas, while John L. Lewis voted for Hoover, as did leaders of several other major AFL unions), while the AFL vocally opposed Perkin's nomination for Secretary of Labor. Thus, neither person's support of the NIRA can be construed as "paying a debt" to organized labor.

Finally, it is clear from the legislative history of the NIRA that the bill was the end product of a series of compromises, with business interests emerging from the behind-doors negotiations as the big winners (Farr 1959). The AFL was the principal advocate of the Black Thirty-Hour Week bill, and it was the bill's passage in the Senate that galvanized Roosevelt to find a substitute recovery measure. From the start, then, the NIRA was pushed by non-AFL interests with non-AFL agendas. Roosevelt formed two informal groups to draw up such a plan, one headed by Raymond Moley (a Columbia economics professor and member of Roosevelt's "Brains Trust") and the second by Sen. Wagner. Both drew considerable counsel from representatives of business interests and their associated plans for "industrial self-government." Labor, to the extent it was involved in the early drafting of the NIRA, was represented by persons from industries outside the "core" of the AFL—coal (Jett Lauck), clothing (Sydney Hillman and Leo Wolman), and railroads (Donald Richberg)—that had themselves been long-time advocates of suspension of the anti-trust laws and various forms of regulation by government or industry trade associations.

Finally, Sen. Wagner's sponsorship and support of the NIRA was also motivated by his realization that Roosevelt's aversion to deficit spending made it unlikely that his goal of expanded public works expenditures would be enacted unless he could tie it to a bill that Roosevelt felt was a high priority. Thus, it can safely be said that Wagner's motivation for supporting the NIRA had much more to do with his goal of promoting additional spending on public works as a pump-priming recovery measure and stopping destructive competition through the codes of fair competition than it did with promotion of unions and collective bargaining per se.

The Origins and Purpose of Section 7(a)

As noted previously, Section 7(a) of the NIRA was the forerunner of the Wagner Act. The origins and purpose of the former are thus of great import for understanding the latter.

The text of Section 7(a) has already been previously quoted and will not be repeated here. Suffice it to note that it mandated that as a part of every code of fair competition:

1. Employees have the right to organize and bargain collectively through representatives of their own choosing and shall be free from the interference, restraint, or coercion of employers in the exercise of these rights;
2. No employee or person seeking employment shall be required to join a company union or refrain from joining a labor organization of his choosing; and
3. Employers shall comply with the maximum hours of labor, minimum wage rates, and other terms and conditions of employment specified in the codes. In the case that employers fail to comply, or are unable to mutually agree as to acceptable minimum wage and maximum hour standards, the president can impose appropriate standards upon the industry and penalties upon violators.

The purpose of Section 7(a) has to be understood in the context of the wider purpose of the NIRA and, more specifically, Title I of the legislation within which Section 7(a) was contained. As noted previously, Title I was directed at correcting imbalances in the structure of prices (including wages and profits) and ending the downward spiral of wages and working conditions due to destructive competition. A logical inference, then, is that Section 7(a) was included because the draftsmen of the act and its supporters in the Congress and executive branch saw the provisions of Section 7(a) as important to accomplishing the broader purpose of Title I. A second possibility also exists, however—that the inclusion of Section 7(a) had less to do with national economic policy and much more to do with politics, such as winning the support of key persons and constituencies during the legislative process or advancing the political and economic agenda of particular interest groups in society.

The evidence suggests that both motives were present but that the economic one was dominant. The economic rationale for Section 7(a) was two-pronged—to end destructive competition and the downward spiral of wages and labor standards it entailed and to shore up wages and shorten work hours in order to promote purchasing power and aggregate demand. With regard to the former, Sen. Wagner stated to the Senate:

> What has dragged industry down more than anything else is the exploitation of labor, cutthroat competition. If you inquire of business men all through the country, the thing they will tell you is, that particularly during these days of unemployment they have suffered because their competitors were able to secure people to work for them for long hours and starvation wages.

With regard to the latter, he stated:

> For several years we floated along on two bubbles, first the illusory prosperity of installment buying and secondly the quixotic policy of selling goods to Europe and lending money to pay for our own goods. When these two bubbles burst the crash came. In retracing our steps to the land of plenty, we must set up a sounder security than bubbles. The only safeguard is a well-planned wage program, dispersing adequate purchasing power throughout the economic system (Lapp 1933).

How was Section 7(a) to help accomplish these goals? The key requirement was to first stabilize wages and labor standards, thus ending the process of deflation and destructive competition. This could be accomplished in one or a combination of three ways: by using legal enactment to establish minimum wages, maximum hours, and other limits on labor standards; by promoting trade unions so that a floor might be placed under competition through collective bargaining agreements; or by suspending the anti-trust laws and allowing firms to enter into wage-fixing agreements. Once wages and labor standards were stabilized, the augmentation of purchasing power then depended on a gradual increase in wages rates (and other forms of labor income, such as unemployment and old age insurance) and possibly a further shortening of hours. This could also be accomplished through the three means earlier cited, although only the former two were realistic alternatives as employers could not be expected to voluntarily raise wages and their own labor costs.

Looking at the provisions of Section 7(a) listed above, it is immediately clear that the draftsmen of the act sought to accomplish the purpose of Title I by using all three instruments of wage stabilization and recovery. The purpose of the first and second provisions—the statement of labor's right to join unions and to practice collective bargaining free of employer interference, and the ban on yellow dog contracts and employer requirements that workers belong to one and only one kind of labor organization (e.g., a company union)—accomplished wage stabilization and recovery by encouraging and protecting trade unions and collective bargaining. The third provision—the mandate that every code of fair competition contain a minimum wage and maximum hour provision, as agreed to by the respective trade associations—also promoted the stabilization goal through a form of industrial self-regulation on the part of business firms. Legal enactment was also present, both directly in the provision that gave the president the authority to unilaterally set the minimum wage and maximum hour standards and indirectly in an executive order issued by Roosevelt ("President's Re-employment Agreement") shortly after passage of the NIRA that set uniform minimum wage and maximum hour levels until individual industry codes could be worked out and approved by the NRA (Roos 1937).

Although all three instruments of wage stabilization and recovery were present in Section 7(a) it is evident that priority was given first and foremost to industrial self-regulation by business firms. This is seen by noting that the primary vehicle specified in Title I to end destructive competition and promote recovery was the code of fair competition—a code to be drafted by business firms acting through trade associations. Since every industry was required to adopt a code of fair competition, and every code was to have minimum wage and maximum hour provisions, it appears that this was intended by the draftsmen of the act to be the principle method chosen to take wages out of competition and put a floor under labor markets.

Collective bargaining was also promoted by Section 7(a), but not nearly to the extent that industrial self-regulation was. Observe, first, that the statement in Section 7(a) affirming the right of workers to join unions and practice collective bargaining did not break significant new ground either in law or principle—this right had been affirmed in a long line of court decisions stretching back nearly a century and was explicitly stated in the Norris-LaGuardia Act (1932), as well as in earlier pieces of legislation such as the Railway Labor Act of 1926 (Bernstein 1950). Second, the prohibition of employer acts of interference in Section 7(a) was relatively weak in that no specific acts were enjoined, no specific penalties for violations given, and no person or agency put in charge of administering this provision. Third, the prohibition of the yellow dog contract was a modest gain for collective bargaining, given that the Norris-LaGuardia Act had already made it unenforceable in court. Finally, although Section 7(a) made it illegal for an employer to require workers to join a company union, it did not make company unions illegal per se. At the bottom of the priority list in Section 7(a) was legal enactment. The only case in which minimum wages, maximum hours, or other terms and conditions of employment could be directly set by government mandate was when a trade association failed to adopt a code of fair competition, or the code agreed upon was deemed unacceptable by the president.

In this view, then, Section 7(a) was included in the NIRA because it was a crucial part of the act's attempt to stop the deflation caused by destructive competition and to promote recovery through stimulation of purchasing power and aggregate demand. Neither could be accomplished without, in Wagner's words, a "well-planned wage program." This well-planned wage program, however, could accomplish its objectives in several ways, and as just demonstrated, the primary path chosen emphasized industrial self-regulation over collective bargaining and legal enactment. It is worthwhile to briefly explore why this mix of policy instruments was chosen. Here, ideology and power politics played an equal or dominant role to considerations of economic efficacy.

The major explanation for the dominance of industrial self-regulation over collective bargaining and legal enactment was that the former had a much larger and politically stronger constituency than the latter two and also enjoyed a greater chance of passing the constitutionality test if challenged in the courts (Farr 1959). Both business groups and most of organized labor, particularly the leaders of the AFL, were committed to voluntarism and for this reason opposed legal enactment as a means of determining wages and other labor standards. While most New Dealers, including key figures such as Roosevelt, Wagner, and Perkins, favored this approach, principally in the form of legislation establishing minimum wages, maximum hours, and government-sponsored unemployment and old age insurance programs, these types of government economic regulation had been declared unconstitutional numerous times by the Supreme Court and, in addition, were actively opposed by both business and labor.

The business community, though fractionated along a number of policy and ideological lines, was for the most part united in wanting to keep out as much "outside" interference in its affairs as possible. As the Depression deepened, however, an increasing number of business leaders reluctantly saw that, if disaster was to be avoided, some type of collective action was necessary to stop the process of deflation. The key requirement, from their perspective, was to make sure that whatever action was adopted to stabilize wages and labor standards did not threaten either profits or control. Not surprisingly, then, the most oft-suggested plan of action from business groups was relaxation or elimination of the anti-trust laws so that firms operating through trade associations could cooperatively establish and enforce minimum wage and maximum hour standards. Even here, however, was an interesting split.

Those companies in oligopolistic industries, such as automobiles and steel, favored industrial self-regulation with only a minimal role played by government and no role for "outside" labor organizations (Gordon 1994). Because these industries were dominated by a relatively few large firms, the conditions were favorable for the companies to use a trade association to serve as an effective coordinator and policeman with regard to maintenance of price and wage standards. Thus, business recovery plans, such as advanced by Swope and the Chamber of Commerce, were largely silent on the issue of wages and hours—not because they were viewed as unimportant but because industry thought these were "internal" matters that they could effectively regulate if government would relax the anti-trust laws and give trade associations power to discipline noncompliant members.

By 1932, however, some companies had reluctantly decided that stabilization and recovery could not be achieved by business alone and that either government or trade unions were also necessary if an effective floor was to be placed under competition in labor markets. These companies were primarily in highly competitive industries, such as bituminous coal and men's clothing, where the presence of thousands of firms made the prospect of effective self-regulation a vain hope (Gordon 1994; Vittoz 1987). Thus, the only hope for stability was that order be forced upon the market through some type of industry-wide planning and coordination mechanism. In this spirit, periodic calls were made by business interests in the bituminous coal industry for creation of a national coal commission with authority to allocate production quotas among firms and set minimum labor standards. Likewise, as the crisis in the industry worsened after 1929 many companies began to rethink their reflexive opposition to trade unionism. Said one coal operator in 1931 (quoted in Farr 1959, p. 28):

> For the past four years these operators who have dispensed with union agreements have had plenty of time to view the experience of running without any fixed wage scale or without having any labor organization to deal with. It must be admitted by everybody that the situation is even worse than when we dealt with the union....Personally, I would rather deal with the United Mine Workers than with these ruthless, wage-cutting operators who are a detriment to the industry.

As we have seen, organized labor was also split on the issue of how best to promote economic stabilization and recovery. The AFL, wed to the doctrine of voluntarism, was hostile to government regulation of markets and labor standards per se (with exceptions, such as workers compensation laws and minimum wages for women and children). The AFL thus found itself allied with business interests in advocating relaxation of the anti-trust laws and various forms of industrial self-regulation, though for the AFL the "self regulation" concept meant joint labor-management coordination and planning of industry along the lines of that promulgated in World War I and espoused in "Industry's Manifest Destiny." Other labor leaders, like Lewis and Hillman, took a more interventionist position, reflecting the chaotic, deteriorating conditions in their respective industries (Fraser 1991). The latter group was more philosophically aligned with Wagner's own views and had greater access to him in the drafting process of the NIRA.

Section 7(a), then, was a compromise that arose out of the conflicting ideologies and political power on the part of business, organized labor, and government. All three groups saw stabilization of wages, hours, and labor standards as crucial to economic recovery. The dominant group of business firms, represented by organizations such and the Chamber of Commerce and National Association of Manufacturers, preferred deleting Section 7(a) altogether from the NIRA on the grounds that industry could best achieve the stabilization objective through relaxation of the anti-trust laws and self-regulation. They were unable to achieve this objective, however, for three reasons. First, Sen. Wagner effectively cast a veto in the drafting process when he told business interests, "no Section 7(a), no bill" (Huthmacher 1968, p. 147). Second, business groups were more strongly opposed to the Black Thirty-Hour Week bill than they were to Section 7(a), and so they saw the latter as an acceptable price to pay to derail the former. Third, since World War I, business men had been touting the virtues of employee representation plans, which they often and somewhat disingeniously referred to as "collective bargaining," and thus found it difficult to oppose Section 7(a) as long as it did not impose a particular form of collective bargaining (e.g., trade unions). Finally, it was strongly felt by many in government, labor, the media, and academic circles (as well as a minority of management people) that, on grounds of economics and equity, if business firms were to be exempted from the anti-trust laws and permitted to stabilize prices, then labor should also be allowed to combine, both to insure that wages did not lag behind prices and because only if workers were organized could they have an effective voice in the drafting and administration of the codes of fair competition.

The fact that Section 7(a) was included at all in the NIRA can thus be interpreted as a defeat for business. It was a modest defeat, however, as in most other respects Section 7(a) was fashioned in a way to make it palatable to corporate America. Thus, as previously noted, the first part of Section 7(a) dealing with unions and collective bargaining did not break much substantive ground, both because the right to join unions and engage in collective bargaining had long since been affirmed in legislation and court decisions and because the prohibition on employer acts of interference with these rights was largely toothless. The second part of Section 7(a) dealing with company unions was disliked but not viscerally, as it did not make illegal company unions but only prohibited companies from making workers join one as a condition of employment. Finally, the third part of Section 7(a) was also made palatable to business by vesting the power to decide minimum wage levels and maximum hours with the trade associations, subject only to government approval.

Viewed from the perspective of organized labor, Section 7(a) was certainly a positive step forward, but it was not a "Magna Carta" for the trade union movement, as AFL President William Green boasted. What Congress and the president were looking for in early 1933 was some means to bring deflation to an end and spur the beginnings of an economic recovery. They were convinced that stabilization of wages, a shortening of hours, and protection of other labor standards (e.g., elimination of child labor) were crucial ingredients to the success of this effort. By including Section 7(a), they were stating, in effect, that unions and collective bargaining were to play a role in this process, albeit a distinctly junior role. The modest role given organized labor reflected, in part, its modest share of the workforce organized (about 10%), the relatively few industries in which it had much presence (e.g., the needle trades, coal, railroads, construction, and printing), and the strong opposition of business groups to union involvement.

An additional factor often overlooked in this regard is the negative attitude held by the bulk of the public and many progressive-liberal reformers toward the organized labor movement of that day. Unions, with certain notable exceptions such as Hillman's Amalgamated Clothing Workers union, were not seen as engines of social reform (Fusfeld 1956; Perkins 1946; Bernstein 1950). Rather, most were regarded as quasi-labor monopolies that were equally or more autocratic than the business firms they tried to organize and were run by labor "bosses" of mediocre talents and sometimes questionable ethics. The public's perception of most unions, therefore, was one of artificially high wages, numerous restrictive work practices, costly strikes over jurisdictional squabbles, and an all too frequent incidence of internal corruption and links to various rackets.

Indicative of this sentiment are the observations recounted in an autobiography by Thomas Elliot (1992) who was a self-professed "New Dealer," worked in the Department of Labor with Francis Perkins, and later became her assistant legal counsel. In personal correspondence to his family, he confided in 1933 (p. 54):

> The two labor representatives on the Board [NIRA Labor Advisory Board] are pretty awful. John L. Lewis is a dishonest thug, but Kirsten [an executive with Filene's Department Stores] thinks he's less harmful on the Board than off. William Green, President of the A.F. of L., is amiable enough, but is forever making great orations on extraneous matters. He nearly upset the applecart yesterday by launching into one of these just when Swope had gained the first real concession from the employers.

He goes on to say (pp. 56-57):

> While I was all for upholding the workers' rights under Section 7(a), and highly critical of employers who denied them those rights, I was not automatically pro-union. Far from it. Frequently I wrote scornfully about the leaders of some of the major A.F. of L. craft unions, especially in the building trades, calling them "a bunch of racketeers in league with a lot of the building contractors." And again: "It's hard to be enthusiastic about organized labor." Those were early comments, but in 1934 I still felt the same way: "I'd like to see equality of bargaining power, but I doubt the efficacy of any program designed to increase the strength of the A.F. of L. as at present constituted. There is a dearth of disinterested labor leaders. If some of the top men could be deported, and Sydney Hillman and Philip Murray and a few like that put in charge, then we'd have a worth-while labor movement."

This opinion was shared by many both within and outside of government. Roosevelt and Perkins, for example, favored protecting the rights of workers to organize and collective bargain but seldom mentioned them in their various speeches and proposals with regard to either labor issues or economic policy and the Depression, while the members of Roosevelt's Brains Trust (Raymond Moley, Rexford Tugwell, Adolph Berle) were either largely ignorant of unions or critical of them (Renshaw 1985). Outside of government, the trade union movement also inspired little confidence as an engine of economic and social reform. Adamic, writing in *Harper's Magazine* (1932), said:

> The body is undoubtedly a sick body. It is ineffectual—flabby, afflicted with the dull pains of moral and physical decline. The big industrialists and conservative politicians are no longer worried by it. Indeed, the intelligent ones see in it the best obstacle—temporary at least—to the emergence of a militant and formidable labor movement.

Similarly, Stolberg (1933, p. 349) said in *Scribner's Magazine*:

> The prestige of the Greens and the Wolls and the Rickerts has been badly shaken by the NRA. The New Deal has brought out they are not merely "conservative" but ridiculously inadequate for these critical times. The old fashioned craft leader is through, for he is helpless to express the increasing restlessness of American labor. The country is full of spontaneous strikes. Wherever one goes one sees picket lines. When Mr. Green opened the national convention of the A.F. of L. with the vision of 25,000,000 Americans "genuinely and actually within the trade union family" under his leadership, the press table shook with long and low laughter.

The title of Stolberg's article from which the above quotation is taken is, "A Government in Search of a Labor Movement." It is a most astute and descriptive title. Given the moribund state of the organized labor movement in early 1933, it would have been naive or hopelessly heroic for the Congress and the Roosevelt Administration to make trade unions the major instrument in the NIRA for effectuating the stabilization of the labor market. That Congress wrote in Section 7(a) owes much to the efforts of a single man—Sen. Wagner—and the fact that labor had already gotten its foot in the political door with Senate passage of the Black Thirty-Hour Week Bill. Once the NIRA and Section 7(a) were in place, however, events developed a logic and momentum of their own that created both a need for a stronger labor movement within the Roosevelt administration, per Stolberg's title, and the fertile conditions necessary for its germination and growth. It is this subject we turn to next.

FROM THE NIRA TO THE WAGNER ACT

Little more than two years elapsed between enactment of the National Industrial Recovery Act in June 1933 and the National Labor Relations Act (Wagner Act) on July 5, 1935. The contention of this paper is that the origins and purpose of the latter are inextricably linked to the macroeconomic origins and purposes of the former. This is amply illustrated by Sen. Wagner's statement to the Senate on behalf of the NLRA in the spring 1935 (NLRB 1985, p. 1412):

> It is a matter of common knowledge that the principles of section 7(a) of the Recovery Act have been flaunted at the very crucial spots where their observance is most essential. This does not inflict injuries upon one group alone. It is unjust to employees who have seen what was handed to them as a new charter being treated as a meaningless gesture. It isunfair to the vast majority of employers who are anxious and willing to obey the law, and who are faced with the destructive competition of those who seek to gain advantage by disobeying it. It is disastrous to every economic interest because it is a main cause for the reappearance of those very tendencies which brought collapse in 1929, and which will certainly bring it again if they are not checked.

The clear implication of this quotation is that in 1935 the senator's focus was still squarely on macroeconomic issues of stabilization and growth and that the NLRA was meant to strengthen those "very crucial spots" in Section 7(a) that were being flaunted by employers and thus endangering the nascent process of economic recovery. The senator also explicitly states that the purpose of the NLRA was not to benefit any particular interest group, such as organized labor, but was intended to serve the community at large by arresting the tendencies toward renewed stagnation and deflation.

To better appreciate the senator's perspective on these matters and the reasons for the drafting of the NLRA by the senator and its passage by the Congress and signing into law by President Roosevelt, it is necessary to explore some of the events that transpired in this two year period.

The Growth of Union Membership

Trade union membership had declined from 5 million to 3.5 million between 1920-1929 and then sunk another half million during the early years of the Great Depression. Even the strongest unions, such as the Mine Workers, were nearly driven to dissolution and bankruptcy (Bernstein 1950). Upon FDR's signing of the NIRA, however, a remarkable turnaround occurred. In the space of six months, unions made up all of the membership losses of the previous three years.

Though a number of academic writers have written about this phenomenon, few have explored in detail workers' motivation for rushing to join unions during the first year of the NIRA period and the process by which this happened. That the NIRA played a pivotal role in this process is clearly revealed by the "night and day" change that took place in union organizing immediately upon its enactment. Illustrative is the experience of the International Brotherhood of Pulp, Sulphite and Paper Mill Workers (IBPSPMW) union. Zieger (1984, p. 67) says of the early NIRA period:

> The upsurge of unionism in the early summer of 1933 startled Brotherhood veterans. Prior to passage of the new legislation [the NIRA], the union's office had been virtually inactive....John Burke [the union president] found the lack of organization perplexing, for, as he observed in February [three months *after* the election of FDR], clearly "everything that the Socialists predicted in the way of breakdown of the capitalist system is coming to pass." Still, "the great mass of wage earners seem[s] to be as difficult to reach as ever."

Within weeks of the passage of the NIRA the situation was completely reversed. Zieger (pp. 68-69) describes it thus:

> Response to the new opportunity to organize came from every section of the country....The international union tried to respond to this unaccustomed demand for its services. "I have so many calls for organizers," Burke declared in July, "that I have neither the men nor the money to take care of all of them." By August the union was running out of dues books, and the printer could not keep abreast of orders for per capita stamps.

What accounted for this tremendous surge in workers' interest in joining unions in the summer of 1933? Why did it occur in 1933 after passage of the NIRA and not in 1932 when Congress passed the Norris-LaGuardia Act, a measure that significantly increased the public support and protection of collective bargaining by banning yellow dog contracts and restricting the use of court injunctions in labor disputes? What made it possible for the United Mine Workers union to completely organize the bituminous coal industry in the space of only six weeks during the summer of 1933, when a few months prior to the NIRA the union was near collapse?

The answers to these questions are multifaceted, but central to all explanations must be the Depression. The Depression set the stage for unionization by creating employment conditions that led to widespread worker discontent with the status quo. Repeated wages cuts, hours reductions, speed-ups, and prolonged joblessness gradually dissipated the goodwill of workers toward their employers and their faith in the promises of welfare capitalism (Brody 1980). A minority of workers, of course, had never believed in the promises of welfare capitalism nor had felt more than hostility toward their employers. But it took three years of depression, and the spread of insecurity and injustice across a large part of the workforce, to make the majority of employees ready to consider alternatives to current institutional arrangements.

Alternative institutional arrangements could take a number of forms, however, and collective bargaining was only one. Prior to the passage of the NIRA, there is little evidence that promotion of greater collective bargaining was, in fact, the preferred institutional change favored by most workers or the American people at large. The platform adopted at the Democratic Party Convention in 1932, for example, made scant mention of unions and gave next to no role to collective bargaining as an instrument of economic recovery. The year 1932 also witnessed a veritable flood of opinions and plans in the press espousing alternative solutions to the Depression. While monetary reform, national economic planning, public works, and other such options all received a wide hearing, encouragement of greater collective bargaining was not a popular or often-heard suggestion, a fact that remained true even in the first months of the Roosevelt Administration (*Nation's Business*, 1932; Rosenof 1975); nor was 1932 marked by any particular increase in union organizing activity or strikes for recognition. Why, then, did the demand for unions suddenly spread across the industrial landscape in the summer of 1933?

The answer has two parts. The first is that the wage cuts, speed-ups, and mass layoffs of the early 1930s embittered many workers and increased their desire for a union and the services it provides (Asher and Edsworth, 1995), while the costs of union joining were reduced (or so it was initially thought) by Section 7(a)'s prohibition of antiunion discrimination. The surge of unionism that followed immediately after the passage of the NIRA was thus partly a reflection of a suppressed or latent demand for collective bargaining on the part of numerous employees which, under the encouragement and protection of Section 7(a), came bubbling to the surface. This dimension of union activity in 1933 is illustrated by Zieger (1984, pp. 69-70) when he says of the IBPSPMW, "Workers surged into the Brotherhood in 1933 and 1934 primarily in hopes of increasing their wages....Discipline on the job, deterioration of working conditions, and callousness on the part of managers also impelled pulp and paper workers toward the union."

The first part of the increased demand for unionism set off by the NIRA was thus "intrinsic" or "organic" in nature in that it represented a demand for the services or benefits of unions for their own intrinsic value (e.g., to raise wages, reduce line speed, protect against arbitrary discipline). Another part of the demand for unions unleashed by the NIRA was largely instrumental in nature and had to do with the act's stated purpose of promoting macroeconomic recovery. The NIRA was introduced with great national fanfare and support of its provisions was often equated with patriotic duty. IBPSPMW President Burke (Zieger 1984, p. 12) observed, for example, "The people of the United States during the summer and fall months of 1933 were stirred into a sort of religious enthusiasm for the N.R.A." Part of this enthusiasm was translated into a demand for unionism, as joining unions and engaging in collective bargaining was suddenly transformed by the NIRA into a crucial component of the president's program to end the Depression and promote recovery. In addition, considerable belief existed in the summer of 1933 that the NIRA *required* some form of collective bargaining (*Business Week* 1933b, p. 9). The net result was that hundreds of thousands of workers rushed to form local unions (and many employers rushed to establish company unions) in order to support the NIRA. Zieger (1984, p. 71) describes this process thus:

> The broader goals that workers brought to local union formation usually had less to do with commitment to organized labor than with a desire to support the New Deal, President Roosevelt, and the NRA. At least two new locals chose names reflecting this commitment, Local 190, representing paper box workers in the Boston area, which took the sobriquet "New Deal," and NIRA Local 159 in Ohio. No corps of organizers rolled through the mill towns and box shops claiming that "the President wants you to join a union," [a reference to tactics used very successfully by John L. Lewis in summer 1933 to organize the coal fields] but throughout the industry workers identified enthusiastically with the Roosevelt program....Workers in every sector seized upon the NRA promise, as a means both of bettering their individual lot and of revitalizing the country. Patriotism fused with self-interest.

The encouragement of unionism by the NIRA was thus quite direct and powerful and was very much tied to the macroeconomic purpose of the NIRA. Largely unremarked upon is a second, complementary way in which the NIRA further boosted the demand for unionism. The NIRA politicized the employment relationship because wages, hours, and other terms and conditions of employment became administratively established through the codes of fair competition. If workers were to gain the higher wages that the NIRA both promised and desired, it quickly became clear that they would have to organize so that their interests were represented in the code hearings in Washington, D.C. It was in this light that AFL organizer Paul Smith stated to a group of workers in summer 1933 (quoted in *Business Week* 1933a, p. 8):

> Your chosen leaders will have as much to say as Harvey Firestone or anyone else when they appear before the President or his qualified representatives....If any of you joins a company union, you do it deliberately and deliberately forfeit the great privilege that is your's.

In a similar vein, AFL organizer William Collins (p. 7) stated:

> [T]he automobile workers can only secure the maximum benefits to which they are entitled under the Industrial Recovery Act through collective action.

The benefits of organization espoused by organizers such as Smith and Collins were soon apparent, as union leaders in organized industries were heavily involved in the drafting of their respective codes of fair competition, and the wage, hour, and labor standards provisions adopted in them were in nearly all respects the terms and conditions existing in union contracts (Roos 1937; Vittoz 1987).

It is impossible to determine the portion of the increase in union membership in 1933-1934 that is accounted for by workers' intrinsic demand for union services versus the instrumental demand generated by the desire to aid the NIRA recovery program and participate in the drafting of the codes of fair competition. What can be said with some certainty are two things. The first is that the intrinsic portion of this demand, while much higher and more visible in 1933-1934 than in earlier years, was nevertheless confined to a minority of the workforce. We know from historical accounts (e.g., Bernstein 1970; Fine 1963; Wolman 1936; Zieger 1977) that many of the new AFL federal unions chartered in the summer of 1933 had disappeared a year later, that in a significant minority of secret ballot elections held in 1933-1934 by the various labor boards created by the Roosevelt Administration workers chose a company union or no representative organization, that in industries such as automobiles and steel union leaders candidly admitted that unions did not have majority support among workers in most of the plants, and that a number of the most visible, confrontative organizing campaigns and strikes were spearheaded by a relatively small cadre of labor militants and political radicals. The second thing that can be said with certainty is that the NIRA was crucial to revitalizing the union movement because it wrapped unions in the flag and made collective bargaining an instrument for promoting economic recovery and thus the general welfare of society.

The Growth of Strikes and Labor Militancy

Although employers in industries such as coal and clothing were quickly organized in the summer of 1933, the same was not true across most other industries. The large companies in mass production, such as General Motors, U.S. Steel, General Electric, and Goodyear, remained strongly opposed to any extension of trade unionism to their operations, in part because they remained convinced that unionism had nothing to offer them with regard to either stabilization or recovery. Thus, these companies sought to maintain the open shop, either through individual dealing with workers or through some form of employee representation plan or "company union."

The increased demand for union representation (both intrinsic and instrumental) described in the previous section collided head on with the intransigence of these employers. The employers responded with the traditional tools of antiunionism, such as firing of union activists, use of labor spies, acts of picket line violence, and so on, or shunted workers into a hastily-built, unilaterally-imposed, company-sponsored employee representation plan. Adding to the frustration of workers was the ineffectiveness and timidity of the American Federation of Labor.

The demand for organization unleashed by the NIRA caught the AFL unprepared and the militancy and spontaneity of the movement caused considerable disquiet among its leaders who feared losing control of the situation to youthful "hotheads." The response of the AFL was to try to channel and contain worker militancy in ways that protected the federation's organizational interests. One method, for example, was to charter independent, directly-affiliated "federal" unions at the local level (Zieger 1977). The AFL gave these new locals only half-hearted support, however, because they were intended to be temporary organizations that soon would be divided up among the AFL's national craft unions. The AFL also intervened in a number of local strikes, brought in a federation staff person to take charge, and effectively elbowed aside the more militant local leadership. The result of such AFL policies was all too often a dissolution or withering of the federal unions, the loss of strikes, and stymied efforts to organize and gain collective bargaining contracts—outcomes that all contributed to mounting frustration and militancy on the part of local rank and file. The average blue-collar worker was thus in the position of being told by its government that labor needed to organize to promote higher wages and economic recovery but found its way blocked by both recalcitrant employers and conservative, sometimes inept, labor leaders.

The final element in this story, and one touched on in the previous section, is the impetus given to strikes and job actions by the labor policies and code administration on the part of the National Recovery Administration. The inauguration of the NIRA promoted strikes by causing workers to expect higher pay increases and steadier work than employers were able and/or willing to deliver. Likewise, the imposition of the minimum wage provisions led to pay compression among factory workers and discontent among the more highly-paid skilled workers. Finally, much as experienced with wartime wage-price controls, when government becomes involved in the wage determination process it inevitably provides an incentive for workers to strike in order to air their grievances and induce government officials to intervene and pressure management to give in to worker demands.

In this respect, the NIRA not only created a demand for union organization, but it also created additional conditions and incentives for strikes. Illustrative are two examples, both taken from accounts in *Business Week* (1933c, p. 12, 1933d, p. 3). The first describes labor unrest in Akron, Ohio, at a plant of the Goodyear Tire and Rubber Co.:

> Akron, geared directly to Detroit, should be used to the twin evils of overtime and layoff. The tire business is seasonal. This year the annual decline, delayed by the belated automotive boom, unfortunately comes at a time when Blue Eagleism [the symbol of compliance with the NIRA codes] runs high. To the unthinking, laying off men just when factory rolls are supposedly increasing under the NRA looks bad. Trouble began when several hundred men walked tight-lipped through the factory gates and wondered out loud what the NRA had done for them. Newspapers asked the same question. Local Congressmen took the matter up with

Washington....Hurrying back from a brief vacation....President Litchfield of Goodyear found a town glowing with rumor, misapprehension, and bad feeling.

The second example comes from Detroit and concerns automobile workers,

In several important cases, the strikers are highly skilled technical workers who have always received more than the minimum wages now going into codes, and who do not see where the codes are doing them any good. Watching their employers increasing sales and, in some cases, meeting higher labor costs at the bottom by cutting in the upper range of the payrolls, they have decided that they are not going to wait for the long run effects of NIRA to reach them....Detroit is full of skilled mechanics who say they are the "forgotten men" of the recovery.

The outbreak of strikes and labor militancy in 1933-1934 put the Roosevelt Administration in a very difficult position. On one hand, worker organization was necessary in order to put a floor under competition and promote the growth in wages that was deemed necessary to fuel purchasing power and aggregate demand. Employer resistance to union organization thwarted this goal and was thus regarded as inimical to the recovery program and, more broadly, the New Deal itself. On the other hand, Roosevelt needed to maintain the cooperation of the business community if the NIRA and codes of fair competition were to have any chance of success. Also, Roosevelt also had to worry that, regardless of who was to blame, the outburst of strikes and labor unrest threatened to derail the struggling economic recovery then underway and destroy the political coalition he had assembled in the early months of the New Deal. The stage was thus set for two years of policy vacillation, ad hoc labor boards, and shifting policy pronouncements that ended up satisfying no one.

Into this void stepped Sen. Wagner with, first, a proposed labor disputes bill submitted in 1934 and, after it was tabled, an expanded and revised version submitted later that year called the National Labor Relations Act. We see, then, that the two major justifications for the Wagner Act cited in the "Findings and Policy" section of the act—promotion of economic stabilization and recovery and reduction of industrial conflict—both had their antecedents in the NIRA. In the case of stabilization and recovery, the antecedent was the theoretical-philosophical rationale put forward for the NIRA based on inequality of bargaining power, destructive competition, and the doctrine of high wages; in the case of industrial conflict, the antecedent came from the heightened expectations, grievances, union organizing efforts, and pressure politics precipitated by the NIRA's codes of fair competition and, most particularly, Section 7(a).

Disillusionment with Business

After a three- to four-month honeymoon period after passage of the NIRA, relations between the Roosevelt Administration and the business community became increasingly strained (Romasco 1983). From the perspective of Roosevelt and

Wagner, self-interested actions of the business community were threatening to torpedo the NIRA and the larger public interest it was intended to serve. As noted in previous quotations given by both FDR and Wagner, it was their view that recovery depended on increased consumer purchasing power which, in turn, was thought to depend on an increase in real wages for workers. Yet, what happened in 1933 and 1934 (Roos 1937) was that prices charged by firms rose first and then continued to rise as fast as wages, thus leaving real wages no higher than before the NIRA was enacted.

The diagnosis from FDR and Wagner's perspective was that much of the blame rested with business and on four counts. First, critics of the NIRA in the Senate had argued that business would use the suspension of the anti-trust laws and codes of fair competition to cartelize markets and charge monopoly-like prices. Although Roosevelt and Wagner had earlier dismissed such fears, and despite language written into the NIRA forbidding monopolistic practices, the fears of the critics appeared to be well-founded. Numerous examples during 1933-1934 were exposed in the press and Congressional hearings of price fixing, bid rigging, and production quotas, all with the seeming intent of forcing up prices and profits.

Second, a growing number of economists were counseling Wagner and Roosevelt that business monopoly was an important reason for the gradual drying up of purchasing power during the 1920s (Hawley 1966; Means 1992, pp. 32-92). Given the rapidity of technological change in both manufacturing and agriculture over the decade, several million workers were displaced, raising fears of growing "technological unemployment." According to neoclassical economic theory, the displaced workers should be reabsorbed as technological change and increased capital investment lead to lower unit production costs, lower prices, and greater product sales due to both the fall in prices and gains in real income. In an influential article titled, "The Trouble With Capitalism Is the Capitalists," published in *Fortune* (November 1935), Harold Moulton, director of the Brookings Institution, long-time economic adviser to Wagner and member of the inner circle who helped Wagner draft the NIRA, claimed that the principle defect in the theoretical chain of events just described was that, due to growing monopoly in the corporate sector, the productivity gains from technological change were not leading to lower prices and higher real wages but rather were going into increased profits—thus skewing the income distribution and shrinking consumer purchasing power. From this point of view then, the NIRA served only further to unbalance the economy, given that it ended up strengthening the market power of corporations and their ability to raise prices far more than it strengthened labor and its ability to advance wages.

Third, while the business community was busy using its new found freedom from the anti-trust laws to line its corporate pockets, businesses at the same time denied to labor use of its new freedoms to practice collective bargaining contained in Section 7(a), thus retarding the needed growth in wages. In case after case, corporations in the major industries subverted attempts of workers to organize through hastily created company unions, violence and physical intimidation and a panoply of anti union tactics such as blacklisting and discharge of union activists. When ordered to cease such activities and hold secret ballot elections, a disturbingly large number of employers either refused or subverted the process.

Finally, it appeared to Roosevelt and Wagner that the business community was guilty of behavior that smacked of both rank hypocrisy and opportunism. When the economy was at its nadir in late 1932 and early 1933, business leaders welcomed government intervention in the market process and pledged to sacrifice short-term self-interest for the good of the whole. By late 1933 when it appeared that recovery was underway, these good intentions seemed to quickly evaporate amidst a rush to raise prices and a growing chorus of complaints and criticisms about the restrictive, "anti business" regulations imposed by the NRA. By late 1934, groups such as the NAM and Chamber of Commerce had largely broken with Roosevelt and were harshly critical of the NIRA (Wilson 1962). Likewise, major corporate leaders, such as Alfred Sloan of General Motors, helped form and support the militantly anti-New Deal and anti-labor Liberty League. It appeared to Roosevelt, then, that much of the business community was drifting steadily to the "right" and could be kept in his political camp only at the cost of largely gutting the New Deal.

Wagner Confronts the Weaknesses of Section 7(a)

The NIRA legislation had created a Labor Advisory Board and Industry Advisory Board to help NRA Administrators Hugh Johnson and Donald Richberg resolve disputes arising out of the drafting and enforcement of the codes of fair competition. Within only two months, however, the volume and complexity of labor-related disputes growing out of Section 7(a) threatened to overwhelm the meager resources and staff of the NRA and its advisory boards. The six board members thus unanimously requested in August 1933 that Roosevelt establish a National Labor Board to mediate conflicts concerning Section 7(a) and that it be chaired by Sen. Wagner. Roosevelt agreed with the suggestions, and Wagner accepted the position.

Wagner's tenure as chair of the NLB lasted less than one year, but it was a thoroughly educating and, to a degree, radicalizing experience. As chairman, he became deeply involved in hundreds of disputes arising out of Section 7(a) and came face to face with both the implacable anti union policies of many employers and the toothless nature of the remedies contained in the NIRA for violations of the right to organize contained in Section 7(a). Over 75 percent of the cases appealed to the NLB, for example, involved interference with workers' organizational activities (e.g., discharge and discrimination of union activists) or refusal to bargain without an independent labor organization, while the lack of enforcement penalties forced Wagner to stand by as major companies either prevented board-sponsored representational elections or refused to abide by the results of such elections.

Wagner's experience with the NLB also provided the laboratory in which he developed and refined many of the legal and administrative principles that were later to go into the NLRA. Early on, for example, the board decided to settle representation disputes through secret ballot elections—a device that later became incorporated into the NLRA. Likewise, the board under Wagner came out in favor of majority representation, rather than the proportional representation schemes favored by NRA administrators Johnson and Richberg, which also was carried over to the NLRA. Finally, Wagner came to develop a keen appreciation for the necessity of having an independent agency with substantive enforcement powers if labor's Section 7(a) rights were to be adequately protected. The result was the National Labor Relations Board in the NLRA.

Company Unions

One of the most controversial provisions of the NLRA is its ban on company unions contained in Section 8(a)(2). This too was a direct outgrowth of the NIRA. In an article in the *New York Times* (March 11, 1934, reprinted in NLRB 1985), Wagner wrote at length on the reason why he favored such a ban. He states:

> The company union....runs antithetical to the very core of the New Deal philosophy. Business men are being allowed to pool their information and experience in vast trade associations in order to make a concerted drive against the evil features of modern industrialism. They have been permitted to recognize the values of unity and the destructive tendencies of discrete activities and to act accordingly. If employees are denied similar privileges, they not only are unable to uphold their end of the labor bargain; in addition they cannot cope with any problems that transcend the boundaries of a single business. The company union has improved personal relations, group-welfare activities, discipline, and other matters which may be handled on a local basis. But it has failed dismally to standardize or improve wage levels, for the wage question is a general one whose sweep embraces whole industries, or States, or even the Nation. Without wider areas of cooperation among employees there can be no protection against the nibbling tactics of the unfair employer or of the worker who is willing to degrade standards by serving for a pittance.

Similar to the other features of the NLRA, we see that Wagner's policy approach to company unions is shaped by his over- arching concern with ending destructive competition and promoting purchasing power. Immediately upon passage of the NIRA in June 1933, numerous companies installed nonunion employee representation plans, or "company unions," in their plants. Two motives predominated. The first was that in the early days of the NIRA it was unclear whether Section 7(a) would be interpreted to mean that collective bargaining was permissible, but not required, or was mandatory. Since, in World War I, the National War Labor Board had ruled that company unions were a form of "collective bargaining," a number of companies in 1933 rushed to put in a nonunion employee representation plan in order to hedge their bets in case the latter interpretation of Section 7(a) prevailed. The second motive, and the one that aroused the ire of Wagner and many other liberal-progressive reformers, was to serve as a union avoidance device. In these companies, the employee representation plans were often facades behind which management manipulated the selection of employee delegates, agenda, and outcomes.

This latter "dominated" type of company union was excoriated by Wagner as a sham since, in his words, true collective bargaining cannot prevail when the employer "sits on both sides of the table." It is interesting to note, however, that Wagner did admit that some company unions were legitimate organizations that served useful functions, such as improved in-plant communication, grievance resolution, and so on. Yet, he wrote Section 8(a)(2) to ban *all* company unions, both good and bad. Why? The quotation above gives two related answers. The first is that the workers in a nonunion representation plan still bargain over wages on an individual basis with the employer and thus continue to suffer from an inequality of bargaining power, making it impossible for them to "uphold their end of the wage bargain." The second reason is that the company union "fails dismally" to take wages out of competition because its reach is limited to one employer in a market of many. We see, then, that Wagner's fundamental motivation for banning company unions is macroeconomic in nature, as they obstruct the development of the "well-planned wage program" he saw as necessary to ending destructive competition and restoring purchasing power (also, see Jacoby 1995).

Though seldom mentioned in the debate over the NLRA, Wagner's position on Section 8(a)(2) entailed a potentially significant contradiction vis-à-vis the other provisions of the act. Once the argument is accepted that company unions should be banned because they interfere with the process of wage stabilization, it would also seem to follow, first, that precedence should be given to industrial unions over craft unions and, second, that collective bargaining should either be made mandatory or the terms and conditions of agreements in unionized firms should be extended to nonunion firms (a practice done in some European countries at the time; see Hamburger 1939). Wagner did not address these issues and no one pressed the matter. Had the birth of the Congress of Industrial Organizations (CIO) occurred before the enactment of the NLRA, rather than afterwards, the craft versus industrial union issue would surely have reared its head. That Wagner did not address these issues no doubt reflected a desire to avoid fracturing the political coalition he had built to support passage of the act as well as his deep commitment to democratic choice. Under the latter interpretation, Wagner could rationalize banning company unions because they were "dominated" and thus not freely chosen, while if workers desired a craft union over an industrial one this was a free choice that should not be abridged—even if it undercut progress toward economic stabilization and recovery.

Industrial Democracy

Sen. Wagner promoted the NLRA as more than just an economic recovery measure. He also made numerous references to the importance of promoting democracy in industry and "making the worker a free man." This was, as just noted, one of the reasons he opposed the dominated company union.

Wagner's emphasis on promoting industrial democracy also had a distinct macroeconomic dimension, however, that is seldom recognized in more recent accounts. Illustrative of this lacuna, for example, are the remarks of Summers (1979, p. 34). He states:

> The purposes of the National Labor Relations Act were many....However, the primary purpose was to give employees an effective voice, through collective bargaining, in determining the terms and conditions of their employment. It echoed the historic declarations that political democracy should be matched by industrial democracy.

Several aspects of these remarks are problematic. First, as this paper has hopefully demonstrated, it is simply not accurate to say that industrial democracy was the primary motivation for the act. Sen. Wagner, his legislative assistant Keyserling, and the great majority of people who testified on behalf of the NLRA gave predominant emphasis in their remarks to the macroeconomic goals of stabilization and recovery. This is also attested to by the language in the "findings and policy" section of the NLRA, which explicitly mentions the stabilization and recovery motives but gives no mention to the motive of industrial democracy per se.

Second, the senator most often used the concept of "industrial democracy" in a more macroeconomic sense than implicitly suggested by Summers. Wagner states on this matter (quoted in Keyserling 1945, p. 13):

> Modern nations have selected one of two methods to bring order into industry. The first is to create a super-government. Under such as plan, labor unions are abolished or become the creatures of the state....The second method of coordinating industry is the democratic method....Instead of control from on top, it insists upon control from within. It places the primary responsibility where it belongs and asks industry and labor to solve their mutual problems through self-government. That is industrial democracy.

The notion of industrial democracy presented here is not a "micro" enterprise level system of worker voice and participation. Rather, it refers to an industry-level system of joint labor-management cooperation in which representatives of workers and firms operating through trade associations and labor unions work out the rules and policies affecting their mutual interests. With government supervision and "veto power" added to the process, the model becomes a tripartite form of "corporatism."

And what was the primary motive for fostering a system of industrial self-regulation? The answer is that it provides the balanced bargaining power necessary to accomplish the stabilization and recovery goals. This is alluded to in the following remarks made by the senator (NLRB 1985, p. 1411),

> In order that the strong may not take advantage of the weak, every group must be equally strong. Not only is this common sense; but it is also in line with the philosophy of checks and balances that colors our political thinking. It is in accord with modern democratic concepts

which reject the merger of all group interests into a totalitarian state. The recovery program did not give employees any rights of organization to which they were not entitled before the program began. But the inauguration of the program has made the protection of these rights imperative.

The meaning of the last sentence is crucial, as it clearly implies that the reason for strengthening the democratic system of "checks and balances" in industry is, in Wagner's view, directly attributable to the need to facilitate the success of the recovery program. Thus, the "macro" form of industrial democracy referenced here is to a significant degree, like the ban on company unions, advocated by Wagner for instrumental reasons—to accomplish improved macroeconomic performance.

The above quotation makes clear that Wagner believed strongly that society is best served by a balance of power between major interest groups. Labor unions were thus a "win-win" from his perspective, as they reduced the bargaining disadvantage of the individual worker in the labor market, and thereby promoted the economic stabilization and recovery goals, and also reduced the worker's unequal power position inside the firm due to the autocratic, master-servant nature of the employment relationship. Had he relied solely on the latter justification for the NLRA, as socially beneficial as it may have been, the chances of the bill being enacted into law would probably have been quite slim (as it was, a contemporary rated the bill's odds of passage as 200-1 against). Though some people today may think the priorities are backward, the hard facts are that in 1935 it was the prospect of ending the Depression, not bringing democracy to the workplace, that made enactment of the Wagner Act possible.

The Supreme Court's Invalidation of the NIRA

Yet another catalyst leading to the Wagner Act was the Supreme Court's ruling in May 1935 that the National Industrial Recovery Act was unconstitutional. In one fell swoop, the centerpiece of the New Deal's economic recovery program came crashing down. Not only did this leave the Roosevelt Administration desperately looking for something to put its place, but it also led to real fears that the nation might slip further back into depression. Within a month of the NIRA's demise, for example, newspapers carried reports that companies were beginning to lengthen work hours and cut wages, while opinion polls revealed that the majority of Americans did not think that the economy had yet entered into a sustainable period of recovery. The issues of macroeconomic stabilization and recovery, the primary catalyst for the NIRA and Section 7(a) in 1933, were thus thrust squarely back on the center stage of political debate in the summer of 1935.

It was in this context that Sen. Wagner framed the necessity for passage of his new labor relations bill, called the National Labor Relations Act, which was introduced in the Senate in March 1935. In an article in the *New York Times* (quoted in Huthmacher 1968, p. 195), for example, he observed that the economic recovery since early 1933 had been frail and halting and attributed the reason to the fact that, "no adequate purchasing power had been built up to sustain it." He went on to say:

> [I]f the more recent quickening of business activity is not supported by rises in wages either we shall have to sustain the market indefinitely by huge and continuous public spending, or we shall meet the certainty of another collapse.

For that reason he maintained that passage of his new labor relations bill constituted:

> [T]he only key to the problem of economic stability if we intend to rely upon democratic self-help by industry and labor, instead of courting the pitfalls of an arbitrary or totalitarian state.

It is also not an accident of history that President Roosevelt publicly declared his support for the NLRA only three days before the Supreme Court's invalidation of the NIRA. For over a year, FDR had withheld his blessing from Wagner's efforts to enact a stronger version of Section 7(a). Now, faced with the likely demise of his original recovery program, growing doubts about the durability and strength of the business upturn, bereft of an alternative recovery program, faced with an increasingly hostile business community, and buoyed by the landslide Democratic victories in the Senate and House elections in 1934, Roosevelt moved off dead center and cast his lot with the Wagner bill. Legislative success was thus assured.

CONCLUSION

It has been more than six decades since the National Labor Relations (Wagner) Act was signed into law by President Roosevelt. It might seem, therefore, that the question, "Why the Wagner Act?," should have been settled long ago. Possibly it once was, but an examination of contemporary writings on the act, as well as recent deliberations on its reform, indicate clearly that a number of modern scholars and experts on labor policy have lost contact with the fundamental rationale for the act and the purpose it was to serve. The objective of this paper has been to reestablish contact with this purpose, as it was originally described by Sen. Wagner and later ably summarized by his legislative assistant, Keyserling, in his 1945 article, "Why the Wagner Act?" That article, I believe, provides the single best summary statement of the answer to, "Why the Wagner Act?" Yet, it and the message contained therein languish in relative obscurity.

And, so, what is the answer to, "Why the Wagner Act?" A full and complete response to this question must acknowledge that the act was supported by a diverse constituency with diverse motives and purposes. Promoting social justice, introducing democracy into the workplace, protecting collective bargaining rights, and stanching labor-management conflict all figured prominently. Each of these rationales had long been touted by supporters of unions and collective bargaining, including Senator Wagner, but none had provided a sufficiently compelling argument to move a majority of congressmen and senators to vote for a NLRA-like bill. Yet in 1935, large majorities in both the House and Senate voted for a near-revolutionary piece of legislation that not only declared collective bargaining to be the *preferred* means for determining the terms and conditions of employment but also created an administrative agency and set of legal procedures and penalties for effective enforcement of labor's right to organize. What can possibly account for this dramatic switch in public policy?

The argument in this paper is that NLRA was a direct outgrowth of the Great Depression and was passed because Sen. Wagner and key supporters made a convincing case that promoting unions and collective bargaining were key ingredients to the Roosevelt Administration's economic recovery program. The manner the act was to accomplish this was, first, by taking wages out of competition in order to short-circuit the process of destructive competition and the downward spiral of wages and working conditions it leads to and, second, to raise wages and redistribute income from capital to labor in order to augment household income, purchasing power, and aggregate demand. Other key parts of the Roosevelt recovery program also involved regulation and/or stimulation of the labor market, such as unemployment insurance, old age insurance, minimum wages, maximum hours, public works, and prohibition of child labor. This package of recovery measures was neither new nor conceptually revolutionary in 1935 for Senator Wagner had advocated the entire package nearly a decade earlier, as had institutional economists such as John R. Commons starting in the 1910s.

No doubt this economic argument was largely academic to shopfloor workers who were battling employers for the right to collective bargain, and it is likely that a number of supporters of the NLRA mouthed it with less than total conviction. Nonetheless, the evidence is incontrovertible that without the Depression and Sen. Wagner's forceful, heart-felt articulation of the macroeconomic rationale for the NLRA the legislation would never have been enacted into law. Given the nation's long-held ideological commitment to individualism and market competition, the considerable political influence business interests exercised in government, and the low regard organized labor was held in by most Americans, passage of the NLRA required an extremely powerful and persuasive explanation for why encouraging and protecting labor unions and collective bargaining would serve the public interest. Ending the ruinous process of deflation and restoring job growth and living standards provided such an explanation, and the American people, pauperized and demoralized by six years of Depression, accepted it.

This view of the origins and purpose of the Wagner Act, while of value for reasons of historical accuracy, is most pertinent as it relates to current-day scholarship and policy debate on the Wagner Act and the role of labor unions and collective bargaining in the U.S. economy and society. A reading of much of the contemporary literature on these subjects (e.g., Freeman and Medoff 1984; Goldfield 1989; Gross 1985; Hirsch and Addison 1986; Posner 1984) strongly suggests that many academics and some policymakers have lost sight of just what was the NLRA's original purpose. Although knowing the original purpose is certainly not the only desideratum for determining the act's current-day economic and social efficacy, it is surely the place to start, per the advice of Keyserling given in the quotation in the introduction to this paper (also, see Lewin, Delaney, and Sockell 1985).

With regard to the academic literature, much of the debate back and forth on the virtues and vices of labor unions and collective bargaining takes place largely independent of the economic theories which Sen. Wagner and most of his New Deal colleagues used to justify the act's encouragement and protection of collective bargaining. Some contemporary proponents of collective bargaining, for example, are wont to justify unions on grounds of "voice" and the economic efficiencies to be gained thereof. Others cite the role of unions in democratizing the workplace, while still others claim collective bargaining and union representation are crucial ingredients for the long term success of the new "high performance workplace" form of work organization. Opponents, on the other hand, are wont to talk about unions as labor cartels, the inefficiencies that come from inflated union wages and restrictive work practices, and corruption and violence fostered by unions.

All of these dimensions of unions and collective bargaining have some element of truth. None, however, captures the essence of why the Wagner Act was enacted or, more importantly, the fundamental purpose for its encouragement and protection of collective bargaining. Confusion is thus bound to occur.

As one example, nearly every academic account recognizes that a central purpose of unions is to raise wage rates. The opponents of collective bargaining immediately graft this fact onto a model of competitive labor markets and decry the inefficiencies that result. Proponents are generally cast on the defensive about union wage gains but try to recover the momentum by looking for indirect benefits (e.g., reduction in turnover, higher productivity, etc.). Both sides miss the fundamental point behind the Wagner Act—that unions are to be encouraged precisely because they *do* raise wages! From Wagner's point of view, the union effect on wages takes two socially desirable forms. One is to use collective bargaining to put a floor under wages, thus preventing the downward nibbling on wages and labor standards that comes from the forces of unequal bargaining power and destructive competition; the second is to use union bargaining power to redistribute income gains from productivity growth from corporate profits to wages, thereby augmenting money wages, real wages, and consumer purchasing power.

My point is not that these positions are necessarily correct; rather, it is that they should at least serve as the starting point for scholarly discussions of the Wagner Act and collective bargaining. This means that the concept of unequal bargaining power—perhaps the most fundamental idea behind the Wagner Act and one almost never referenced by opponents and proponents of unions alike—has to be seriously examined and then re-evaluated in light of today's much-changed economy (for exceptions, see Kaufman 1989, 1991, 1993; Reynolds 1984, 1991). This also means that the concept of destructive competition—also almost totally neglected by both sides to the debate—needs to be put back on center stage, as does the corollary "doctrine of high wages." Finally, it is common for modern-day scholars to examine the case for and against unions using the tools of microeconomic theory and in a microeconomic context of individual firms and markets. If anything is revealed by the analysis in this paper, however, it is that the fundamental reason for enactment of the NLRA had little to do with microeconomics—it was inspired by macroeconomic concerns and had macroeconomic objectives: to end the Depression by stabilizing the wage-price structure and boosting real wages and purchasing power.

This lacuna in the academic literature is also reflected in recent debates on labor policy and labor law reform. Mention was made in the introduction of this paper to the recent deliberations and reports of the Commission on the Future of Worker-Management Relations (1994, 1995). Although the NLRA was the principal piece of legislation examined by the commission, scant discussion is given to the origins and purpose of the act in either its fact-finding report or final report of recommendations. Both reports restate the language of Section 1 of the NLRA that it is the purpose of the act to promote and protect collective bargaining and worker self-organization, then offer only the barest of explanations for *why* these continue to serve the national interest. If the commission can not articulate a persuasive answer to this fundamental question, then is it surprising that its various recommendations to strengthen the NLRA's protection of collective bargaining are greeted with little enthusiasm?

And what if the commission had given serious consideration to the macroeconomic purpose of the NLRA? On one hand, it would have given the commission an opportunity to make the same case for the NLRA that Sen. Wagner made for it 60 years ago; namely, that it continues to serve the national interest by stabilizing wages and employment standards and ensuring that a portion of super-normal profits arising from monopolistic elements in product markets and the ongoing process of productivity growth are redistributed to workers as higher wages, incomes, and purchasing power. The building blocks necessary to construct this case are readily available, though as noted below there are equally compelling arguments on the opposite side.

The commission could have noted, for example, that the 15-year drift toward greater income inequality in the United States parallels the same trend so evident in the 1920s. It could have further noted that, even as productivity rebounded in the 1990s and corporate profits reached an all-time high, the level of real wages of the average American worker stagnated. Much as Sen. Wagner did in 1935, the commission could have described the adverse impact that this growing maldistribution of income has on both the macroeconomic balance between demand and supply and the social balance between low and high income groups. Finally, the commission could also point to collective bargaining's role not only in restoring a demand-supply balance but also in stabilizing wages and employment standards from the downdrafts of intense competition brought on by deregulation and globalization. Surely workers and even managers from industries such as airlines, meatpacking, and temporary help could have been found who would testify to the "downward escalator" that competition has subjected their wages and working conditions and the potentially beneficial role that collective bargaining can play in taking wages out of competition.

This is one set of arguments that the commission might have put forward had they sought to more effectively articulate why the NLRA still serves the national interest. Of course, raising the macroeconomic rationale for the Wagner Act would also invite a counter-response from critics of the legislation. The critics might note that one year after the passage of the NLRA, Keynes (1936) published the *General Theory of Employment, Interest, and Money*. Two years after passage of the NLRA, the Roosevelt Administration tried to balance the budget and precipitated a severe economic downturn (May 1981). Out of this confluence of theory and practice evolved relatively quickly a commitment to a new policy approach to macroeconomic stabilization and recovery—compensatory fiscal policy (with counter-cyclical monetary policy given renewed emphasis later on). From the perspective of the Roosevelt Administration, most economists, and the public at large, the use of Keynesian-inspired demand management policies seemed to offer a far easier and more effective method to stabilize the economy and regulate aggregate demand than did the earlier generation of New Deal recovery legislation (the NIRA and later the Wagner Act, Social Security Act, and Fair Labor Standards Act). And, importantly, Keynesian fiscal and monetary policy operates with less disruption to both the supply side of the economy (e.g., no strikes as with collective bargaining) and existing institutional arrangements in the labor market.

If one subscribes to this perspective, a number of fundamental questions then have to be addressed, such as:

- If government fiscal and monetary policies can stabilize the macroeconomy and keep the nation closer to full employment, then what is the continued rationale for a depresssion-era law that seeks to do the same through encourgement and protection of collective bargaining?
- If the macroeconomic justification for the Wagner Act is no longer compelling, are there alternative institutional forms, such as works councils or mandatory employee handbooks, that can deliver the other social benefits of unions (e.g., protection of workers' rights, a mechanism for voice in the workplace, etc.) but do so more effectively and/or efficiently?
- Is there still a rationale for the NLRA when it is premised on an inequality of power in the wage determination process that may have been substantially reduced or eliminated by full employment demand management policies?

- When the federal government is able to keep the economy much closer to full employment, does the industry-wide collective bargaining facilitated by the Wagner Act change from a social virtue because it protects wages and labor standards from destructive competition to a social evil because it promotes cost- push inflation and various inefficiencies on the supply side?
- Does it make sense to continue the ban on nonunion forms of employee representation when the original purpose of doing so—facilitating collective bargaining and taking wages out of competition—may have either been made redundant by Keynesian full employment policies or impossible to achieve by the globalization of markets?
- What does the globalization of markets imply about the entire strategy behind the NLRA? Even if we grant the desirability of taking wages out of competition in order to protect American living standards and working conditions, is it realistic to think that collective bargaining can perform this function when many product markets are international in scope and thus beyond the reach of American-based unions?

These types of questions by critics of the NLRA, as well as the arguments cited above in favor of the act, need to be addressed and answered as they get to the core purpose of the NLRA and its continued relevance to an economy and society on the verge of entering the 21st century. Unfortunately, in my view, neither in the published reports of the Dunlop Commission, in most other policy forums, or in much of the academic literature are these kinds of issues given serious consideration. It is as if we have lost contact with what the original purpose of the Wagner Act was all about. And, as Keyserling stated over 50 years ago, to ignore the original purpose of the act is to invite confusion and poor policy choices. This we already have in ample supply.

ACKNOWLEDGEMENT

The author wishes to acknowledge the valuable comments of Robert Zieger, Charles Whelan, and Jack Blicksilver on an earlier draft of this paper.

REFERENCES

Adamic, L. 1932. "The Collapse of Organized Labor." *Harper's Magazine* (January), pp. 167-178.
Arnold, P. 1982. "Ambivalent Leviathan: Herbert Hoover and the Positive State." Pp. 109-136 in *Public Values and Private Power in American Politics*, edited by J. David Greenstone. Chicago, IL: University of Chicago Press.
Asher, R., and R. Edsforth with R. Boryczka. 1995. "The Speedup: The Focal Point of Workers' Grievances, 1919-1941." Pp. 65-98 in *Autowork*, edited by R. Asher and R. Edsforth. Albany, NY: SUNY Press.
Barber, W. 1985. *From New Era to New Deal: Herbert Hoover, the Economists, and American Economic Policy, 1921-1933*. New York: Cambridge University Press.

Barenberg, M. 1993. "The Political Economy of the Wagner Act: Power, Symbol, and Workplace Cooperation." *Harvard Law Review* 106 (May): 1381-1496.

Bernstein, I. 1950. *The New Deal Collective Bargaining Policy.* Berkeley: University of California Press.

_____ . 1970. *Tubulent Years: A History of the American Worker, 1933-1941.* Boston: Houghton-Mifflin.

Brody, D. 1980. *Workers in Industrial America: Essays in the 20th Century Struggle.* New York: Oxford University Press.

Byrne, T. 1951. *The Social Thought of Robert F. Wagner.* Unpublished Ph.D. dissertation. Washington, D.C.: Georgetown University.

Business Week. 1933a. "What About Labor?" (July 15), pp. 7-8.

Business Week. 1933b. "Recovery Act Catechism II" (July 22), p. 9.

Business Week. 1933c. "Akron and NRAI" (September 23), p. 12.

Business Week. 1933d. "Striking at Recovery" (October 7), p. 3.

Casebeer, K. 1987. "Holder of the Pen: An Interview With Leon Keyserling on Drafting the Wagner Act." *University of Miami Law Review* 42 (November):285-363.

Clark, J. M. 1923. *Studies in the Economics of Overhead Costs.* Chicago: University of Chicago Press.

Commission on the Future of Worker-Management Relations. 1994. *Fact Finding Report.* Washington, DC: U.S. Department of Labor and U.S. Department of Commerce.

Commission on the Future of Worker-Management Relations. 1995. *Report and Recommendations.* Washington, DC: U.S. Department of Labor and U.S. Department of Commerce.

Commons, J. 1921. "Industrial Relations." Pp. 1-16 in *Trade Unionism and Labor Problems,* edited by John R. Commons. New York: Augustus Kelley.

Elliot, T. 1992. *Recollections of the New Deal: When the People Mattered.* Boston: Northeastern University Press.

Farr, G. 1959. *The Origins of Recent Labor Policy.* Boulder: University of Colorado Press.

Fine, S. 1963. *The Automobile Under the Blue Eagle; Labor, Management and the Automobile Manufacturing Code.* Ann Arbor: University of Michigan Press.

Finegold, K., and T. Skocpol. 1984. "State, Party, and Industry: From Business Recovery to the Wagner Act in America's New Deal." Pp. 159-192 in *Statemaking and Social Movements: Essays in History and Theory,* edited by C. Bright and S. Harding. Ann Arbor, MI: University of Michigan Press.

Fraser, S. 1991. *And Labor Will Rule: Sidney Hillman and the Rise of American Labor.* New York: The Free Press.

Freeman, R., and J. Medoff. 1984. *What Do Unions Do?* New York: Basic Books.

Fusfeld, D. 1956. *The Economic Thought of Franklin D. Roosevelt and the Origins of the New Deal.* New York: Columbia University Press.

Goldfield, M. 1989. "Worker Insurgency, Radical Organization, and New Deal Labor Organization." *American Political Science Review* 83 (December): 1257-1284.

Gordon, C. 1994. *New Deals: Business, Labor, and Politics in America, 1920-1935.* New York: Cambridge University Press.

Graebner, W. 1980. *A History of Retirement: The Meaning and Function of an American Institution.* New Have: Yale University Press.

Greer, T. 1958. *What Roosevelt Thought: The Social and Political Ideas of Franklin D. Roosevelt.* East Lansing: Michigan State University Press.

Gross, J. 1985. "Conflicting Statutory Purpose: Another Look at Fifty Years of NLRB Law." *Industrial and Labor Relations Review* 39 (October):7-18.

Hacker, L. 1934. "The New Deal is No Revolution." *Harper's Magazine* 168 (January), pp. 121-133.

Hamburger, L. 1939. "The Extension of Collective Bargaining Agreements to Cover Entire Trades and Industries." *International Labour Review* 40 (August): 153-194.

Hawley, E. 1966. *The New Deal and the Problem of Monopoly: A Study in Economic Ambivalence.* Princeton, NJ: Princeton University Press.

_____. 1987. "Neo-Institutional History and the Understanding of Herbert Hoover." Pp. 67-84 in *Understanding Herbert Hoover: Ten Perspectives*, edited by L. Nash. Stanford, CA: Stanford University Press.

Hirsch, B., and J. Addison. 1986. *The Economic Analysis of Unions*. Boston: Allen and Unwin.

Hogler, R. 1993. "Employee Involvement and Electromation, Inc.: An Analysis and a Proposal for Staturoy Change." *Labor Law Journal* (May): 261-274.

Hoover, H. 1952. *The Memoirs of Herbert Hoover*. New York: MacMillan.

Huthmacher, J. J. 1968. *Senator Robert F. Wagner and the Rise of Urban Liberalism*. New York: Atheneum.

Jacoby, S. 1985. *Employing Bureaucracy: Managers, Unions, and the Transformation of Work in American Industry, 1900-1945*. New York: Columbia University Press.

_____. 1995. "Current Prospects for Employee Representation in the U.S.: Old Wine in New Bottles?" *Journal of Labor Research* 16 (Summer): 387-397.

Kaufman, B. E. 1989. "Labor's Inequality of Bargaining Power: Changes Over Time and Implications for Public Policy." *Journal of Labor Research* 10 (Summer): 185-199.

_____. 1991. "Labor's Inequality of Bargaining Power: Myth or Reality?" *Journal of Labor Research* 11 (Spring): 151-166.

_____. 1993. "The Evolution of Thought on the Competitive Nature of Labor Markets." Pp. 148-203 in *Labor Economics and Industrial Relations: Markets and Institutions*, edited by C. Kerr and P. Staudohar. Harvard, MA: Harvard University Press.

Keynes, J. M. 1936. *The General Theory of Employment, Interest, and Money*. New York: Harcourt, Brace.

Keyserling, L. 1945. "Why the Wagner Act?" Pp. 000-000 in *The Wagner Act:After Ten Years*, edited by L. Silverberg. Washington, DC: Bureau of National Affairs.

Kochan, T., H. Katz, and R. McKersie. 1986. *The Transformation of American Industrial Relations*. New York: Basic Books.

Lapp, J. 1933. *The First Chapter of the New Deal*. Chicago: Prescott.

Layton, E. 1971. *The Revolt of the Engineers: Social Responsibility and the American Engineering Profession*. Cleveland, OH: Case Western University Press.

Lewin, D, J. Delaney, and D. Sockell. 1985. "The NLRA at Fifty: A Research Appraisal and Agenda." *Industrial and Labor Relations Review* 39 (October): 46-75.

Linder, M. 1990. "The Minimum Wage as Industrial Policy: A Forgotten Role." *Journal of Legislation* 16(2): 151-171.

Marshall, F. R. 1992. "Work Organization, Unions, and Economic Performance." Pp. 287-315 in *Unions and Economic Competitiveness*, edited by L. Mishel and P. Voos. Washington, DC: Economic Policy Institute.

May, D. 1981. *From New Deal to New Economics: The American Liberal Response to the Recession of 1937*. New York: Garland Publishing.

McKelvey, J. 1952. *AFL Attitudes Toward Production 1900-1932*. Ithaca, NY: Cornell University.

Means, G. 1992. *The Heterodox Economics of Gardiner Means*, edited by F. Lee and W. Samuels. Armonk, NY: M.E. Sharpe.

Mikva, A. 1986. "The Changing Role of the Wagner Act in the American Labor Movement." *Stanford Law Review* 38 (April):1123-1140.

Millspaugh, P. 1988. "America's Industrial Relations Experiment: Legal Scholarship Assesses the Wagner Act." *St. Louis University Law Journal* 32 (Spring): 673-711.

Mitchell, D.J.B. 1986. "Inflation, Unemployment, and the Wagner Act: A Critical Appraisal." *Stanford University Law Review* 38 (April): 1065-1095.

Moulton, H. 1935. "The Trouble With Capitalism is Capitalists" *Fortune* 12 (November), pp. 77.

National Labor Relations Board. 1985. *Legislative History of the National Labor Relations Act, 1935*, Vols. 1 and 2. Washington, DC: Government Printing Office.

Nation's Business. 1932. "A Panorama of Economic Planning." (February), pp. 29-32.

Perkins, F. 1946. *The Roosevelt I Knew*. New York: Viking.

Plotke, D. 1996. *Building A Democratic Political Order: Reshaping American Liberalism in the 1930s and 1940s*. New York, NY: Cambridge University Press.

Posner, R. 1984. "Some Economics of Labor Law." *University of Chicago Law Review* (4, Fall):988-1011.

Renshaw, P. 1985. "Organized Labor and the Keynesian Revolution." Pp. 214-235 in *Nothing Else to Fear: New Perspectives on America in the Thirties*, edited by S. Baskerville and R. Willett. Manchester, UK: Manchester University Press.

Reynolds, M. 1984. *Power and Privilege: Labor Unions in America*. New York: Universe Books.

_____. 1991. "The Myth of Labor's Inequality of Bargaining Power." *Journal of Labor Research* 12 (Spring): 167-183.

Romasco, A. 1983. *The Politics of Recovery: Roosevelt's New Deal*. New York: Oxford University Press.

Roos, C. 1937. *NRA Economic Planning*. New York: Da Capo Press.

Rosenof, T. 1975. *Dogma, Depression, and the New Deal: The Debate of Political Leaders Over Economic Recovery*. Port Washington, WA: Kennikat Press.

Schwarz, J. 1970. *The Interregnum of Despair: Hoover, Congress, and the Depression*. Urbana: University of Illinois Press.

Slichter, S. 1929. "The Current Labor Policies of American Industries." *Quarterly Journal of Economics* 43 (May):393-435.

Stolberg, B. 1933. "The Government in Search of a Labor Movement." *Scribner's Magazine* 6 (December), pp. 345-350.

Summers, C. 1979. "Industrial Democracy: America's Unfulfilled Promise." *Cleveland State Law Review* 28 (1):29-49.

Tomlins, C. 1985. *The State and the Unions*. New York: Cambridge University Press.

Troy, L. 1990. "Will a More Interventionist NLRA Revive Organized Labor?" *Harvard Journal of Law and Public Policy* 13 (Spring): 583-633.

U.S. Congress. 1929-1930. *Congressional Record*, 71st Congress, 2nd Session.

U.S. Congress. 1927-1928. *Congressional Record*, 70st Congress, 2st Session.

Vittoz, S. 1987. *New Deal Labor Policy and the American Industrial Economy*. Chapel Hill: University of North Carolina Press.

Weiler, P. 1990. *Governing the Workplace*. Cambridge, MA: Harvard University Press.

Wilson, W. 1962. "How the Chamber of Commerce Viewed the NRA: A Re-Examination." *Mid-America* 44 (April):95-108.

Wolman, L. 1936. *Ebb and Flow of Trade Unionism*. New York: National Bureau of Economic Research.

Zieger, R. 1977. *Madison's Battery Workers 1934-1952: A History of Federal Labor Union 19587*. Ithaca: New York State School of Industrial and Labor Relations.

_____. 1984. *Rebuilding the Pulp and Paper Workers' Union, 1933-1941*. Knoxville: University of Tennessee Press.

Zinn, H. 1966. *New Deal Thought*. Indianapolis: Bobbs-Merrill.

THE ROLE OF LOYALTY IN EXIT AND VOICE:

A CONCEPTUAL AND EMPIRICAL ANALYSIS[1]

David Lewin and Karen E. Boroff

ABSTRACT

This paper analyzes the effects of employee loyalty to the firm on employee exercise of voice through grievance filing and employee intent to leave-exit-the firm. Using survey data obtained from samples of employees in two large firms, one unionized and the other nonunion, logistic regression analyses find that loyalty is negatively related to both the use of voice and intent to exit the firm. The findings contradict propositions drawn from exit-voice-loyalty theory as well as procedural justice-distributive justice theory.

Grievance procedures are virtually always present in unionized firms (Lewin and Peterson 1988; U.S. Bureau of Labor Statistics 1981) and are increasingly common in nonunion firms (Delaney, Ichniowski, and Lewin, 1989; Delaney, Lewin, and Ichniowski 1989; Ichniowski and Lewin 1988). Some studies of grievance

Advances in Industrial and Labor Relations, Volume 7, pages 69-96.
Copyright © 1996 by JAI Press Inc.
All rights of reproduction in any form reserved.
ISBN: 1-55938-925-7

procedures have sought to identify the characteristics of grievance filers and to assess the effectiveness of grievance procedures. Other research has examined the link between grievance procedures and organizational outcomes, such as employee turnover and productivity, and between grievance procedures and individual outcomes, such as performance appraisal ratings and promotion rates (Lewin 1992; Lewin and Peterson 1988; Peterson and Lewin 1991b). In the case of nonunion grievance procedures, recent research has also focused on union avoidance and other competing rationales for the emergence of such procedures (Feuille and Delaney 1993).

Most of this research has been conducted by organizational behavior and economics specialists, with the former emphasizing the determinants of grievance filing and individual outcomes associated with grievance procedure usage and the latter emphasizing organizational outcomes associated with grievance procedures. Rarely have these two perspectives been combined in a single study. This is surprising because a major paradigm underlying *both* schools of thought is Hirschman's (1970) well-known model of exit, voice, and loyalty.

This lack of conceptual integration is disturbing, but in addition there is a growing body of evidence indicating that Hirschman's model does not adequately explain why individuals file grievances (i.e., use voice) or why individuals subsequently opt to quit (i.e., exit) in the face of a voice option. Consequently, this paper attempts to advance the multidisciplinary integration of research on grievance procedures and to provide a fuller "test" of Hirschman's model than has been attempted heretofore. Our principal emphasis in this regard is on the role of loyalty in the exit-voice nexus, and our data are drawn from both unionized and nonunion settings.

EXISTING RESEARCH

In his model of exit, voice, and loyalty, Hirschman sets forth two different dependent variables and suggests that they are mutually exclusive. These are (1) the decision to complain about a perceived deteriorated condition one has experienced in an organization (i.e., "voice") and (2) the decision to remove oneself from this worsening condition (i.e., "exit"). One intervening explanatory variable that predicts whether voice or exit behavior will be observed is the individual's loyalty to the firm—"the likelihood of voice increases with the degree of loyalty" (Hirschman 1970, p. 77). Hirschman does not expressly define loyalty, but by his own words it is clearly something different from "exit." If one were to graph the relationship among the three variables, one might draw a line ranging from "low loyalty" to "high loyalty." At the low end of the loyalty spectrum would be the "exit" point, while at the high end of the spectrum would be the "voice" point.

Hirschman's model is bounded by an important concept, which is captured in the subtitle of his book: "...*Responses to Decline in Firms, Organizations and*

States." More pointedly, Hirschman informs the reader that "the initial assumption is a *decline* in the performance of the firm or organization" (1970, p. 31, emphasis added). Thus, exit and voice are options to be weighed once one has experienced deterioration, perceived or actual, in one's relationship to an organization. It is at this point that the interrelationships among exit, voice, and loyalty become operative. As is explained further below, this insight has rarely, if ever, been used by researchers to frame their studies of grievance procedures.

Hirschman's model, which was developed to explain varieties of consumer (customer) behavior, has broad appeal to many disciplines. We focus, however, on how the model has been adapted to explain the behavior of individuals in the employment relationship. Hirschman's thesis has been used by labor economists primarily to analyze the behavior of labor unions (Freeman 1980; Freeman and Medoff 1984; Miller and Mulvey 1991). The dominant finding that emerges from this work is that, by providing employees a "voice" mechanism, unionism reduces voluntary employee turnover, that is, quits. Only a small portion of this research, however, treats grievance procedures (as distinct from unionism) as a voice mechanism. The standard empirical approach in this regard is to compare quit rates within industries among workers who are and are not covered by grievance procedures. In this work, moreover, little conceptual attention is given to the distinction between grievance procedure coverage and usage (Ichniowski and Lewin 1987; Peterson and Lewin 1991a), and none of the work appears to test for the effects of grievance procedure usage (or grievance issues, settlements, and outcomes) on employee quits—that is, exit.

Another major limitation of this research, one of particular relevance to the present inquiry, is the failure to distinguish between employees who have and have not experienced unfair treatment at work. That is, researchers have not attempted to identify and separate those individuals who perceive themselves to have experienced a deterioration in their employment relationship from all other employees. Thus, the boundary condition established by Hirschman in the explication of his model has not been adopted or empirically tested by industrial relations researchers. In addition to this limitation, there has been no attempt in previous research to conceptualize or test for loyalty in the context of the exit-voice framework. Put differently, the work of labor economists on grievance procedures provides a comprehensive treatment of exit (quits), a partial but importantly incomplete treatment of voice, and virtually no treatment of loyalty.

Equally troublesome is the knowledge gap in the organizational justice literature. Here, scholars emphasize that individuals' perceptions of procedural justice strongly influence their perceptions of and attitudes toward resulting (distributive) outcomes (Folger and Greenberg 1985; Greenberg 1990; Sheppard, Lewicki, and Minton 1992). Procedural justice focuses on the mechanisms or processes through which resource allocation decisions are made, while distributive justice focuses on the outcomes of such resource allocation decisions and the criteria used to make them (Delaney and Feuille 1992).

The concept of organizational justice appears to be supported by a body of scholarly work which indicates that fairness is a major contributor to the effective functioning of organizations (Greenberg 1990; Kahneman, Knetsch, and Thaler 1986a, 1986b; Sheppard, Lewicki, and Minton 1992).

Relatedly, individual perceptions of the fairness of resource allocation decisions depend on both the outcomes of and procedures used to make these decisions—that is, on distributive justice and procedural justice. For example, several studies have shown that the citizens of some nations strongly prefer an adversarial to an inquisitorial system for resolving legal disputes (Folger and Greenberg 1985; Lind and Tyler 1988; Thibaut and Walker 1975). Adversarial systems are used in the United States and Britain and in arbitration proceedings and apparently are preferred by the parties to disputes in these settings because they allow the disputants to control the collection and presentation of evidence (i.e., they allow voice). Inquisitorial systems (which are widely used in Continental Europe), by contrast, give judges or other authorities control over the collection and presentation of evidence as well as over decisions.

Research also shows that organizational members more readily accept organizational decisions which affect them when the processes used to make such decisions are perceived to be fair (Greenberg 1990; Sheppard, Lewicki, and Minton 1992). Perceptions of organizational fairness, in turn, significantly influence employee attitudes. For example, the perceived fairness of performance appraisals may depend more on the procedures used to make appraisals than on the actual content of the appraisals. Relatedly, employees who have meaningful input into the appraisal process perceive the process to be fairer than employees who have little or no input into the appraisal process (Folger and Greenberg 1985). Further, Sheppard and his colleagues found that the availability of mechanisms for employees to provide input into workplace-related organizational decisions were positively associated with employee attitudes toward the organization (Sheppard, Lewicki, and Minton 1992). This finding is consistent with Sheppard's earlier (1984) work showing that the type of conflict resolution procedure used by an organization is more important in determining employee-disputant satisfaction with an outcome than is the outcome itself.

More narrowly, perceptions of fairness of justice also appear to play a key role in the context of grievance procedures. To illustrate, Ewing (1989) found that about nine of every 10 respondent subscribers to the *Harvard Business Review* agreed with the proposition that employees should have some type of grievance procedure to present their complaints to top management; Kochan (1979) found that union members assigned grievance handling the highest priority in ranking issues and activities that unions should pursue; and Fryxell and Gordon (1989) concluded that employee belief in the procedural and distributive justice afforded by grievance systems was a strong predictor of employee satisfaction with the unions that represented them.

Nevertheless, scholarly work on the application of organizational justice concepts to grievance procedures gives relatively little attention to the determinants of employee perceptions of the grievance procedure (Peterson and Lewin 1991b) and gives virtually no attention to the relationship between employee perceptions of the grievance procedure and employee use of the procedure—that is, the exercise of voice in the employment context. Instead, the organizational justice literature concentrates on the positive influence of perceived procedural fairness on employee attitudes—analogous perhaps to the dominant emphasis in the labor economics literature on the positive effects of grievance procedures (a form of organizational justice) on employee turnover.

In summary, Hirschman's well-known exit-voice-loyalty model has *not* been robustly tested in the context of the employment relationship, and this remains so despite the "parallel" work of numerous scholars on procedural and distributive justice. In addition, if the model itself has not been robustly tested, one can also call into question the outcomes and conclusions of research which purportedly rest on the underlying model.

Further, while Hirschman's model as well as those of procedural and distributive justice scholars have been only partially tested empirically, there is a developing body of evidence which suggests that the use of voice brings about additional deterioration in one's relationship with the firm. Indeed, Feuille and Delaney (1993) review eight studies, some set in unionized firms and others in nonunion firms, in which individuals who opted to use voice—that is, grieved—suffered adverse organizational consequences when compared to their counterparts who did not use voice. These consequences included lower performance ratings and lower promotion rates.

Furthermore, after having filed grievances, the grievants had higher turnover rates than nongrievants, which is clearly at odds with Hirschman's main thesis. Because loyalty was neither conceptualized nor measured in any of these studies, however, it is not possible to conclude definitively that, all else equal, it is the more loyal employee who opts to voice a complaint and the less loyal employee who exits the firm.

Research on "whistleblowers" further distorts *a priori* expectations drawn from the Hirschman model. Whistleblowers view their actions as ultimately loyal, but loyal to whom is an open question. Typically, these individuals, having blown the whistle, subsequently experience punishment, including being fired by management (Elliston, Keenan, Lockhart, and Van Schaick 1985; Westin, Kurtz, Robbins, and the Educational Fund for Individual Rights 1981). All in all then, in research on the employment relationship, we are confronted both with conceptual gaps in the application of Hirschman's model and with empirical findings that do not square with it. Yet many researchers appear to accept this model as valid, continue to use it to frame their inquiries, and fail to incorporate insights drawn from the literature on procedural and distributive justice into their research. We hope both to avoid and to overcome these limitations in the present study.

THE MODEL

Hirschman (1970, p. 77) posits that:

> [The] two principle determinants of the readiness to resort to voice when exit is possible [are]:
> (1) the extent to which customer-members are willing to trade off the certainty of exit against the uncertainties of an improvement in the deteriorating product; and
> (2) the estimate customer-members have of their ability to influence the organization.

From these propositions, we obtain the variables required to define, operationalize, and test Hirschman's model in a workplace setting. First, the model predicts the conditions under which "the use of voice"—the dependent variable, P(Voice)—will occur in the employment relationship. Second, in predicting the use of voice, the availability of an exit option must be controlled. Put differently, there is no decision for an employee to make between exit and voice if an employee does not believe that a viable exit option exists in the first place.

Third, Hirschman specifies factor (1) above as the loyalty component. He contends that "the first factor is clearly related to that special attachment to an organization known as loyalty" (1970, p. 77). Put this way, Hirschman is less than precise in articulating his loyalty concept, defining it as a tradeoff between exit and voice. In essence, the researcher is left with a virtual tautology—the likelihood to use voice depends on one's loyalty, which is the tradeoff between using voice or exiting. Alternatively, one can cast loyalty as some other scholars have done, such as "giving public and private support to the organization" or "practicing good citizenship" (Rusbult, Farrell, Rogers, and Mainous 1988, p. 601)—or, in Hirschman's words, the "special attachment." We opt to interpret loyalty in this latter fashion, stressing the "organizational commitment" element of the construct. As such, we conceptualize loyalty as the degree to which a person identifies with an organization. In so doing, we purposely differentiate loyalty from organizational satisfaction, a position supported by research on organizational satisfaction and commitment (Bateman and Strasser 1984; Becker 1992; Brooke, Russell, and Price 1988; Curry, Wakefield, Price, and Mueller 1986). Nevertheless, and as will be subsequently discussed, in one of the studies reported below we also control for satisfaction, given its influence on the propensity of individuals to quit organizations (Carston and Spector 1987; Mobley, Horner, and Hollingsworth 1978; Mowday, Koberg, and McArthur 1984).

Fourth, as Hirschman suggests in factor (2)above, the likelihood of using voice is also a function of how effective the mechanism is perceived to be for channeling one's complaint. If individuals feel that they can influence (change) the organizationally-induced "deteriorated state" through the available voice mechanism, then they are more likely to use voice and less likely to exit the firm. Therefore, factor (2) is a measure of how effective the voice mechanism is perceived to be. Thus, Hirschman posits that both loyalty and perceived complaint mechanism effectiveness will be positively related to the use of voice and, at the same time, negatively related to exit (quitting the firm).

The key assumption that underlies Hirschman's entire model, as emphasized earlier, is a deterioration in one's relationship with the organization. From this perspective, it follows that not all members of an organization will contemplate exiting the firm or using voice; only members who have experienced some (perceived) deterioration or, more pointedly, injustice will consider whether to respond through voice or exit. Stated differently, as a deteriorated state or "discontent" rises among employees, both the exercise of voice and the use of exit are likely to increase. But for a given deteriorated state or level of discontent, voice and exit will presumably be inversely related, as posited by Hirschman. By limiting our analysis to those employees who believe that they have been unfairly treated at work, we are in effect attempting to control for the deteriorated or discontented state and thereby provide the most direct test of the exit-voice tradeoff proposition as well as of the effects of loyalty on both exit and voice.[2]

From this, we can specify the following functional model:

$$P(\text{Voice}) = f(\text{loyalty, effective voice mechanism}). \qquad (1)$$

Here, $P(\text{Voice})$ is the likelihood that an individual will use voice. However, since Hirschman (1970, p. 37) argues that "voice can be a substitute for exit," one's likelihood to exit the firm, $P(\text{Exit})$, can also be predicted from this functional equation. So,

$$P(\text{Exit}) = f(\text{loyalty, effective voice mechanism}). \qquad (2)$$

The anticipated relationships between the independent and dependent variables differ as between these two equations. In equation (1), both loyalty and perceptions of an effective voice mechanism are hypothesized to be positively related to the use of voice. In equation (2), the less loyal employee and the employee who perceives the voice mechanism (grievance procedure) to be ineffective in correcting injustices is more likely to exit the firm. In the first study reported later, we shall refer to employee loyalty as LOYALTY, and to the employees' perception of the voice mechanism as GRIEVERATING. In the second study, we shall again refer to employee loyalty as LOYALTY but will use PERQUAL to refer to the employee's perception (of the quality) of the voice mechanism.

Note that the inclusion of a perceived grievance procedure effectiveness or quality variable in the analysis is germane to the issue of the type of voice that is exercised by employees. To some, grievances or formal complaints represent "negative" types of voice, whereas suggestions made by employees in the context of a suggestion plan or quality circle represent "positive" types of voice. If loyal employees are most likely to use positive rather than negative types of voice, then an inverse relationship between loyalty and grievance filing would be expected. In this study, we were unable to obtain data about suggestion plans, quality circles, and other potential voice mechanisms. But the inclusion of GRIEVERATING and PERQUAL, respectively, in the first and second studies reported below provide partial measures of employees' perceived grievance procedure positivity (negativity).[3]

THE EMPIRICAL EQUATIONS

As noted in our introduction, the study of grievance filing behavior has predominantly been the domain of organizational behavioral scholars, while the study of quit behavior has largely been the domain of labor economists. Drawing upon the research from these respective disciplines, we can identify the control variables that should be included in each of the functional equations in order to estimate P(Voice) and P(Exit).

Control Variables for Equation (1)

First, and perhaps the most challenging variable from a conceptual perspective, is individuals' membership status within the union (UNIONMBR) that represents them, which has been shown to be associated with grievance filing propensity (Boroff 1993). Yet, the very reason that individuals join unions may be to secure collective voice. So, the use of voice can arguably be conceived of as both a dependent and an independent variable (Intriligator 1978; Lee 1978). In the former case, union membership can help explain the likelihood to use voice; in the latter case, voice can be an explanatory variable for union membership. To address this endogeneity of union membership and voice, we shall subsequently estimate a system of simultaneous equations using the first of two data sets obtained for this study. At this juncture, though, we merely recognize union membership as an important control variable.

Beyond union membership, there are several other individual characteristics that have been associated with the use of voice. Minorities (MINORITY) and employees with greater length of employment or service in a firm (SERVICE) are more likely than others to use the grievance process (Boroff 1990). By contrast, the use of voice has been shown to be negatively associated with the age (AGE) and the education (EDUCATION) level of grievants. Further, men are more likely than women (MEN) to file grievances (Ash 1970; Lewin and Peterson 1988), and employees with relatively high occupational status (HIGHOCCUP), all else equal, are less likely to voice a complaint than relatively low occupational status employees (Boroff and Lewin 1994). Additionally, Boroff (1993) has observed that grievance filing is lower among individuals who fear organizational punishment (REPRISAL) or who exhibit overall satisfaction with the firm (SATISFACTION).

Control Variables for Equation (2)

The second equation, the likelihood to exit the firm, or $P(\text{Exit})$, has its own set of control variables which are drawn from the literature on job mobility. In this literature, union membership (UNIONMBR) has been shown to be negatively related to quit behavior (Bartel 1979; Freeman and Medoff 1984). But, we are again confronted with a potential endogeneity issue if UNIONMBR is included as an independent variable in explaining the propensity of individuals to exit a firm. Unions attempt to secure economic rents for their members, thereby lowering the probability that union members will exit (quit) the firm. At the same time, individuals may join unions in order to obtain such economic rents. So, as will be done with equation (1), we shall subsequently estimate a simultaneous equation version of P(Exit) in order to minimize potential estimation bias, again using one of the two data sets obtained for this study.

Other variables have also been shown to be associated with employee propensity to exit the firm. Younger persons (AGE) and men (MALE) are more likely to quit their jobs; higher pay (WAGES) reduces the probability of quitting (Blau and Kahn 1981); single women are more apt to quit their jobs than their married counterparts (MARRIED) (Viscusi 1980); better-educated workers (EDUCATION) are less likely to quit than poorly-educated workers (Weiss 1984); and fringe benefits (BENEFITS) are negatively associated with turnover rates (Mitchell 1983). Additionally, the effect of minority status (MINORITY) on quit behavior is indeterminate (Boroff and Ketkar 1994; Sicherman and Galor 1990); the length of employment (SERVICE) has been found to be negatively related to quit behavior (Bartel 1979; Freeman and Medoff 1984); and employee satisfaction (SATISFACTION) with the firm is also negatively related to the propensity to exit the firm (Carston and Spector 1987; Mobley et al. 1978, Mowday et al. 1984).

In sum, the conceptual framework from which our estimating equations are derived distinguishes among employees who have and have not experienced unfair workplace treatment and identifies grievance procedure usage (the exercise of voice) and the intent to exit among those who have experienced unfair workplace treatment as the main dependent variables. Further, the framework incorporates employee loyalty to the firm and employee perception of the quality of the grievance procedure as main independent variables, as well as the control variables described above. All of this constitutes a more comprehensive test of Hirschman's model than has been attempted heretofore.

DATA AND EMPIRICAL ESTIMATION

To test for the likelihood of employee use of voice and employee intent to exit the firm, P(Voice) and P(Exit) respectively, we rely on two unique data sets. Concerning the first of these, a survey instrument was administered in October 1991 to a random sample of nonmanagement employees of a large, U.S.-based multinational telecommunications firm.[4] Individual employees worked in the firm's manufacturing and services divisions and were represented by one of two unions, each of which had negotiated an agency shop provision in its contract with the firm. The two unions have represented employees of the firm for more than 50 years.

The respondents answered a series of questions concerning their attitudes toward their employer, the union that represented them, and the grievance procedure under which they operated as well as their use of the grievance procedure. The survey instrument's construction and subsequent administration was guided by Dillman (1978); of 8,100 surveys mailed, 3,160 were completed and returned, representing a response rate of 39 percent.

Concerning the second data set, a survey instrument was administered in mid-1987 to 1,300 nonmanagerial employees of a large, U.S.-based multinational firm that specializes in overnight mail and freight delivery.[5] At the time of the survey, this firm was entirely nonunion but maintained a multi-step grievance procedure which we refer to as the Company Complaint Procedure (CCP). The CCP was instituted early in the company's history, in part for the express purpose of remaining nonunion, and managerial personnel as well as employees are eligible to file written complaints via the CCP. Under this procedure, complaints are "heard" by employees' peers, company officials, or both. Final binding decisions are made at the last step of the procedure by senior company officials; put differently, this procedure does not culminate in arbitration.

For administration of the survey instrument in this firm, 900 surveys were randomly distributed to employees irrespective of their actual use of the CCP, while the remaining 400 surveys were distributed to known employee users of the CCP.[6] Special procedures were taken to ensure the confidentiality of the CCP users as well as the anonymity of all respondents.[7] A total of 579 fully usable surveys were completed and returned to the researchers for a response rate of 43 percent.

For the first of these two firms, the average survey respondent was about 43 years old and had about 13 years of schooling. Moreover, 49 percent of the respondents were female, 17 percent were minority group members, and 67 percent were married; they averaged some 17.6 years of work experience and earned approximately $31,500 annually from employment with this firm. The respondents were employed in such jobs as tester, payroll clerk, operator, technician, data systems clerk, and service representative. These data were used to estimate the P(Voice) and P(Exit)equations.

Estimating P(Voice)

If we were we to measure P(Voice) using a single equation, it would be as follows (regression coefficients are surpressed):

$$P(\text{Voice}) = B_0 + \text{GRIEVERATING}_1 + \text{LOYALTY}_2 + \text{EXITOPTION}_3 + \\ \text{UNIONMBR}_4 + \text{SATISFACTION}_5 + \text{REPRISAL}_6 + \qquad (3) \\ \text{EDUCATION}_7 + \text{MINORITY}_8 + \text{HIGHOCCUP}_9 + \\ \text{SERVICE}_{10} + \text{AGE}_{11} + \text{MALE}_{12} + e_1.$$

However, because of the endogeneity of $P(\text{Voice})$ and the UNIONMBR variable, we first estimate the likelihood of being a union member as a function of voice and then estimate $P(\text{Voice})$ as a function of union membership.

The literature on correlates of union membership is extensive (see, e.g., Heneman and Sandver 1983; LeLouarn 1980; for respective literature reviews; Fiorito and Greer 1986; Gordon and Long 1981; Hills 1985; Leigh and Hills 1987). Since our main interest is in controlling for the determinants of union membership in order to avoid biased estimates of the effects of loyalty on voice and exit, we first estimate union membership using $P(\text{Voice})$ as an independent variable together with the personal characteristics variables that the received literature indicates are associated with union membership (Blinder 1972; Getman, Goldberg, and Herman 1976; Kochan 1978; Uphoff and Dunnette 1956).

Next, we estimate P(Voice) as a function of respondents' perceptions of the effectiveness of the grievance process and their loyalty to the firm, controlling for the perceived viability of the exit option, union membership status, and employee satisfaction with the firm. We also control for employee concerns about reprisal for filing grievances and for length of service with the firm. Because the demographic variables that are used to predict union membership are the same as those used to predict the likelihood to use voice, we omit them from the estimate of $P(\text{Voice})$.

Estimating P(Exit)

Based on the independent variables previously specified, a single empirical equation measuring $P(\text{Exit})$ would be as follows:

$$P(\text{Exit}) = B_0 + \text{GRIEVERATING}_1 + \text{LOYALTY}_2 + \text{EXITOPTION}_3 + \\ \text{UNIONMBR}_4 + \text{SATISFACTION}_5 + \text{EDUCATION}_6 + \qquad (4) \\ \text{MINORITY}_7 + \text{BENEFITS}_8 + \text{WAGES}_9 + \text{SERVICE}_{10} + \\ \text{MALE}_{11} + \text{AGE}_{12} + \text{MARRIED}_{13} + e_1.$$

Again, however, because of the interrelationship between $P(\text{Exit})$ and UNION-MBR, we create two equations which will be solved simultaneously. The likelihood of an employee being a member of the union is estimated in the same manner as reported previously. $P(\text{Exit})$ is then estimated as a function of the grievance rating and respondents' loyalty to the firm, again controlling for the viability of the exit option as well as for respondents' union membership status, satisfaction with the company, length of service in the firm, marital status, and benefit levels.

Operationalizing the Variables

All of the variables in equations (3) and (4) were constructed from responses to the questions contained in the aforementioned survey instrument. Appendix A summarizes the questions we relied upon to form the empirical measures for these equations (and variants thereof). Some variables, such as EDUCATION, AGE, and SERVICE, were formed straightforwardly; however, others required more complex construction. In equation (3), the dependent variable P(Voice) measures whether an employee actually filed one or more grievances in response to perceived unfair treatment. The effectiveness of the grievance process, GRIEVERATING, was measured by a question that asked respondents to rate the "quality" of the grievance (voice) mechanism. LOYALTY was created from three statements included in the survey that collectively measure the respondent's attachment to the firm. These statements have frequently been used in research on employee loyalty (Rusbult et al. 1988). The viability of the exit alternative, EXITOPTION, was formed from two survey questions which have often been used in research on job mobility (Price and Mueller 1981, 1986).

In equation (4), the dependent variable P(Exit) measures the degree to which an employee intends to leave (exit) the firm. It was constructed from responses to two survey questions in which employees indicated the degree to which they had considered and continue to consider leaving (exiting) the firm.

RESULTS FOR DATA SET #1

Prior to estimating these equations, we censored the data to include only those employees who perceived themselves to have experienced unfair treatment; this was done in order to comport with the "deteriorated state" condition of Hirschman's model.[8] This procedure reduced the sample for analysis to approximately 950 employee respondents. The employees of this firm who indicated that they had experienced some unfair treatment were more likely to be male, union members and to have more work experience with the firm, higher earnings, more education, lower satisfaction with and loyalty to the firm, a lower rating of grievance procedure effectiveness (quality), and greater perceived exit options than employees who did not report experiencing unfair treatment.

Estimating Equation (3)—The Determinants of Voice

Following the approach outlined above, we first used a two-stage least squares procedure to estimate the probability of an employee in the aforementioned telecommunications company being a union member and the probability of an employee filing a grievance (i.e., exercising voice). We then used a logistic regression procedure to generate reduced form estimates of these probabilities, and con-

Table 1.   Logistic Regression Estimates of P(Voice) and
P(Exit), Data Sets #1 and #2
(Changes in Probabilities)

	Data Set #1		Data Set #2	
Dependent Variable	P(Voice)	P(Exit)	P(Voice)	P(Exit)
Independent Variable:				
Grievrating	.007	−.078***	NA	NA
Loyalty	−.067***	−.078**	−.102**	−.203**
Exitoption	−.013	.263***	NA	NA
Satisfaction	.007**	−.241***	NA	NA
Reprisal	−.013**	NA	NA	NA
Education	−.007**	−.014**	−.024	.113
Minority	.019**	.042**	.256	NA
Wages	.099**	.178**	NA	NA
Service	−.222	−.021***	NA	−.081
Sex	−.013*	−.050***	.237	.356
Married	NA	.050	NA	NA
Perqual	NA	NA	−.040	−.186**
Age	NA	NA	−.240	NA
Highoccup	NA	NA	.158	−.049
P(Exit)	NA	NA	1.09**	NA
P(Voice)	NA	NA	NA	−.980**
Constant	.620**	2.59***	1.86	−.186
Psuedo F-statistic	3.50***	5.24***	1.90***	12.150***
N	958	978	220	223

Notes: *Significant at $p = < .10$.
           **Significant at $p = < .05$.
           ***Significant at $p = < .01$.

verted these to changes in probabilities evaluated at the mean of the dependent variable in equation (3) (Schmidt 1978). Because the results of the two procedures were very similar, and also because our main focus is on the determinants of P(Voice), not union membership, we limit the discussion to the changes in probabilities derived from the reduced form estimates of equation (3); these are shown in column 1 of Table 1.[9] Note that (for reasons discussed in Appendix A) the variable WAGES served as a proxy for the variable HIGHOCCUP and that due to colinearity with the variable SERVICE the variable AGE was dropped from these estimates.

In column 1 of Table 1, we observe an unexpected and significantly negative coefficient on LOYALTY. This indicates that employees who are *more* loyal to the firm are *less* apt to grieve in the face of unfair treatment than employees who are *less* loyal to the firm. Moreover, this finding emerged when controlling for employee fear of reprisal for filing a grievance,[10] employee belief about the viability of an exit option (i.e., leaving the firm), and other variables. The coefficient on the GRIEVERATING variable has the expected sign but is not statistically significant. Thus, among employees who have experienced unfair treatment in the workplace, perceived effectiveness (or quality) of the grievance procedure does not influence the probability of their actually using the procedure—exercising voice.

Estimating Equation (4)—The Determinants of Exit Intent

Note that the variable BENEFITS was omitted from equation (4) because negotiated benefits do not vary among represented employees of this firm except by seniority, which is measured by the variable SERVICE. Here, too, WAGES serving as a proxy for HIGHOCCUP and AGE was omitted from the analysis due to its colinearity with SERVICE. The changes in probabilities for the independent variables resulting from logistic estimation of the reduced form of equation (4) are shown in column 2 of Table 1.

In this case, we observe the expected negative and significant relationship between LOYALTY and P(Exit). In addition, the negative and significant coefficient on perceived effectiveness (quality) of the grievance process (GRIEVRATING) comports with our a priori expectation. Further, perceived availability of job opportunities in the labor market (EXITOPTION) is, as expected, significantly positively related to P(Exit), and seniority or work experience with the firm (SERVICE), employee satisfaction with the firm (SATISFACTION), education and sex(female status) are, also as expected, significantly negatively related to P(Exit). Among other control variables, occupational status (proxied by WAGES) and marital status (married) are, uexpectedly, significantly positively related to exit intent, as is minority status, in data set #1.

RESULTS FOR DATA SET #2

Here, as before, the data were censored to include only those employees who perceived themselves to have experienced unfair treatment. This procedure reduced the sample for analysis to approximately 220 employee respondents. The employees of this firm who indicated that they had experienced some unfair treatment were more likely to be male and to have more work experience with the firm, higher earnings, more education, lower satisfaction with and loyalty to the firm, and a lower rating of grievance procedure quality (effectiveness) than employees who did not report experiencing unfair treatment.

Because the employees included in data set #2 were not unionized, it was not necessary to perform two-stage least squares estimation of P(Voice) and P(Exit). In addition, certain variables for which data were available from data set #1 were not available from data set #2; these included EXITOPTION, SATISFACTION, and REPRISAL. Further, HIGHOCCUP was entered directly into the analysis of data set #2 using a five-point scale of the respondent's occupational position in the firm. A complete list and descriptions of the variables used to test data set #2 is contained in Appendix B.

Before proceeding to estimate P(Voice) and P(Exit) using data set #2, the potential influence of an employee's intent to leave (exit) the firm on the filing of a CCP (i.e., the exercise of voice) merits attention. Perhaps because of the widespread use by labor economists of Hirschman's exit-voice-loyalty framework, exit (or quitting or intent to leave) is overwhelmingly treated as a dependent variable. However, intent to leave may itself moderate relationships with other independent variables and the use of voice in the employment context.

On the one hand, such intent may spur employees to file grievances because they are less likely than those who do not intend to leave to be concerned about potential negative consequences of grievance decisions. On the other hand, intent to leave may reduce the likelihood of grievance filing because employees who have such intent are less concerned than employees who do not have such intent about the potential positive consequences of grievance decisions (Feuille and Delaney 1993). In any case, previous work by Boroff (1990) suggests that employee intent to leave the work organization does influence the likelihood of grievance filing. Consequently, and also because measures of EXITOPTION and REPRISAL were not available from data set #2, we include an intent to leave variable $P(\text{Exit})$ in a second estimate of $P(\text{Voice})$, with $P(\text{Exit}) = 1$ if the respondent employee intends to leave the firm, and $P(\text{Exit}) = 0$ if the respondent employee does not intend to leave the firm.[11]

Unlike $P(\text{Voice})$, which measures actual behavior, $P(\text{Exit})$ reflects the attitudes of respondent employees. In both cases, however, the dependent variable is binary. Consequently, the correct functional form of the estimating procedure is one which constrains the probability function to between zero and 1 (Aldrich and Nelson 1984). For consistency with equations (3) and (4) but modified to take account of the somewhat different variables included in data set #2 from those included in data set #1, the estimating equations for $P(\text{Voice})$ and $P(\text{Exit})$, using data set #2, are as follows:

$$P(\text{Voice}) = B_U + \text{LOYALTY}_1 + \text{PERQUAL}_2 + P(\text{EXIT})_3 + \\ \text{AGE}_4 + \text{MALE}_5 + \text{EDUCATION}_6 + \text{HIGHOCCUP}_7 + \\ \text{MINORITY}_8 + e_1. \tag{5}$$

$$P(\text{Exit}) = B_U + \text{LOYALTY}_1 + \text{PERQUAL}_2 + P(\text{VOICE})_3 + \\ \text{MALE}_4 + \text{EDUCATION}_5 + \text{HIGHOCCUP}_6 + \\ \text{SERVICE}_7 + e_1. \tag{6}$$

Column 3 of Table 1 presents the changes in probabilities for the independent variables included in equation (5) derived from logistic estimation of this equation. Observe that LOYALTY is significantly inversely associated with the probability of using voice—P(Voice). In other words, among employees who believe that they have experienced unfair treatment in this organization, the more loyal the employee the lower the likelihood of using the CCP. This finding is again contrary to the proposition embedded in Hirschman's model that loyalty and the use of voice are positively correlated—but is consistent with Birch's (1975) expected relationship between these two variables. It also comports with evidence produced by Boroff (1991) in a related study.

Also observe from column 3 of Table 1 that PERQUAL is inversely (though insignificantly) associated with the probability of using voice. That is, the higher the perceived quality of the CCP the less likely is the employee to file a written complaint. It is possible that this relationship is moderated by employees' previous experiences with the CCP. Specifically and consistent with other research (Boroff 1990), employees who previously filed written complaints and who subsequently lost the decisions made in those cases may rate the CCP lower than employees who won their decisions or who did not file complaints. It is not possible to test this relationship here because the model underlying equation (5) will not converge if decision outcome (OUTCOME) is included as a right-hand side variable (OUTCOME varies only when P[Voice] = 1, and there are no outcomes when P[Voice] = 0). Nevertheless, this finding is consistent with (1) concepts of procedural justice (Sheppard, Lewicki, and Minton 1992), (2) the distinction between coverage and use of certain third-party dispute settlement procedures, such as arbitration (Delaney 1983), and (3) other empirical evidence drawn from studies of grievance procedure effectiveness in unionized settings (Lewin and Peterson 1988).

The results of estimating equation (5) also show that P(Exit) is significantly positively associated with the use of voice. In other words, among employees who have experienced unfair treatment, those who intend to leave the firm are more likely to file a written complaint than those who intend to stay with the firm. As before, this finding is contrary to the expected relationship derived from Hirschman's (1970) model. Using this data set, it is not possible to determine whether the propensity to exit (stay with) the firm preceded the use of voice or whether the actual use of voice influenced employee-complainants' intent to exit (stay with) the firm.[12] In any case, these caveats do not negate the finding of a positive relationship between P(Exit) and P(Voice), or the judgment that this finding is contrary to expectations derived from the exit-voice model.

In equation (6), P(Exit) serves as the dependent variable with P(Voice) included as an independent variable. Changes in probabilities for the independent variables included in equation (6) which resulted from logistic estimation of this equation are shown in column 4 of Table 1. Observe that both LOYALTY and PERQUAL are significantly inversely associated with the probability of an employee's intent to leave the firm. In other words, the more loyal the employee and the higher the employee's perceived quality of the CCP, the lower is the employee's intent to leave the firm. Of the control variables included in this equation, none are significantly related to P(EXIT).

Data set #2 also provides an opportunity to examine the effect of voice (filing a written complaint) on the intent to leave (exit from) this nonunion company. Clearly, the central proposition derived from Hirschman's (1970) work is that the use of voice will be negatively correlated with exit, and (just as clearly) the central finding from labor economists' studies of unionism is that unions reduce employee quits. Is this prior theoretical and empirical research supported by the results from econometric testing of data set #2?

The answer to this question is "no," based on the results of estimating equation (6), again as shown in column 4 of Table 1. The use of voice (more precisely, the probability of using voice by filing a complaint under the CCP) is significantly positively associated with employee intent to leave the firm. This finding is consistent with the results of other recent studies of nonunion grievance systems (Boroff 1991; Lewin 1987, 1992).

As with the empirical findings from testing the P(Voice) equation (5), the findings from testing the P(Exit) equation may be moderated by employees' experiences with using the CCP—specifically, by the outcomes of decisions rendered under this grievance-like system. However, a separate regression estimate of equation (6) which incorporated this variable found no significant association between OUTCOME and P(Exit) (t-value = 0.50). In addition, and because PERQUAL and OUTCOME were significantly positively correlated (r = 0.38, alpha = 0.0001), another P(Exit) equation was estimated which included OUTCOME and excluded PERQUAL. Again, no significant association between OUTCOME and P(Exit) resulted from this estimate.

DISCUSSION

How do the findings from this study illuminate the relationships among exit, voice, and loyalty? First, in the face of unfair treatment and controlling for an exit option in both a unionized and nonunion firm, it is *less* loyal employees who are more likely to use voice *and* to exit the firm—but these may not necessarily be the same "less loyal" employees! By itself, employee loyalty to the firm does not distinguish between the use of voice and the intent to exit the firm. Instead, employees' fear of reprisal for using voice negatively influences the probability that an employee (in the unionized firm) will actually exercise voice. At the same time, perceived effectiveness (quality) of the voice mechanism coupled with the availability of alternative employment opportunities strongly influence, in opposite directions, an employee's intent to leave the firm.

In addition, the findings from this study enhance our understanding of who does *not* use voice and who does not intend to exit the firm. Keeping in mind that we have included in our multivariate analyses only those employees who have experienced unfair treatment (and who therefore might be most likely to exercise voice), the more loyal the employee the less likely is the employee to exercise voice *and* to intend to leave the firm. Further, fear of reprisal for exercising voice is significantly inversely related to the probability of employees (in the unionized firm) actually exercising voice, and these "unfairly" treated loyal employees might arguably be said to suffer in silence.

Conceptually, these results and interpretations are compatible with theoretical propositions offered by two political scientists. For example, in critiquing Hirschman's framework, Barry (1974) argues that loyalty may be unrelated or even inversely related to the exercise of voice. He criticizes Hirschman's concept of loyalty for being an "ad hoc equation filler" (Barry 1974, p. 95) lacking substantive content. According to Barry, loyalty cannot be directly observed but instead is invoked as an explanation of why some people who could be expected to quit do not, in fact, do so. Barry further proposes that once a customer (and presumably an employee) decides to stay with the firm (i.e., fails to exit), there is an additional choice to be made between voice and silence. Proceeding from Barry's amended version of Hirschman's model, loyalty may well be uncorrelated with voice but positively correlated with silence.

Another political scientist, Birch (1975), goes further in judging loyalty to belong to a family of concepts which also includes allegiance and fidelity. He illustrates this with reference to a "loyal party member," a term which "...is normally applied to the man who accepts what his leaders decide, not to be the constant critic" (Birch 1975, p. 74). Birch further observes that when a manager refers to one of his employees as a "loyal worker," he is unlikely to be referring to a shop steward. Birch concludes that Hirschman is "simply wrong" about the voice-inducing property of loyalty in both economic and political contexts. It follows, says Birch (1975, p. 75), that "loyalty and voice are correlated inversely rather than positively."

The statistical findings produced in this study appear to support these political science-based arguments. If voice and exit are on the same side of the "low loyalty" spectrum, we may ask if there is a positive association between the two. More pointedly, does an employee's use of voice subsequently render the employee more likely to exit (or to consider exiting) the firm? Our answer to this question is, "perhaps, but not necessarily." Admittedly, this is an equivocal answer to the question, but one which we believe is warranted at this stage of our research.

Consider once more the finding that the viability of the exit option (the availability of employment opportunities elsewhere) is positively associated with intent to exit the (unionized) firm, while length of service is negatively associated with intent to exit the firm (both in unionized and nonunion settings). It is possible, of course, for an employee's assessment of available labor market opportunities to change over time. However, given the negative association between $P(\text{Exit})$ and SERVICE, as each year goes by, it becomes increasingly improbable that an employee will exit the firm. This suggests that intent to exit the firm does not necessarily or solely flow from the use of voice. Further, in the unionized firm, we found an insignificant correlation between employee intent to exit the firm and employee use of voice ($r = 0.00041$ at $p = 0.99$). Therefore, it does not appear that an employee's use of voice provides a "springboard" to the employee's intent to exit the firm.

Going further, examination of the relationship between grievance outcomes—specifically, grievances lost by employees[13]—and intent to exit the (unionized) firm revealed only a slight and marginally significant positive association between these two variables ($r = -0.07$ at $p = 0.13$). Finally, we conducted a multivariate analysis (not shown here) in which the use of voice was regressed on subsequent intent to exit the (unionized) firm[14]; again, no significant result was observed (standardized beta = 0.008; t-statistic = 0.3).

By contrast, in the nonunion firm included in this study the use of voice (i.e., the probability of using the CCP) was significantly positively associated with employee intent to exit the firm (Column 4 of Table 1) and, as noted earlier, this result remained significant when the outcomes of grievance decisions were taken into account. Perhaps the absence of a union to represent employees in this firm is part of the "explanation" of this finding, but other factors, including fear of reprisal for using the grievance (complaint) system in this firm, which we were not able to measure, may also be at work here. What may be most appropriately concluded at this point is that the unequivocal proposition derived from Hirschman's (1970) exit-voice-loyalty model, namely that (the use of) voice and (intent to) exit are inversely correlated is not supported, indeed, appears to be contradicted, by this study.

CONCLUSIONS

The findings from this study provide some new insights into the relationships among exit, voice, and loyalty in an employment context. Using behavioral and perceptual data from samples of employees in one large unionized firm and one large nonunion firm who have experienced unfair workplace treatment, we found consistently strong negative relationships between employee loyalty and actual use of the grievance procedure. This relationship is opposite to that derived from Hirschman's (1970) exit-voice-loyalty model. However, we also found consistently strong negative relationships between employee loyalty and employee intent to leave (exit) the firm. This relationship is consistent with that derived from the exit-voice-loyalty model. Putting these two sets of findings together, we conclude that employee loyalty translates into "silence." Further, because this analysis is one of the first to have focused exclusively on employees who (believe that they) have experienced unfair treatment, we believe that it may be *strongly* concluded that loyal employees "suffer in silence" rather than exercise voice.

We noted earlier that prior studies have not fully specified or tested the exit-voice-loyalty framework. In particular, those studies have ignored loyalty altogether (or have assumed that it is somehow embodied in voice), have rarely examined the actual use of voice, and have failed to distinguish between employees who have and have not experienced unfair workplace treatment. Consequently, the findings of this study (and related studies: Boroff 1990, 1991; Lewin 1987, 1993; Lewin and Peterson 1988, 1991) call into question both the conceptual foundations and the empirical validity of the exit-voice-loyalty framework as it applies to the employment relationship.

Further, the findings from this study also have certain implications for research on organizational justice. Recall that employee perceptions of the effectiveness (quality) of the grievance procedure were insignificantly associated with P(Voice) and significantly inversely associated with P(Exit). This suggests that the more employees perceive such a procedure to be just or fair, the less likely the are to (intend to) leave the firm. At the same time and for the unionized employees included in this study, the fear of reprisal for using the grievance procedure was significantly negatively associated with the use of the procedure—even though these are unionized employees who presumably have legal protection (under the National Labor Relations Act) against such reprisals. Employee concerns about reprisal for exercising voice surely blur the distinction between procedural and distributive justice. Given this finding, the sharp distinction between these two types of organizational justice that has been made by many scholars warrants rethinking and perhaps reconceptualization.

However, even if and as additional research into organizational justice in the context of the employment relationship is undertaken, more conceptual and empirical work needs to be done on the issues of exit, voice, and loyalty taken up here. For example, in this study we were unable to determine whether intent to leave the firm preceded or followed the filing of grievances, though we do know that these two phenomena did not occur simultaneously. Consider the possibility that the filing of grievances, especially by employees who (say that they) have experienced unfair treatment, may reflect an accumulation or progression of incidents about which action (grievance filing) is finally taken. If an "accumulation" or "progression" story is indeed at work here, then grievance (or complaint) filing may well signal the employee's intent to leave the firm rather than remain with the firm. This matter warrants further investigation (using longitudinal rather than cross-sectional research designs). So, too, does the proposition that a voice mechanism operating in a unionized or nonunion context reduces the probability of an employee quitting (or intending to exit) the firm. Not only was evidence to support this proposition not found in the present study, some evidence to the contrary was adduced!

Finally, this study underscores the importance of distinguishing between employees who have and have not experienced unfair workplace treatment and of perceptual data in the analysis of grievance/complaint systems. Recognition of the former should spur researchers to formulate new and revise existing models of workplace dispute resolution, while recognition of the latter should lead researchers to strengthen their primary research design and data collection efforts. It is also possible, and from our perspective, desirable, that such initiatives will foster closer links among scholars in economics, organizational behavior, and industrial relations, who have in common theoretical and empirical interests in workplace dispute resolution.

APPENDIX A

Variables In Equations (3) and (4)

P(Voice) measures the likelihood of an employee having used the grievance process. It equals 1 if the employee filed a grievance in response to perceived unfair treatment and 0 otherwise. It is operationalized with the following questions from the survey instrument: "Have you ever experienced unfair treatment by management?" and "Did you file a grievance to correct this unfair treatment?"

P(Exit) measures a respondent's self-reported (future) intent to leave the firm. It is operationalized as an index ranging from 1 (no expressed intent) to 5 (high expressed intent) and was formed from the following disagree/agree questions: "I am seriously considering quitting this firm for an alternative employer," and "During the next year, I will probably look for a new job outside this firm." Cronbach's alpha for these items was 0.8.

GRIEVERATING measures the employee's perceived effectiveness (or quality) of the grievance procedure. The grievance procedure rated by the employee was the one contained in the collective bargaining agreement between the union that represented the employee and the company. This variable is operationalized with the following question from the survey instrument: "Overall, how would you rate the grievance procedure where you work?" with the rating scale ranging from 1 (poor) to 5 (excellent).

LOYALTY measures the employee's loyalty to the firm and is operationalized following the procedures developed by Rusbult and associates (1988). Specifically, the following disagree/agree questions were used to construct an index for this variable which ranges from 1 (least loyal or low loyalty) to 5 (most loyal or high loyalty): "I generally say good things about this firm even when other people criticize it," "I sometimes wear clothing (hat, jacket, pin, etc.) that bears the firm's logo or symbol," and "The people in charge of this firm generally know what they're doing." Cronbach's alpha among these items was 0.7.

EXITOPTION represents the employee respondent's assessment of the viability of his/her exit option and is based on measures of employment opportunity developed and reported by other researchers (Price and Mueller 1981, 1986). Specifically, the following disagree/agree questions were used to form an index for this variable ranging from 1 (poor exit options) to 5 (good exit options): "It is possible for me to find a better job with another employer than the one I have now with this firm," and "Acceptable jobs with other employers can always be found." Cronbach's alpha for these variables was 0.7.

UNIONMBR is coded 1 if the respondent is a member of one or the other of the two unions that represent employees of this firm, 0 otherwise.

SATISFACTION measures the employee's satisfaction with the firm and is based on the following disagree/agree question, ranging from 1 (strongly disagree) to 5 (strongly agree): "I am satisfied with the firm as an employer."

REPRISAL is the degree to which protection from reprisal for filing a grievance is important to the employee respondent. This variable is operationalized with one survey question containing nine items which the respondent ranked from 1 = not at all important to 9 = most important. One of these items was "no reprisal for filing a grievance."

EDUCATION measures the self-reported years of formal schooling completed by the employee respondent.

MINORITY measures the self-identified ethnic status of the respondents. It equals 1 if the respondents said they were a member of a minority group, 0 otherwise.

WAGES represents the employee respondent's self-reported annual earnings. For the unionized employees of this firm, higher annual earnings implies higher occupational ranking so that WAGES are effectively a proxy for an occupation variable (see also Boroff and Lewin 1996).

SERVICE is the number of years the employee respondent has been employed by the firm.

SEX is the gender of the respondent, coded 1 = female, 0 = male.

AGE is the age of the respondent in years.

MARRIED is coded 1 if the respondent reported being presently married, 0 otherwise.

APPENDIX B

Variables In Equations (5) and (6)

P(Voice) measures the probabililty of the respondent's filing a complaint, with 1 = experienced unfair treatment and filed a complaint, 0 = experienced unfair treatment and did not file a complaint.

LOYALTY measures the degree of loyalty of the respondent on a 1 = least loyal, 16 = most loyal scale. This index was based on employees' responses to five questions asking about how they would react to a work order that violates government safety regulations, their preferences for a union or outside representative (such as an attorney) to advocate their complaints under the CCP, their choice among four alternative company programs for dealing with workplace complaints (including the CCP), and their confidence in the firm's senior management. For further detail about the construction of this LOYALTY index, see Boroff and Lewin (1994).

PERQUAL measures the respondent's perceived quality of the Company Complaint Procedure (CCP) on a 1 = lowest quality, 10 = highest quality scale.

P(Exit) measures the repondent's intent to leave the firm, with 1 = intent to leave, 0 = no intent to leave.

AGE is the age of the respondent in years.

SEX is the gender of the respondent, coded 1 = female, 0 = male.

EDUCATION measures the self-reported years of formal schooling completed by the employee respondent.

HIGHOCCUP measures the employee respondent's occupational position in the firm on a 1 = lowest ranking, 5 = highest ranking scale.

MINORITY measures the self-reported ethnic status of the employee respondent, with 1 = racial minority, 0 = otherwise.

SERVICE is the number of years the employee respondent has been employed by the firm.

ACKNOWLEDGMENT

The authors thank Baichun Xiao, Associate Professor at Seton Hall University, for his comments on portions of the empirical analysis contained in this paper.

NOTES

1. This paper draws from an attempts to integrate the findings reported in Boroff and Lewin (1994, 1996; also see Lewin and Boroff 1994).

2. A referee for the first draft of this paper makes the point that the issue of estimating the exit-voice tradeoff is "identical to the one of estimating the trade off between wages and fringe benefits. Individuals with higher bargaining power have higher wages *and* fringe benefits (emphasis in the original). If we do not adequately control for bargaining power, we often get a positive coefficient for fringe benefits in a wage equation. If we can control for bargaining power, then a negative tradeoff results, as theoretically expected." In the present paper, limiting the analysis to those employees who have experienced unfair workplace treatment—or discontent—can be said to provide the type of control recommended by this referee. In addition, and as is more fully explained in the following text, we also include in data set #1 a variable measuring employee satisfaction (SATISFACTION) with the firm.

3. This point was raised by an external referee to whom we are indebted for doing so.

4. These data are more fully described in Boroff and Keefe (1991).

5. This survey was designed by Prof. Alan Westin of Columbia University, with the assistance of Prof. David Lewin. A detailed description of this firm's company complaint procedure (CCP) is contained in Westin and Feilu (1988).

6. The identification of CCP users was determined by a review of written complaint files. These confidential data were provided to the researchers by the firm's vice president of human resources, to whom we express our appreciation.

7. From the completed surveys, we were able to determine who among the respondents perceived themselves to have experienced unfair workplace treatment and who actually used the CCP in the face

of unfair treatment. Specifically, the survey included the following question: "Within the past year, do you feel that you personally have experienced unfair treatment by management?" ("yes"—"no")

Respondents were also asked, "Have you ever filed a CCP yourself?" ("yes"—"no") Further, all respondents irrespective of their use of the CCP were asked to rate the quality of the CCP. The relevant question was: "Overall, on a scale from 1 to 10, with 10 being 'excellent,' 5 being 'average,' and 1 being 'poor,' how would you rate the CCP?"

8.   The relevant survey question was: "Have you ever experienced unfair treatment by management?"

9.   Similarly, columns 2-4 of Table 1 present changes in probabilities for the independent variables included in equations (4), (5), and (6), respectively, which were also evaluated at the means of the dependent variables in each of those equations. The reduced form logistic estimates of equations (3)-(4) are available on request from the authors and may also be found in Lewin and Boroff (1994). The full results of the two-stage least squares estimates of the P(Voice) as well as the P(Exit) equations (the latter being more fully discussed later in the text) are also available on request from the authors and may be found in Boroff and Lewin (1996).

10.   In a study of a nonunion complaint procedure, Boroff (1991) found that fear of reprisal was a predictor of perceived complaint procedure effectiveness. Hence, it might be argued that GRIEVER-ATING captures employee concerns about reprisal and that REPRISAL should not be included in our model. However, the correlation between GRIEVERATING and REPRISAL was –0.02, and colinearity was not present. Furthermore, fear of reprisal is only one of several predictors of grievance procedure effectiveness (Boroff 1993; Lewin and Peterson 1988).

11.   The specific question asked whether or not the respondent expected to be working for this firm three years from now, with the answers constrained to "yes" and "no."

12.   Two factors support an inference that intent to exit the firm precedes the decision to use voice. First, in a related study, Boroff (1991) found that nonusers of the CCP feared reprisal for filing written complaints whereas users of the CCP did not. The absence of fear of reprisal may stem from previously formed intentions to leave the firm. Second, and as will briefly be discussed later, intent to leave the firm is unrelated to the outcomes of complaint settlement decisions. This may indicate that the complainant's intention to leave the firm was formed prior to using the CCP.

13.   Respondents who grieved were asked to report the outcomes of their grievances. Their choices were: "I won my grievance," "I lost my grievance," "There was a compromise," "My grievance is still pending," and "My case was dropped." From the responses to this question, a three-point scale was created ranging from 1 = "I lost my grievance" to 3 = "I won my grievance." Grievances that were settled through compromise were valued at the midpoint of the scale, while pending cases and dropped cases were excluded from the analysis.

14.   As noted earlier, andas we constructed it, the use of voice reported by respondents to our survey occurred in the past. But we also asked the respondents about their *future* intent to exit the firm. In this way, we sought to ensure that we were not measuring the same point in time for "voice" and "exit." It can be argued, of course, that an employee considers the exit option even before perceived unfair treatment occurs (and thus before voice is exercised). Even so, in light of the absence of a significant association between exit and voice, we believe that using VOICE as an independent variable in the estimation of P(Exit) does not result in correlated error terms.

REFERENCES

Aldrich, J. H., and F.D. Nelson. 1984. *Linear Probability: Logit* and Probit Models. Beverly Hill, CA: Sage Publications.

Ash, P. 1970. "The Parties to Grievances." *Personnel Psychology* 23: 13-37.

Barry, B. 1974. "Review Article: *Exit, Voice, and Loyalty.*" *British Journal of Political Science* 4: 79-107.

Bartel, A. 1979. "The Migration Decision: What Role Does Job Mobility Play?" *American Economic Review* 69: 775-786.

Bateman, T. S., and S. Strasser. 1984. "A Longitudinal Analysis of the Antecedents of Organizational Commitment." *Academy of Management Journal* 27: 95-112.

Becker, T. E. 1992. "Foci and Bases of Commitment: Are They Distinctions Worth Making?" *Academy of Management Journal* 35: 232-244.

Birch, A. H. 1975. "Economic Models in Political Science: The Case of *Exit, Voice, and Loyalty.*" *British Journal of Political Science* 5: 69-82.

Blau, F., and L. Kahn. 1981. "Race and Sex Differences in Quits by Younger Workers." *Industrial and Labor Relations Review* 35: 563-577.

Blinder, A. S. 1972. "Who Joins Unions?" Working Paper No. 36. Industrial Relations Section, Princeton University.

Boroff, K. E. 1990. "Loyalty—A Correlate of Exit, Voice, or Silence?" Pp. 307-314 in *Proceedings of The Forty-second Annual Meeting* (Atlanta, December 28-30, 1989). Madison, WI: Industrial Relations Research Association.

———. 1991. "Measuring the Perceptions of the Effectiveness of a Workplace Complaint Procedure." Pp. 93-102 in *Advances in Industrial and Labor Relations*, Vol. 5, edited by D. Sockell, D. Lewin and D. B. Lipsky. Greenwich, CT: JAI Press.

———. 1993. "The Probability of Filing a Grievance—Does Union Membership Make a Difference?" Pp. 251-259 in *Proceedings of the Forty-fifth Annual Meeting* (Anaheim, January 5-7). Madison, WI: Industrial Relations Research Association.

Boroff, K. E., and J. Keefe. 1991. *Technical Report Of The Employment Security Project.* South Orange, NJ: W. Paul Stillman School of Business, Seton Hall University.

Boroff, K. E., and K. Ketkar. 1994. "Investigating Career Flexibility Among Union-Represented Employees." Pp. 268-278 in *Proceedings of the Forty-sixth Annual Meeting* (Boston, January 3-5). Madison, WI: Industrial Relations Research Association.

Boroff, K. E., and D. Lewin. 1994. "The Relationships Among Loyalty, Voice and Intent to Exit in Grievance Filing—A Conceptual and Empirical Analysis." Revised Working Paper No. 211. Institute of Industrial Relations, University of California, Los Angeles.

———. 1996. "Loyalty, Voice, and Intent to Exit a Union Firm: A Conceptual and Empirical Analysis." Revised Working Paper No. 268. Institute of Industrial Relations, University of California, Los Angeles.

Brooke, P. B., Jr., D. W. Russell, and J. L. Price. 1988. "Discriminant Validation of Measures of Job Satisfaction, Job Involvement, and Organizational Commitment." *Journal of Applied Psychology* 73: 139-145.

Carston, J. M., and P. E. Spector. 1987. "Unemployment, Job Satisfaction, and Employee Turnover: A MetaAnalytic Test of the Muchinsky Model." *Journal of Applied Psychology* 72: 75-80.

Curry, J. P., D. S. Wakefield, J. L. Price, and C. W. Mueller. 1986. "On the Causal Ordering of Job Satisfaction and Organizational Commitment." *Academy of Management Journal* 29: 847-858.

Delaney, J. T. 1983. "Strikes, Arbitration, and Teacher Salaries: A Behavioral Analysis." *Industrial and Labor Relations Review* 36: 431-446.

Delaney, J. T., and P. Feuille. 1992. "The Determinants of Nonunion Grievance and Arbitration Procedures." Pp. 529-538 in *Proceedings of the Forty-fourth Annual Meeting* (New Orleans, January 3-5). Madison, WI: Industrial Relations Research Association.

Delaney, J. T., C. Ichniowski, and D. Lewin. 1989. "Employee Involvement Programs and Firm Performance." Pp. 148-158 in *Proceedings of the Forty-First Annual Meeting* (New York, December 28-30, 1988). Madison, WI: Industrial Relations Research Association.

Delaney, J. T., D. Lewin, and C. Ichniowski. 1989. *Human Resource Policies and Practices of American Firms*, BLMR No. 137. Washington, DC: U.S. Department of Labor, Bureau of Labor-Management Relations and Cooperative Programs.

Dillman, D. A. 1978. *Mail and Telephone Surveys: The Total Design Method*. New York: Wiley.

Elliston, F. J., J. Keenan, P. Lockhart, and J. van Schaick. 1985. *Whistleblowing: Managing Dissent In The Workplace*. New York: Praeger.

Ewing, D. W. 1989. *Justice on the Job: Resolving Grievances in the Nonunion Workplace*. Boston: Harvard Business School Press.

Feuille, P., and J. T. Delaney. 1993. "The Individual Pursuit of Organizational Justice: Grievance Procedures in Nonunion Workplaces." Pp. 187-232 in *Research in Personnel and Human Resource Management*, Vol. 10, edited by G.R. Ferris and K.M. Rowland. Greenwich, CT: JAI Press.

Fiorito, J., and C. Greer. 1986. "Gender Differences in Union Membership, Preferences, and Beliefs." *Journal Of Labor Research* 7: 145-164.

Folger, R., and J. Greenberg. 1985. "Procedural Justice: An Interpretive Analysis of Personnel Systems." Pp. 141-183 in *Research in Personnel and Human Resource Management*, Vol. 3, edited by K.M. Rowland and G.R. Ferris. Greenwich, CT: JAI Press.

Freeman, R. B. 1980. "The Exit-Voice Tradeoff in the Labor Market: Unionism, Job Tenure, Quits and Separations." *Quarterly Journal of Economics* 94: 643-673.

Freeman, R. B. and J. L. Medoff. 1984. *What Do Unions Do?* New York: Basic Books.

Fryxell, G.E., and M.E. Gordon. 1989. "Workplace Justice and Job Satisfaction as Predictors of Satisfaction With Union and Management." *Academy of Management Journal* 32: 851-866.

Getman, J. G., S. Goldberg, and J. Herman. 1976. *Union Representation Elections: Law and Reality*. New York: Russell Sage Foundation.

Gordon, M., and L. Long. 1981. "Demographic and Attitudinal Correlates of Union Joining." *Industrial and Labor Relations Review* 20: 306-311.

Gordon, M. E., and S. J. Miller. 1984. "Grievances: A Review of Research and Practice." *Personnel Psychology* 37: 117-146.

Greenberg, J. 1990. "Looking Fair vs. Being Fair: Managing Impressions of Organizational Justice." Pp. 111-157 in *Research in Organizational Behavior*, Vol. 12, edited by B.M. Staw and L.L. Cummings. Greenwich, CT: JAI Press.

Heneman, H. G., III, and M. H. Sandver. 1983. "Predicting the Outcome of Union Certification Elections: A Review of the Literature." *Industrial and Labor Relations Review* 36: 537-559.

Hills, S. 1985. "The Attitudes of Union and Nonunion Male Workers Toward Union Representation." *Industrial and Labor Relations Review* 38: 179-194.

Hirschman, A. O. 1970. *Exit, Voice And Loyalty*. Cambridge, MA: Harvard University Press.

Ichniowski, C., and D. Lewin. 1987. "Grievance Procedures and Firm Performance." Pp. 159-193 in *Human Resources and the Performance of the Firm*, edited by M. M. Kleiner, R. N. Block, M. Roomkin and S. W. Salsburg. Madison, WI: Industrial Relations Research Association.

_____. 1988. "Characteristics of Grievance Procedures: Evidence from Nonunion, Union and Double-Breasted Businesses." Pp. 415-424 in *Proceedings of the Fortieth Annual Meeting* (Chicago, December 28-30). Madison, WI: Industrial Relations Research Association.

Intriligator, M. D. 1978. *Econometric Models, Techniques, and Applications*. Englewood Cliffs, NJ: Prentice-Hall.

Kahneman, D., J.L. Knetsch, and R.H. Thaler. 1986a. "Fairness and the Assumptions of Economics." *Journal of Business* 59: S285-S300.

_____. 1986b. "Fairness as a Constraint on Profit Seeking: Settlements in the Market." *American Economic Review* 76: 728-741.

Kochan, T. 1978. "Contemporary Views Of American Workers Toward Trade Unions." Research Report to the U.S. Department of Labor.

_____. 1979. "How American Workers View Labor Unions." *Monthly Labor Review* 102: 23-31.

Lee, L.F. 1978. "Unionism and Wage Rates: A Simultaneous Equations Model With Qualitative and Limited Depended Variables." *International Economic Review* 19: 415-433.

Leigh, D., and S. Hills. 1987. "Male-Female Differences in the Potential for Union Growth Outside Traditionally Unionized Industries." *Journal of Labor Research* 8: 131-142.

LeLouarn, J.Y. 1980. "Predicting Union Vote from Worker Attitudes and Perceptions." Pp. 72-82 in *Proceedings of the Thirty-Second Annual Meeting* (Atlanta, December 28-30, 1979). Madison, WI: Industrial Relations Research Association.

Lewin, D. 1987. "Dispute Resolution in the Nonunion Firm: A Theoretical and Empirical Analysis." *Journal of Conflict Resolution* 31: 467-502.

_____. 1992. "Grievance Procedures in Nonunion Workplaces: An Empirical Analysis of Usage, Dynamics and Outcomes." *Chicago-Kent Law Review* 66: 823-844.

_____. 1993. "Conflict Resolution and Management in Contemporary Work Organizations: Theoretical Perspectives and Empirical Evidence." Pp. 167-209 in *Research in the Sociology of Organizations*, Vol. 12, edited by S.A. Bacharach, R.L. Seeber and D.J. Walsh. Greenwich, CT: JAI Press.

Lewin, D. and K. E. Boroff. 1994. "The Role of Loyalty in Exit and Voice: A Conceptual and Empirical Analysis." Paper presented to the Fourth Bargaining Group Conference, Centre for Industrial Relations, University of Toronto, October.

Lewin, D., and R. B. Peterson. 1988. *The Modern Grievance Procedure In The United States.* Westport, CT: Quorum.

_____. 1991. "Behavioral Outcomes of Grievance Settlement in Unionized Businesses." Working Paper No. 198, Institute of Industrial Relations, University of California.

Lind, E.A., and T.R. Tyler. 1988. *The Social Psychology Of Procedural Justice.* New York: Plenum.

Miller, P., and C. Mulvey. 1991. "Australian Evidence on the Exit/Voice Model of the Labor Market." Industrial and Labor Relations Review 45: 45-57.

Mitchell, O. 1983. "Fringe Benefits and the Cost of Changing Jobs." *Industrial And Labor Relations Review* 37: 70-78.

Mobley, W. H., S. O. Horner, and A. T. Hollingsworth. 1978. "An Evaluation of Precursors of Hospital Employee Turnover." *Journal of Applied Psychology* 63: 408-414.

Mowday, R. T., C. S. Koberg, and A. W. McArthur. 1984. "The Psychology of the Withdrawal Process: A Cross-Validation Test of Mobley's Intermediate Linkages Model of Turnover in Two Samples. *Academy of Management Journal* 27: 79-94.

Peterson, R. B., and D. Lewin. 1991a. "Lessons from Research on Unionized Grievance Procedures: A Critical Review and Appraisal." Working Paper No. 210. Institute of Industrial Relations, University of California, Los Angeles.

_____. 1991b. "The Grievance Procedure and Personal Outcomes." Working Paper No. 208, Institute of Industrial Relations, University of California, Los Angeles.

Price, J. L., and C. Mueller. 1981. "A Causal Model of Turnover for Nurses." *Academy of Management Journal* 24: 543-565.

_____. 1986. *Absenteeism and Turnover of Hospital Employees.* Greenwich, CT: JAI Press.

Rusbult, C. E., D. Farrell, G. Rogers and A. G. Mainous, III. 1988. "Impact of Variables on Exit, Voice, Loyalty and Neglect: An Integrative Model of Responses to Declining Job Satisfaction." *Academy of Management Journal* 31: 599-627.

Schmidt, P. 1978. "Estimation of a Simultaneous Equations Model With Jointly Dependent Continuous and Qualitative Variables: The Union-Earnings Equation Revisited." *International Economic Review* 19: 453-465.

Sheppard, B. 1984. "Third Party Conflict Intervention: A Procedural Justice Framework." Pp. 141-189 in *Research in Organizational Behavior*, Vol. XX, edited by B.M. Staw and L.L. Cummings. Greenwich, CT: JAI Press.

Sheppard, B., R. J. Lewicki, and J. Minton. 1992. *Organizational Justice.* Lexington, MA: Lexington Books.

Sicherman, N., and O. Galor. 1990. "A Theory of Career Mobility." *Journal of Political Economy* 98: 169-192.

Thibaut, J., and L. Walker. 1975. *Procedural Justice: A Psychological Analysis.* Lexington, MA: Lexington Books.

Uphoff, W. and M. D. Dunnette. 1956. "Understanding the Union Member." Bulletin No. 18, Industrial Relations Center, University of Minnesota.

U.S. Bureau of Labor Statistics. 1981. *Characteristics of Major Collective Bargaining Agreements, January 1, 1980.* Bulletin No. 2095. Washington, DC: U.S. Department of Labor, Bureau of Labor Statistics.

Viscusi, W. K. 1980. "Sex Differences in Worker Quitting." *Review of Economics and Statistics* 62: 388-398.

Weiss, A. 1984. "Determinants of Quit Behavior." *Journal of Labor Economics* 2: 371-387.

Westin, A. F., and A. G. Feliu. 1988. *Resolving Employment Disputes Without Litigation.* Washington, DC: Bureau of National Affairs.

Westin, A. F., H. I. Kurtz, A. Robbins, and the Educational Fund for Individual Rights. 1981. *Whistle-blowing: Loyalty and Dissent in the Corporation.* New York: McGraw-Hill.

UNIONIZATION, EMPLOYEE REPRESENTATION, AND ECONOMIC PERFORMANCE:
COMPARISONS AMONG OECD NATIONS

Morris M. Kleiner and Chang-Ruey Ay

ABSTRACT

This study examines the relationship between the major labor market institutions, which are unions and works councils, on national economic performance. The study first reviews the theoretical role of corporatist policies on economic efficiency. Next, the analysis modifies a standard production function to account for institutional factors such as unionization and mandated employee representation. The empirical results from the specified model, using a pooled cross-section time series approach for 14 OECD countries over thirty-years, show that nations with relatively low levels of uniozation and strong forms of joint consultation do somewhat better on productivity growth and investment activity. The generally small efficiency impacts of labor market institutions suggest that employee voice concerns should dominate the policy discussion on the optimal types of employee representation for economically advanced nations.

Advances in Industrial and Labor Relations, Volume 7, pages 97-121.
Copyright © 1996 by JAI Press Inc.
All rights of reproduction in any form reserved.
ISBN: 1-55938-925-7

INTRODUCTION

The potential economic effects of labor market and legal institutions which provide employee representation have been a long-standing issue in industrial relations (Perlman 1928). Furthermore, some economists have argued that institutions in the economic system are the most important determinants of economic performance (North 1994). It has been stated that unions, which are generally viewed as the most visible labor market institution for providing employee representation, increase aggregate productivity by enhancing voice at the workplace, lowering turnover rates, and providing greater worker participation (Freeman and Medoff 1984). Freeman and Medoff go on to state that unions have two faces—a "voice" face that promotes the positive aspects of the institution and a negative "monopoly" face that reduces productivity. A contrary view of unions as a labor market institution concludes that unions are just another form of economic monopoly engaged in rent capture, which should be discouraged since it causes gross economic inefficiencies for both firms and countries (Simons 1948). Since unions traditionally are perceived as the most economically significant labor market institution, their impact is likely to be important in both product and capital markets (Eberts and Groshen 1991). Empirical studies of the economic impact of unions on the U.S. economy, however, have found either slight negative impacts (Defina, 1983; Rees 1963; Stevens 1995) or modest positive effects (Freeman and Medoff 1984).

In many advanced economies, the role of employee voice through mandated works councils has been accepted as sufficiently valuable to these societies that it has been legally mandated in private sector organizations. For example, the European Union has recently adopted rules requiring multinational companies to set up works councils in all member countries except Britain (Reuters 1994). Typically, workers with these legislated rights can elect a representative to meet with management in work organizations with five or more employees. In some countries, members of the works council can have a place on the board of directors of the organization if there are 200 or more employees.[1]

In most of these countries, works councils are independent of trade unions but tend to work closely with them, especially in dealing with issues of enforcement of both rights and interest disputes. Further, a high percentage of elected members of the works council are also union members. Given the high level of both information-sharing and consultation rights under legally mandated works councils, they would appear to epitomize the voice aspects of industrial relations that may enhance economic efficiency (Levine and Tyson 1990). In most of the countries where works councils are legally mandated, these institutions work closely with unions on both economic and worker rights issues. Although there has been considerable descriptive work on how works councils operate (e.g., Rogers and Streeck 1995), the economic performance aspects have been largely ignored.[2]

With few exceptions, empirical tests of the efficiency-enhancing impacts of unions have used the firm or industry as the unit of analysis (Freeman 1988). The argument for this neoclassical economic approach is that the firm's objective function is assumed to maximize profits, and productivity is closely tied to this goal. For this to be the objective of a nation, more heroic assumptions need to be made about national goals. It is reasonable, however, to assume that nations would prefer higher levels of overall productivity, investment, and long-run wealth enhancement to lower ones. Furthermore, the efficiency enhancing impacts of any policy that promotes industrial relations institutions would likely use aggregate economic performance as a major criteria in its evaluation. The objective of this study is to examine the impact of union density and government policies regarding employee voice, such as government-mandated employee participation, on the economic performance of the more highly developed nations that are members of the Organization for Economic Cooperation and Development (OECD). This analysis will provide another arena for the examination of union and statutory works councils at an aggregate level. This approach is consistent with earlier economic evaluations of unions on aggregate performance in the United States by Rees (1963), Defina (1983), and Freeman and Medoff (1984). It provides additional evidence of the impact of unionism and mandated participation on economic outcomes such as investment and productivity. Moreover, this study also can serve as a point of departure for more in-depth country-specific analyses of the impact of unions and works councils on economic performance.

In the remainder of this paper, we first describe the assumed relationship between labor market institutions and economic performance. We also review the potential impacts of "corporatist" government policies on economic efficiency.[3] Second, we specify a standard production function that is used often in the economic development literature and modify it to account for institutional variables such as union and nonunion labor, as well as mandated employee representation statutes and other forms of employee voice such as voluntary joint-consultation. We detail the variables in the data set and state their linkage to the specified model. Next, we provide estimates from the model, including several sensitivity tests used in our econometric specifications. We conclude by briefly examining the effect of employee representation and unions in two of the countries in our sample.

LABOR MARKET INSTITUTIONS AND ECONOMIC PERFORMANCE

To examine why economic performance may differ among national economies, we will go beyond conventional specifications and include institutional labor market factors. One important institutional factor is the "collective action" of coalitions, a factor which has been used in recent economic performance analyses (e.g., Calmfors and Driffill 1988; Olson 1988). Within this context, interest groups in the labor market are assumed not only to move resources away from the production process but also to slow the reaction of the economy to external shocks. Consistent with this approach, Bruno and Sachs (1985) find that excessive real-wage growth, which led to a major shift in income from owners of capital to labor, played a role in slowing down productivity growth since 1970. This implies that it is desirable to capture the effect of institutions that coordinate influences of various coalitions on prices (or wages) in the operation of labor markets.

Furthermore, Olson (1965, 1982) provides a plausible explanation of the difference in the growth of productivity among countries with his hypothesis that "distributional coalitions" lead to less efficiency. In his model, the "actors" follow Pareto efficiency in welfare economics in which workers and employers achieve an optimal situation in which no one can become better off without making anyone else worse off (Henderson and Quandt 1971). Neither worker nor employer has enough power to generate a distorted effect in a competitive market economy. They are confined to producing and exchanging goods and services to realize a goal of profit maximization. However, once some actors begin to organize (e.g., trade unions) to pursue their own benefits while others remain within the original competitive framework, institutional constraints are created on both the supply and demand sides of the labor market, leading to potential distortions of the market economy.

If, however, the government believes that worker organizations in the labor market are bound to do the economy more harm than good, it will intervene in the market through other types of institutional constraints, such as laws to remove barriers to free competition, or a system of interest intermediation to encourage compromises among interest groups. If some "institutions" can distort markets, other "institutions" can enforce competition in the market or bring about outcomes similar to those of competitive markets.

Olson (1982) predicts that the longer the periods of stability of a democratic economy, the greater the number and the denser the network of the coalitions will be and, hence, the lower rate of its economic growth. There is, however, one critical exception to the general connection between slowdown and the accumulation of distributional coalitions. It is the "encompassing organization" (Olson 1982). Because encompassing organizations contain a large proportion of the total population within their jurisdictions, they "have some incentive to make the society in which they operate more prosperous, and an incentive to redistribute income to their members with as little excess burden as possible, and to cease such redistribution unless the amount redistributed is substantial in relation to the social cost of the redistribution" (Olson 1982, p. 53). In other words, if a trade union or works council is encompassing, the collective interest of the union becomes almost identical with the national interest. It can pursue the general interest while at the same time pursuing its own particular interest. Thus, encompassing trade unions are not necessarily antisocial and do not necessarily harm economic efficiency. One example of this phenomenon is Sweden where between 80 percent and 90 percent of the workforce belongs to a union, and the interest group objectives are consistent with national ones. An encompassing trade union could have a strong voice effect and weak monopoly power, to use the analysis provided by Freeman and Medoff.

As a result, if what matters for economic growth is the presence of encompassing groups and the degree to which a group has this feature is a function of labor market institutions and industrial culture, then countries with institutional structures that encourage this process will have higher economic growth. In a study of trade union wage restraint among the OECD countries, Crouch (1985) concludes that "once economic actors have become organized, the sociopolitical context most likely to be consistent with relative freedom from economic distortion will be one that encourages coordination of action and centralization of organization rather than one that tries to reproduce among organized interests situations analogous to a free market" (p. 137).

A further explanation of the rationale for the effectiveness of works councils is offered by Freeman and Lazear (1995). They argue that there is a difference between private and public gains. For business, with its emphasis on profit maximization, there is a premium on having some information from employees, but the optimal level of consultation and power sharing is low. For society, however, the level of optimal consultation and employee power is higher for productivity maximization. Therefore, for society to maximize output, some level of joint consultation should be encouraged through incentives developed by the government.

CATEGORIES OF EMPLOYEE INVOLVEMENT AND CONSULTATION

In this section, we identify three types of collective employee participation at the workplace and describe their possible impact on economic performance. This categorization provides an empirically tractable grouping of the different degrees of government-mandated or encouraged participation, as well as interest group intervention on the operation of markets.

In Figure 1, we provide a method of categorizing the nations in our sample by the type of statutory provision dealing with worker rights to information and consultation. The major source of the categorization is the existence of a statutory provision. The countries on continental Europe like Austria, Denmark, France, Germany, the Netherlands, Norway and Sweden, since 1977, all have formal provisions mandating participation. The others have no mandatory provisions but can have employee participation through the national or industry collective bargaining agreement. Sweden, from 1946 through 1976, had this type of employee involvement program. The other countries in our sample have no formal statutory provisions on joint consultation, but Japan has a program through long-standing custom with their employers and unions (see Morishima 1991).

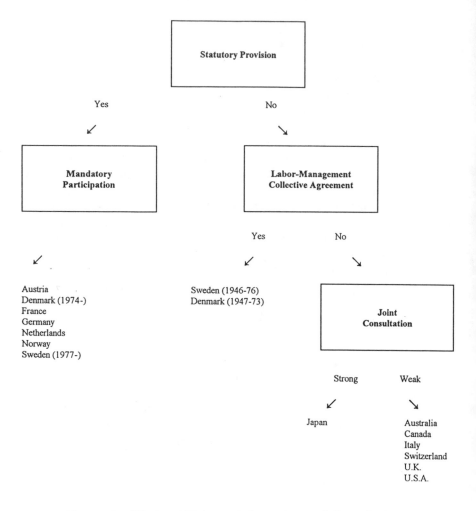

Figure 1.   Workers' Rights to Information and Consultation
(Employee Involvement in Mangement as of 1990)

To guarantee workers' voice in the governance of the shop floor and the firm, some countries, such as France, the Netherlands, and Norway, statutorily require employers to take the initiative in establishing works councils. However, in Germany, Austria, and Denmark works councils must be set up at the employees' initiative. Typically, legally-mandated employee participation statutorily was monitored by works councils in these Western European countries. These institutions' representative bodies were elected by all workers at a particular workplace for a given size firm. Rights of collective worker participation and representation are institutionalized at the workplace through legislation and are usually performed by works councils.[4]

Another voluntary type of employee participation is the system of labor-management joint consultation. Labor-management consultation committees are optional in this system. Japan is the representative country with strong joint consultation between employees and employers; in contrast, the United States is characterized as a country with weak joint consultation arrangements consistent with generally adversarial labor relations. In this case, there is virtually no required joint consultation.

To the extent that there are distinct groups of employee involvement, the categories that we have identified can be classified as statutory mandated, the collective agreement type, and the strong and weak joint consultation type. To the extent that they fit into the Olson model, the strong joint consultation model is the one which may have evidence of "encompassing" relationships. The weak joint consultation means free markets with coalitions.

To the extent that granting the participation rights to workers would put constraints on management, slow the speed of adjustment to the external environment, and hinder the optimal use of capital stock and labor, these policies would reduce productivity. On the other hand, voice and consultation on job-related issues can result in higher levels of productivity consistent with the Freeman and Lazear model.

In Table 1, we present the institutional characteristics of the nations in our study. In Column 1 we present the average percent of workers organized in each country in our analysis over the period of our study. Next, we present whether the country has a statutory provision for employee participation. The final column indicates whether there is a provision involving voluntary employee participation. It is not surprising to see that countries with high levels of unionization also tend to have statutory provisions mandating some form of works councils. It is important, however, to point out that unions often do not favor works councils, and many cases actively oppose them (Rogers and Streeck 1995). For example, in the United States and England, unions have actively opposed works councils, in part, due to the perceived competition from this institution for members.

MODEL SPECIFICATION

To initially model the effects of unionism and alternative forms of representation on productivity, we begin with the same approach used at the firm level to estimate the factors that influence productivity levels, changes, and investment. We then model the country-specific effects with the assumption that economic output in a nation is a function of the availability of capital, the amount of useable land, quan-

Table 1. Mandated and Voluntary Employee Representation in OECD Countries*

Country	Union Density[1] (%)	Statutory Provision for Employee Participation (Year Mandated)	Voluntary Employee Participation
Austria	59.9	Works Councils ($N^2 > 5$) Supervisory Boards (board-level)	
Australia	51.9	None[3] (compulsory wage arbitration)	Joint Consultative Committee
Canada	33.1	Occupational Health and Safety Committee[4]	Mandate consultation on this issue
Denmark	71.3	Board of Directors[5] ($N > 50$) (1974)	Cooperation Committees
France	19.1	Employee Delegates ($N > 10$) Works Councils ($N > 50$) Health and Safety Committee ($N > 50$) Training Committee ($N > 300$) Economic Committee ($N > 1,000$) Direct Expression Groups ($N > 50$) Board of Directors	
Italy	43.6		Works Councils
Japan	32.3	None	Strong Joint Consultative Comittee
Netherlands	36.5	Works Councils ($N > 35$) Supervisory Boards	
Norway	62.1	Works Councils and/or Cooperation Committee Board of Directors	
Sweden	80.5	Co-determination Committee [Act of Co-determination at Work (MBL) in 1976] Board opened in 1987	Works Councils (1946-1976) (established on legally binding central agreements and terminated in 1976)

Switzerland	32.1	None	Works Councils
United Kingdom	46.7	None[6]	Joint Consultative Committee
United States	23.2	None	Weak Joint Consultative Committee (1935 Wagner Model)
West Germany	38.4	Works Councils (N>5) (1972) Supervisory Boards	

Notes: *Although this table does not cover rights and obligations, it should be noted that the role of works councils varies greatly between countries.

1. Average union density from 1960 to 1989 in percent.
2. N means the number of company employees.
3. In 1984, employers were required to consult with their employees before introducing major changes to work method or to organizational structure.
4. For some provinces only, not nationwide policy.
5. Under the 1974 statute, companies with more than 50 employees can elect representatives to the Board of Directors.
6. The Labor Government (1974-1979) proposed a White Paper on board-level representation, but failed to bring it to parliament before its 1979 general election defeats.

tity and quality of labor, and the institutional structure of the country, including the extent of the unionization of the labor market. Consequently, a variation of the Cobb-Douglas production function can be used as the basis of our theoretical model. The basic production function is presented as follows:

$$Q = f(K, L, La),$$
(1)

where Q is the quantity of output, K is capital input, L is labor, and La is the quantity of arable land as a natural resource. Productivity, the output per unit of input, is determined by the amount and quality of inputs of capital, labor, and land. The basic specification of this model is similar to the one applied by Bergson (1987) in his cross-national examination of comparative productivity, using varying assumptions regarding constant versus increasing returns to scale and their role in total factor productivity. A further modification of this production function was implemented by Brown and Medoff at the firm level to distinguish between union and nonunion labor (Brown and Medoff 1978). More specifically, they specified the labor function as:

$$L = f(Ln, cLu)$$
(2)

where Ln is non-unionized labor, Lu is unionized labor, and c is the parameter reflecting differences in the productivity of union and nonunion labor. In the model, if c is greater than 1, then union labor is more productive than nonunion labor.

Next, by substituting (2) into the Cobb-Douglas production function, we have the following relationship:

$$Y = AK (Ln + cLu)^{1-\alpha-\beta} La^{\beta},$$
$$\text{where } \alpha + \beta < 1 \text{ and } \alpha, \beta > 0,$$
(3)

Then:

$$\frac{Y}{L} = AK^{\alpha} L^{-\alpha-\beta} [1 + (c-1)u]^{1-\alpha-\beta} La^{\beta}$$

$$= A\left(\frac{K}{L}\right)^{\alpha} [1 + (c-1)u]^{1-\alpha-\beta} \left(\frac{La}{L}\right)^{\beta}$$

$$\text{where } \frac{Lu}{L} = u.$$

In order to estimate the basic model derived from the initial production function in equation (4), we can specify the following equation in a manner similar to the approach taken by Brown and Medoff to estimate the following[5]:

$$ln(Y/L) = lnA = \alpha \ ln \ (K/L) = \beta \ ln(La/L) + (1-\alpha-\beta) \ (c-1) \ U + \varepsilon. \qquad (5)$$

This equivalent equation to (3) makes output per worker depend on capital per worker and union labor, holding land constant. We also have developed a second-order Taylor series on this extended Brown-Medoff production function to account for nonlinearities. Further, we modify the model to examine the role of labor market institutions on productivity growth by including the role of legislated works councils.

We also estimate alternative specifications of our production function that include nonconstant returns to scale,[6] a nonlinear relationship between unionization and measures of economic performance. Freeman (1988) and (1992), for example, finds a nonlinear relationship between independent variables like unionization and corporatist policies, and dependent variables involving measures of labor market performance in OECD countries. Performance was highest when there were either very low or very high levels of corporatism.

Political scientists and institutionally-focused economists have also argued, through country-specific cases, that national corporatist economic policies can have significant economic effects on macroeconomic labor market outcomes (Crouch 1985; Freeman 1992; Wilensky 1991). Government, through policies like social welfare payments, centralized bargaining, and other social legislation (e.g., labor courts and abolition of employment-at-will), can affect the labor market. An interesting empirical question is whether these government policies have a negative impact on the efficiency of the labor market. Our model, therefore, will examine the role of unionism and various forms of employee representation on economic performance through an examination of their impact on productivity levels, productivity changes and investment outcomes of the countries in our sample.

DATA AND METHODS

The information used to estimate variations in the production function were obtained for the period from 1960 to 1989 to allow for long- term economic effects. The data set was gathered from 14 OECD countries. The major reason for not including more countries in our investigation were the limitations on union density information and our desire that the countries in our sample be at similar states of development. The data was obtained from the International Labor Organization Yearbook, OECD Historical Statistics, World Bank Reports, and the United Nations Yearbook for various years. All the economic data were converted to constant 1985 U.S. dollars using the OECD purchasing parity estimates (Summers and Heston 1988). However, as a check on the robustness of our results, we also estimated these models using standardized World Bank algorithms for exchange rates of tradeable goods and found no major changes in the qualitative results (Dollar and Wolff 1988). All labor force data conversions used U.S. Bureau

Table 2. Means and Standard Deviations for
Variables in the OECD Sample

	1960-1989 14 Country Group	
	Mean	Standard Deviation
GNP (000)	562,920	888,510
Gross Domestic Investment (000)	122,840	171,320
Population (000)	44,002	58,222
GNP Per Worker (000)	25.31	6.52
Investment Per Worker (000)	8.21	26.96
Growth of Productivity Per Hour	32.25	176.71
Education (Years)	8.05	2.39
Labor Force (000)	20,127	27,311
Hourly Wage	6.90	1.54
Unemployment Rate (%)	5.52	3.70
Arable Land (Hectares) (000)	22,780	47,204
Mandatory Works Councils	.35	.48
Strong Joint Consultation	.16	.37
Weak Joint Consultation	.49	.50

of Labor Statistics definitions to make the values comparable over the time period and across countries.[7]

The grand means and standard deviations for the major economic and labor force variables for the different country and year groupings are presented in Table 2. In addition to these economic and labor force variables, we also collected information on unionization as well as the statutory presence in each nation of formal employee representation through works councils. Since most forms of mandated participation in these OECD nations were enacted during the 1950s and 1960s, and none of the countries repealed their participation legislation, this variable is a constant over time (except for Sweden).[8] However, this variable may also be controlling for labor market "corporatism" in government policies adopted by each of these countries (Crouch 1985). Furthermore, Blanchflower and Freeman (1992) showed that all major measures of corporatism, which often include measures of mandated worker participation, are highly correlated for advanced OECD nations. They also demonstrated that corporatist levels are correlated with both union growth in the 1970s and to some extent union decline in the 1980s.[9]

The union membership density data reflect both the general upward movement in unionization among OECD nations during the 1970s and the downward trend throughout the 1980s (Visser 1991).[10] An example is the United Kingdom, which had a 15.8 percent growth in membership from 1970 to 1979 and a 20.9 percent decline from 1980 to 1989. Although union density is only one of several measures of union bargaining power on productivity, it has been shown to have important economic impacts on factor prices, especially at the establishment level, and we have no reason to think that the impacts would be any different at the national level (Reilly 1992). Further, we will also test for the impact of legislated "voice effects" as presented by Freeman and Lazear (1995) through mandatory works council programs and legislated programs of employee participation on boards of directors for the countries in our sample (Bain 1992).

The principal dependent variables, aggregate productivity and growth rates, and aggregate investment are measured as GNP per worker and investment per worker. The wage-rate variable is the adjusted average hourly wage in manufacturing in each of the countries. The land variable is the number of square hectares of arable land in the country. The hour variable is the total hours worked in manufacturing in the country for the year in question. Finally, unemployment is measured as the average annual civilian unemployment rate in the country using U.S. Bureau of Labor Statistics equivalent estimates.

Table 3. Definition of Categories of Unionization and Employee Representation

Category of Unionization and Representation	Illustrative Countries	Proportion of Total in Each Category
Weak Joint Consultation with Low Union Density	USA, Switzerland, Canada 1960-1980	19.3%
Weak Joint Consultation with Medium Union Density	Australia, UK, Italy	21.4%
Weak Joint Consultation with High Union Density	Sweden 1960-1975, Norway 1960-1965, Austria 1960-1973, Denmark 1960-1973	9.9%
Strong Joint Consultation with Low Union Density	Japan	7.1%
Strong Joint Consultation with Medium Union Density	—	—
Strong Joint Consultation with High Union Density	Norway 1966-1972, Austria 1974- 1989	5.5%
Mandatory Councils with Low Union Density	Canada 1981-1989, France	9.3%
Mandatory Councils with Medium Union Density	Germany, Netherlands	14.2%
Mandatory Councils with High Union Density	Sweden 1976-1989, Denmark 1974-1989, Norway 1973-1989	13.3%
		100%

The joint consultation and union density categories were developed using the groupings shown in Table 3. Weak joint consultation countries included the United States, Switzerland, and Canada from 1960-1980. Weak joint consultation and medium union density had Australia, England, and Italy, whereas weak joint consultation with high union density included Sweden from 1960-1975, Norway 1960-1965, and Austria 1960-1973. The only nation with strong joint consultation and low density was Japan. Norway (1966-1972), Denmark (1960-1973), and Austria (1974-1989) had strong joint consultation with high union density. Mandatory consultation with low density had Canada 1981-1989 and France, whereas medium density with mandatory councils included Germany and the Netherlands. Finally, mandatory councils with high union density had Sweden 1976-1989, Denmark 1974-1989, and Norway 1973-1989.

Our data contain characteristics of both cross-section and time-series information. Fixed- and random- effects models are the most often employed methods in pooled data analysis. In general, these are appropriate methods when the number of cross-section units is large and the number of time periods is small. When the reverse is the case, we need to consider the assumptions imposed on the disturbances. Because the number of cross-section observations in our data set is small (only 14 countries) and the number of time periods is relatively large (30 years), we follow Kmenta's (1986) procedure in order to estimate the impact of labor market institutions on economic performance (i.e., there are no cross-section and time-period effects in the residual, and this term is assumed to be both serially correlated and cross-sectionally heteroskedastic).

ESTIMATES FROM THE MODEL

In Tables 4-6, we present estimates of the impact of union density and the type of works council legislation or arrangement on key elements of economic performance, specifically productivity, productivity growth, and investment activity. To the extent that institutional factors influence economic activity, these outcome measures, which include productivity and investment, measure the efficiency aspects of these policies. The tables presented below show alternative econometric specifications with different definitions of the measures of labor market institutions and control variables which include interaction terms, as well as varying definitions of the dependent variables. The data, as discussed earlier, includes annual information for all nations in our study for the 1960 through 1989 period for a total of 406 observations. All of the estimates presented correct for heteroskedasticity and serial correlation. The estimates for the impact of works councils and unions are interpreted relative to the omitted reference category, the United States, which has the lowest union density and/or weakest provisions for employee representation.[11]

In Table 4 we present the impact of union density and mandated participation on productivity per worker, productivity growth per hour, and the logarithm of invest-

Table 4.   Impact of Various Forms of Worker Representation on
Measures of Performance, 14 OECD Nations, 1960-1989

	Dependent Variables*		
Independent Variables	(1) Log of Productivity Per Worker	(2) Productivity Growth Per Hour	(3) Log of Investment Per Worker
Union Density (UD)	.064 (.079)	−.012* (.005)	−.347* (.091)
Strong Joint Consultation	.020 (.016)	.002 (.004)	.038 (.046)
Mandatory Works Councils	.017 (.012)	−.006 (.004)	−.027 (.025)
Log Gross Domestic Product (GDP) Per Worker			1.13* (.045)
Log Gross Capital Per Worker	.305* (.031)	.332* (.023)	
Log Land Per Worker	−.034* (.012)	.021* (.006)	
Unemployment Rate (%)	−.0001 (.002)	−.0007 (.0004)	−.044* (.003)
Education (Years)	.071* (.008)	.761* (.172)	
Constant	1.32 (.096)	.016* (.004)	−1.54* (.144)
Durbin-Watson Statistic	1.24	2.0	1.92
R^2	.99	.66	.98

Notes: *Indicates significant at the .95 confidence level or higher.
Correcting for heteroskedasticity and serial correlation.
Standard errors are in parentheses.
Estimates derived using nonconstant returns to scale showed no significant changes in the
qualitative results.

ment per worker for the nations in our sample using standard economic production function models (Allen, 1988). In the first column, we present the impact of mandatory works councils and strong joint consultation from the model in Figure 1 on the logarithm of productivity per worker relative to the weakest form of consultation with controls for capital per worker, land per worker, unionization, education, average years of education, and unemployment rates.[12] The estimates for productivity levels are consistent with other results by Rees, Defina, Freeman and Medoff, and Stevens by showing small impacts of unionization on overall productivity. Further, these estimates show that statutory or strong joint consultation have only modest impacts on aggregate productivity levels.[13]

In the second column of Table 4 we show the relationship between the same independent variables and the growth in productivity per average hour in manu-

Table 5. Impact of Aggregate Economic Various Forms of Worker Representation on Measures of Performance, 14 OECD Nations, 1960-1989

Independent Variables[a]	Dependent Variables*		
	(1) Log of Productivity Per Worker	(2) Productivity Growth Per Hour	(3) Log of Investment Per Worker
Weak Joint Consultation with Low Union Density is the Reference Group			
Weak Joint Consultation with Medium Union Density	-.277* (.038)	.007* (.003)	.135* (.069)
Weak Joint Consultation with High Union Density	-.185* (.036)	.010* (.003)	.106* (.054)
Strong Joint Consultation with Low Union Density	-.370 (.245)	.021* (.007)	.336* (.067)
Strong Joint Consultation with High Union Density	-.102* (.034)	.003 (.005)	-.011 (.049)
Mandatory Councils with Low Union Density	.013 (.023)	.011* (.003)	.058 (.041)
Mandatory Councils with Medium Union Density	-.141* (.061)	.0008* (.003)	.014 (.043)
Mandatory Councils with High Union Density	-.142* (.035)	-.004* (.002)	.059 (.052)
Log Gross Domestic Product (GDP) Per Worker			1.15* (.041)
Log Gross Capital Per Worker	.322* (.034)	.313* (.022)	
Log Land Per Worker	-.033* (.009)	.022* (.007)	

Unemployment	.004*	−.001*	−.045*
	(.002)	(.0004)	(.003)
Education	.030*	.625*	
	(.009)	(.182)	
Constant	1.70	.007*	−1.77
	(.093)	(.002)	(.137)
Durbin-Watson Statistic	1.08	2.10	1.89
R^2	.99	.74	.98

Notes: *Indicates significance at the .95 confidence level or higher.

[a]Employee representation categories only include those groups for which there are nations that fit into the definitions. High union density included nations with 60 percent or greater; medium had 30 percent to 60 percent and low included nations with 30 percent or less. All estimates are relative to the United States, which had low unionization and weak joint consultation.

Standard errors are in parentheses.

Estimates derived using nonconstant returns to scale showed no significant changes in the qualitative results.

facturing. The results show a modest negative impact of mandatory works councils and unionization. The signs and significance of the control variables are consistent with prior studies estimates of production function equations. The third column of this table shows the relationship between unionization and the other institutional variables and the logarithm of investment per worker. We do not use controls for land or education levels based largely on theory and their omission from other cross-country investment studies (Levine and Renelt 1992). In addition, we use GDP per worker rather than the capital stock variable.[14] The estimates show that there is a negative impact of union density on aggregate investment per worker, which is consistent with firm and industry-level studies of the relationship between unionization and investment behavior (Hirsch 1991).

Table 5 presents estimates of the effect of the interaction of alternative forms of joint consultation policies and union density as categorical variables on the productivity per worker, productivity growth per hour, and the logarithm of investment per worker for the 14 countries in our sample. The categories for unionization uses Hirsch's (1991) groupings as follows: below 30 percent were low, between 30 percent and 60 percent were grouped as medium, and above 60 percent were termed high. The estimates provided in Table 5 used the same set of control variables as in Table 4. The results in column 1 of Table 5 show that none of the alternative forms of employee representation do better than the reference group (i.e., the United States) on productivity levels; and all of the groups perform worse, except for Canada and France, and they had similar impacts with mandated councils and low union density. For example, having mandatory works councils and high union density are associated with a 0.14 percent reduction in average productivity levels. This result is consistent with Rees and Stevens' estimates of union impacts in the United States. Overall, these coefficients suggest that fewer labor market institutions are associated with somewhat higher levels of productivity, but the optimal form is not clear from these results nor are the results large by any standard metric.

In column 2 of Table 5, the dependent variable is the annual growth in productivity per hour. The results show that low union density with strong joint consultation, like the Japanese system, is associated with the highest growth in productivity. Except for countries with mandatory works councils and high levels of unionization, all of the other forms of labor market institutions are associated with faster growth in productivity relative to weak joint consultation and low union density.

In column 3 of the same table, estimates are shown for the logarithm of investment per worker as the dependent variable. In a manner similar to Table 4, the estimates control for gross domestic product per worker as well as the annual unemployment rate in the country. The institutional form that has the highest statistically significant impact on investment per worker is strong joint consultation with low union density, which is estimated relative to the omitted group of weak joint consultation with low union density. The estimated impact of this set of labor

Table 6.   Interaction Impacts of Various Forms of
Worker Representation on Measures of Aggregate Economic
Performance, 14 OECD Nations, 1960-1989[a]

	Dependent Variables*		
Independent Variables[b]	Log of Productivity Per Worker	Productivity Growth Per Hour	Log of Investment Per Worker
Medium Union Density	.010	.005	.012
	(.010)	(.003)	(.020)
High Union Density	.026	.003	−.083
	(.018)	(.004)	(.041)*
Strong Joint Consultation	−.405	.015	.256
	(.236)	(.008)	(.057)*
Mandatory Works Councils	.032	.008*	−.009
	(.019)	(.003)	(.031)
Strong Joint Consultation with High Union Density	.459	−.021*	−.315*
	(.235)	(.009)	(.069)
Mandatory Works Councils with Medium Density	−.081	−.014*	−.063
	(.060)	(.004)	(.033)
Mandatory Works Councils with High Union Density	−.004	−.022*	−.026
	(.026)	(.005)	(.044)
Log Gross Capital Per Worker Growth of GDP Per Hour Log GDP Per Worker	.233*	.311*	1.131*
	(.030)	(.030)	(.040)
Log Land Per Worker	−.053*	0.21*	—
	(.012)	(.009)	
Unemployment	.001	−.002*	−.042*
	(.002)	(.0004)	(.003)
Education	0.71*	.587*	
	(.008)	(.205)	
Constant	1.653*	.150*	−1.650*
	(.084)	(.004)	(.125)
R^2	.99	.75	.98
Durbin-Watson Statistic	1.25	1.98	1.85

Notes: *Indicates significance at the .95 confidence level.
[a]Estimates for union density are relative to low union density and estimates for employee representation are relative to weak joint consultation.
[b]Standard errors are in parentheses, and nonconstant returns to scale showed no significant changes in the qualitative results.

market institutions is 0.34 percent on per worker investment levels. All of the alternative forms of labor market institutions presented in Table 5 do as well or better than no joint consultation with low union density.

In Table 6 we show models similar to the ones presented in Tables 4 and 5. However, as part of these estimates, we present separate estimates for union density and employee representation along with the interaction effects. For example, the total impact of medium union density with mandatory works councils can be estimated by summing the coefficients for the three estimates presented in Table 6 (i.e., medium density, mandatory works councils, and medium density and mandatory works councils or 0.95 percent for the overall impact on the productivity level). In a similar manner, the impact of high union density and strong joint consultation with interaction impacts on investment per worker is −0.10 percent. These estimates show that, although the forms of employee representation matter statistically, the form of the labor relations institution's magnitude is relatively small in influencing economic activity.

COUNTRY-SPECIFIC EXAMPLES AND SIMULATIONS

Countries like Sweden, Germany, and Austria, which have medium to high levels of unionization and mandated works councils, have recently been concerned with declining investment activity due in part to the high-wage policies associated with these institutions (Freeman and Gibbons 1993). In Sweden, for example, during recent national negotiations, the government suggested that pension funds be controlled by union leaders so that they might have a greater incentive to put a higher percentage of national GNP into capital formation, which is consistent with the Olson model of encompassing relationships.

For Sweden, the only country in our sample that changed its policies from one of joint consultation to mandated works councils, we are able to estimate the potential impacts of a change in the labor statute that mandates participation. In Table 7, we estimate the impact of a change from a policy of joint consultation to one of mandated works councils in 1977 on productivity per worker and investment per worker with the use of a categorical variable for the change in the statute. Using the same econometric specification as the ones in the earlier analysis, we find that there is a statistically significant but small negative impact on productivity of 0.04 percent of moving from a joint consultation policy to one that requires works councils in larger firms. The impact of the change to mandated regulation on investment per worker is also negative but insignificant. The estimates from our model in the Swedish case of the movement to a mandated form of employee involvement suggested small but negative impacts on both aggregate productivity and investment.

In contrast to Sweden, Japan, which has relatively low levels of unionization but voluntary joint consultation bodies in over 70 percent of all establishments, was able to maintain high levels of investment and continuing productivity growth. The ability to maintain adequate returns to the owners of capital and to provide workers with sufficient levels of involvement and information-sharing appears to result in economic efficiency gains.

Part of the Japanese commitment to voluntary employee involvement are human resource policies that include high participation in formal and informal problem

Table 7. Impact of a Change From Joint Consultation to
Mandatory Works Councils on Productivity and Investment,
$N=29$: The Case of Sweden*

Productivity *Log GDP Per Worker*	
Log Capital Gross Per Worker	.67*
	(.20)
Unemployment Rate	−.16*
	(.01)
Log Land Per Worker	−.03
	(.22)
Unionization/Labor Force	−.40
	(.47)
Education	.10*
	(.04)
Consultation Statute	−.04*
	(.02)
Constant	−.56
	(.76)
Durbin-Watson	1.42
Adjusted R^2	.99
Investment *Log Investment Per Worker*	
Log Gross Domestic Product	1.64*
	(.25)
Unemployment Rate	−.07*
	(.02)
Unionization/Labor Force	−1.87*
	(.51)
Education	.03
	(.04)
Consultation Statute	−.05
	(.05)
Constant	−2.25*
	(.42)
Durbin-Watson	1.93
Adjusted R^2	.88

Notes: Standard errors are in parenthesis.
    * Indicates significance at the .95 confidence level.

solving, sharing of financial information, and regular meetings with union and management representatives (Morisihama 1991). Even though joint consultation is voluntary in Japan, for large firms there have been no documented cases of firms repealing an employee involvement program following its establishment. Furthermore, the leadership of the joint consultation committees are selected by the workers. At least for the period of our study, the institutional form of the organization of labor within large firms in Japan was associated with higher levels of economic performance.

To further illustrate the effects of the industrial relations system on economic performance, we present a simulation of the impact of the U.S. economic behavioral relationship within the Japanese-style employee representation system. Using a standard decomposition model, we estimated the potential economic impact if the United States shifted to a Japanese-style system. More specifically, we use the models specified in equations (3) and (4) and presented in Tables 4 and 5 to estimate country-specific equations using a time-series model with 29 observations for the United States and Japan. In this simulation, we assume that differences in the residuals between predicted ($\hat{X}$) and actual productivity growth per hour (X) are due to the differences in the industrial relations system and the other unobservable factors that are assumed to be normally distributed. The estimates for the productivity growth decomposition analysis shows that the U.S. productivity per hour growth rate could have been 9.9 percent higher if it had the Japanese industrial relations structure, all else equal. This result is consistent with our cross-country regression estimates and with observed productivity growth rates in both countries during the 1960-1989 time period.

CONCLUSIONS

This paper has attempted to present the results of an exploratory study of the impacts of unionization and alterative forms of joint consultation on measures of national productivity and investment. Consistent with single country studies, these results have found that the impacts though often statistically significant are relatively small. Our results show that countries, like Japan, that have relatively low levels of unionization and strong forms of joint consultation are able to enhance productivity growth and investment relative to the United States which has low unionization, weak forms of joint consultation, and an adversarial labor-management relationship. Nations with mandated works councils and high levels of unionization, however, did not achieve efficiency gains as measured by productivity levels, productivity growth, or investment activity.

Of course, the use of cross-section and time-series analysis for nations has innate methodological problems. Issues of the potential endogeneity of the institution of unions and the form of joint consultation may never be completely addressed in a macroeconomic model like the one presented here. The use of single-country studies, like a more detailed study of countries like Sweden, where changes occur in either the level of unionization or the type of works council statute, may provide more precise insights into the efficiency effects. Firm performance studies, where some firms have employee representation and others do not, can further enhance our understanding of the role of joint consultation on economic efficiency. Further, studies of multinational firm performance in different institutional environments would further the field's knowledge of the issues raised in this paper. In conclusion, to the extent that employee representation promotes industrial democracy and worker satisfaction at the workplace, this impact should dominate any small efficiency gains or losses that this or other studies has shown exist as a consequence of employee voice at the workplace.

ACKNOWLEDGMENTS

The authors would like to thank Dennis Ahlburg, John Budd, Richard Freeman, Tzu-Shian Han, Morley Gunderson, and Jonathan Leonard for helpful comments, as well as discussants at the University of Minnesota and at the Fourth Bargaining Group Conference, Toronto, Ontario, Canada.

NOTES

1.   This is the typical standard in both Austria and Germany (Kindley 1992).

2.   An exception to this rule has been firm-level examinations of the impact of works councils on firm performance in Germany by Addison, Kraft, and Wagner (1993) and in South Korea by Kleiner and Lee (in press).

3.   Freeman (1988) notes that Europeans often complain about the inflexibility of government policies causing labor market inefficiencies. Others in the United States see the Japanese policy of playing a heavy role in industrial policy and industrial relations as a key to productivity growth. There does not seem to be a clear consensus on this issue.

4.   In Sweden, an act on co-determination at work (MBL) was introduced in 1977 to replace the Works Councils Agreement between SAF, LO, and TCO in 1946.

5.   Both derivations and estimates of the "extended" Brown-Medoff production function using a first- and second-order Taylor series expansion and the empirical results from this specification are available from the authors. The Taylor series used in this case was

$$ln\ (1 = \lambda) = \lambda - \frac{\lambda^2}{2},$$

$$\text{where } \lambda = (c-1)u,$$

$$\text{therefore } \lambda^2 = (c-1)^2 u^2, \text{where } \lambda^2 \text{ approaches } 0.$$

6.   In deriving nonconstant returns to scale, we estimate the model with the logarithm of the total work force included in the productivity equation. This specification results in no substantive changes in the basic results of the productivity equations.

7.   Conversions to Bureau of Labor Statistics definitions were made for several of the OECD nations for the following labor force variables: unemployment, labor force participation, and wage rates.

8.   This does not suggest that there were no changes in the legislation over time. For example, the initial German Works Council legislation was passed in 1952, but it has been significantly amended to provide significantly greater worker participation through provisions added in 1972, 1976, and 1988 (Rogers and Streeck 1995).

9.   In some of our estimates, we will also attempt to control for unobserved country-specific effects through the use of dummy variables. This "fixed-effect" approach controls for different laws

and customs as well as the industrial and public institutions that may affect productivity differently in ways that we may not have captured directly in our specified model.

10.   Although trade union membership and the number covered are obviously not the same, and the results do show some divergence on a country by country basis, the membership/coverage gap within countries remained remarkably consistent during the period analyzed (Visser 1991).

11.   In fact, employee representation in the United States without unions has questionable legal status. Further, alternative specifications with only capital and land per worker were also estimated and showed similar results to those presented in the tables.

12.   Alternative specifications with only capital and land per worker were also estimated and showed similar results to those presented in the tables.

13.   Additional specifications that included unionization and unionization-squared and categorical variables for high and medium levels of unionization showed no qualitative differences from the results presented in Tables 4-6. Furthermore, estimates using 10 and nine nation subsets of the sample resulted in similar qualitative results. We also estimate Granger Causality Models for unionization, with both productivity and investment and the F-tests were significant in both directions. These estimates are available from the authors.

14.   We also estimated the model with average education, and it did not change the qualitative results for the labor institution variables.

REFERENCES

Addison, J. T., K. Kraft, and J. Wagner. 1993. "German Works Councils and Firm Performance." Pp. 309-338 in *Employee Representation: Alternatives and Future Directions*, edited by B. Kaufman and M. Kleiner. Madison, WI: Industrial Relations Research Association.

Allen, S. 1988. "Productivity Level and Productivity Change Under Unionism." *Industrial Relations* 27 (Winter): 94-113.

Bain, T. 1992. "Employee Voice: A Comparative International Perspective." Paper presented at the Industrial Relations Research Association, January.

Bergson, A. 1987. "Comparative Productivity." *American Economic Review* 77(3): 342-57.

Blanchflower, D., and R. B. Freeman. 1992. "Unionism in the United States and Other Advanced OECD Countries." *Industrial Relations* 31(1) 56-79.

Brown, C., and J. Medoff. 1978. "Trade Unions in the Production Process." *Journal of Political Economy* 86(3) 355-78.

Bruno, M., and J. D. Sachs. 1985. *The Economics of Worldwide Stagflation*. Cambridge, MA: Harvard University Press.

Calmfors, L., and J. Driffill. 1988. "Bargaining Structure, Corporatism and Macroeconomic Performance." *Economic Policy* 6 (April): 14-61.

Crouch, C. 1985. "Conditions for Trade Union Wage Restraint." Pp. 105-139 in *The Politics of Economic Stagflation*, edited by L. N. Lindberg and C.S. Maier. Washington, DC: Brookings Institution.

Defina, R. H. 1983. "Unions, Relative Wages and Economic Efficiency." *Journal of Labor Economics* (October)1(4): 408-429.

Dollar, D., and E. N. Wolff. 1988. "Convergence of Industry Labor Productivity Among Advanced Economies, 1963-1982." *Review of Economics and Statistics* 70: 549-558.

Eberts, R. W., and E. L. Groshen. Eds. 1991. *Structural Changes in U.S. Labor Markets: Causes and Consequences*. Armonk, NY: M.E. Sharpe.

Freeman, R. B. 1988. "Labor Market Institutions, Constraints, and Performance." NBER Working Paper, Cambridge, MA.

_____. 1992. "On the Economic Analysis of Labor Market Institutions and Institutional Change." Harvard Institute of Economic Research Discussion Paper No. 1587.

Freeman, R., and R. Gibbons. 1993. "Getting Together and Breaking Apart: The Decline of Centralised Collective Bargaining." NBER Working Paper No. 4464, September.

Freeman, R., and E. Lazear. 1995. "An Economic Analysis of Works Councils." Pp. 27-52 in *Works Councils*, edited by J. Rogers and W. Streeck. Chicago: University of Chicago Press.

Freeman, R. B., and J. L. Medoff. 1984. *What Do Unions Do?* New York: Basic Books.

Henderson, J. M., and R. E. Quandt. 1971. *Microeconomic Theory*. New York: McGraw-Hill.

Hirsch, B. T. 1991. *Labor Unions and the Economic Performance of Firms*. Kalamazoo, MI: Upjohn Institute.

Kindley, R. 1992. "Labor's Role in the Emergence and Reproduction of Austrian NeoCorporatism." Ph.D. dissertation, Duke University.

Kleiner, M. M., and Y. M. Lee. In press. "Effective Works Councils and Unionization: Lessons From South Korea." *Industrial Relations*.

Kmenta, J. 1986. *Elements of Econometrics*. New York: Macmillan Co.

Levine, D., and L. Tyson. 1990. "Participation, Productivity and the Firm's Environment." Pp. 183-244 in *Paying for Productivity: A Look at the Evidence*, edited by A. S. Blinder. Washington, DC: Brookings Institution.

Levine, R., and D. Renelt. 1992. "A Sensitivity Analysis of Cross-Country Growth Regressions." *American Economic Review* 82(4): 942-963.

Morishima, M. 1991. "Information-Sharing and Firm Performance in Japan." *Industrial Relations* (Winter): 37-61.

North, D. C. 1994. "Economic Performance Through Time." *American Economic Review* 89(3): 359-368.

Olson, M. Jr. 1982. *The Logic of Collective Actions*. Cambridge, MA: Harvard University Press.

_____. 1982. *The Rise and Decline of Nations: Economic Growth, Stagflation, and Social Rigidities*. New Haven: Yale University Press.

_____. 1988. "The Productivity Slowdown, the Oil Shocks, and the Real Cycle." *Journal of Economic Perspectives* 2(4): 43-70.

Perlman, S. 1928. *A Theory of the Labor Movement*. New York: The Macmillan Company.

Rees, A. 1963. "The Effects of Unions on Resource Allocation." *Journal of Law and Economics*, 6 (October): 69-78.

Reilly, K. 1992. "Does Union Membership Matter: The Effect of Establishment Union Density on the Union Wage Differential." Working Paper, Department of Economics, University of Waterloo.

Reuters. 1994. News release, September 22.

Rogers, J., and W. Streeck. Eds. 1995. *Works Councils*, Chicago: University of Chicago Press.

Simons, H. C. 1948. *Economic Policy for a Free Society*. Chicago: University of Chicago Press.

Stevens, C. 1995. "The Social Costs of Rent Seeking by Labor Unions in the United States." *Industrial Relations* 34(2) (April): 190-202.

Summers, R., and A. Heston. 1988. "A New Set of International Comparisons of Real Product and Price Levels: Estimates for 130 Countries." *Review of Income and Wealth* 34(1) (March) 1-28.

Visser, J. 1991. "Trends in Trade Union Membership." Pp. 97-134 in *Employment Outlook*. Paris: Organisation for Economic Co-Operation and Development.

Wilensky, H. L. 1991. "The Nation-State, Social Policy, and Economic Performance." Institute of Industrial Relations Working Paper 25, University of California, Berkeley.

SUCCESSOR UNIONS AND THE EVOLUTION OF INDUSTRIAL RELATIONS IN FORMER COMMUNIST COUNTRIES

Derek C. Jones

ABSTRACT

Using new survey data for samples of union leaders in Estonia, the Czech Republic, Bulgaria, and Russia for 1991-1994, the hypothesis that successor unions are incapable of reform is rejected. Evidence is found in all countries of evolution away from arrangements that characterized the old unions. Changes include: more decentralized union structures, an increasing emphasis on job-related concerns, and more variability in the profile and compensation of union leaders. There is no relationship between a union leader's membership in the Communist Party and political beliefs. Together these changes point to greater democracy within successor unions. Also, whereas unions without precursors have low levels of membership, high levels of membership characterize successor unions. On average, the extent of employee par-

Advances in Industrial and Labor Relations, Volume 7, pages 123-143.
ISBN: 1-55938-925-7

ticipation is quite limited and has not changed much during transition. However, the nature and extent of change also varies across countries, and no one system of industrial relations seems to be emerging. Thus, differences exist in the extent to which patterns of privilege persist, especially for union leaders who were officials in the former official unions and/or members of the Communist Party. In a concluding section, we conjecture on reasons for differences across countries and also consider policy implications of our findings.

INTRODUCTION

As part of the immense political and economic changes in the former communist countries, trade unions have often emerged as imfluential actors. Important powers of unions in the evolving systems of industrial relations include deep involvement in the wage determination process, both in the emerging systems of collective bargaining and as partners in incomes policies. Frequently unions exercise enormous political influence at all levels, and they articulate programs on the national stage on behalf of labor; often these activities have been at odds with the policies of different governments.[1] The need to better understand the new unions in transition economies also follows from the growing evidence from studies of other countries that particular forms of trade unions, in conjunction with other particular kinds of human management resource practices, often may have substantial effects on firm and national economic performance (e.g., Kleiner and Ay 1994; Morishima 1994).

While some accounts of changes in unions in transition economies have appeared,[2] the available data are often quite limited and are seldom based on fieldwork. In this paper, by using new survey data for unions in four countries, hypotheses concerning the nature of change in unions during the early stages of transition toward a market economy are examined. Data are mainly for union leaders in large cities—St. Petersburg, Sofia, Tallinn, and Prague. The new data enable us to both improve on existing studies and to provide more systematic evaluation of potential changes in successor unions in several areas.

In particular, evidence is presented on the question of whether the unions that have succeeded the former (official) unions are making changes from the old communist ways of doing things. Since the situations in most transition economies are remarkably fast changing, the factual bedrock guiding researchers in the area of changing industrial relations is unusually fragile, and it is not surprising that often there is acute controversy on these matters. For example, concerning successor unions, some (e.g., AFL-CIO 1993) argue that typically successor unions are *incapable* of reform. Acceptance of this position implies that a genuine independent labor movement must be based on unions without precursors. However, other conceptions of the processes of institutional and organizational change are possible. Conceptual frameworks based on an evolutionary paradigm (e.g., Murrell 1992) imply that real though gradual change is possible in organizations (such as successor unions) that are adapting to a radically different environment, although constraints may serve to hamper the pace of change.[3] In turn, these paradigms may have profoundly differing implications for the design of the new industrial relations. For reasons including the potential for huge economic costs associated with new institution building, the evolutionary paradigm implies that in some cases it may be more prudent to build on parts of the old system (e.g., Stark 1992).

In the next section, we review key aspects of the institutional framework in the survey countries, describe the surveys, and briefly discuss our conceptual framework. Building on earlier work for Russia (Jones 1995b) evidence is assembled under several headings—membership, structure, functions, leadership, democracy, and compensation. Findings on these topics are presented in the main sections of the paper. In a concluding section, after conjecturing on reasons for differences in the new systems of industrial relations in survey countries, we consider policy implications.

INSTITUTIONS, CONCEPTUAL FRAMEWORK, AND THE DATA

Until about 1990, essentially all employees in the planned economies of Eastern and Central Europe were members of the old, official unions.[4] These official unions were postulated to have dual functions. First, trade unions were subservient to the Communist Party and, like many other institutions, were an integral part of the centrally administered system. At enterprise and industry level, this meant that a key task of union officials was to ensure that plan targets were fulfilled. The fact that unions had no separate identities had several implications for the structure and functioning of the labor movement. For example, these "official" unions were the only unions, were organized along industry (branch) lines, and were strongly centralized. Top union leaders were likely to be members of the Communist Party and were believed to be almost as well paid as top administrators (directors) of enterprises.

The second function of unions, albeit within this framework, was to represent the interests of individual members. However, in practice, to the extent that union leaders (at branch and enterprise levels) directly served the separate interests of members, most believe this was done mainly by social and welfare activities, especially handling social security claims and disbursing holiday vouchers. In a system of central planning, union leaders were not involved in functions traditionally associated with Western-style collective bargaining. Moreover, typical protest forms like strikes and slowdowns were completely prohibited.

But even before the late 1980s, there had been many attempts to reform unions, including efforts to improve member involvement in achieving production targets and in protecting members' interests. Yet most scholars have concluded that such innovations did not produce basic changes (e.g., Petkov and Thirkell 1991; Slider

1987; Van Atta 1989). In all countries under study, the critical step in changing this "transmission-belt" model took place in late 1989 or 1990. Thus, in the former Czechoslovakia, the reconstruction of trade unions which began in 1989 was followed in March 1990 with the dissolution of the old unions and the establishment of a new federation, the Czech and Slovak Confederation of Trade Unions (CSKOS).[5]

To provide more systematic evidence on labor unions in former communist countries, separate surveys were administered to samples of union leaders in four countries. The countries selected were chosen to reflect differences both in conditions at the beginning of reform (e.g., concerning population and levels of external indebtedness) and in policies adopted during early transition (e.g., on privatization) (for details of policies, see EBRD 1994). By using a common instrument to examine change in such disparate cases the objective was to see whether or not during these early stages of transition any general patterns of change were evident.

In such times of extraordinary rapid change, official data collection procedures essentially had collapsed and no official (independent) data on the scope and nature of unionism throughout the four countries were systematically available. Moreover, for similar reasons, even union records on matters such as the number of workplaces at which employees were represented were incomplete, and hence it was impossible to draw representative samples. Since information was usually more reliable for the large or capital cities, and also because branch unions usually had their headquarters in those locations, it was decided to extend the initial survey of union leaders in St. Petersburg to unions in Sofia, Prague, and Tallinn. By using union records, samples comprised at least one respondent from all of the branch unions in each location, with the balance (in fact, the bulk) of respondents being at the local level. The data were collected using both postal and face-to-face collection methods.[6] The St. Petersburg survey (the first administered) resulted in 101 usable responses—a 33 percent response rate. The comparable figures for Sofia, Estonia, and Prague are respectively 116 (93%), 91 (57%), and 51 (57%). In St. Petersburg, about 60 percent of respondents had leadership positions at the local (enterprise rather than the branch) level; the comparable figures for Sofia, Tallinn, and Prague are 73 percent, 80 percent, and 85 percent.

Since there is no generally accepted theory of comparative change in industrial relations for the former communist countries, in designing the instrument the focus is on those features that were hallmarks of the old, official unions—domination by the Communist Party, centralization, and unions with dual functions. Areas of inquiry are also stimulated by drawing on conceptual frameworks designed to illuminate cross-national differences in collective bargaining in market economies (e.g., Clegg 1976) as well as criteria used to judge key aspects of the evolution of collective bargaining (e.g., formal indicators of democracy in unions as used by Taft 1962). Survey design was also affected by practical considerations. To study change in unions, it was important to study not only those aspects about which something was known in the past but also for which information might be forthcoming currently. Eventually, the questionnaire was designed to capture information on several themes—membership, structure, functions, leadership, compensation, and democracy.

In Table 1, we note some features of the firms in which the local union leaders whom we sample were located. Reflecting industrial organization in large industrial firms in these former communist countries, union officials were mainly representing workers in old established state firms. However, some changes had begun. In 1991, nearly all Russian firms were state-owned (with modest representation of leased firms); a year later, about three in 10, while remaining state-owned, were now joint stock organizations. That is, they had begun the process of "commercialization" a necessary first step before privatization (Bim, Jones, and Weisskopf 1993). The data in Table 1 also show that the average size of an enterprise in these countries was falling. This is especially apparent for Bulgaria in which fully 71 percent of sample firms were now employing fewer than 500 workers compared to the large average size reported for earlier years (Jones and Parvulov 1995).

These shifts had major implications for labor markets. This stormy picture is reflected in the enormous diversity in the dynamics of employment at the level of individual enterprises in the survey (Table 1). Thus, whereas in the Czech Republic in the average firm employment fell by 9 percent between 1991-1992, in Sofia changes in employment were almost twice as big.

FINDINGS

Union Membership: Successor and Alternative Unions

While union membership was almost automatic in the old unions, recently the decision to be a union member has become a matter of a choice. One might, therefore, expect membership rates in successor unions in all of these countries to have fallen significantly. However, aggregate data provided by the successor bodies sometimes indicate that this was not the case. For example, in Estonia and the Czech Republic, membership in the alternative unions was calculated to be less than half of 1 percent of the labor force.[7]

To provide partial checks on these sometimes in-house data, union density was estimated for successor unions in survey enterprises. Typically, this was found to quite high (Table 1). While there has been loss of membership on average in about three in four firms surveyed in all countries except Bulgaria, at least 70 percent of employees belonged to a union. Even in Bulgaria, the average union density was almost 70 percent.[8] Equally, we see that the St. Petersburg levels are considerably higher than in most other former communist countries.[9]

In the new environment, it might also be expected that there would have been significant switching by members to the new alternative unions, particularly in

Table 1.   Characteristics of Sample Firms

Firm Characteristic	Czech	Estonia	Bulgaria	Russia
% State Owned	97	93	91	94
Average Employment	1057	1414	537	9518
% < 500	24	52	71	21
% 500-2500	64	41	26	47
% over 2500	12	8	3	33
Average % Change in Employment 1991-1992	−9	−12	−17	−14
% > 0	9	4	8	6
% 0 to −10% decline	46	35	28	19
% to decline > −10%	46	61	76	64
Union membership as % of employment				
% < 69	24	28	54	4
70 - 79	24	7	13	4
80 - 89	8	19	10	11
90 - 100	44	47	24	89

Notes: Data are for union leaders at enterprise level.
All data are from the author's surveys.

places where the impetus for the new unions was thought to be especially strong, for example, St. Petersburg (see Temkina 1992) and Bulgaria where the new union, Podkrepa, played an important political role as opposition under the old regime. To gauge the importance of alternative unions, respondents were asked to estimate membership in unions other than their successor union. Often this was reported to be tiny. In St. Petersburg, membership in new unions never amounted to more than 2 percent of the workforce. Based on this evidence for the St. Petersburg region, it does not appear that membership in alternative unions or multiple unionism at the same plant were strong phenomena. In both the Czech Republic and Estonia, the reported membership levels in alternative unions are even lower, virtually nonexistent.

But in Bulgaria, the percentage of employees in other unions (mainly Podkrepa) was significant—estimated to average 28% in June 1993. However, this compares with 38% in December 1991, indicating that there has been some erosion in the membership commitment to Podkrepa. Also, at the same time, on average, the number of unions without precursors at an enterprise had grown from 1.2 in 1992 to 1.4 in 1993.

Table 2. Characteristics of Union Leaders

Union Leader	Czech	Estonia	Bulgaria	Russia
Age (years)	45	48	44	47
% Male	83	39	58	88
% Currently Married	83	79	93	84
Years in Previous Job	17	14	17	15
% Higher Education	33	32	47	78
% Former Member of CP	19	53	na	52
% Current Member of CP	3	na	na	23
% Never Member of CP	78	47	na	25
% Left-Wing Sympathies	12	55	56	16
% Right-Wing Sympathies	46	27	2	18
% Centrist Sympathies	41	18	42	66

Note: All data are from the author's surveys.

Who Are the Union Leaders?

In the old unions, the perception[10] is that the typical union leader was, first and foremost, a member of the communist party. Leaders were apt to be male, well-educated, middle-aged, and not to hail from a blue-collar background. To determine a profile of leaders in successor unions, summary statistics are presented in Table 2.

In important respects, including age, marital status, and work experience, the profile is remarkably similar in the four countries. Thus, the mean age for union leaders ranges from 44 to 48. However, there are also substantial differences, notably in gender and educational qualifications. Whereas in Russia 88 percent of union leaders are male, in Sofia only 58 percent are male and in Estonia 39 percent. Also, the available data on occupational backgrounds indicate a picture that is often quite varied. Thus, in Russia *all* union leaders had previously belonged to the technical or managerial end of the spectrum. By contrast, in the three other survey countries, at least 24 percent of respondents had previously been unskilled or semi-skilled workers.

Data are sometimes available concerning respondents' affiliation with the Communist Party (Table 2). The responses reveal that, whereas in St. Petersburg, 25 percent of union officials had never been party members, in Estonia the comparable figure was much higher at 45 percent, and even higher in the Czech Republic (data are not available on this question for union leaders in Sofia). While 23 percent of Russian officials were members of the party when it was outlawed (or had joined the successor body), no one in the Estonian sample and only 3 percent of Czech officials were members. When three types of political affiliation were identified, our findings also indicate sharp differences in the pattern of political sympathies (Table 2).

Sometimes these profiles of the average union leader can be put into broader contexts. Since women make up about half of the local labor force (Gendler and Gildingersh 1992), a disproportionately small share of union leaders in St. Petersburg are women, especially at the level of president. The under representation of women in Russian leadership positions is a phenomenon that is observed in many other countries (including the United States). For Bulgaria, however, our data indicate that women are very well-represented as leaders in successor unions. The fact that so many union leaders are female means that the extent of female representation is probably more advanced in these former communist countries (and especially Estonia and Bulgaria) than is typical in many western countries.

Union Functions: What Do Union Leaders Do?

The changes ushered in by the advent of perestroika mean that the framework within which unions function has dramatically changed. Fundamentally, the system of central planning (including central wage fixing) has formally collapsed. However, typically the state still strongly influences the wage bargain—for example, in the Czech Republic and in Bulgaria through an "excess wages" tax. Nevertheless, exactly what are to be the new ways of determining wages and employment (and the role of unions therein) remains unclear. At the time of the survey, in most countries (e.g., Russia) there was no new labor code in place, though often the existing codes have been amended (as in the Czech Republic.). Also, successor unions usually inherited substantial assets, especially infrastructure such as kindergartens, houses, and vacation centers. While complex questions of asset ownership often await final resolution, of interest here is how union leaders serve their members by administering these assets (and thus constraining how unions might otherwise allocate their scarce resources.)

To gather new data on what successor unions actually do in the new, evolving context, union leaders were asked to evaluate a variety of tasks in order of the priority they assigned when deciding how to allocate their time and other union resources. The pattern that emerges from this exercise (Table 3) is very similar in all countries. For Russia, consistently ranked as most important are improving or protecting pay, helping members solve problems and grievances on the job, protecting job security, and improving safety and health at work. In Estonia and the Czech Republic, pay was clearly identified as the most pressing problem. But in Bulgaria issues of pay were ranked behind grievance settlement in overall importance. Moreover, while job security is one of the top issues in Russia and clearly the third most important matter in Bulgaria, for Tallinn and Prague, perhaps reflecting tighter local labor markets, job security does not appear to be a pressing issue.

Table 3. How Union Leaders Allocate Time ad Resourc es

Function	Czech	Estonia	Bulgaria	Russia
1. Pay	70	74	56	1
2. Grievances	64	62	64	2
3. Health and Safety	28	15	5	6
4. Information	14	17	16	5
5. Benefits	17	5	12	7
6. Running the Union	0	13	11	8
7. Job Security	0	2	27	3
8. Social Security	6	6	2	4
9. Collecting Dues	0	0	5	11
10. Holidays	3	0	1	12
11. Organizing New Members	0	5	0	9
12. Product Distribution	0	1	2	10

Notes: For all countries except Russia, entries are the percent of respondents ranking that function as being of first or second most importance. For Russia, entries are the rank ordering of functions. (Thus, "1" indicates that respondents most frequently ranked that function as being of primary or secondary importance.)

All data are from the author's surveys.

Union functions are as follows:
   1 = improving or protecting pay.
   2 = helping members solve problems and grievances on the job.
   3 = improving safety and health at work.
   4 = keeping members informed.
   5 = improving or protecting benefits.
   6 = improving the way the union is run.
   7 = protecting job security.
   8 = administering social security.
   9 = collecting dues.
   10 = arranging for holidays at union-owned facilities.
   11 = organizing non-union workers.
   12 = distributing products or consumer goods.

In Russia, the issue which consistently ranked as being of lowest priority is arranging for holidays at union-owned facilities. While for many Russian union leaders, distributing products or consumer goods is a low priority, in all other surveyed countries, product distribution was viewed as the least important issue.

Union Structure and Employee Involvement

In all countries, reflecting their origins with the old unions, the members of the new confederations overwhelmingly are branch unions. But in most countries, the union structure is no longer based *only* on a small number of large industrial unions. In Russia, in addition to 33 branch (industry) members, now there are four independent unions, each representing workers at huge enterprises. They had chosen to directly affiliate (rather than be represented, as in the past, through a branch.). In Bulgaria, while most unions were industrial, reflecting competing unions within sectors, the number of federated unions had grown to more than 70 in CITUB. A similar process occurred in the former Czechoslovakia, where 63 unions have federated to CSKOS. By contrast, the number of federations in Estonia had fallen to 25. In part, this reflects the disbanding of unions that formerly consisted almost entirely of Russian nationals or Russian-speaking Estonians— for example, in the airline industry.

Especially in Bulgaria, where unions without precursors are a real factor, there is also evidence that fresh structures to facilitate cooperation among unions are emerging. Thus nearly all respondents report that, where multiple unions exist, joint bodies have been established to facilitate cooperation between the principals—Podkrepa and CITUB.

Another important change, evident in all of the countries, concerns the process of de-emphasizing the role of the central organs in successor unions. This is indicated, for example, by personnel cuts. Staff at the confederation in St. Petersburg has been reduced from 100 in 1992 to 30 in September 1993. At CITUB, staff at the central headquarters has fallen dramatically (Jones 1992). Similar processes have occurred at the branch and, where appropriate, individual union levels.[11]

Formerly, diverse structures (e.g., production committees) existed in enterprises in tandem with the machinery of the old union. Apparently important changes are underway, concerning the relation of successor union structures and these inherited, formally nonunion bodies. In most cases it seems that shop-level production committees have been discontinued. But often brigades remain in place, though today brigade leaders are more likely than in the past to be union officials. And at the plant level, the labor collective often continues to be an important body. For example, in Russia the labor collective played the key role in choosing options for medium and large firms that were privatized (Bim et al., 1993).

Evidence is also found of the existence of new structures through which trade union leaders participate with management. Thus, in the Czech Republic, respondents reported that in 10 percent of cases management visited trade union meetings and that in 60 percent of firms surveyed there were joint meetings between union leaders and managers. In Bulgaria, the extent of cooperation was even higher, frequently through special commissions; in 4 percent of cases, union representatives sat on the board of management. Also from enterprise visits in Russia, the strong impression gained is that quasi-co-determination arrangements have often emerged and that they are an important mechanism in the decision-making process.

To gauge the impact of these structures for employee involvement in Estonia, Sofia, and Prague, union leaders reported their perceptions of the extent of employee involvement on various issues. While data for union leaders in St. Petersburg were unavailable, as part of another exercise information was collected on top managers' assessments of employee influence for a separate sample of 80 manufacturing firms in St. Petersburg.

Table 4.   Employee Participation

	Bulgaria		Estonia		Czech		Russia	
	1993	1992	1994	1993	1993	1992	1993	1991
Day to Day Work	1.76	3.35	1.40	1.40	1.23	1.19	1.51	1.74
Wage and Benefits	2.19	3.31	2.20	2.22	1.94	1.29	2.37	2.56
Selection of Production Managers	2.67	1.70	1.12	1.19	1.14	1.20	1.82	2.34
Privatization	3.43	1.78	1.28	1.3	1.45	1.41	2.87	3.08
Employment Decisions	2.41	2.49	1.6	1.62	1.84	1.90	1.69	1.81

Notes: All data are from the author's surveys.
The figures are averages on a six-point scale where:
1 =   Management decides; no worker role.
2 =   Management decides; workers make suggestions.
3 =   Management decides; some information provided.
4 =   Management decides; but consults workers.
5 =   Management and workers share power and decide together.
6 =   Workers decide alone.

These data, reported in Table 4, show that typically the level of perceived employee influence is quite restricted — the average is usually about two (on a six-point scale). Typically this fell well short of power-sharing so that it is management that is in the driving seat during early transition. Where employees have some influence (a response other than one), normally this is limited to their making suggestions or receiving information. However, while the average level of participation is low, there is variation in the level of employee influence across countries and across issues. For example, on average it is employees in the Czech Republic who have the least amount of participation and employees in Bulgaria and Russia who typically have a greater level of involvement. While employees in the Czech Republic always do not see much difference in employee involvement by issue, in 1992 Bulgarian employees perceived that typically they had more influence over wages and benefits and on work organization and least influence over strategic issues, such as decisions concerning privatization (e.g., privatization options). Normally, no strong trends in employee participation are evident over time.[12]

Union Democracy

The available accounts indicate that the old unions were deeply bureaucratized and undemocratic (e.g., for Russia, see Ruble 1981). Moreover, other bodies that existed alongside unions in the old structures were viewed in a similar light. Thus, formerly there was a limited level of employee autonomy in brigades and a high level of formalism characterized elections of brigade leaders.[13] Also, Ruble (1981, p. 33) observed that production conferences were a failed institution insofar as they did not enhance employee participation.

Table 5. Bureaucratization and Union Democracy

Characteristic	Czech	Estonia	Bulgaria	Russia
Months Since Last Election	19	27	14	23
Candidates for Position	5	2	2	2
Months as Union Officer	31	45	27	36
% Newly Elected	77	38	46	66
% Where Members Can Access Membership List	75	90	100	95
Months Between Membership Meetings	8	9	5	0
% Elected at:				see note
Place of Work	72	66	29	b. below
Union Meeting Hall	6	15	56	see note b. below
Elsewhere	22	20	15	see note b. below
Union Leader Average Hourly Compensation	27 krowns	43 kroons	30 leva	299 rubles
Union Leader Hours Worked Per Month	132	94	66	166

Notes: a. All data are from the author's surveys and are averages unless otherwise stated.

b. In Russia 12% were elected at general meetings, 65% at a conference, 12% at a plenary and 10% at a presidium.

Diverse evidence that attempts to gauge democracy in successor unions which operate in a new context is presented, much of it in Table 5.[14] We begin by considering evidence on *elections*. In most cases, respondents reported that union rules required elections no less than every five years. And findings (Table 5) on the timing of the last elections for the incumbents' current position indicate that, on average, leaders were last elected between 14 and 27 months ago. However, the data are also quite varied. Thus, in 22 percent of cases for Estonia, officials report that it was at least four years since they were last elected. Table 5 also indicates that Russia was exceptional insofar as elections typically were held in fairly structured settings, such as conferences. By comparison, in the Czech Republic and Estonia, the vast majority of leaders were elected at the workplace.

In all countries, on average there were at least two candidates for each position This implies that typically there was some open competition for leadership positions. By this yardstick, Estonia was least democratic with only one candidate competing for a post in 49 percent of cases, compared to 35 percent of cases in Russia, 43 percent in the Czech Republic, and 24 percent in Bulgaria (Table 5). But it was still unusual to have several candidates competing for a position. (The exception is the Czech Republic where in almost 25 percent of cases there were at least six candidates for a position.)[15]

Turning to measures of *incumbency/tenure*, the average time that respondents had held their position in successor unions varied from 27 to 45 months (Table 5). In addition, there was much variation within countries. This was especially the case in Russia where 15 percent of respondents had held office for more than six years—that is, well before the reform process began in earnest. But elsewhere, no new leaders have held office for more than six years. These indications of greater levels of democracy in the Czech Republic and relatively lower levels in Estonian unions are reinforced by data on the extent to which leaders report that they were newly elected to that office.

Data on the number of jobs current leaders held previously sometimes indicate substantial turnover. In Russia, for one in five union leaders this was their first job in any union, and 28 percent of respondents had previously held only one union position. In Estonia, while 17 percent had not held a job in the old unions, 10 percent of today's leaders had held 4 or more jobs in the old unions, suggesting more entrenchment than in Russia. By this yardstick, again things have changed most in the Czech Republic where no current leaders had held four or more jobs in the old unions, and 58 percent had held no job in the old union structures. In sum, the data on tenure indicate potentially conflicting trends. They reveal tendencies both for many union officials to have risen through the ranks,[16] as well as for much new blood to have appeared recently in successor unions.

In 75 percent to 100 percent of cases, leaders reported that all members were able to see copies of the union membership lists (Table 5). Also the data indicate that membership meetings occurred quite frequently and that typically there are good turnouts at these meetings—in all countries average attendance by the membership exceeded 60 percent.

Leaders' Compensation and Effort

Hours worked by union leaders varied considerably within and across countries (Table 5). While Russian and Czech leaders typically worked the longest, least average effort is expended by union leaders in Bulgaria and Estonia. The average monetary compensation (wages plus bonuses) for leaders also varies considerably (on an estimated hourly basis).[17] Thus, in Russia the average was almost 300 rubles per hour (in February 1993 rubles). But there was much dispersion in these figures. Thus, the average Bulgarian leader earned 2,530 leva per month, or about 30 leva per hour. But the hourly rate ranged from below 5 leva per hour to more than 100 leva per hour.

Various exercises were undertaken to see whether current earnings of union leaders reflect past differences, especially political affiliation and union experience. For example, in the old unions it was widely believed that membership in the Communist Party had a positive influence on a union leader's salary. For Russia, various exercises indicated that such differences did persist (Jones 1995b).[18] In addition, we calculated earnings for those who had and those who did not have a position as a union leader in the past. In Bulgaria, these data show that those who were former trade union leaders and now had a full-time leadership position did not receive greater earnings than those who had never had union office in the past (5,223 leva per month compared with 5,250 leva per month). And in Estonia, we find that former union leaders earn less than those who are new to the job as a union leader.

One clear change that has occurred concerns the earnings of union leaders relative to previously important reference groups, such as senior managers. For Russia, Jones (1995b) reports that, in the past, union leaders typically earned about 70 percent to 90 percent of what a director earned. But by 1993, this had changed dramatically in all countries, and union leaders seldom earned more than one-third if the salary of a top manager. However, union leaders' wages continue to be linked to average worker earnings. In other words, the fall in relative earnings of union leaders fundamentally reflects the improved position of managers relative to all other groups. Similar processes appear to be at work in the other countries. Thus, in Bulgaria comparisons with other survey data (Jones, Kato, and Avramov 1995) show that earnings of union leaders relative to those of top managers have fallen dramatically.

CONCLUSION AND IMPLICATIONS

By using new survey data on union leaders in four countries, we do not find support for the hypothesis that unions that have succeeded the old unions are *incapable* of reform. Compared to the standard portrayal of the old unions, the evidence points to greater decentralization and democracy within successor unions. The characteristics of today's union leaders suggests movement away from the profile of leaders in the old unions. In particular, the role of membership in the Communist Party (and its successors) has diminished considerably. Today's union leaders and confederations clearly have functions that are very different than those of their predecessors. The priorities of union leaders today are quite different from tasks stressed previously and relate to issues of more central concern to workers—for example, wages and job protection. Formal union structures are more decentralized than in the past and quasi-co-determination arrangements are emerging. However, seldom do these formal and informal structures lead to employees perceiving that they have substantial input in enterprise decision making during transition.

Relative to enterprise managers, there has been substantial erosion in union leaders' compensation. Unlike the homogeneity that characterized the past, there is significant variation in compensation and effort among union leaders. By diverse measures, today's unions are more democratic than those in the past and when compared with other bodies that existed alongside unions in the old structures. Much new blood has appeared in leadership positions, and the average tenure of union leaders has fallen. Past or present membership in the Communist Party is not related to the likelihood of a leader being newly elected. No evidence is found of a relationship between a union leader's status concerning the Communist Party and political beliefs.

One implication of this finding of changes in successor union leaders and their behavior concerns comparable findings for change in managers and enterprise behavior. Most of the relevant research (e.g., Ash and Hare 1994; Blasi 1994) conclude that the astonishing changes in economic policies, including privatization, have produced a disappointingly slow degree of change in key aspects of management in these transition economies, such as managerial turnover. Similar findings have been found concerning executive compensation systems and the managerial labor market (Jones and Kato in press). When judged against this benchmark of limited managerial change, it does not seem that changes in unions have been slower; on the contrary, it seems reasonable to conclude that often there has been swifter and more extensive change in union personnel and practices.[19]

Together with findings reported on these and other issues for other countries (such as the development of independent employers associations), our findings suggest some movement in the direction of a Western type of industrial relations. At the same time, we also observe that there are important differences in the pace and extent of change in unions (and other aspects of industrial relations) across countries. It does not seem that a single type of industrial relations system is emerging in former communist countries. Union differences exist in respects including: membership levels (union density has declined everywhere but remains extremely high in Russia); the importance of alternative unions (in many countries, including the Czech Republic and Russia, the trade union movement is effectively dominated by successor unions; but in some countries, including Bulgaria, Hungary, and Poland, while successor unions are the most important unions, unions without precursors are also significant); the extent of union democracy (in Russia, a somewhat slower pace of democratic change and a persistence of past patterns of privileges that is especially strong). Also, there are differences in areas not examined in this paper, though reported elsewhere, such as the extent of cooperation between government and unions (e.g., Swiatkowski 1994).

While the principal task of this paper was to provide evidence on changes in successor unions, perhaps the more intriguing research issue is to account for these and other differences in the emerging systems of industrial relations. While much more work both on applied and theoretical questions is needed, especially for systems that are in a state of flux, to provide a modest stimulus to thinking on this topic, we offer the following conjectures.

Differences in *initial starting conditions* appear to be playing an important role. For example, the fact that in Russia the former system was in place for a longer period than elsewhere is probably related to the slower pace of change in Russian industrial relations—for example, a comparatively higher rate of entrenchment and influence by the old guard within unions. Similarly, the more Western orientation of Estonia and the Czech Republic may have produced quicker changes in certain areas, such as in union democracy. Analogously, differences, both in patterns of political conflict under communism and in ways in which the political revolutions occurred, are shaping features of the new industrial relations. Nationality issues also appear to be leaving their mark on the way in which systems are evolving—in the surveyed countries, this is probably of most importance in Estonia.

In addition, *differences in policies* across countries probably have been important in producing different environments within which varying systems of industrial relations are emerging.[20] For example, while all countries suffered sharp drops in output, this was especially pronounced in Bulgaria and least severe in the Czech Republic; also, there were significant differences in the timing of these movements in aggregate output. In turn, in most labor markets, unemployment quickly appeared, accompanied by rapid inflation and declining real wages. However patterns vary considerably with unemployment (and inflation) being especially acute in Bulgaria and Russia (though official measures of unemployment have remained relatively low in Russia, there is abundant evidence of widespread underemployment and intense fear of unemployment). By comparison, unemployment and inflation have been much more modest in Tallinn and Prague. These differences probably help to explain the different attention union leaders have devoted to issues of job security in the various locations. In all countries, there has been substantial growth in the private sector, especially in employment levels, though again at different rates. Indeed, in the early 1990s, plural forms of enterprise organization began to appear in all former communist countries, and discussion of privatization was underway.[21] The lower level of unionization in Bulgaria and the greater strength of alternative unions there, relative to Russia and the Czech Republic, likely reflect differences in labor market conditions.

Also, *differences in the strategies pursued by employers and unions* will likely have played an important part. Thus, the low levels of unionization in Estonia in part probably result from fairly strident policies pursued by many new private employers. In turn, these policies have been nurtured in an environment where privatization policies have successfully encouraged foreign capital investment.

Our findings also have several potential implications for policy. One implication arises from the observation that this is a key time of transition in the industrial relations systems in Eastern and Central Europe and that, once systems are set in place, major modifications are often quite difficult to make (Katz, Kuruvilla, and Turner 1994). In all countries, a critical issue concerns the respective roles that the successor unions and the new independent unions should be encouraged to play at this vital stage. For example, in Russia the AFL-CIO will not support or cooperate with FNPR successor unions because it is claimed they have not (and, some would argue, cannot) really changed their nature and functions. A similar position has been adopted concerning CITUB in Bulgaria, where the AFL-CIO essentially supports only Podkrepa.[22] On balance, our findings cast doubt on this argument. We provide evidence of progressive changes in actual practices and sustained membership in successor unions in all countries where plural unions exist. Successor unions appear to be genuine trade unions. Hence, our findings imply it may not be either socially or economically optimal to clear away all vestiges of the old institutional arrangements. On the contrary, the St. Petersburg experience suggests that in facilitating the emergence of a tripartite system it is possible (and perhaps more efficient) to gradually build on the old system (Stark 1992). At minimum, successor unions are a good complement to the newer (alternative) unions which, while attracting the lion's share of attention by Western analysts, have tended to remain quite weak in practice during the early transition. Especially during times of economic uncertainty and political polarization, support is crucial for those institutions that have a measure of popular acceptance but which are struggling with problems posed by unfamiliar environments and the need to continue the processes of internal reform. Attempting to shape policy in the direction of an "institutional big bang" may not only be impossible but potentially destabilizing.

Other implications concern the design of new labor codes and the potential role of employee involvement in enterprise decision making. The available evidence (including the findings reported in this paper as well as other work by the author; e.g., Jones 1995a does not support those (e.g., Burawoy and Krotov 1992) who hypothesize that the firm in a transition economy is typically worker controlled. At the same time, there is some evidence indicating that certain "participatory" institutions are emerging spontaneously, and there is a volume of evidence to suggest that such institutions may be desirable on grounds of economic efficiency (e.g., Ben-Ner and Jones 1995; Levine and Tyson 1990). In such circumstances, it may be sensible to legislate to put such changes on a firmer footing. For example, there is evidence that quasi-co-determination arrangements are emerging automatically in countries such as Russia and that union strength in the contemporary global economy is closely linked to the existence of institutions for plant and firm-level participation (e.g., Turner 1992). To reinforce and regularize these developments, labor codes might be amended so as to require union-based mechanisms for employee representation on the board or works councils.

However, the situation is very dynamic, and unions face important challenges in an uncertain environment, especially because of challenges arising from privatization. Another important test for successor unions in most of these countries arises from the ending of trade unions' responsibility for administering social security funds.[23] An added potential trial concerns the matter of ownership of assets accumulated by the former unions. In Russia, this has not yet been addressed in ways comparable to its treatment in other countries. At the same time, in most former communist countries, even after the loss of assets to rival unions (and the state), one finds that membership commitment to successor unions continues. This is the case, for example, in Poland and Hungary. Hence, for the foreseeable future in these former communist countries, there is no reason to believe that these challenges will lead to members switching away from successor (and to alternative) unions, though further erosion in union membership levels is likely.

ACKNOWLEDGMENTS

For helping to facilitate this work I acknowledge the assistance of several institutions including: the Leningrad Confederation of Trade Unions; the Association of Estonian Trade Unions; the Trade Union Research Institute (Sofia); CERGE, Charles University, Prague; the National Council on Soviet and East European Affairs; and CEET, ILO, Budapest. For constructive discussions on these issues I thank Yevgeny Makarov, Kari Tapiola, Leonid Gordon, Richard Freeman, Peter Dorman, Kelly Smith, Jeffrey Pliskin, Krastyo Petkov, Yuri Arroyo, Trevor Bain, Morley Gunderson, Anil Verma, Maria Vavrejnova, Jan Svejnar, Vambo Veer, Eiki Nestor, Larry Bush, Guy Standing, Patrick LaCombe, Dan Abele and other participants at a seminar at the Kenan Institute where an earlier version of the paper was presented. Kosali Ilayperuma provided capable research assistance. The author acknowledges support from NCEESRand NSF SBR 9511465.

NOTES

1.   For example, in Russia leaders of successor unions were vocal in their condemnation of the decision of the Yeltsin Administration to close the Parliament in September 1993. In Bulgaria, both the successor unions (CITUB) and the new confederation (Podkrepa) supported general strikes which helped to unseat different administrations (Jones 1992).

2.   Informative accounts of some innovations in labor market institutions during the early stages of transition in former communist countries have appeared. Thus, in Russia the tendency toward decentralization within successor unions and the emergence of alternative labor unions have been documented (e.g. Clark, Fairbrother, Burawoy, and Krotor 1993; Silverman, Vogt, and Murray 1992. For changes in Bulgaria, see Jones (1992) and for the Czech Republic, Tomer (1991). For more general accounts, see Freeman (1994).

3.   For a related but more general argument that reflects the basic processes of institutional change, see Kuruvilla and Erickson (1994).

4.   For a description of the union-monopoly model, see Jones (1992). For informative accounts of trade unions in the former USSR, see Ruble (1981), and Pravda and Ruble (1986).

5.   In Bulgaria, the leaders of the old unions, the Bulgarian Trade Unions, seized the opportunity presented by the fall of Zhivkov to declare independence from the Communist Party. Shortly afterward, the old unions were disbanded, and in February 1990 a new confederation of independent trade unions (CITUB) was established (see Jones 1992). In Estonia, the analogous key conference for the new unions was in April 1990. In Russia, in September 1989 delegates at a congress of the old "official" unions declared their independence from the Communist Party; a year later, the centralized structure of the old arrangements was overturned, at both national and regional levels (see Jones 1995b).

6.   To check on the accuracy of the survey data that are largely self-reported, several methods were used including visits to enterprises and interviews with local researchers. These checks did not reveal any obvious biases in the data. As such, a rough estimate is that each survey covers about 20 percent of workers in that labor market. Thus in the greater St. Petersburg area, I calculate that firms in which data for union officials are available employed about 885,000. This compares with a potential labor force estimated at 3.1 million and employment of 2.525 million for the city of St. Petersburg alone (estimates derived from Gendler and Gildingersh 1992).

7. These estimates are based on data provided in an interview with Eiki Nestor and in a personal communication from Igor Tomes.

8. In some cases, reported union membership exceeded the labor force. (These observations are not included in the reported figures. Had they been, such cases would have represented 17.5 percent of responses.) It is not clear whether these represent delays in removing former members from the rolls or actual figures reflecting released or retired workers retaining union membership and possible instances of multiple membership.

9. For details on union membership in Western European countries, see Blanchflower and Freeman (1992). See Freeman (1994) for information for other East European countries.

10. Unfortunately there do not seem to be precise data with which one can make comparisons. This impression of the profile of the average union leader under communism comes from several sources, for example, Granick (1954).

11. Thus, at a shipyard in St. Petersburg at the end of 1993, the staff was half as large as it was in 1991. During the same period, the labor force fell by 11 percent.

12. In other work (e.g., Jones 1995a), some of these issues are examined more deeply for Bulgaria by using a larger data set. The findings reported earlier that workers on average have minimal control in firm level decision making in this former Communist country are reaffirmed. Moreover, no marked changes in patterns of individual influence during early transition are found.

13. For Russia, see Van Atta (1989) and Slider (1987). For Bulgaria, see Petkov and Thirkell, (1991) and Jones and Meurs (1991).

14. In so doing, we note that there is a long history of examining this theme for Western trade unions (see, e.g. Edelstein and Warner 1976). Furthermore, these and other studies that attempt to measure democracy in other organizations indicate that there is no single ideal indicator or measure and that there are obvious problems in interpreting some of the evidence. For example, long tenure in office or few candidates for a position may imply either a strong and popular incumbent (whom no one wants to challenge) or an entrenched incumbent with considerable resources.

15. Similar formal indicators of democracy have been used in evaluating unions elsewhere. In his classic study of American unions, Taft (1954) found that on average 23.4 percent of offices were contested. If similar formal indicators are used in St. Petersburg, then contemporary Russian successor unions would probably be judged at least as democratic as were U.S. and U.K. unions in these studies.

16. Evidence on some of these matters is also available from visits to unions and enterprises. In Bulgaria, there appeared to be active participation by all present at meetings of CITUB.

17. They also vary, of course, depending on the particular union job, especially whether it is at the branch or the local level. In addition, total compensation includes "fringes" and not just money earnings. Efforts to systematically collect information for union leaders on the money value of various kinds of income in kind (e.g., subsidized food and transportation) and other unpaid privileges were largely unsuccessful.

18. These included calculations of mean compensation by Communist Party status and estimation of compensation equations with controls for other factors such as the leader's age, hours of work, tenure as a union leader, level of education, and form of ownership.

19. In future research, it will be important to see whether these patterns persist and to examine their implications for theory and practice concerning firm behavior, especially consequences for wage and employment adjustment.

20. In turn, these may interact with differences in economic outcomes. For example, the fact that Bulgaria has one of the highest unemployment rates and one of the steepest falls in the labor force, may arguably be linked to the early establishment of tripartite mechanisms in Bulgaria and its having a divided labor movement. For details on policy and outcomes, see EBRD (1994).

21. For an account of the different forms of enterprise organization in Russia and the former U.S.S.R. during this period, see Bim, et al. (1993). For Bulgaria, see Jones and Parvulov (1995); for Estonia, see World Bank (1993); and for the Czech Republic, the relevant essay in Estrin (1994).

22.   With funds primarily provided by the U.S. government, the AFL-CIO has a strong presence in Russia. While no support is provided to FNPR unions, significant assistance has been given to the unions without precursors. While there does not appear to be an AFL-CIO presence in Estonia, in the Czech Republic the AFL-CIO does support the new unions, the bulk of which are really successor unions.

23.   In Russia, in the aftermath of the events surrounding the dissolution of the Parliament in September 1993, this right was taken away from trade unions. There is some suggestion that, compared to successor unions, alternative unions were often more dependent on such funds as a source of revenue. It has also been suggested that, again compared to successor unions, alternative unions were often disbursing a smaller fraction of such funds for social security purposes. If so, this development will be especially hard on the alternative unions.

REFERENCES

AFL-CIO. 1993. *Report to the Board of Directors, Free Trade Union Institute, 1991-1992.* Washington, DC: Author.

Ash, T. N., and P. G. Hare. 1994. "Privatization in the Russian Federation: Changing Enterprise Behaviour in the Transition Period." *Cambridge Journal of Economics* 18: 619-634.

Ben-Ner, A., and D. C. Jones. 1995. " Productivity Effects of Employee Ownership: A Theoretical Framework." *Industrial Relations* (October): 532-554.

Bim, A., D. C. Jones and T. Weisskopf. 1993. "Privatization in Russia." Pp. 252-278 in *Privatization in Central and Eastern Europe*, edited by S. Estrin. London: Longmans.

Blanchflower, D.G. and R.B. Freeman 1992. "Unionism in the United States and Other Advances OECA Countries" *Industrial Relations*, v. 31, #1, 56-79.

Blasi, J. 1994. "Corporate Ownership and Corporate Governance in Russia: 1994 Findings." Presented at the 1995 IRRA Meetings, Washington, January 8.

Burawoy, M., and P. Krotov. 1992. "The Soviet Transition From Socialism to Capitalism:Worker Control and Economic Bargaining in the Wood Industry." *American Sociological Review* 57 (February): 16-38.

Clarke, S., P. Fairbrother, M. Burawoy and P. Krotov. 1993. *What About the Workers?* London: Verso.

Clegg, H. 1976. *Trade Unionism Under Collective Bargaining.* Oxford: Blackwell.

Edelstein, J. D., and M. Warner. 1976. *Comparative Union Democracy.* New York: Wiley.

EBRD. 1994. *Transition Report for 1994.* October, London: Author.

Estrin, S. Ed. *Privatization in Central and Eastern Europe* London: Longmans.

Freeman, R. 1994. "What Direction for Labor-Market Institutions in Eastern and Central Europe?" Pp. 1-29 in *The Transition in Eastern Europe,* vol. 2 edited by O. Blanchardm K.A. Froot and J.D. Sachs, NBER and Chicago University Press Chicago.

Gendler, G., and M. Gildingersh. 1992. "Unemployment in St. Petersburg." *RFE/RL* 1(40): 57-59.

Granick, D. 1954. *Management of the Industrial Firm in the USSR.* New York: Columbia University Press.

Jones, D. C. 1992. "The Transformation of Labor Unions in Eastern Europe: The case of Bulgaria." *Industrial and Labor Relations Review* 45(3): 452-470.

_____. 1995a. "Employee Participation During the Early Stages of Transition: Evidence From Bulgaria." *Economic and Industrial Democracy* 16: 111-135.

_____. 1995b. "On Successor Unions in Transitional Economies: Evidence From St. Petersburg." *Industrial and Labor Relations Review,* 49(1): 39-57.

Jones, D.C., and T. Kato. In press. "The Determinants of Chief Executive Compensation in Transitional Economies: Evidence From Bulgaria." *Labour Economics.*

Jones, D.C., and T. Kato, and S. Avramov. 1995. "Managerial Labor Markets in Transitional Economies" *International Journal of Manpower,* 16: 14-24.

Jones, D.C., and S. Parvulov. 1995. "Industrial Organization in a Restructuring Socialist Economy: Evidence From Bulgaria." *Empirica.* 22: 23-46.

Katz, H. C., S. Kuruvilla, and L. Turner. 1993. "Trade Unions and Collective Bargaining: Suggestions for Emerging Democracies in Eastern Europe and the Former Soviet Europe." Pp. 187-208 in *Double Shift*, edited by B. Silverman, R. Vogt, and M. Yanowitch. Sharpe.

Kleiner, M., and C. R. Ay. 1994. "Employee Representation and Economic Growth: Theory and Evidence From Advanced Countries." Mimeo, University of Minnesota and presented at the Fourth Bargaining Group Conference, Toronto, October.

Kuruvilla, S., and C. Erickson. 1994. "Critical Junctures in the Transformation of Industrial Relations Systems: A Comparative Study of Nine Countries." Mimeo, Cornell University and presented at the Fourth Bargaining Conference, Toronto, October.

Levine, D., and L. Tyson. 1990. "Participation, Productivity and the Firms' Environment." Pp. 183-2370 in *Paying for Productivity*, edited by A. Blinder. Washington, DC: Brookings.

Morishima, M. 1994. "The Evolution of HRM Policies and Practices in Japan." Mimeo, University of Illinois and presented at the Fourth Bargaining Group Conference, Toronto, October.

Murrell, P. 1992. "Evolution in Economics and in the Economic Reform of the Centrally Planned Economies." Pp. 35-53 in *The Emergence of Market Economies in Eastern Europe*, edited C. Clague and G. C. Rausser. Cambridge, MA: Blackwell.

Petkov, K., and J. Thirkell. 1991. *Labor Relations in Eastern Europe*. London: Routledge.

Pravda, A., and B. Ruble. 1986. *Trade Unions in Communist States*. London: Allen and Unwin.

Ruble, B. 1981. *Soviet Trade Unions*. Cambridge: CambridgeU.P.

Silverman, B., R. Vogt, and M. Yanowitch. 1992. *Labor and Democracy in the Transition to a Market System*. NY: Sharpe.

Slider, D. 1987. "The Brigade System in Soviet Industry." *Soviet Studies* 39(3): 388-405.

Stark, D. 1992. "Path Dependence and Privatization: Strategies for East and Central Europe." *East European Politics and Societies* 6:17-54.

Swiatkowski, A. 1994. "Transformation of the Industrial Relations in Central and Eastern Europe: Insider's Summary Report." Mimeo, Jagiellonski University, Poland.

Taft, P. 1954. *The Structure and Government of Trade Unions* Cambridge, MA: Harvard.

Temkina, A. 1992. "The Workers' Movement in Leningrad, 1986-91. *Soviet Studies* 42(2): 209-236.

Tomes, J. 1991. "Social Reform: A Cornestone in Czechozlovakia's new economic structure" *International Labour Review*, v. 130, #2, 191-198.

Turner, L. 1992. *Democracy at Work: Changing World Markets and the Future of Unions*. Ithaca, NY: Cornell University Press.

Van Atta, D. 1989. "A Critical Examination of Brigades in the USSR." *Economic and Industrial Democracy* 10: 329-340

World Bank. 1993. *Estonia: The Transition to a Market Economy*. Washington, DC: Author.

THE EVOLUTION OF WHITE-COLLAR
HUMAN RESOURCE MANAGEMENT IN
JAPAN

Motohiro Morishima

ABSTRACT

The author, using qualitative interview and quantitative questionnaire data, documents the evolution of Japanese white-collar human resources management (HRM) and investigates what variables are related to Japanese firms' divergence from the traditional patterns of HRM policies as characterized by long-term employment and *nenko*-based appraisal. The analyses show that two emergent clusters of firms with divergent HRM policies can be identified in the sample: one characterized by long-term employment and competitive performance-based appraisal and the other by policies of employment externalization and competitive performance-based appraisal. These firm clusters are found to show predictable relationships to firms' adoption of specific HRM practices. Finally, the factors that are associated with the emergence of these clusters include workforce demographics, firm performance, and firms' institutional characteristics.

Advances in Industrial and Labor Relations, Volume 7, pages 145-176.
Copyright © 1996 by JAI Press Inc.
All rights of reproduction in any form reserved.
ISBN: 1-55938-925-7

145

INTRODUCTION

The Japanese human resource management (HRM) system has recently been submitted to a variety of academic as well as nonacademic debates as to its effectiveness in managing valued corporate resources. The discussion has been both supportive and critical. On one hand, some researchers have emphasized the ability of the Japanese HRM system to develop workers' problem-solving ability and high commitment to employing organizations (Florida and Kenney 1991; Koike 1988; Lincoln and Kalleberg 1990). On the other hand, others have denounced what they view as work intensification, management by stress, and lack of worker freedom and autonomy (Kawahito 1991; Parker and Slaughter 1988). Yet, most of these assessments have one thing in common: they are assessments of the Japanese HRM system as applied to production workers in manufacturing industries. Relatively little has appeared in the literature on the Japanese HRM system for white-collar workers (but see Pucik's 1989). Despite the noteworthy effectiveness of Japanese HRM systems for production workers (Koike 1988), the effectiveness of HRM systems for white-collar employees has not been established either by academic research or by practice.

Yet, in the early 1990s, the Japanese are becoming increasingly critical of their white-collar HRM system. The discussion has become even more heated in the current recession which is the worst since the end of World War II. As companies have resorted to a range of cost-cutting measures, debates have also flared as to whether the modifications introduced by firms will change the basic character of white-collar HRM (Befu and Cernosia 1990; Berggren 1994).

In this paper, I examine the evolution of Japanese HRM policies as applied to white-collar employees. Based on the examination of pressures and constraints on Japanese employers attempting to modify their white-collar HRM, predictions are made that, between the two sets of rules that characterize Japanese white-collar internal labor markets (ILMs), changes are more likely with regard to the rules of employee appraisal and reward, relative to the other set regarding long-term employment and employment security. Examination of interview and anecdotal evidence and a data set obtained from approximately 1,600 firms shows that the traditional type of HR system—characterized by HRM policies of long-term employment and appraisal and reward based on skill development—still exists in the majority of firms. The study, however, finds that two other clusters of firms with divergent HR policies also exist among sample firms: one (called the Competitive Appraisal HRM cluster) that maintains the traditional long-term employment but emphasizes highly competitive performance-based appraisal and the other (called the Transformed HRM cluster) that abandons both of the traditional ILM rules by emphasizing employment externalization and highly competitive performance-based appraisal. Hypotheses regarding the demographic, economic, and institutional factors inducing this divergence are examined using the data set.

RULES OF JAPANESE WHITE-COLLAR ILMs

The system of internalized white-collar HRM developed in Japan after World War II was based on two important principles: (1) long-term employment and internal skill development and (2) evaluation based on skill development (*nenko* evaluation).[1]

Long-Term Employment and Internal Skill Development

Long-term employment meant not only that employees enjoyed strong employment security, but that also the skills necessary for the execution of their tasks were developed internally. From the early systematic descriptions of Japanese employment (e.g., Abegglen 1958), long-term employment practices have been pointed out, under the rubric of such terms as "permanent employment" and "life-time employment." In essence, Japanese "life-time" employment refers to the practice of hiring employees fresh out of school without previous work experience and keeping them until forced retirement at around age 60.

Two questions are: is the degree of long-term employment stronger or weaker among white-collar workers, relative to the workforce in general, and are long-term employment practices declining over time. Table 1 shows the distribution of employee tenure in the overall male workforce and in male employees in manufacturing. In this table, data for three periods—1972, 1982, and 1992—were collected and broken down by firm size and employee category.

Data indicate that Japanese white-collar workers are more likely to stay with one firm than is the general workforce. More importantly, employment tenure is increasing for both white- and blue-collar workers, contrary to the alleged "demise of permanent employment" theme (Befu and Cernosia 1990). The increase in employee tenure is, however, smaller among white-collar workers relative to their blue-collar counterparts.

One of the most important implications of long-term employment practices in Japan is their ability to encourage firms to invest in intra-firm training (Cole 1992). According to Koike (1993), training for white-collar workers in large Japanese firms is quite similar in principle to that for blue-collar workers, which has been discussed at length in previous literature (Cole 1992; Koike 1988;). Extensive OJT is used to train workers through learning-by-doing, while Off-JT is used to supplement this process with systematic and codified knowledge about the firm, industry and functions of which they are in charge. One major finding worth noting, however, is that for white-collar positions early-career training is a long process that might last up to 10 years, involving a number of assignments within a broadly defined specialization (Koike 1993; Pucik 1989).

Evaluation Based on Skill Development (*Nenko* Evaluation)

In this paper, the term *nenko* does not refer to the simple use of seniority or tenure as the basis of promotion and advancement; it refers to the use of skill devel-

Table 1. Employee Tenure: 1972, 1982 and 1992 By Firm Size, Men Only
(In Percent; Column Sums Equal 100)

Years with Current Employer	Firm Size In Persons								
	1000+			10-999					
	1972	1982	1992	1972	1982	1992	1972	1982	1992
Men (All Industries)									
0-2	17.5	12.9	14.9	31.5	22.6	22.9			
3-4	11.1	5.6	6.3	15.3	10.6	10.4			
5-9	21.2	17.5	14.7	23.5	21.5	18.6			
10-19	27.8	36.3	25.4	23.1	30.2	25.2			
20-29	17.5	21.2	28.6	6.0	12.6	17.1			
30+	5.0	6.5	10.1	0.7	2.5	5.8			
Blue-Collar (Manufacturing)									
0-2	17.6	11.9	16.4	33.6	22.0	24.3			
3-4	15.6	3.9	4.2	16.1	8.8	9.6			
5-9	23.5	16.8	13.4	22.4	20.5	17.7			
10-19	27.9	39.8	23.4	21.5	31.9	23.0			
20-29	13.2	20.9	31.2	5.8	13.8	18.5			
30+	2.1	6.6	11.3	0.7	3.0	6.9			
White-Collar (Manufacturing)									
0-2	13.1	9.6	12.6	20.8	14.8	16.3			
3-4	9.9	3.9	5.7	13.2	7.6	8.4			
5-9	19.9	14.5	15.6	24.5	18.9	18.1			
10-19	34.1	37.8	22.4	30.5	35.3	25.7			
20-29	18.5	26.6	30.9	9.9	19.2	22.3			
30+	4.5	7.7	12.8	1.1	4.2	9.2			

Source: Basic Wage Structure Survey, 1972, 1982, 1992.

opment as the basis of employee evaluation. Since it is usually assumed that white-collar skills are developed through a long process of internal training, the length of tenure is often used as a proxy for the level of skill development.

In Japanese firms, employees have been assessed and their pay and promotions generally determined by a scheme called the skill-grade system which, using a set of very detailed criteria, assesses each employee as to what he/she is capable of performing, not what he/she actually performs (Koike 1991). In this scheme, employees' capabilities are considered to be formed on the basis of cumulative on-the-job experience and internal training and, therefore, strongly related to their tenure. A survey conducted by the Ministry of Labour (MOL 1990) shows that out of approximately 6,000 firms with 30 or more employees, 80 percent used the skill-grade pay scheme to determine at least some portion of their employees' take-home pay. It is almost 100 percent for large firms with 1,000 or more employees.

Typically, an employee spends three to four years completing a whole set of skills in a given grade before advancing to the next skill-grade. Advancement to a higher skill-grade is based mostly on supervisory assessment of an employee's learning and carries an increase in pay. Moreover, since many firms require advancement to a certain skill-grade as a precondition for promotion to managerial positions (i.e., to be promoted to the position of, say, section head, one must be at least in grade, say, A5), this system takes on an added incentive value.

Taken together, these two "rules" of Japanese white-collar ILMs have served to ensure an adequate flow of skills throughout the organization, especially the supply of firm-specific skills. They also created incentives for employees to work hard, develop attachment to the corporation and most importantly to maintain the motivation to improve their skills.

PRESSURES AND CONSTRAINTS FOR CHANGE IN JAPANESE WHITE-COLLAR HRM

Recently, however, several important circumstances developed to create an environment that substantially reduced the benefits of an internalized white-collar HRM system based on these two principles. Below, four major factors are described as pressures for change. At the same time, there are constraints that were imposed on Japanese employers in changing their HRM policies. Combined, the existing pressures and constraints suggest the direction of change in Japanese HRM.

Productivity Lag

While Japan built its economic powerhouse on blue-collar productivity through such mechanisms as the lean production system, its white-collar productivity has lagged behind Western nations by, according to some estimates, more than 50 percent (Hori 1993). According to a 1992 study by the Japan Productivity Center (JPC), in white-collar dominated industries such as banking and finance, and wholesale and retail, Japanese productivity is two-thirds to three-quarters of that observed in the United States and 80 percent to 90 percent of that in Germany and the United Kingdom (JPC 1992). In contrast, the JPC study shows that, in the auto manufacturing and electrical appliance industries—two industries where Japanese manufacturing has been globally competitive—Japanese productivity levels are very similar to those observed in the United States and Germany. Also, in the most carefully conducted study of white-collar productivity differences to date, Hori (1993) estimates that in wholesale and retail, a Japanese firm with an average level of productivity needs to improve its productivity by more than 20 percent to be competitive with comparable U.S. firms in the same industry.

The reason for the low productivity levels among white-collar employees is, in part, due to the lack of appropriate performance measurement schemes. As noted earlier, the Japanese model of HRM is premised on the assumption that firms recruit candidates with the largest learning potential, provide them with continuous training opportunities, and reward them according to the degree to which they have acquired internally relevant job-related skills. Yet, since learning takes on such an important meaning, performance itself and, more importantly, the task of measuring it are often neglected (Nonaka 1988). Also, since compensation based on the level of learning is likely to be relatively stable, it tends not to reflect fluctuations in the levels of employees' actual contributions to the organization.

Organizational Demographics: *Dankai* Bulge and White-Collar Redundancy

The second factor demanding change in white-collar employment practices is the maturing of the *dankai* (baby-boom) generation. The demographic structure of the Japanese workforce, especially among white-collar employees, has a bulge in the middle which has overloaded the ranks of middle management and is now at the peak of its earning curve. In the Japanese white-collar HRM system, the increase of employees in the middle management level creates a number of problems, including increased overhead cost, demotivation due to early career plateau, and the lack of promotion opportunities for junior employees. Overhead is increased because, in a reward system based on skill development, senior employees are likely to have learned more and therefore are entitled to receive higher pay.

Moreover, since the middle management bulge creates a lower selection ratio, a larger number of employees reach their career plateau at an earlier stage than before. Similarly, junior employees are discouraged since the positions they are intended to be promoted to remain occupied by their more senior colleagues who themselves have nowhere to go. Since the incentive mechanism in the Japanese intra-company training system has depended heavily on regular advancement concordant with employees' skill advancement (Yashiro 1991), the viability of the Japanese training system is also likely to be undermined.

Finally, not even counting the middle management bulge, Japan's white-collar workforce is generally expanding at a much higher rate than are blue-collar workers. According to government statistics, blue-collar employment has decreased from 10.4 percent of the entire workforce in 1980 to 7.2 percent in 1990. Over the same period, the white-collar workforce has increased from 43.1 percent to 48.6 percent (Hori 1993). At Sony, the manufacturing headcount increased by 6 percent during the eight-year period 1984-1992, but the overhead personnel increased by 139%. An increasing number of firms are experiencing "overstaffing" in their white-collar ranks. In a 1993 survey by the JPC, 72.5 percent of 305 leading firms reported overstaffing of their white-collar workforce (JPC 1994).[2]

Slow Growth and the Changing Nature of Competition

One prevailing factor inducing Japanese employers to change their HRM practices is the slower growth of the Japanese economy (and consequently of individual firms). The Japanese economy, which grew by an average of 10 percent annually up to the 1970s, maintained approximately 5 percent to 6 percent growth in the 1980s. In the 1990s, the growth is expected to be as low as 1 percent annually.

As a result, the nature of competition in the Japanese economy has shifted from that based on market share to that based on profitability. It has long been argued that Japanese firms have relied heavily on market share as a criterion of their effective performance (Clark 1979). When the economy and the markets were growing, emphasizing market share and de-emphasizing profitability made sense since the practice allowed firms to invest in capital, research and development, and human resources for future growth. Fixed costs associated with internalized employment arrangements were quickly absorbed by increased sales. Stockholders were also relatively quiet hoping for long-term capital gains.

When sales growth slowed down along with the maturing economy, the cost of fixed employment arrangements became more visible. Firms became much more sensitive to profit margins than before, especially with the bursting of the bubble economy in the late 1980s. Instead of long-term benefits, firms have begun to emphasize short-term cost reductions that will immediately be reflected in profit figures. Internalized HRM arrangements for white-collar employees that involve fixed (and increasing) costs were chosen as one of the targets of cost reduction. Since efforts have always been under way to improve the operational efficiency and numerical flexibility of production workers even during the economic growth period (as well as the fact that the economy itself was becoming less and less manufacturing-based), changes are usually targeted on white-collar employment practices.

Changing Management Values

The fourth factor concerns the values held by the enterprises' managers. The strategic choice literature has suggested that employment systems depend not only on external market and institutional pressures but also on how management views the costs and benefits of various employment practices in meeting these external pressures (Osterman 1994). Management values are, therefore, important determinants in the selection of HRM policies and practices.

In Japan, the available evidence, summarized in Table 2, suggests that there have been divergent trends in how employers view the two ILM rules that have held together the traditional Japanese employment system. While firms still value long-term employment, they appear to be moving away from using *nenko* as the basis for human resource decisions. Specifically, *nenko*-based advancement and pay determination practices, which received support from a majority of firms in 1987, had lost their popularity in 1993.

Constraints: Employment Security

Thus, Japanese employers are under enormous pressure to change their HRM practices for white-collar employees. Long-term employment and assessment based on ability growth (*nenko* assessment) could both be targets of massive changes. There are, however, constraints imposed on Japanese employers which

Table 2. Japanese Firms' Support for "Traditional" HRM Policies

	Percent That Support	
	Long-Term Employment	*Tenure-Based Practices*
	"Is your policy to maintain employment of regular-status (*seishain*) workers until retirement?"	"Do you use tenure as the most important criterion in human resource decisions?"
Asked in 1987[a]		
Currently Support	89.6	59.4
Asked in 1993[b]		
Currently Support	90.3	20.3
Support in the Future?[c]	65.7	1.4

Notes: a. Source: MOL (1987); N = 629. The sample is restricted to large firms (employment > 1,000).

   b. Source: RECRUIT (1993); N = 319. The sample is restricted to large firms (employment > 1,000).

   c. The questions for future support asked whether the respondents will continue to support the policy in the future.

may restrict their choices. Two major factors are the strong employment security afforded to white-collar employees and the characteristics of work organization.

There are at least four reasons why employment security continues to be strongly protected in Japanese labor markets. First, Japanese employment security is firmly grounded in legal precedents set by the Japanese court, which has made it almost impossible for employers to terminate or layoff their regular-status employees without the employees' (or their unions') consent (Tackney 1994). Second, as shown in Table 2, recent evidence indicates employment security for regular-status workers is also strongly supported by management values.

Third, employment security has always been the most important bargaining item on Japanese labor unions' agenda. The bitter strikes that Japanese firms have experienced with their generally cooperative labor unions have involved threats to employment security of core workers (Gordon 1985). Fourth, both long-term employment and employment security are explicit policies of the Japanese government. For example, the Ministry of Labour, using its unemployment insurance funds, subsidizes up to two-thirds of wages for employees in companies that engage in temporary shutdowns of operations instead of layoffs or terminations.[3]

Constraints: Work Organization

Japanese work organizations are usually designed to require employee involvement through such means as quality control circles and team production (Cole 1992), and greater participation of middle- to low-level managers in firms' strategic decision making (Nonaka 1988). What has often been described as consensus or collective decision making (such as *ringi* decision making) in white-collar workplaces takes advantage of information collected and possessed by individual employees, since it assures that ideas created on the basis of information at lower levels of an organization find a way to upper-level management. White-collar workers are also encouraged to engage in extensive information sharing among functionally separated positions (Clark 1979; Morishima 1995a).

The primary purpose of Japanese decentralization practices is to make effective use of the information and knowledge possessed by employees directly involved in the operation, an aspect which Aoki (1993) refers to as information participation. According to Aoki, participation increases firms' capabilities in problem solving and decision making by increasing the total amount of information that the organization can utilize. He conjectured that this aspect of Japanese management creates "information rent" which can be used to increase the value of the firm.

One important condition for effective information participation is that employees possess a high degree of firm-specific knowledge, skills, and abilities (KSAs) regarding operational processes. Thus, employee participation and decentralization of decision making is one important reason for enhancing learning and knowledge development in Japanese organizations (Aoki 1993). Theories of Japanese work organization argue that this level of firm-specific knowledge and skills can only be acquired through a long process of on-the-job training buttressed by periodic off-the-job learning, with the acquisition process driven by the system of skill-based assessment (Aoki 1993; Koike 1988). To the extent that Japanese organizations continue to take advantage of employees' information participation, changes in the two principles of Japanese ILMs are constrained.

Summary

Summarizing the arguments presented in this section, Japanese employers face pressures to reduce the cost of and introduce flexibility in their internalized white-collar HRM practices, namely because of (1) lower productivity and lack of performance measurement for white-collar employees, (2) increases in middle management ranks, (3) slow growth and the heightened sensitivity to profit performance, and (4) changing management values emphasizing performance over skill development. In contrast, constraints placed on Japanese employers are strong white-collar employment security and work organization.

Thus, the predicted changes in Japanese white-collar employment practices, given these pressures and constraints are twofold:

1. Of the two rules of Japanese ILMs, the rule regarding assessment and reward (*nenko* assessment) will be more likely to be modified.
2. With regard to long-term employment and internal training, employers will devise a way to maintain the benefits of internalized employment practices, while reducing the fixed cost associated with internalized practices. Employers are most likely to reduce the size of permanent employment and put more employees on a contingent status.

CHANGES IN JAPANESE WHITE-COLLAR HRM

Can the changes predicted in the previous section be found in Japanese white-collar HRM? In this section, the predicted changes are examined by use of anecdotal and interview evidence on the experience of several firms.

Introduction of Pay- and Promotion-for-Performance

There is currently an increasing move toward more performance-based appraisal practices for white-collar employees. This move is most visible in the compensation arrangements for middle and senior managers, although a number of firms have also tried to introduce management-by-objectives (MBO) for their non-managerial white-collar employees.

For example, Fujitsu, the second largest computer manufacturer in the world, put all of its 6,000 middle and senior managers on strict MBO compensation as of

April 1, 1993, where up to 30 percent of their annual pay could be variable depending on their performance assessment. Fujitsu is planning to introduce MBO-style compensation to its non-managerial white-collar administrative work-force and computer hardware and software engineering employees within the next year. At Hino Truck Manufacturing, MBO-type compensation is being introduced for all its 200 managers, whose annual pay may vary up to 50 percent depending on their performance.

All Nippon Airways (ANA), Japan's second largest passenger carrier, went even further and put all of its 6,800 white-collar administrative and technical employees on MBO, including those not in management positions. The uniqueness of ANA's MBO practice, however, is that, for white-collar employees with relatively short tenure (less than nine years), skill development goals are specifically designed into the goal setting process. In this sense, for junior employees, ANA's model represents a transitional model from the skill-grade scheme to more performance-oriented practices.

According to a 1993 RECRUIT survey ($N = 319$), 46.4 percent of large firms (defined as employment > 1,000) reported using some type of MBO practice, while 67.5 percent of larger firms (employment > 3,000; $N = 123$) reported using such practices (RECRUIT 1993). A JPC survey conducted in 1993 indicates that, of firms using MBO practices for managers, 10.1 percent determine all managerial pay changes (increases and decreases) on the basis of goal attainment (JPC 1994). Given that this practice was not even discussed in a 1987 MOL survey, this figure must be considered substantial.

Similarly, another practice is that junior employees with short tenure (usually within the first five years) are assigned to managerial or supervisory positions on the basis of potential and performance (Hanada 1987; Nonaka 1988). Consequently, status differentiation is created in the early years, sometimes even leading to inversion of firm tenure and rank (i.e., superiors having shorter firm tenure than subordinates). This practice contrasts with what many observers had noted in Japanese organizations: that formal status differentiation among junior employees in the same cohort (defined by year of entry, education, occupation, and gender) occurred only after seven to 10 years of *nenko*-tied, largely simultaneous advancement (Clark 1979).

Two surveys conducted in different years suggest that the timing at which firms introduce status differentiation may be moving toward earlier stages of white-collar employees' careers. In a MOL survey conducted in 1987, more than 20 percent reported introducing multiple careers with different pay and promotion levels after 10 years, and more than 40 percent between five and 10 years. In a Japan Institute of Labour (JIL) survey conducted in 1993, the proportion of firms that introduced differentiation after 10 years dropped to 7.6 percent and between five and 10 years to 33.1%. In this survey, the largest proportion of firms (46.3 percent) reported three years as the hallmark year for introducing status differentiation (JIL 1993).

Use of Externalized Employment Arrangements

Employment externalization has been proceeding in a similar manner in Japan (Morishima 1995b) as has been the case in the United States (Pfeffer and Baron 1988) and other countries (Thurman and Trah 1990). Given the existence of strong employment security and the proven benefits of internalized employment practices, however, when Japanese firms attempt to increase employment flexibility and control labor cost, their choice has often been limited to creating multiple contractual arrangements within the firm workforce, all designed to introduce segments of the firm workforce that have weaker employment protection than previously assumed for regular-status workers (Nihon Keizai Shimbunsha 1993). In particular, Japanese firms have begun to externalize their employment not only through the use of part-timers and temporaries but also by hiring limited-contract employees[4] and sorting employees (based on performance and potential) into segments with different levels of employment security. Through the increased use of contingent employees (part-timers and temporaries) and employees with weaker employment security, firms pursue the goals of cost control and deployment flexibility, while expecting other outcomes such as skill enhancement and commitment maximization from their permanent, regular-status workers (Morishima 1995a).

For example, Nitto Denko, a manufacturer of industrial equipment, announced in June 1993 that it will sort its white-collar employees, after four years of tenure, into those who will advance in some specialty and those who will advance in general management. At Sumitomo Rubber, new recruits are expected to be designated at the time of hiring to one of two career tracks similar to those used at Nitto Denko on the basis of management judgement and employee preference. In Japanese firms, specialist positions have usually carried weaker employment protection than those making progress through the management hierarchy. In both cases, firms' intention is to identify those who will have weaker employment security very early in their tenure.[5]

Simultaneously, many firms have started to engage in a variety of activities to remove senior members from their white-collar workforce permanently, thus departing from their previous paternalistic practice of transferring senior employees out of the parent firm but locating for them employment in a related firm (i.e., *shukko*; see Sato 1994). Programs used to remove senior employees range from early voluntary retirement to aggressive career counseling[6] (Sato 1994). Thanks to corporate efforts to introduce flexibility into their white-collar employment practices, Japanese white-collar employment now shows a much wider variety of "shades" from the strongly protected to the only weakly protected.[7]

QUANTITATIVE EVALUATION OF EMERGING HRM POLICIES

Interview and anecdotal evidence indicates that Japanese employers have begun to introduce performance-based pay and promotion practices as an important component of their white-collar HRM system and, to a lesser degree, introduce changes in long-term employment practices. In this section, a recent large-scale survey is used to examine the nature of changes in Japanese white-collar HRM practices. Three questions are investigated.

First, is it possible to identify clusters of firms with different degrees of divergence in HRM policies and practices from the traditional pattern? Second, as evidence of the relationship between firms' HRM policies and their actual practices, is actual adoption of performance-based and externalization practices related to firms' HRM policies? Third, given the discussion presented earlier on the pressures and constraints of HRM change, can we identify the factors that influence the degree to which firms pursue these alternative HRM policies?

The Survey

The data on which the following analyses are based come from a survey which a private management consulting firm conducted under contract with the Japanese Ministry of Labour. The author participated as one of the project members upon the the consulting firm's request.

A sample was drawn from a data file retained by the consulting firm for the purpose of corporate rating. An advantage of using this data base was the availability of financial performance measures which were used in explaining firms' HRM policies. Another advantage was that the file included firms that were not listed on stock exchanges in addition to those listed. The sampling allowed the researchers to examine HRM policies of medium-sized firms whose employment sizes range between 100 and 1,000. The minimum size of firm employment for inclusion was 100 regular-status employees.

The original data file contained approximately 6,000 firms in various industries. To increase homogeneity in industry characteristics, two samples were drawn, one containing firms in manufacturing and the other in service (retail and wholesale). Since Japanese HRM policies and practices tend to be determined at the corporate level and uniformly applied throughout the entire white-collar workforce, the sampling unit was determined to be the firm as opposed to establishments. Moreover, this practice allowed the matching of questionnaire data to corporate financial data.

Initially, 3,788 firms were selected using the criteria described above. Questionnaires were sent to all of these firms in February 1994. After one telephone follow-up, a total of 1,618 firms returned usable questionnaires, producing a response rate of 42.7 percent. Questionnaires were sent to the top HRM officer of each firm, who was asked to fill out the questionnaire or forward it to the person he/she deemed appropriate. Because of the centralization of white-collar HRM activities in Japanese firms (Morishima 1995a), it was considered that corporate HRM staff were knowledgeable about not only HRM policies but also practices at the workplace level. Interviews conducted prior to questionnaire construction also showed that corporate staff had strong control over white-collar HRM practices at the workplace level. In addition to HRM policies and practices, the survey instrument contained questions on such firm characteristics as workforce composition by gender and occupation, regular-status employee turnover rate, unionization, and subjective measures of performance relative to competitors. A measure of management values was also available.

Measures of HRM Policies

Based on interviews conducted by the researcher with more than 30 firms and a review of previous large scale sample surveys (e.g., MOL 1987; RECRUIT 1993), the eight questions listed in the appendix were created to measure the two dimensions of HRM policies along which changes are expected to be occurring: competitive performance-based appraisal and employment externalization. In the questionnaire, the eight HRM policy questions were posed as polar items (traditional and emerging), and the respondents were asked to indicate how close their firms' HRM policies were to each end. The measure was a four-point scale, with higher points indicating closeness to emerging patterns. A factor analysis with varimax rotation bore out the expected two-factor structure of the eight items (see the appendix).

The first dimension, called competitive appraisal, refers to the degree to which firms' HRM policies diverge from the previous practice of assessing and rewarding employees on the basis of ability progression to a more competitive appraisal policy based mainly on performance. The first two questions highly loaded on this factor directly refer to this dimension. The remaining two questions converged on this factor were derived from the interviews conducted by the author. First, interviews made it clear that firms that are attempting to introduce more competitive performance-based appraisal policies were also required to move from structuring pay hierarchy on the basis of employees' career stages to compensation based on the hierarchy of jobs. Under the previous policy, expectations regarding one's ability ranking were formulated on the basis of his/her career stage. "What the person should have learned by the Nth year in the company" was the criterion of employee appraisal. In the new practice, performance expectations were formulated by comparing his/her outputs to the expected outcomes in a job. Thus, job content becomes the basis for pay hierarchy. Second, interviews showed that those companies that shifted to competitive appraisal also considered employees' careers as individualized, with individuals progressing at different speeds and in different directions.

The second dimension of HRM policies was employment externalization. The first three questions converged on this factor are straightforward. They all tap on different actions taken by Japanese firms to externalize employment and introduce flexibility in their regular-status white-collar workforce. Hiring mid-career employees with work experience departs from the previous practice of hiring fresh school graduates and increases firms' staffing flexibility. Interviews revealed that the fourth item in this set also related to employment externalization since more specialized training indicates that firms no longer consider the firm white-collar ILM as one large labor market within which employees are trained to perform a broad segment of jobs (see Morishima 1995a for more details on this point). Specialized training is a move toward accepting a more segmented internal labor market within the firm labor force, with each segment being associated with different degrees of employment security and externalization.

Clustering of Firms Based on HRM Policies

As the next step to identify firms which pursue alternative HRM polices, the two scale scores derived from the two HRM policy factors in the appendix were subjected to cluster analysis. (For cluster analyses, the four items highly loaded on each factor were averaged to produce scale scores. Every firm, thus, obtained one scale score for the competitive appraisal factor and another other for the employment externalization factor.[8]) The theoretical rationale for deriving these clusters was that firms develop their HRM systems by combining HRM policies (Butler, Ferris, and Napier 1991; Schuler 1987). The purpose of this analysis was to identify clusters of firms that used some combination of the two HRM policies.[9]

After several tries, the analysis yielded a three-cluster solution. Figure 1 shows the plotting of the two HRM policy scale means; Table 3 shows the highlights of the HRM systems of the firms in the three clusters. In Figure 1, higher scores on the HRM policy variables (which are on four-point scales) indicate stronger emphasis on emerging policies (i.e., higher externalization and higher performance-based appraisal). Relative to the overall mean of the two scales, Cluster 1, which included 57 percent ($N = 919$) of the sample, is characterized by slightly lower levels of both externalization and competitiveness in appraisal. However, the deviations from the mean of the total sample were modest. Cluster 1 represents firms that follow relatively "traditional" patterns of high employment security and assessment based on *nenko* and will be called the "Traditional HRM" cluster. Cluster 1 will be used as the referent category in the following analyses.

Cluster 2 (32%) has firms that are high on competitive appraisal but do not appear to emphasize externalization. This cluster is called the "Competitive Appraisal HRM" cluster. Cluster 3 (11%) includes firms that are high on both externalization and competitive appraisal and is called the "Transformed HRM" cluster. This cluster includes firms that are the most deviant from the traditional patterns of Japanese white-collar HRM. While the relative proportion of the firms is by no means nationally representative, these results, which indicate that a relatively small number of firms have adopted externalization policies as opposed to making their employee assessment and reward policies more competitive, are consistent with previous surveys on changes in Japanese HRM. For example, data presented earlier in Table 2 showed that Japanese firms are more likely to change their

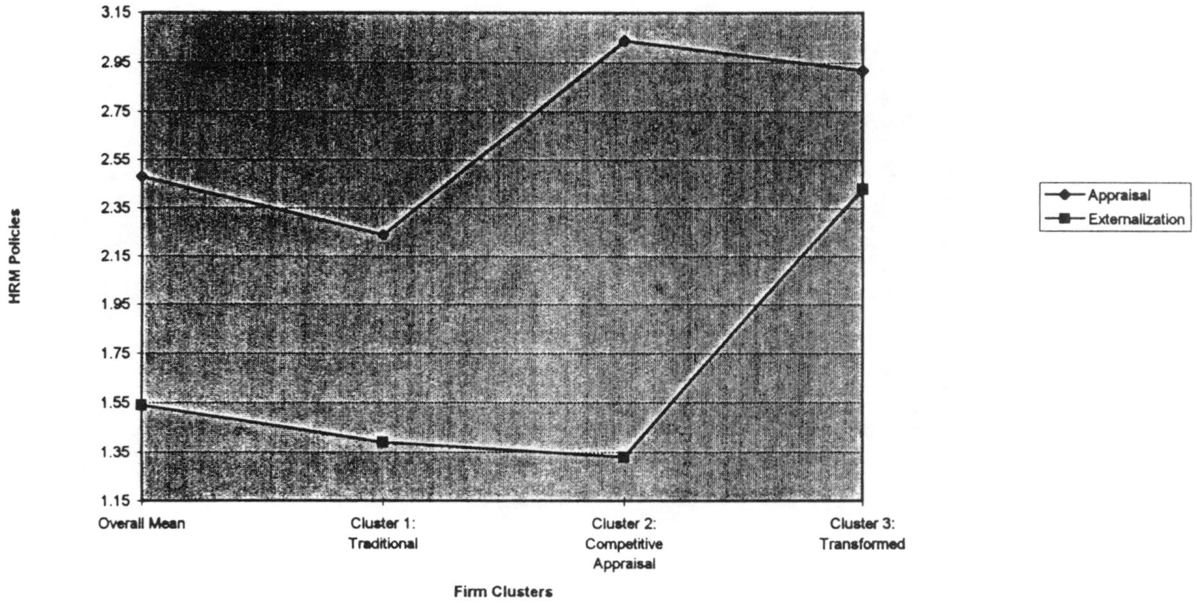

	Appraisal	Externalization	N
Overall Mean	2.48	1.54	1,618
Cluster 1: Traditional	2.24	1.39	919
Cluster 2: Competitive Appraisal	3.04	1.33	524
Cluster 3: Transformed	2.92	2.43	175

Note: Higher scores indicate divergence from traditional patterns.

Figure 1. HRM Policy Means

160

Table 3.   HR Policy Characteristics of Firms in the Three Clusters

Firm Cluster Based on HRM Policies	Description of HR Policies	% of Firms in Cluster (N=1,618)
1. Traditional HRM	Long-term employment and *nenko*-based appraisal and reward	56.8%
2. Competitive Appraisal HRM	Long-term employment and competitive performance-based appraisal and reward	32.4%
3. Transformed HRM	Employment externalization and competitive performance-based appraisal and reward	10.8%

assessment and reward policies than to change their employment structure. Thus, it is reasonable to expect that transformed HRM (Cluster 3) represents a small minority of firms that have instituted wholesale restructuring of their HRM systems.

One other observation about Figure 1 is that the analysis did not produce a cluster that has high externalization and low competitiveness (i.e., the opposite of Cluster 3), leading to a speculation that when Japanese firms attempt to change their HRM policies they start with those relating to appraisal and reward. This observation is consistent with previous findings that Japanese long-term employment in principle has remarkable resilience to downturns in economic conditions (Dore 1989). Also in Figure 1, the means for the three clusters and the entire sample are generally higher for changes toward competitive appraisal than externalization (although since these scores are not on absolute scales, these comparisons are not entirely reliable).

RELATIONSHIPS BETWEEN FIRM CLUSTERS AND HRM PRACTICES

The next question is whether these firm clusters are related to firms' adoption of specific HRM practices that characterize firms' HRM policies. Since these clusters represent groups of firms with different combinations of HRM policies, their use of specific HRM practices might be in part determined by their cluster affiliation. Although it is not possible to expect a perfect matching of policies and practices, since adoption of practices tends to be influenced by institutional and other factors that are not directly related to firms' HRM policy positions, we may expect to find correlations between firm clusters and selected practices that are most representative of the two policies that serve as the basis for firms' HRM clustering.

Eight specific practices were chosen with which to examine the predicted relationship between firm clusters and HRM practices. For the competitive appraisal policy, use of management-by-objectives (MBO) for white-collar workers, use of individual incentive bonuses, creation of fast promotion tracks, and early selection of managerial candidates were chosen. These four practices are often described in previous literature as representing a move toward more competitive, performance-based appraisal practices (RECRUIT 1993).

For the externalization policy, increases in the use of part-timers and temporaries, use of limited-term contract employees, early retirement programs, and use of outplacement services were examined as sample practices. Since part-timers and temporaries have always been used by Japanese firms (Morishima 1995b), the "increase in their use" was the question posed to respondents. Similarly, early retirement programs have also been used in previous recessions in Japan (Rohlen 1979). However, early retirement programs were relatively rare in the 1980s when the economy was strong. Thus, no qualification was introduced for this item. The other two practices are relative newcomers to Japanese firms' externalization practices (RECRUIT 1993). In all cases, respondents were asked to indicate whether a specific practice was applied to regular-status white-collar workers.

Table 4 shows the results of a cross-tabulation between firms' clusters and adoption of HRM practices. Since the data do not control for a number of factors that might influence firms' adoption of specific HRM practices (e.g., unionization, workforce demographics, etc.), the relationships between clusters and adoption rates are not particularly strong. However, two patterns emerge from this table which seem to suggest that these firm clusters might be related to their HRM practices.

First, the competitive appraisal and transformed HRM clusters, both of which have relatively high scores on this dimension, have slightly higher adoption rates for most competitive appraisal practices than the overall mean.[10] Stronger supporting evidence for the prediction is found in the creation of fast promotion tracks, which is more frequent both in the competitive appraisal HRM and transformed HRM clusters than the overall mean. Similarly, transformed HRM has much higher adoption rates for management-by-objectives and early selection practices than the overall mean. In both cases, however, adoption rates for competitive appraisal HRM are similar to or lower than the overall rate, which indicates that, while firms in this cluster have a policy of competitive appraisal, they are slow to institute specific practices that support this policy. One reason, as argued by Nihon Keizai Shimbunsha (1993), may be that a firm needs to have a relatively active outflow of human resources to support competitive appraisal policy. Otherwise, individuals who lose out in the competition may be stuck within the firm, burdening the firm with lower-caliber and presumably demotivated workers. Thus, firms might need to have intentions to institute *both* policies to adopt competitive appraisal practices, a pattern shown by firms in the transformed HRM cluster.

Second, stronger evidence of the relationship between cluster affiliation and HRM practice adoption comes from externalization practices. Specifically, for all four practices, the adoption rate is highest for transformed HRM, the only cluster with a relatively high mean score for the externalization policy. Thus, although

Table 4. Relationships between Firm Clusters and Selected HRM Practices

HRM Practice	Overall Adoption Rate	Adoption Rate for		Chi-Square
		Transformed HRM	Competitive Appraisal HRM	
Competitive Appraisal				
Use of Management–by–objectives	61.3%	90.0%	61.6%	83.44***
Use of Individual Incentive Bonus	79.6%	81.6%	81.2%	3.17
Creation of Fast Promotion Track	54.5%	65.3%	61.9%	50.45***
Early Selection of Managerial Candidates	31.7%	47.7%	21.9%	144.41***
Employment Externalization				
Increased Use of Part-Timers and Temporaries	71.4%	78.6%	63.7%	30.87***
Use of Limited–Term Contract Employees	21.9%	72.1%	21.7%	301.59***
Early Retirement Programs	52.7%	64.7%	34.2%	153.65***
Use of Outplacement Services	39.8%	59.5%	31.9%	49.85***

weak, there is a predictable relationship between firms' adoption rate and their cluster affiliation.

CORRELATES OF EMERGING HRM POLICIES AND FIRM CLUSTERS

The next step is to understand why these new HRM policies are being adopted by some Japanese firms and not by others. In this section, two sets of analyses are presented. The first analysis regressed the two HRM policy scales (used in the cluster analysis) on the independent variables using OLS. Second, binomial logit models were estimated to test the effects of independent variables on the probability that a given firm belongs to the competitive appraisal HRM cluster (Cluster 2) over the traditional HRM cluster (Cluster 1), or the transformed HRM cluster (Cluster 3) over the traditional HRM cluster (Cluster 1), respectively. Cluster 1 was used as the reference category because it contains firms that most closely follow the traditional patterns of long-term employment security and *nenko* appraisal.

The independent variables are intended to test many of the explanations that have been offered as determinants of emerging HRM policies. Consistent with the review in an earlier section of this paper, three categories of explanatory variables are examined: (1) demographic, (2) firm performance and (3) institutional.

Workforce Demographics

As noted earlier, one of the reasons offered for firms adopting externalization and competitive appraisal practices involves the characteristics of firms' workforce demographics. In particular, a high average age of white-collar employees and a large proportion of administrative employees (in the pool that includes other types of white-collar employees such as engineers and specialists) are often cited as prime reasons for firms to attempt to change their HRM policies (Kawakita 1993a; RECRUIT 1993). High average age usually translates into high labor costs due to the concentration of employees in expensive pay categories, while a high proportion of administrative employees indicates that a firm has large overhead costs. Since the productivity of these administrative employees is questionable at best (Hori 1993), firms are likely to externalize these employees and/or boost their productivity through competitive appraisal. In addition, the level of turnover among white-collar regular-status employees was considered. While this factor has not been extensively considered in previous literature, it might be expected that firms that are experiencing high turnover may not perceive the need to introduce flexibility into their employment arrangement through externalization. Thus, turnover is expected to have a negative association with the degree of externalization.

Firm Performance

In any type of change in HRM policies, factors associated with firms' performance are critical (Osterman 1994). In particular, since the current calls for change in Japanese employment practices are strongly motivated by low white-collar productivity and heightened sensitivity to profit levels (made worse in the recent recession that Japanese firms have been experiencing since 1991 or the last year of the so-called prosperous "bubble" period), factors related to productivity and profitability are important. In this study, three performance measures were included to explain firms' adoption of emerging HRM policies. First, productivity changes between 1991 and 1993 were calculated. The productivity measure used here was gross sales per employee obtained from firms' financial statements, with the 1991 value subtracted from the 1993 value.[11] Second, profit change was measured in a similar way as the difference between 1991 and 1993. The profit measure used here was approximate due to the lack of market-based measures for those firms whose stocks are not traded on the exchanges. Firms' total profits in a given year over capital in the same year was used as the measure. As expected, descriptive statistics shown in Table 5 indicate that on average sample firms have experienced declines both in productivity and profits.

Finally, one perceptual measure of firm performance was taken from the questionnaire. In this question, respondents were asked to indicate whether their firms' performance was: (5) much higher, (4) somewhat higher, (3) about the same, (2) somewhat lower, or (1) much lower than the companies which they consider as competitors. In general, firms that were experiencing declines in performance were expected to adopt emerging HRM policies.

Institutional Characteristics

The five independent variables included in this set are institutional and technological characteristics of the firm as well as management's value orientation. These factors act as both pressures for and constraints on change. First, unionization was expected to have negative effects on the adoption of new policies, since unions are likely to resist changes because of the potential impact on their membership. Historical evidence suggests that Japanese unions have played an important role in shaping the current HRM system in Japan, especially by emphasizing employment security for core workers (Morishima 1995a). Thus, unions are likely to resist changes that may reshape the negotiated order, in particular when they threaten members' employment security.

Second, the expected effects associated with whether a firm is a manufacturing organization (as opposed to retail and wholesale) are ambiguous. Previous literature suggests that, on one hand, firms in the service industry are more likely to adopt externalization and competitive appraisal policies because of high industry competition, lack of institutional resistance from blue-collar HRM which is

Table 5. Variable Definitions and Basic Statistics

Variable	Definition	Mean (S.D.)
Competitive Appraisal	Average of Four Items in Factor 1 from Appendix (4-point scale)	2.48 (0.42)
Employment Externalization	Average of Four Items in Factor 2 from Appendix (4-point scale)	1.54 (0.42)
Avg. Age of Employees	Average Age of White-Collar Employees	36.59 years (3.22)
% of Admin. Employees	Percentage of Administrative Staff Within the White-Collar Workforce	22.40% (13.36)
Annual Turnover	Annual Turnover of Regular-Status Employees (*Seishain*)	4.89% (1.87)
Change in Productivity	Change in Sales per Employee from 1991 to 1993 (million yen)	−18.89 million yen (69.85)
Change in Profitability	Change in Gross Profits per Unit of Capital from 1991 to 1993	−4.40 (18.12)
Relative Performance	Perceptual Measure of Performance Relative to Competitors (5-point scale; higher scores indicate better performance.)	2.80 (1.11)
Union Dummy	1 = Union is Present 0 = No Union	0.86 (0.34)
Manufacturing Dummy	1 = Manufacturing; 0 = Retail and Wholesale	0.56 (0.50)
Size Dummy 1	1 = Firm Has 100-300 Employees	0.08 (0.26)
Size Dummy 2	1 = Firm Has 301-1000 Employees	0.19 (0.39)
Capital/Labor	Gross Total of Property, Plant, and Equipment per Employee	1.35 million yen (6.33)
Mgt. Value	Management Value Emphasizing Profits over Employee Well-Being (4-point scale; higher scores indicate emphasis on profits.)	2.85 (0.55)

heavily dominated by traditional Japanese HRM patterns, and employees seeking more competitive appraisal and flexible employment patterns (MOL 1987). More-over, manufacturing firms have been more likely to take advantage of information participation by their employees (Aoki 1993; Koike 1988); constraints imposed by the type of work organization may be stronger in the manufacturing sector. On the other hand, manufacturing firms which have been harder hit by the recent recession and the stronger yen might be more likely to adopt emerging HRM policies.

Third, another variable with ambiguous predictions was capital-labor ratio, here defined as total property, plant, and equipment assets over the size of employment. On one hand, more capital-intensive firms are less likely to see the need for changes because of the relatively low contribution that human resources make to performance. These firms may be the ones that have long engaged in labor to capital substitution, thus removing the constraints imposed by work organization and technology. On the other hand, because of the low importance of human resources, these firms may be quicker to abandon traditional HRM policies that are designed to provide firms with a large supply of highly-skilled and committed employees (Morishima 1995a).

Fourth, the size of the firm is also expected to have effects. It was expected that, since traditional patterns of Japanese employment and HRM arrangements were initially created in the large-firm sector, smaller firms would be quicker to depart from the large-firm sector norm. Thus, pressures for conformity and the quest for legitimacy may lead to a stronger tendency to maintain traditional HRM patterns in the large-firm sector. Also, smaller firms are more likely to experience competition and feel the effects of the recession due to the lack of slack resources. In this study, two size dummies were created: one representing firms that employ 100 to 300 employees and the other representing firms with employment size of 301 to 1,000. Firms with employment larger than 1,000 were used as the reference category.

Fifth, management's value with regard to the tradeoff between company profits and employee well-being was also adopted from the questionnaire data. In this item, respondents were asked to locate the firms' position on a four-point scale which ranges from "emphasizing employee well-being over company profits" to "emphasizing company profits over employee well-being."[12] It was expected that firms that emphasize company profits were more likely to adopt externalization and competitive appraisal policies.

Results

Results of the OLS and logit analyses are presented in Tables 6 and 7. Table 6 shows the coefficients for the OLS estimation regarding the two HRM policies, and Table 7 shows the logit results on the probability that a firm is in competitive appraisal HRM or transformed HRM, respectively, over traditional HRM. For the analyses shown in Table 6, the competitive appraisal and employment externalization scores created for the cluster analyses were used as dependent variables. I assumed that these two scales represented the degree to which firms adopted these two HRM policies and treated the scales as continuous variables.

For the analyses presented in Table 7, the dependent measures were dichotomous variables representing one of the two nontraditional clusters (1 = competitive appraisal HRM or Transformed HRM) versus the traditional cluster (0 = traditional HRM). The first column shows the results of the logit analysis examin-

Table 6.   OLS Results for HRM Policies[a] (Standard Errors in Parentheses)

Variables	Competitive Appraisal (Mean = 2.48)[b]	Employment Externalization (Mean = 1.54)[b]
Intercept	3.843***	1.060***
	(0.143)	(0.102)
Avg. Age of	0.025***	0.002
Employees	(0.003)	(0.002)
% of Admin.	0.003***	0.005***
Employees	(0.0008)	(0.0006)
Log of Annual	0.119	−0.103***
Turnover	(0.018)	(0.013)
Change in	−0.0004**	−0.002***
Productivity	(0.0002)	(0.0001)
Change in	−0.005***	−0.002***
Profitability	(0.0005)	(0.0004)
Relative	0.029***	−0.009
Performance	(0.009)	(0.007)
Union Dummy	−0.105***	−0.237***
	(0.034)	(0.024)
Manufacturing	0.014	−0.143***
Dummy	(0.025)	(0.017)
Size Dummy 1	0.257***	0.483***
	(0.045)	(0.032)
Size Dummy 2	−0.047	0.182***
	(0.029)	(0.021)
Capital/Labor	0.009***	−0.0004
	(0.002)	(0.001)
Mgt. Value	0.184***	0.262***
(Emphasize Profits)	(0.019)	(0.014)
R^2	.200	.609
F	32.839***	205.199***
N	1,594	1,594

Notes: *.05 < p < .10; ** .01 < p < .05; *** p < .01.
   a. Dependent variables are two HRM policy scales computed as averages of the items in the two
       factors shown in the appendix. The scales were assumed to be continuous and analyzed by OLS.
   b. Means are based on a four-point scale.

ing the probability of a firm being in competitive appraisal HRM over traditional HRM, and the second column examines the probability of a firm being in transformed HRM over traditional HRM. Firms in transformed HRM and in competitive appraisal HRM were excluded in the analyses shown in the first and second columns, respectively. Using subsamples with only two possible choices permitted direct comparisons of competitive appraisal HRM against traditional HRM, and transformed HRM against traditional HRM, and more straightforward interpretations of the coefficients.[13]

Table 7.   Bivariate Logit Results for Firm Cluster Affiliation

Variables	Competitive Appraisal HRM over Traditional HRM		Transformed HRM over Traditional HRM	
	Logit Coeff. (S.E.)	Marginal Effect[a]	Logit Coeff. (S.E.)	Marginal Effect[a]
Intercept	−9.991*** (1.034)		2.517 (2.520)	
Avg. Age of Employees	0.179*** (0.025)	0.041	0.165*** (0.061)	0.022
% of Admin. Employees	0.042*** (0.007)	0.010	0.036*** (0.011)	0.005
Log of Annual Turnover	0.232** (0.135)	0.054	−0.935*** (0.305)	−0.126
Change in Productivity	−0.055*** (0.005)	−0.013	−0.019*** (0.0005)	−0.003
Change in Profitability	−0.060*** (0.008)	−0.014	−0.029 (0.039)	−0.004
Relative Performance	0.264*** (0.070)	0.061	0.068 (0.198)	0.023
Union Dummy	−0.438 (0.284)	0.101	−0.788** (0.368)	−0.106
Manufacturing Dummy	−0.716*** (0.191)	−0.166	−0.837** (0.405)	−0.112
Size Dummy 1	0.798* (0.466)	0.184	2.572*** (0.495)	0.346
Size Dummy 2	0.764*** (0.225)	0.177	0.612 (0.478)	0.082
Capital/Labor	1.056*** (0.170)	0.244	2.213*** (0.053)	0.297
Mgt. Value (Emphasize Profits)	1.462*** (0.155)	0.338	2.067*** (0.435)	0.278
−2 Log L	1400.787		470.19	
N	1,443		1,094	

Notes: *.05 $< p <$ .10; ** .01 $< p <$ .05; *** $p <$ .01.
   a. Changes in probability of being in Competitive Appraisal HRM or Transformed HRM over Traditional HRM.

Several conclusions may be drawn directly from these results which are generally robust across different types of analyses. First, both average age of the white-collar workforce and percent of administrative employees are generally associated with adoption of emerging HRM policies as well as with a firm being in a cluster other than the traditional HRM cluster, the referent category representing traditional HRM patterns. A one year increase in the average age of the white-collar workforce is associated with 4.1 percent and 2.2 percent increases in the probability that a firm is in the competitive appraisal HRM and Transformed HRM clusters, respectively. Similarly, a 5 percent increase in the proportion of administrative employees is associated with 5.0 percent and 2.5 percent increases in the same probabilities. These findings are consistent with previous arguments that firms with a heavy labor cost burden due to an older workforce and a bloated white-collar administrative workforce tend to be motivated to change their HRM policies and practices (Kawakita 1993b). One exception to this observation is that average age of the white-collar workforce was not significantly associated with the degree to which firms externalize their employment.

The third demographic variable, employee turnover, is as predicted negatively associated with externalization. In addition, it is positively associated with the probability that a firm is in competitive appraisal HRM and negatively with the probability that a firm is in transformed HRM. The difference between the competitive appraisal and transformed HRM clusters is that externalization policy appears to be much more advanced in transformed HRM (see Figure 1).

The second conclusion is that both firm performance variables are associated with HRM policies and firm clustering. Specifically, since change variables were measured as 1993 minus 1991, the larger the decline in 1993 relative to 1991, the more likely firms have adopted emerging HRM policies and also belong to competitive appraisal HRM or transformed HRM. Change in profitability was not significantly associated with the probability that a firm is in transformed HRM in logit analyses, indicating that firms in this cluster may not have been reacting to declining profits. Productivity declines appear to be stronger determinants of HRM shifts.

In contrast, the perceptual measure of performance (relative to the firms that the firms themselves consider as competitors) showed modest effects. It was associated positively with the degree to which a firm has a competitive appraisal policy and the probability of a firm being in competitive appraisal HRM over traditional HRM.

Third, among the institutional factors, unionized and manufacturing organizations, respectively appear to be associated with more traditional patterns of HRM policies. That manufacturing firms have lower levels of emerging HRM policies and lower probabilities of belonging to competitive appraisal HRM or transformed HRM indicates that while manufacturing has been severely hit by the current recession, it is still the firms in the service industry that have taken the lead in adopting emerging HRM policies. Manufacturing firms are approximately 11 percent to 17 percent less likely to be in transformed HRM or competitive appraisal HRM over traditional HRM, *ceteris paribus*. Manufacturing organizations' slow response may be in part due to the existence of blue-collar HRM that is strongly grounded in traditional Japanese HRM (Morishima 1995a). Since it has been common for Japanese firms to apply similar HRM techniques to both blue- and white-collar workforces (Koike 1988), HRM changes may be more difficult in manufacturing than in service organizations where blue-collar workforces do not exist. It may also be due to the institutional pressures for conformity and legitimation, given the prevalence and success of the traditional HRM practices in the manufacturing industry.

Similarly, union effects indicate that unions generally act as a deterrent to management efforts to diverge from traditional patterns of employment. Specifically, since the union dummies show significant relationships to the probability that a firm is in the transformed HRM cluster but not in competitive appraisal HRM, the coefficients suggest that unions are less likely to resist changes in appraisal and reward practices than employment security policies. The findings are consistent with Japanese unions' historical emphasis on employment security for their core workers (Morishima 1995a).

As predicted, smaller size firms generally had higher degrees of competitive appraisal and externalization policies as well as higher probabilities of being in competitive appraisal HRM and transformed HRM over traditional HRM. For the comparison between transformed HRM and traditional HRM, the probability that a firm is in the transformed HRM cluster is almost 35 percent higher in the smallest firm-size category, relative to the large-firm sector. An exception to this statement is that mid-sized firms (employment of 301 to 1,000) were not significantly more likely to have competitive appraisal policies or to be in transformed HRM over traditional HRM. Thus, firm size effects tend to be more pronounced among firms with smaller employment size (employment ≤ 300).

Capital intensity, when significant, was associated with higher degrees of competitive appraisal and higher probabilities of firms being in competitive HRM and transformed HRM. Capital intensive firms, which rely less on skilled and committed individuals than labor intensive firms, may be in a better position to depart from traditional patterns of Japanese HRM. These firms may have been substituting capital for labor, thus removing the constraints imposed by work organization and technology.

Finally, management values were strongly associated with a firm's adoption of the competitive appraisal policy, the externalization policy, and the probabilities that a firm is in competitive appraisal HRM or transformed HRM. These effects are substantial since a one point increase on a four-point scale changes the probability that a firm is in competitive appraisal HRM or transformed HRM by 34 percent or 28 percent, respectively. These findings reinforce the importance of management values in the determination of HRM policies and practices and are strongly consistent with previous research (Osterman 1994). Independent of firm performance variables and institutional factors, employers who place relative emphasis on employee well-being (over company profits) are less likely to depart from traditional patterns of Japanese white-collar HRM.

CONCLUSIONS

Through the use of anecdotal evidence, interviews conducted by the author, and quantitative analyses of a firm-level data set, this study has attempted to document the evolution of Japanese white-collar HRM. Specifically, three findings are most important. First, the evolution is occurring along the two key dimensions of Japanese HRM: long-term employment security and *nenko*-based appraisal. With regard to long-term employment security, the policy itself is not being abandoned, but due to the labor cost implications of this policy in these times of an aging workforce and slower firm growth, Japanese firms are devising a variety of ways to work around the constraints imposed by long-term security. Various attempts to externalize segments of their workforce are under way.

In contrast, stronger changes are occurring regarding *nenko* practices in that firms have started to introduce a more performance-based assessment policy as well as to treat employees' careers as individualized with differentials in career attainment being created according to their performance records. The current quantitative evidence suggests that this category of change is much more pervasive than the externalization practices (see Figure 1).

The second conclusion is that, while Japanese HRM might be changing, not all firms are uniformly moving in the same direction. Rather, firms appear to be adopting alternative combinations of these emerging policies in formulating their HRM systems. In particular, a cluster analysis indicated that firms might be classified into three groups: the traditional HRM cluster which still maintains "traditional" patterns of employment security and *nenko*-based policies, the competitive appraisal HRM cluster which maintains employment security for the regular-status workers but emphasizes performance-based assessment and individualized careers, and the transformed HRM cluster which has deviated from the traditional pattern the most with strong competitive appraisal as well as externalization policies. These firm clusters, which are based on combinations of HRM policies, were related to the adoption of specific HRM practices representing competitive appraisal and externalization.

The third conclusion is that the differences among firms in HRM policies and the probabilities of their cluster affiliation could be predicted in a rather straightforward way by firms' workforce demographics, performance conditions, and various characteristics of the firm itself. In particular, firms that have larger labor cost burdens due to high average age and a high proportion of administrative employees are more likely to have adopted emerging HRM policies. Firms whose financial performance is declining, as measured by productivity and profit changes, tend to adopt emerging policies. Finally, institutional factors such as unionization and management values which emphasize company profits over employee well-being are also associated with emerging HRM policies. Unionized firms and firms whose management stresses employee well-being over profits are less likely to have diverged from the traditional pattern of HRM.

Theoretically, the evidence presented in this paper shows that, although Japanese firms still maintain highly structured internal labor markets (though weakening), the rules by which pay and promotions are assigned to individual employees have shifted from the previous reliance on *nenko* practices. In the language of the internal labor market literature, changes in administrative rules and procedures represent the emergence of an alternative internal labor market arrangement (Osterman 1988, chap. 4).

Although this study made progress in documenting the current status of Japanese white-collar HRM, a word of caution is in order. Based on the author's institutional knowledge, the claims about "emergence" and "new" HRM practices were permissible. But the final test of such claims requires time-series observations of the phenomena. Also, studies need to be conducted to corroborate even the current images depicted in this study. Until such studies are accumulated, these claims remain as working hypotheses to be tested in future research.

APPENDIX

Factor Structure of Human Resource Management Policies

Questionnaire Item	Factor 1 Competitive Appraisal	Factor 2 Employment Externalization
Emphasize Seniority vs. Performance* in Employee Appraisal	.818	−.067
Ability Ranking vs. Performance Appraisal* is the Most Important		
Factor in Pay Determination	.867	.079
Individuals' Career Stage vs. Job Content* as the Basis of Pay Hierarchy	.522	.093
Career Paths Are Not vs. Are* Individualized	.508	.011
Hiring of Fresh School Graduates Is vs. Is Not* the Main Hiring Method	.048	.511
The % of Contingent Workers Is Not vs. Is* Increasing	−.209	.580
The Firm Has vs. Does Not Have* a Policy of Employing Regular-Status Workers Until Forced Retirement	.163	.391
Employees Receive Broad vs. Specialized* Training	.109	.735
Eigenvalue	1.927	1.420
Proportion of Variance Explained	24.1	17.8
Cronbach's alpha	.61	.62

Note: *s indicates emerging policies.

ACKNOWLEDGMENT

The author acknowledges with gratitude the comments received from Nancy Bartter, John Budd, Morley Gunderson, Hitoshi Mitsuhashi, Tom Roehl, Anil Verma, and the participants of the Fourth Bargaining Group Conference. Comments received at HRM seminars at Rutgers University, Ohio State University, and the University of Illinois are also appreciated.

NOTES

1.   Another important component of the Japanese employment structure is the enterprise union, a topic which will not be discussed in detail in this paper.

2.   There have been a number of estimates regarding so-called "hidden unemployment" or "in-house redundancy" which refers to redundant employees who are retrained due to long-term employment policies. The estimates have grown from one million at the end of 1992, to 2 million in the middle of 1993, to 5-6 million in December 1993 (Hori 1993). Since the Japanese unemployment figure was 2.9 percent with approximately 2 million people unemployed at the end of 1993, if these "internally redundant" employees were pushed out to external labor markets, the unemployment rate could skyrocket to close to 10 percent, a figure comparable to those observed in European countries.

3.   The MOL sometimes exercises its strong "bureaucratic" muscle in maintaining the policy of long-term employment, sometimes even intervening in decisions made by private corporations. When a medium-sized machine manufacturer announced in early 1994 that it was lowering its forced retirement age from 60 to 55, the MOL intervened strongly and the company was forced to reverse its decision.

4.   Multi-year, limited-term employment contracts are illegal in Japan. All employment contracts have to be either up to one year or unlimited. Therefore, employers have begun to devise a variety of ways to work around this law, including promising employees that their one-year contracts will be renewed twice.

5.   Previously such "specialist" designation came only after employees reached their mid-40s (Pucik 1989).

6.   Sometimes called *katatataki* or "tapping-on-the-shoulder."

7.   When asked, "Do you believe that you will be able to work for this company until retirement," only 36.5 percent of male white-collar college graduates responded affirmatively (Morishima 1994).

8.   The reliability of these scales (estimated by Cronbach's alpha) was low: 0.61 for the competitive appraisal scale and 0.62 for the employment externalization scale.

9.   The procedure followed three steps. First, two scales were created by summing the four items highly loaded on each factor in the appendix. The correlation between the two scales was small at $r=0.116$ ($p<0.001$) and, therefore, warranted the use of the two scales as separate variables. Second, each firm scores on each scale were standardized and submitted to a cluster analysis, using the between-groups linkage technique. This procedure employed the squared Euclidean distances of the group means as the basis of clustering firms. Third, cluster means of each HRM policy scale were calculated and used to interpret the characteristics of firms' HRM systems.

10.   The reason for the lack of significant finding for the use of individual incentive bonus might be that respondents may have confused the term "individual incentive bonus" with the Japanese annual bonus practice.

11.   Productivity measures used in this study were not obtained solely for white-collar workers. However, since Japanese firms have made consistent efforts to increase blue-collar productivity, especially in poor economic times, any decrease in overall productivity levels is likely to be attributed to white-collar productivity declines.

12.   The author is aware of the possibility that company profits and employee well-being may not be tradeoffs. However, the question was posed as a choice, given that they are tradeoffs.

13.   For this type of investigation, multinomial logit analyses are more methodologically appropriate but more difficult to interpret. The results of the multinomial logit analyses do not substantively change the conclusions and are available from the author.

REFERENCES

Abegglen, J. C. 1958. *The Japanese Factory: Aspects of Its Social Organization.* Glencoe, IL: Free Press.

Aoki, M. 1993. "The Motivational Role of an External Agent in the Informationally-Participatory Firm." Pp. 229-247 in *Markets and Democracy: Participation, Accountability and Efficiency,* edited by S. Bowles, H. Gintis, and B. Gustafsson. New York: Cambridge University Press, pp. 229-247.

Befu, H., and C. Cernosia. 1990. "Demise of 'Permanent Employment' in Japan." *Human Resource Management* 29: 231-250.

Berggren, C. 1994. *"Toward Normalization? Japanese Competitive Position and Employment Practices after the Heisei Boom."* Paper presented at the Industrial Relations Research Association Meetings, Boston, January 3-5.

Butler, J. E., G. R. Ferris, and N. K. Napier. 1991. *Strategy and Human Resources Management.* Cincinnati, OH: South-Western Publishing Co.

Clark, R. C. 1979. *The Japanese Company.* New Haven: Yale University Press.

Cole, R. E. 1992. "Issues in Skill Formation in Japanese Approaches to Automation." Pp. 187-209 in *Technology and the Future of Work,* edited by P. S. Adler. New York: Oxford University Press.

Dore, R. P. 1989. "Where We Are Now: Musings of an Evolutionist." *Work, Employment and Society* 3: 425-446.

Florida, R., and M. Kenney. 1991. "Transplanted Organizations: The Transfer of Japanese Industrial Organization to the U.S." *American Sociological Review* 56: 381-398.

Gordon, A. 1985. *The Evolution of Labor Relations in Japan: Heavy Industry, 1853-1955.* Cambridge, MA: Harvard East Asian Monographs.

Hanada, M. 1987. "Tournament Mobility of Japanese Firms' Promotion Systems and Strategic Human Resource Management." *Organizational Science* 21 (Summer): 44-53 (in Japanese).

Hori, S. 1993. "Fixing Japan's White-Collar Economy: A Personal View." *Harvard Business Review* (November-December)71: 157-172.

Japan Institute of Labour. 1993. *"Staffing and Promotion of White-Collar Workers in Large Firms."* JIL Research Report No. 37 (in Japanese). Japan Institute of Labour (Tokyo).

Japan Productivity Center. 1992. *International Comparison of Labor Productivity.* Tokyo: Japan Productivity Center.

Japan Productivity Center. 1994. *Survey Report on the Future of the Life-Time Employment System* (in Japanese). Tokyo: Japan Productivity Center (in Japanese).

Kawahito, H.. 1991. "Death and the Corporate Warrior." *Japan Quarterly* 38: 149-157.

Kawakita, T. 1993a. "Prospects on the Management of White-Collar Careers." Pp. 25-67 in *Changes in the Management of White-Collar Careers: A Report Submitted to the Ministry of Labour,* edited by Y. Sano. Tokyo: Ministry of Labour.

————. 1993b. *"Diversity and Human Resource Management in Japan."* Paper presented at the Japan Institute of Labour-University of Illinois Institute of Labor and Industrial Relations Conference on "The Change of Employment Environment and Human Resource Management in the U.S. and Japanese Labor Markets," Tokyo, October 5.

Koike, K. 1988. *Understanding Industrial Relations in Modern Japan.* London: Macmillan.

————. 1991. *"Learning and Incentive Systems in Japanese Industry."* Mimeo, Faculty of Management, Hosei University, Tokyo.

————. 1993. "Human Resource Development Among College Graduates in Sales and Marketing." Pp. 42-64 in *An International Comparison of Professionals and Managers,* JIL Report No. 2, edited by K. Koike. Tokyo: Japan Institute of Labour.

Lincoln, J. R. and A. L. Kalleberg. 1990. *Culture, Control and Commitment: A Study of Work Organization and Work Attitudes in the United States and Japan*. New York: Cambridge University Press.

Ministry of Labour. 1987. *Prospects on Changes in Japanese Employment Practices: Survey Report* (in Japanese). Tokyo: Ministry of Finance Printing Office.

Ministry of Labour. 1990. *Comprehensive Survey on Pay and Working Hours* (in Japanese). Tokyo: Ministry of Finance Printing Office.

Morishima, M. 1994. *"Firms' HRM Strategies and Employee Attitudes."* Mimeo (in Japanese). Faculty of Policy Management, Keio University, Fujisawa.

_____. 1995a. "The Japanese Human Resource Management System: A Learning Bureaucracy." Pp. 119-150 in *HRM in the Pacific Rim: Institutions, Practices, and Values*, edited by L. Moore and P. D. Jennings. Berlin and New York: Walter de Gruyter, pp. 119-150.

_____. 1995b. *"Externalization of Employment as a Response to Internal Labor Market Constraints."* Manuscript under review, Tokyo.

Nihon Keizai Shimbunsha. Ed. 1993. *Japanese-Type Personnel Management Is No More* (in Japanese). Tokyo: Nihon Keizai Shimbunsha.

Nonaka, I.. 1988. "Self-Renewal of the Japanese Firm and the Human Resource Strategy." *Human Resource Management* 27: 45-62.

Osterman, P. 1988. *Employment Futures*. New York: Oxford University Press.

_____. 1994. "How Common is Workplace Transformation and Who Adopts It?" *Industrial and Labor Relations Review* 47: 173-188.

Parker, M., and J. Slaughter. 1988. *Choosing Sides: Unions and the Team Concept*. Boston: South End Press.

Pfeffer, J. and J. N. Baron. 1988. "Taking the Workers Back Out." Pp. 257-303 in *Research in Organizational Behavior*, edited by B. M. Staw and L. L. Cummings. Vol. 10. Greenwich, CT: JAI Press.

Pucik, V. 1989. "Managerial Career Progress in Large Japanese Manufacturing Firms." Pp. 257-276 in *Research in Personnel and Human Resources Management*, Suppl. 1, edited by A. Nedd, G. R. Ferris and K. M. Rowland. Greenwich, CT: JAI Press.

RECRUIT. 1993. *A Survey on Japanese Personnel Systems and Employee Development* (in Japanese). Tokyo: RECRUIT Co.

Rohlen, T. P. 1979. "Permanent Employment Faces Recession, Slow Growth, and an Aging Workforce." *Journal of Japanese Studies* 5: 235-272.

Sato, H. 1994. "Employment Adjustment of Middle-Aged and Older White-Collar Workers." *Japan Labor Bulletin* 33(2): 5-8.

Schuler, R. S. 1987. "Personnel and Human Resource Management Choices and Organizational Strategy." *Human Resource Planning* 10: 1-17.

Tackney, C. 1994. "A Perspective on the Postwar Court Struggles of Japanese Labor." *Nanzan Management Review* 8: 497-526.

Thurman, J. E. and G. Trah. 1990. "Part-Time Work in International Perspective." *International Labour Review* 129: 23-40.

Yashiro, A. 1991. "Changes in the Structure of Intra-Company Promotion Systems." Pp. 137-158 in *New Visions of Employment Management* (in Janpanese), edited by K. Kikuno and T. Hirao. Tokyo: Chuo Keizai.

THE FINANCIAL POWER OF
PUBLIC-EMPLOYEE UNIONS

Marick F. Masters and Robert S. Atkin

ABSTRACT

Industrial relations research generally associates union density with power. This perspective discounts the potential relevance of financial resources. The purpose of this chapter is to examine the financial resources of 11 major public sector unions. Using data from the unions' financial disclosure forms filed with the Department of Labor, the chapter explores the unions' assets, net wealth, income, and financial performance in terms of standard accounting ratios. The data show that public sector union wealth and income grew significantly during the 1980s. Significant inter-union differences exist in financial resources and performance, and union membership would appear to be only one of several possible explanatory factors. Conclusions and research implications are discussed.

Industrial relations research generally associates union density with organizational strength. The growth in public employee organizations thus signifies more power. An increasing body of research, however, adds financial resources as

Advances in Industrial and Labor Relations, Volume 7, pages 177-205.
Copyright © 1996 by JAI Press Inc.
ISBN: 1-55938-925-7

important components to union economic and political clout (Masters and Atkin 1995b; Sheflin and Troy 1983; Willman 1990; Willman and Morris 1995; Willman, Morris, and Aston 1993). According to this view, the financial resources of public sector unions deserve scrutiny because they may independently affect organizational capacity to influence important decisions. According to Sheflin and Troy (1983, p. 149), "[t]he level of unions' assets and net income provide a significant measure of their ability to finance strikes and organizational and political activities." In this regard, they have observed that aggregate public employee union finances did not keep pace with observed membership growth in the 1970s.

To date, little research exists on union finances in either the public or private sector (Bennett 1991; Clark and Gray 1991). Sheflin and Troy's (1983) aggregate public sector union data have not been updated, Nor has the literature examined public employee union finances on a disaggregated basis. Further, industrial relations research has generally neglected to analyze the financial management of unions in terms of standard accounting measures (see Allison 1975; Masters and Atkin 1993a, 1993b, 1995a; Sandver 1978, for exceptions).

This study partially fills the void by providing a comprehensive analysis of the finances of 11 major public employee unions in three governmental sectors: (1) federal executive branch (i.e., general schedule [GS] and wage grade [WG] employees), (2) federal postal service, and (3) state and local.[1] It presents a sizable body of data which provides insights on several questions which bear on the institutional strength of these 11 unions (at least at the national/international level). Finances are relevant to understanding unions *qua* organizations in several important respects. First, "labor union's finances impact the strategic choices available to its leaders" (Weil 1994, p. 154). Second, it provides insights as to how well a union is being managed. Financial mismanagement may spell trouble for union leaders with the rank and file (Bok and Dunlop 1970). Finally, it signals to management (public or private) how well unions are financially equipped to take a strike or layoff, both of which interrupt the flow of income (Weil 1994).

Specifically, the study focuses on six questions covering the 1981-1993 period:

1. What are the unions' aggregate financial bases (assets, income, net wealth), and how have they changed over time?
2. To what extent are the unions dependent on member-based income (e.g., dues)?
3. How well have the unions managed their finances, as measured in terms of standard accounting measures, such as solvency and liquidity?
4. What are the unions' relative financial capacities to serve their members based on their financial resources?
5. What is the relationship between union membership and financial wealth and income?
6. To what extent are there differences in the unions' financial power across the three governmental sectors?

The unions studied are the largest bargaining representatives in each sector:

Executive Branch: American Federation of Government Employees (AFGE)
National Federation of Federal Employees (NFFE)
National Treasury Employees Union (NTEU)
Postal Service: American Postal Workers Union (APWU)
National Association of Letter Carriers (NALC)
National Rural Letter Carriers Association (NRLCA)
State and Local: American Federation of State, County, and Municipal
Employees (AFSCME)
American Federation of Teachers (AFT)
International Association of Fire Fighters (IAFF)
National Education Association (NEA)
Service Employees International Union (SEIU)

The source of financial data is each union's annual LM-2 form, which must be filed with the Department of Labor as per the Labor-Management Reporting and Disclosure Act of 1959 (LMRDA) and other labor relations statutes (these statutes, a discussed later, regulate federal executive branch and postal sector labor relations).

The paper is organized as follows. Section 2 reviews the literature on union finances. Section 3 describes the data. Section 4 provides some background information on the unions in terms of their membership and representation levels. It also briefly discusses the various public policy contexts within which they operate, particularly the statutes regulating executive branch and postal service labor relations. Section 5 reports the unions' financial bases as measured by total assets, total income, and net wealth (i.e., assets minus liabilities). Section 6 explores the unions' principal sources of liquid assets and their dependence on member-based income, and Section 7 analyzes financial performance in terms of standard accounting measures. In Section 8, the paper examines the relationship between union membership and financial resources. Section 9, the last section, discusses conclusions and research implications of the data.

LITERATURE REVIEW

Despite the fact that unions have access to billions of dollars in assets, "the issue of union finances has been largely ignored" (Bennett 1991, pp. 1-2). The limited research in this area per se falls into three principal categories: union corruption, financial resources, and financial performance analysis. A fourth may be added that deals with the impact of union expenditures. A brief review of this literature follows.

Table 1 identifies selected works in each of the four categories. The union corruption research focuses on financial misconduct—both illegal and unethical—

Table 1. Selected Works on Union Finances

Research Category	Focus	Selected Works
Union Corruption	Examines evidence as to corrupt financial practices in unions and the rationale and content of law regulating union finances.	Hoxie (1921) Esty, Taft, and Wagner (1964) Stein (1964)
Financial Resources	Examines data on the balance sheets and income statements of unions.	Troy (1975) Sheflin and Troy (1983) Troy and Sheflin (1985) Willman (1990) Willman, Morris, and Aston (1993) Bennett (1991) Masters and Atkin (1995b)
Financial Performance	Examines various finances in terms of accounting ratios.	Allison (1975) Sandver (1978) Masters and Atkin (1993a; 1993b; 1995a) Willman, Morris, and Aston (1993) Willman and Morris (1995)
Impact of Union Expenditures	Examines impact of union organizing and political spending	Block (1980) Kau and Rubin (1981) Voos (1983; 1984; 1987) Masters and Zardhoohi (1987)

among labor organizations and the resulting need to regulate union financial activity. Hoxie (1921) recognized the financially corrupt nature of some unions, which he labeled as predatory. Stein (1964) reported extensively on the findings of the McClellan Committee of the U.S. Senate, which investigated union misconduct in many areas in the 1950s. In commenting on the Committee's findings, which led to the passage of the LMRDA in 1959, Stein (1964, p. 135) noted that "[t]he novelty, if any, in the McClellan Committee investigations....is the innumerable varieties of corruption." As previously mentioned, the LMRDA required that unions make extensive public financial disclosures, and it also imposed fiduciary responsibilities on union officers.[2] Studies like Stein's, which appeared in the 1964 Industrial Relations Research Association research volume, edited by Estey, Taft, and Wagner (1964), provide detail on the legal rationale and content of the LMRDA.

The financial resources research is an institutional body of work which examines the balance sheet and income statement information provided by unions in their LM-2 financial disclosure forms. For example, Sheflin and Troy (1983) analyze the aggregate assets, revenues, liabilities, and disbursements of unions for selected years during the 1960s and 1970s. Bennett (1991) partially extends their work into the 1980s, examining aggregate revenues among private sector unions. Similarly, Willman (1990), Willman and associates (1993), and Willman and Morris (1995) analyze aggregate and disaggregate financial data among British trade unions.

Research on financial performance applies standard accounting measures to analyze the financial health of unions. Allison (1975) and Sandver (1978) use three common accounting ratios (solvency, liquidity, and reserve) to analyze the finances of selected local and federal sector unions, respectively.[3] Masters and Atkin (1993a, 1993b, 1995a, 1995b) have conducted similar analyses among both selected public and private sector unions. Willman (1990) and Willman and associates (1993) use a broader array of accounting measures in a longitudinal analysis of post-World War II British trade union finances, finding that "that unions have experienced considerable financial difficulties, particularly since the mid-1960s" (William 1990, p. 323).

The research on union financial resources and performance has yielded some noteworthy though tentative conclusions. First, unions may improve their financial positions during times of membership losses (Bennett 1991; Willman et al. 1993). The loss in membership, in fact, and attendant dues revenues, may cause unions to become more sophisticated financial managers and to take certain related steps (e.g., raising dues) to generate more money. Second, unions differ in terms of how they allocate resources across various organizational levels. Sheflin and Troy (1985) found that unions, on average, allocated finances relatively equally between the national and local levels, respectively, but financial centralization or decentralization among unions is correlated with "the decentralization of collective bargaining" (Troy 1975, p. 136) among unions. In other words, bargaining structure will influence the financial strength of national unions. Beyond this point, however, little research has been done on the determinants of interunion financial differences (see Masters and Atkin, 1995b, for an exploratory analysis of this issue). Third, unions in the United States have tended to invest money in rather liquid forms of assets (e.g., U.S. Treasury securities) to help finance strikes and other emergencies (Sheflin and Troy 1983; Troy 1975). In this regard, public sector union wealth (net assets) has tended to lag behind private sector union counterparts.

A fourth category of research examines the impacts of union expenditures. In particular, Block (1980) and Voos (1983, 1984, 1987) have examined the relationship between union organizing expenditures and union successes in securing new members. Block (1980, pp. 101-102) "has suggested that one of the main reasons that union membership as a percentage of the private labor force and employment has declined in recent years is because unions...have not placed a high priority on organizing." With respect to public sector unions, which have grown to represent a considerable block of government employees, the implication of this finding is clear: they will face continually difficult tradeoffs between allocating money to serve current members, on the one hand, and pouring funds into organizing new units, on the other hand, in what is already a relatively densely unionized industry sector. If they opt to neglect the latter, they may, according to Block's (1980) analysis, go down a path of eventual decline á la their private sector counterparts.

Political expenditures have also been linked to legislators' votes on important public policy questions. Kau and Rubin (1981) and Masters and Zardkoohi (1987) have established an empirical relationship between union political action committee (PAC) contributions and legislators' votes on key issues. While unions may not use their treasury money to make PAC contributions, they are permitted under federal election laws to use such money to *raise* PAC funds on a voluntary basis from their members (Epstein 1976, 1980). Furthermore, unions may spend dues money to lobby lawmakers and promote "nonpartisan" political education. Thus, the financial condition of unions may have important political implications.

In sum, various strains of research have explored union finances. Generally speaking, however, the research has neglected to examine U.S. unions—private and public sector—on a disaggregated basis. Few studies have explored the variation in public sector unions' finances during the 1980s and more recently.

DATA

As previously noted, data on union finances were obtained from annual financial disclosure reports mandated under the LMRDA. The law covers labor organizations at the local, regional, and national/international levels that represent employees engaged in industry (29 U.S.C. 402). It encompasses private sector labor organizations regulated by the National Labor Relations Act and the Railway Labor Act, as well as predominantly public employee unions which also represent some employees in private industry. The Federal Service Labor-Management Relations Statute, which regulates labor relations among GS and WG employees, and the Postal Reorganization Act apply disclosure requirements to unions under their respective jurisdictions (see 5 U.S.C. 7120; 29 U.S.C 1209)

Department of Labor regulations have required labor organizations with $100,000 or more in annual cash receipts to file an LM-2 report within 90 days of the close of their fiscal years.[4] The LM-2 form includes several accounting statements and schedules. Detailed breakdowns of assets, liabilities, receipts, and disbursements are reported for each organization's preceding fiscal year. LM-2s are available for public inspection and purchase for the cost of copying (29 U.S.C 431).

For the purposes of this study, the first two pages of the public employee unions' *national* organizations' reports were purchased for each year in the 1981-1993 period. Page one includes information on dues rates or ranges (to the extent actually reported on this page rather than an attachment to the form) while page two provides breakdowns of assets, liabilities, receipts, and disbursements. The national level focus is justified on three grounds. First, the national level is substantively important because if its organization-wide strategic decision-making perspective. Second, the sheer number of local and regional organizations across these unions (which total well into the thousands) makes a disaggregated analysis of their finances impractical.[5] Also, many of the local and regional affiliates of the state and local employee unions are not covered by the LMRDA.[6] Finally, as previously mentioned, previous research indicates that a substantial portion of the financial activities of unions occur at the national or international levels (Sheflin and Troy 1983).[7] While this might be less the case for some public sector unions, due to their decentralized organizational structure, the nationals still conduct a nontrivial part of the unions' overall operations.

Union financial data are reported below in real amounts. They are adjusted according to the Consumer Price Index (CPI-U 1982-1984=100). To assess the extent to which free riding in bargaining units may strain the unions' financial resources, union representation were obtained (to the extent available). Representation data for executive branch and postal unions are from biennial reports prepared by the U.S. Office of Personnel Management (various years). Unfortunately, disaggregated union representation data are not available at the state and local level, although the AFT did furnish information for selected years (the AFT provided data in correspondece dated September 29, 1993).

Data on union membership were obtained from two sources. First, self-reported union data were obtained from Gifford (various years). Second, AFL-CIO-reported data for affiliates of the federation are also available in Gifford (various years).[8]

BACKGROUND

Public employee unions operate in government sectors which differ significantly in terms of employment levels and labor relations policy. Employment level affects the unions' potential organizing bases, and public policies create different incentives for government employees to join unions (Masters and Atkin 1989, 1990). The unions' finances may thus vary somewhat accordingly, especially to the extent that revenues depend on membership.

Representation and Membership

Table 2 reports the representation data for executive branch and postal service unions. The data show that the AFGE and APWU have clearly dominant positions within their respective areas. The AFGE represented more than twice the number of executive branch employees than the NFFE and NTEU combined throughout the 1981-1993 period. The NTEU's representation base, however, has increased significantly, making it the second largest bargaining representative since 1991. Together, the three executive branch unions have represented more than 70 percent of the GS and WG employees who belong to bargaining units.

Table 2.   Federal and Postal Sector Union Rpresentation
(in thousands)

Year	Executive Branch				Postal Service			
	Total Rep.[1]	AFGE	NFFE	NTEU	Total Rep.[2]	APWU	NALC	NRLCA
1981	934	691	136	107	565	306	198	61
1983	927	686	136	105	570	305	198	67
1985	941	689	149	103	587	310	206	71
1987	959	685	152	122	655	348	231	76
1989	960	675	148	137	678	355	242	81
1991	940	642	146	152	655	336	234	85
1992 (Dec.)	961	665	147	149	600	300	213	87

Notes: [1]Sum of the number of employees represented by the three executive branch unions.
[2]Sum of the number of employees represented by the three postal unions.

Source: Sources: U.S. Office of Personnel Management 1981, 1983, 1985, 1987, 1989, 1991, 1992.

Within the postal service, the APWU until recently has represented more than the NALC and NRLCA combined, reflecting its broader occupational base. Unlike the occupationally homogeneous letter carriers' unions, the APWU is an amalgam of previously existing craft and industrial-type unions among postal employees (Loewenberg 1980). The NALC and NRLCA, however, have experienced nontrivial growth in terms of the number of employees they represent. The three postal unions account for more than 90 percent of the total number of postal employees belonging to bargaining units.

Public sector union membership data are reported in Table 3. Two observations are noteworthy. First, sizable differences exist both within and between sectors in terms of membership levels. Across sectors, the state and local unions have the largest memberships, reflecting the much greater number of employees at that level of government. In 1991, 84 percent of the civilian public sector workforce in the United States was employed by state and local governments. Second, membership levels, particularly in the executive branch, are substantially below representation levels. Significant free-riding exists among federal sector bargaining units. In other words, the overwhelming majority of federal employees represented by unions have chosen not to join the union representing them. As to free-riding in state and local bargaining unions, limited available data suggest that nontrivial amounts of free-riding are present there.[9] Table 4 reports free-riding rates for executive branch and postal service unions.

Public Policy Contexts

Executive branch and postal unions operate under two distinct federal labor relations statutes: Title VII of the Civil Service Reform Act of 1978 (the Federal

Table 3. Public-Employee Union Membership
(in thousands)

Year	AFGE	NFFE[1]	NTEU[1]	APWU	NALC	NRLCA	AFSCME	AFT	IAFF	NEA	SEIU
1981	223	40	53	249	151	63	957	461	144	1,684	579
1983	204	52	55	246	175	60	959	456	142	1,692	589
1985	199	45	59	232	186	58	997	470	142	1,700	688
1987	157	45	65	230	200	63	1,032	499	142	1,700	762
1989	156	45	75	213	201	66	1,090	544	142	2,000	762
1991	151	30	74	228	210	82	1,191	573	151	2,000	881
1993	149	30	74	249	210	81	1,167	574	151	2,100	919

Note: [1]NFFE and NTEU reported their membership in Gifford (various years) for 1991 and 1993 as their representation members, which are considerably higher than actual membership, due to free riding. For these two years, the unions membership was estimated by dividing union dues revenues by dues rates (see Masters and Atkin 1995a).

Source: For AFL-CIO affiliates, bienniel AFL-CIO reports as published in Gifford (various years); for NFFE, NTEU, NRLCA, and NEA, union self-reported membership, as reported in Gifford (various years).

185

Table 4. Free-Riding Rates[1]

	Executive Branch				Postal Service		
Year	AFGE	NFFE[2]	NTEU[2]	APWU	NALC	NRLCA
1981	.68	.70	.50	.19	.24	.00
1983	.70	.62	.48	.19	.12	.10
1985	.71	.70	.43	.25	.10	.00
1987	.77	.70	.47	.34	.13	.00
1989	.77	.70	.45	.40	.17	.00
1991	.76	.79	.51	.32	.10	.03
1992 (Dec.)	.78	.79	.50	.17	.01	.07

Notes: [1]Free-riding rates are estimated by dividing representation minus membership by representation:

$$\frac{\text{total representation} - \text{membership}}{\text{total representation}}$$

Representation numbers are from U.S. Office of Personnel Management, 1981, 1983, 1985, 1987, 1989, 1991, 1992). Membership data are from the AFL-CIO for affiliated unions and from union self reports for other unions in Gifford (various years).

[2]Membership data are estimated for NFFE and NTEU in 1991 and 1992 as reported in Table 3.

Table 5.   Public-Policy Provisions in the Federal Government Sector

Policy Dimensions	PRA	FSLMRS
Basic Organizing and Bargaining Rights	Grants Employees the Right to Unionize and Bargain Collectively	Grants Employees the Right to Unionize and Bargain Collectively
Scope of Bargaining	Permits Bargaining Over Wages, Hours, and Selected Fringes	Prohibits Bargaining Over Economic Items
Impasse Resolution	Grants Parties the Right to Binding Arbitration	Parties May be Granted Binding Arbitration if Approved by Federal Service Impasses Panel
Union-Security	Union Security Arrangement Prohibited	Union Security Arrangement Prohibited

Source: Loewenberg (1980); Schneider (1988).

Service Labor-Management Relations Statute, or FSLMRS) and the Postal Reorganization Act of 1970. State and local unions operate under a myriad of different labor relations policies (Schneider 1988). Differences exist not only between but also within states, as particular groups of state and local employees (e.g., teachers and protective service employees) may be covered by separate statutes.[10] Because of the variety of state-enacted policies, it is impractical to compare policies across all three sectors. Thus, the comparison focuses on similarities or differences in policy provisions between the executive branch and postal service in these specific areas: basic organizing and bargaining rights, scope of bargaining, impasse resolution, and union security.

Table 5 highlights the major policy provisions. Both policies grant basic organizing and bargaining rights, but the FSLMRS is much more restrictive regarding the scope of bargaining.[11] It forbids bargaining over major economic items such as wages and fringes, while the PRA makes many such items negotiable. Both statutes ban strikes, but the PRA allows for the binding arbitration of impasses. Each statute prohibits union-security agreements. In sum, the fundamental differences revolve around the scope of bargaining and impasse resolutions procedures.

TOTAL ASSETS, INCOME, AND NET WEALTH

A union's total assets and revenues represent the principal financial resources to provide goods and services to its rank-and-file. The net wealth of a union, as measured by total assets minus total liabilities, constitutes a measure of the financial reserves that may be available for whatever purposes deemed necessary if they are sufficiently liquid (a point discussed later). Negative net wealth presumably cannot be sustained for unlimited periods of time without jeopardizing the institutional viability of a labor organization. Tables 6-8 report the real total assets, income, and net wealth of the public employee unions.

Table 6. Real Total Assets
(in millions)

Fiscal Year[1]	Executive Branch			Postal Service			State and Local				
	AFGE	NFFE	NTEU	APWU	NALC	NRLCA	AFSCME	AFT	IAFF	NEA	SEIU
1981	6.73	1.25	3.23	8.66	8.64	1.10	16.83	6.88	1.70	37.09	18.71
1982	5.36	1.05	3.54	13.12	10.14	1.91	16.45	8.28	1.70	39.53	19.38
1983	6.32	1.00	3.22	15.17	14.16	2.81	17.55	11.69	2.84	40.37	20.32
1984	17.28	1.14	2.82	15.61[2]	16.03	4.01	15.72	14.91	3.51	39.79	21.77
1985	22.43	2.86	2.96	14.45	20.74	4.88	18.15	16.58	3.11	38.93	22.24
1986	22.42	3.07	3.58	17.42	22.49	4.72	18.23	16.74	2.83	40.95	24.27
1987	22.76	2.63	4.33	17.88	23.39	5.16	22.70	17.45	3.39	42.45	23.25
1988	21.10	2.35	4.64	16.60	25.53	5.30	20.45	19.01	3.47	44.48	19.70
1989	19.12	2.01	4.90	15.21	26.88	4.29	22.55	20.16	4.13	51.65	20.69
1990	17.56	1.89	5.32	15.27	28.86	3.81	15.25	20.92	4.23	66.11	25.00
1991	16.12	1.87	5.44	16.74	29.15	7.07	20.36	23.25	5.50	88.63	31.82
1992	15.73	1.81	3.59	16.53	32.28	6.76	19.79	30.06	6.23	89.20	32.30
1993	16.16	1.42	3.81	17.76	33.76	6.24	23.47	39.37	6.91	88.35	31.90

Notes: [1]The unions' fiscal years are as follows: AFGE, SEIU (January 1 - December 31); NFFE (July 1 - June 30); NTEU, IAFF (October 1 - September 30); APWU (June 1 - May 31 through FY 1984; January 1 - December 31 FY 1985 and subsequent years); NALC (April 1 - March 31); NRLCA (July 1 - June 30); AFSCME (January 1 - December 31); AFT (July 1 - June 30); NEA (Sept. 1 - Aug. 31).
[2]The APWU changed fiscal years in 1984-1985 period. Data in tihis and subsequent tables are from the fiscal year ending May 31, 1984.

Source: LM-2 financial forms.

Assets

The data in Table 6 reveal vast differences in the unions' real assets. Each union ended the 1981-1993 period with more assets than it had at the beginning, although growth was uneven in several cases. For instance, while AFGE's assets in 1993 were more than double the reported amount in 1981, they were significantly less than the 1987 peak.

The data also show an unclear relationship between total assets and union membership. The NEA has had a sizable lead in total assets throughout the period, consistent with its vastly greater membership level. However, its asset advantage does not correspond with its membership lead. For example, while it had more than nine times as many members as the NALC did in 1993, it had less than three times as much in total assets. More to the point, some of the smaller unions (in terms of membership) have had greater asset bases. The NALC, for example, has reported more real assets than the AFSCME and AFT since 1984, despite a smaller membership base. This may be due, in part, to relative differences in the centralization of bargaining and finances within the unions. The NALC operates exclusively in the postal service, compared to the decentralized state and local unions which function across thousands of governmental lines.

The executive branch unions as a whole have had the lowest asset bases across the three sectors. In 1993, for instance, the state and local unions' assets surpassed $166 million compared to the postal unions' $58 million and the executive branch unions' $21 million. The NFFE, in particular, has had a relatively small amount of real total assets throughout most of the period in comparison to any of the other public employee unions. Its real assets have generally been significantly below $3 million. In addition, its total assets in 1993 were less than half the amount reported in 1986, indicating a continual diminution in its overall wealth.

Table 7 reports the unions' real total income from all sources, including receipts to be transmitted to locals and on behalf of members and receipts from the sale of financial assets.[12] The data reveal some interesting patterns. First, total income fluctuated widely among several unions. It exhibited a bell-shaped trend for AFGE and NFFE, but more consistent growth among postal unions. Second, income varies widely across sectors. In this regard, for their membership size, the postal unions have apparently generated quite a lot. The NEA, in contrast, would appear to generate relatively little for its size. But such a comparison may be misleading, in part because of how the unions are financially structured. For instance, the NEA would appear relatively decentralized in terms of both bargaining and financial operations, as the national received only 24 percent of the union's total revenue at all organizational levels in 1993 (Brimelow and Spence 1995).

Net Wealth

Table 8 reports the unions' real net wealth (i.e., total assets minus total liabilities). The data show clearly that executive branch unions in general have had rel-

Table 7. Real Total Income
(in millions)

Fiscal Year	Executive Branch			Postal Service			State and Local				
	AFGE	NFFE	NTEU	APWU	NALC	NRLCA	AFSCME	AFT	IAFF	NEA	SEIU
1981	20.29	2.58	7.80	16.38	30.70	1.91	139.38	34.24	6.53	100.66	30.62
1982	19.75	2.73	9.17	22.59	34.77	4.27	115.10	39.07	5.98	90.74	44.66
1983	19.38	3.25	10.57	45.52	38.04	2.90	109.63	35.46	8.14	93.55	22.73
1984	18.78	3.57	9.98	40.91	33.54	6.71	132.32	33.67	7.92	96.44	30.35
1985	23.19	3.74	9.44	56.94	38.63	6.54	97.87	43.48	7.49	97.61	34.79
1986	39.98	3.91	8.15	60.32	55.41	6.65	136.83	45.88	7.63	107.84	32.35
1987	22.47	3.62	8.54	65.31	54.57	7.11	139.69	41.94	7.28	115.33	39.13
1988	18.59	3.59	9.16	59.55	120.03	7.95	222.81	51.76	7.76	117.95	41.97
1989	18.38	2.75	9.65	62.79	106.23	7.60	357.40	46.28	8.83	125.66	55.26
1990	17.18	2.97	9.88	62.22	78.39	7.65	164.94	52.57	9.12	134.40	42.08
1991	17.54	2.45	9.41	62.89	69.90	12.55	67.71	52.26	9.64	145.73	43.93
1992	18.58	2.83	10.25	64.70	77.36	9.54	67.24	56.71	10.33	169.81	43.84
1993	21.22	2.70	10.95	66.16	59.22	8.45	68.19	63.09	10.60	130.64	44.12

Source: LM-2 financial forms.

Table 8. Real Net Wealth
(in millions)

Fiscal Year	Executive Branch			Postal Service			State and Local				
	AFGE	NFFE	NTEU	APWU	NALC	NRLCA	AFSCME	AFT	IAFF	NEA	SEIU
1981	3.95	.15	2.48	8.28	6.92	.19	11.79	3.38	.40	24.44	18.55
1982	2.04	-.11	2.58	12.41	9.33	.86	12.00	4.68	.89	24.02	19.23
1983	1.84	-.11	2.17	11.25	10.39	1.51	11.39	8.16	1.22	26.45	20.32
1984	-.19	.16	2.05	12.32	13.39	1.98	10.12	11.00	1.79	26.42	21.74
1985	-.69	2.18	2.17	11.42	15.03	2.52	11.32	9.93	1.82	26.17	22.22
1986	2.00	1.80	2.69	13.76	17.17	2.84	11.64	9.39	1.60	28.84	24.08
1987	1.17	1.56	3.37	13.43	18.10	3.04	13.39	11.54	2.53	29.56	22.73
1988	.27	1.27	3.68	12.59	19.63	2.87	11.60	13.24	2.28	28.56	18.70
1989	.38	.97	3.72	13.51	21.04	2.65	12.59	14.06	2.86	28.90	20.03
1990	.06	.52	4.17	13.46	22.02	2.38	4.33	14.03	2.87	28.62	21.69
1991	-.51	.71	3.12	14.92	23.62	2.36	6.40	13.48	3.64	29.29	28.14
1992	1.37	.76	1.69	14.59	26.83	2.15	7.90	20.00	3.99	28.11	29.43
1993	2.82	.45	1.59	16.16	28.48	1.70	10.23	26.67	4.92	27.09	28.10

Source: LM-2 financial forms.

atively little net wealth. In some years, in fact, the AFGE and NFFE have actually had negative net wealth, meaning that their total liabilities have exceeded total assets. In fact, the combined net wealth of the executive branch unions was only slightly above $4 million in 1993.

In contrast, the postal unions as a whole have amassed considerably more wealth, exceeding $40 million in 1993. The NALC's wealth more than quadrupled between 1981 and 1993, making it the wealthiest public employee union at the end of this period.

Again, membership does not guarantee financial advantage, at least at the national union level, further suggesting that other factors may explain inter-union differences. In this regard, bargaining centralization is probably an important factor. While the NALC had more wealth than the 2.1 million member NEA in 1993, the latter union, as noted, has highly decentralized organizational and bargaining structures. The NALC, in contrast, represents one bargaining unit in the U.S. Postal Service and, as will be discussed later, serves as a financial conduct for its affiliated branches or locals.

Across the entire period, the state and local unions' situations have differed. The AFT, IAFF, NEA, and SEIU ended the period with greater net wealth than they had at the start. AFSCME ended the period with slightly less wealth, but its situation has fluctuated widely since 1989 (AFSCME's income levels reflect volatile business-related transactions)

ASSET AND INCOME SOURCES

The sources of union assets and revenues affect financial flexibility and power. As in the case of businesses and other types of organizations, unions that maintain relatively large amounts of assets in highly liquid form presumably have more flexibility in the deployment of their assets. A union which has mainly fixed assets such as land or property may have to undergo prolonged and complicated financial transactions to convert these assets into cash.

With regard to income, unions that depend primarily on member-based revenues may have less flexibility, as decreases in membership levels can only be offset by raising dues, which is likely to be unpopular (Bok and Dunlop 1970). Private sector unions, like the UAW, which have diversified their income bases are financially better able to withstand extensive membership decreases.[13] However, union income that is pre-obligated either in terms of transmittal to affiliates or members reduces financial flexibility.

Liquid Assets

Table 9 shows the percentage of assets held in relatively liquid form: that is, (1) cash, (2) accounts receivable, and (3) U.S. Treasury securities. The data show that

Table 9. Public Sector Unions' Liquid Assets, Selected Years[1]

(number = percentages)

	AFGE			NFFE			NTEU			APWU			NALC			NRLCA			AFSCME			AFT			IAFF			NEA			SEIU		
	C	A	T	C	A	T	C	A	T	C	A	T	C	A	T	C	A	T	C	A	T	C	A	T	C	A	T	C	A	T	C	A	T
1981	.06	.24	.25	.08	.07	.00	.24	.09	.58	.65	.04	.00	.13	.01	.00	.55	.22	.00	.43	.16	.00	.65	.21	.00	.32	.02	.02	.19	.38	.00	.21	.00	.17
1986	-.01	.12	.00	.01	.03	.00	.28	.13	12	.81	.05	.00	.01	.17	.00	.57	.02	.00	.33	.17	.00	.64	.07	.00	.33	.16	.00	.30	.39	.00	.20	.00	.14
1990	.02	.10	.00	.03	.06	.00	.38	.12	.00	.80	.03	.00	.08	.18	.00	.49	.05	.00	.07	.27	.20	.56	.22	.00	.49	.18	.00	.15	.31	.00	.05	.19	.18
1993	.04	.12	.00	.08	.12	.00	.30	.09	.09	.86	.04	.00	.03	.09	.02	.22	.05	.00	.14	.20	.39	.68	.18	.00	.63	.10	.01	.12	.24	.00	.10	.21	.18

Note: [1]C = cash; A = accounts receivable; T = U.S.Treasury securities. The numbers are the percentage of total assets held in each category.

Source: Unions' LM-2 financial disclosure forms.

193

the AFGE, NFFE, and NALC would seem to be relatively nonliquid in terms of how they hold their assets. In major contrast, APWU, AFT, and IAFF appear quite liquid, holding much larger portions of their assets in cash. Since 1990, AFSCME and SEIU have held relatively sizable portions of their assets in U.S. Treasury securities. In sum, significant differences exist within each sector in terms of the portion of total assets held in liquid form and in the distribution across cash and treasury securities. Given that some of these unions (e.g., AFGE and NTEU) have small nominal amounts of assets to begin with, their liquid reserves would seem to be relatively meager.

Income Sources

As member-based organizations, unions may depend heavily on membership for income. Thus, their dependence on member-based income suggests their financial vulnerability to a declining membership, which has occurred among two executive branch unions. Member-based income consists of six items enumerated on the LM-2 form: dues, per capita tax, fees, fines, assessments, and work permits.[14]

The unions' member-based incomes are reported in Table 10. Generally speaking, the executive branch and state and local employee unions have depended substantially on member-based revenues for their total income. Each of these eight union's received almost two-thirds or more of their overall receipts from such sources in 1993. On the surface, however, the postal unions would seem relatively less dependent. For instance, these three unions derived two-thirds or more of their income nominally from other sources (as did AFSCME until 1990). What accounts for this apparent discrepancy is that much of the postal unions' income is obligated for transmittal to local or regional affiliates or for disbursement on behalf of union members.[15] For instance, in 1993, the APWU received 57 percent of its total income for transmittal to affiliated organizations. For NALC and NRLCA, the corresponding figures were 54 percent and 28 percent; NRLCA received 31 percent of its income for transmittal on behalf of members (for accounts predesignated for members). Between 1981 and 1990, AFSCME received somewhere between 50 percent to 83 percent of its annual income from the sale of fixed assets or other investments, receipts which were almost equally reflected in disbursements for the purchase of such assets or investments. If these revenue sources are deleted from total receipts, then the postal unions and AFSCME would appear comparably dependent on member-based income.

FINANCIAL PERFORMANCE

The previous data demonstrate sizable inter-union variation in financial resources. The data, however, do not assess financial performance in a strict accounting sense. Various accounting measures of financial performance indicate the relative

Table 10. Public Sector Unions' Real Member-Based Income, Selected Years[1]
(in millions)

Year	AFGE $	%	NFFE $	%	NTEU $	%	APWU $	%	NALC $	%	NRLCA $	%	AFSCME $	%	AFT $	%	IAFF $	%	NEA $	%	SEIU $	%
1981	14.73	.73	2.09	.81	4.31	.55	15.03	.92	12.47	.47	1.58	.83	40.66	.29	24.06	.70	5.21	.80	75.73	.75	16.67	.54
1986	12.40	.31	2.28	.58	5.77	.71	22.93	.38	16.23	.29	2.19	.33	46.37	.34	34.19	.74	6.40	.84	90.44	.84	28.92	.88
1990	12.00	.70	2.10	.71	7.65	.77	23.35	.36	19.13	.24	2.11	.27	54.42	.33	38.12	.72	7.25	.79	102.22	.76	34.21	.81
1993	13.74	.65	2.60	.96	7.69	.70	22.53	.34	17.50	.29	2.49	.29	53.33	.78	42.66	.68	8.29	.78	114.60	.88	38.19	.86

Note: [1]Member-based income is the sum of dues, per capita taxes, assessments, fees, fines, and permits enumerated on the LM-2 forms. Numbers in the left column are the various member-based revenues (in millions); right-hand column numbers are the percentage of total revenues from member-based income.

Source: Unions' LM-2 financial disclosure forms.

195

capacities of unions to withstand interruptions in income and to avoid dependency on loans and other costly sources of money.

Three standard accounting measures of financial performance are presented: solvency, liquidity, and reserve. Each is a ratio which reflects different aspects of financial health. Solvency is the ratio between real *adjusted* revenues and real *adjusted* disbursements. Adjusted receipts are equal to total receipts minus (1) transmittals to locals and for members on their behalf and (2) receipts from the sale of fixed assets. Adjusted disbursements are equal to total disbursements minus (1) disbursements to affiliates and on behalf of members and (2) disbursements for the sale of fixed assets. An insolvent union is deficit financing current expenditures. As Willman (1990, p. 320) states, "insolvency...cannot be sustained indefinitely." Unlike the federal government, unions do not have the seemingly endless capacity to borrow money to finance operations.

Liquidity is measured here as current assets divided by current liabilities. Unions with current assets greater than current liabilities presumably have more unencumbered financial resources to use for various purposes. Current assets include cash, accounts receivable, and U.S. Treasury securities. Current liabilities consist of accounts payable and other liabilities, both of which are specific items provided in the LM-2 form.

The third accounting ratio is the financial reserves of a union. The reserve ratio is a measure of the relative "working capital" of an organization. In other words, it indicates the money an organization has left over at the end of a fiscal year to maintain operations during the next year. It thus shows the relative capacities of unions to withstand interruptions in income. It "is a safeguard against the sudden experience of a strike or high levels of unemployment" (Willman 1990, p. 320). Reserves are commonly measured in terms of current assets minus current liabilities divided by essential expenditures. Given that LM-2 forms do not provide a basis for distinguishing between essential and nonessential expenditures, *adjusted* expenditures or disbursements (as defined above) are used in the denominator to calculate this ratio. Adjusted disbursements are used because they delete transmittals and disbursements for the purchases of fixed assets, neither of which are made for general operating purposes of the national.

The public employee unions' solvency ratios are reported in Table 11. The data show that the unions have tended to operate close to or slightly above solvency (i.e., 1.00). But five unions (AFGE, NFFE, NTEU, AFT and NRLCA) have had several technically insolvent years. Most unions have also had nominally small liquidity ratios, and two executive branch unions (AFGE and NFFE) have had ratios less than 1.00 for several years between 1981 and 1993, indicating that their current liabilities exceeded current assets. APWU and SEIU have displayed high rates of liquidity versus current liabilities.

The unions' reserve rates also vary considerably but in a pattern somewhat similar to liquidity. APWU and SEIU have consistently maintained solid reserve levels. The data indicate that they had sufficient unencumbered liquid assets to

Table 11. Public Sector Unions' Financial Performance,[1] Selected Years

Year	AFGE			NFFE			NTEU			APWU			NALC			NRLCA		
	S	L	R	S	L	R	S	L	R	S	L	R	S	L	R	S	L	R
1981	1.01	1.86	.09	1.01	.50	-.08	1.07	3.92	.43	1.08	16.22	.37	1.15	.74	-.04	1.09	.92	-.04
1986	.87	.67	-.03	1.07	.12	-.02	1.09	2.24	.17	1.04	4.13	.48	1.76	.76	-.08	.89	1.49	.27
1990	1.01	.91	-.01	1.02	.29	-.15	1.08	2.34	.20	1.04	7.04	.42	1.21	1.65	.21	.87	1.45	.19
1993	1.04	1.83	.08	1.07	1.01	.00	.99	.83	-.05	1.08	9.92	.57	1.14	.91	-.03	.83	.75	-.14
[2]	3	6	6	4	12	12	4	2	2	0	0	0	0	9	9	6	3	3

<1.00 # <1.00 # <.00[2]

Year	AFSCME			AFT			IAFF			NEA			SEIU		
	S	L	R	S	L	R	S	L	R	S	L	R	S	L	R
1981	1.09	1.98	.2	1.04	1.77	.09	1.03	1.00	.00	1.07	1.69	.10	1.12	48.83	.41
1986	1.09	1.39	.05	1.13	2.25	.19	1.00	1.30	.04	1.04	2.33	.16	1.05	131.18	.27
1990	.98	.75	-.04	1.07	2.38	.22	1.01	2.13	.17	1.09	1.31	.06	1.06	4.30	.21
1993	1.16	1.30	.07	1.26	2.68	.48	1.09	2.52	.31	1.02	1.20	.04	1.00	4.71	.30
[2]	1	1	1	0	0	0	1	0	0	1	0	0	1	0	0

Notes: [1] Solvency is the ratio between adjusted income (total receipts minus receipts collected for transmittal to affiliates and for disbursement to members and receipts from the sale of fixed assets) and adjusted disbursements (total disbursements minus disbursements for transmittals and on behalf of members and for the purchase of fixed assets); liquidity is the ratio between current assets (cash + accounts receivable + treasury securities) and current liabilities (accounts payable plus "other liabilities"); reserve is the ratio between current assets minus current liabilities and adjusted disbursements.

[2] The numbers under the respective columns refer to the number of years between 1981 and 1993 in which (a) solvency was below 1.00, (b) liquidity was below 1.00, and (c) reserve was below .00.

Source: Unions; LM-2 financial disclosure forms.

maintain nearly one-third and more than a half, respectively, of their annual operating requirements for 1993. Other unions, such as AFGE, NFFE, and NTEU, did
not have such a luxury. In fact, AFGE and NFFE had reserve ratios less than zero
in six and 12 of the reported years, respectively. In those years, the unions'
adjusted disbursements exceeded their unencumbered liquid assets.

UNION MEMBERSHIP AND FINANCIAL TRENDS

What is the relationship between union membership and financial trends? In an
analysis of the wealth and income of 28 of the largest private and public sector
unions in the United States, Masters and Atkin (1995b) found that membership
was significantly and positively correlated with union wealth and income, while
controlling for bargaining centralization and private sector location (vis-á-vis public sector) as predictors. But research (Bennett 1991; Willman et al. 1993) suggests
that union finances might improve during periods of membership decline.

Table 12 reports the percentage change (comparing 1993 to 1981) in the public
sector unions' membership, wealth, total income, adjusted income, and member-
based income. It shows that the unions which lost members (AFGE and NFFE)
had more total income in 1993 than 1981. NFFE in fact, had more wealth, adjusted
income, and member-based income, while AFGE losses on these financial dimensions were proportionately less than their one-third membership decline. These
data suggest that unions may improve their finances or prevent them, at a minimum, from decaying as much.[16]

The relationship between union finances and membership, however, is not a per-
fectly inverse one. The public sector unions that had more membership in 1993
than 1981 also had relatively more adjusted income and member-based income.
For the unions as a whole, net wealth grew by 85 percent, from $80 million to $148
million, between 1981 and 1993 or more than three times as much as the 24 percent hike in total membership (which grew from 4.6 to 5.7 million). Their adjusted
income climbed by 51 percent to $381 million, and their member-based revenues
increased by 50 percent as well. Thus, their financial resources grew by more than
their membership growth would necessarily imply.

In sum, membership decay need not imply financial decay, but financial gain
may outpace membership advances. As a whole, these unions would seem to have
taken various measures to enhance their financial base during this 13-year interval.

CONCLUSIONS AND IMPLICATIONS

The data permit several conclusions and yield implications for a future agenda of
research. First, in the 1980s, the finances of these 11 national public sector unions
grew considerably, outpacing their combined membership expansion. This trend is
an apparent reversal of the one which Sheflin and Troy (1983, p. 155) observed in

Table 12. Public Secor Union Membership and Finances, 1981-1993

Measures[1]	AFGE	NFFE	NTEU	APWU	NALC	NRLCA	AFSCME	AFT	IAFF	NEA	SEIU
Membership	-.35	-.25	.29	.00	.39	.28	.22	.24	.05	.25	.59
Wealth	-.28	2.07	-.36	.96	3.11	8.02	-.13	6.89	11.36	.10	.51
Total Income	.05	.05	.40	3.04	.93	3.43	-.51	.84	.62	.30	1.44
Adjusted Income	-.15	.08	.42	.65	.44	.81	.46	.85	.64	.40	1.21
Member Income	-.07	.24	.78	.50	.40	.57	.31	.77	.59	.51	1.29

Note: [1]Wealth, total income, adjusted income, and member income are measured as defined in text.

Source: Membership from Gifford (various years) and financial data from unions' LM-2 financial disclosure forms.

the 1960s and 1970s, when "public sector unions were unable to enlarge their funds as rapidly" as membership growth. A possible explanation is that the pace of membership growth had decelerated in the 1980s, enabling the unions to catch up financially.

Second, significant variation exists on all financial dimensions. At the national level, these 11 unions have shown vastly different levels of financial resources and performance. These differences would seem to be partly attributable to some combination of membership size, bargaining centralization, and governmental context (with its attendant labor relation policy framework). In the main, the executive branch unions would appear—at least in nominal terms—to be the financially weakest, but there are still great differences both within and between governmental sectors.

Third, these financial differences suggest varying capacities to represent union members. Table 13 reports the wealth, total income, and adjusted income per union member for each of the unions. Interestingly, it shows that, on a per-member basis, the executive branch sector unions are not as disadvantaged in terms of income as their nominal totals might indicate. In this regard, some of the bigger state and local unions would appear relatively worse off. But given the fact that executive branch unions represent a lot more employees than they have as dues-paying members, caution must be exercised in reading too much into these comparative figures. Illustratively, while the AFGE had $108 in adjusted income *per union member*, its corresponding figure *per represented employee* was less than one-fourth of that total. Parenthetically, the presidentially appointed National Partnership Council (NPC) recently issued a report recognizing the financial implications of free riding in the executive branch and the strain it imposes on the unions' capacities to service bargaining units (the NPC was formed October 1, 1993, by Clinton's E.D. 12871) The NPC stated that "[u]nder that [FSLMRS] statute..., employees are not obligated to join the union and pay membership dues or otherwise help defray representational expenses from which they benefit. The arrangement has consequences for labor relations and partnership—union's ability to pay for costs related to representation of employees is greatly diminished" (NPC 1994, p. 20).

Fourth, this research lends further credence to two previous findings on union finances. It suggests, as do Bennett (1991) and Willman and associates (1993), that union finances may improve notwithstanding membership losses. Also, it suggests that unions among public employees have generally lagged behind private sector counterparts in amassing money at the national level (cf. Masters and Atkin 1995b; Sheflin and Troy 1983). For instance, while these 11 public employee unions accounted for 43 percent of the membership of the largest 28 U.S.-based unions in 1993, they comprised (at least at the national level) only 8 percent of the total wealth and 17 percent of total income (Masters and Atkin 1995b). Again, it should be emphasized that this discrepancy may be due in part to greater decentralized bargaining and financial operations.

Table 13. Public Sector Union Real Financial Resources Per Member[1]

Financial Resource[2]		AFGE	NFFE	NTEU	APWU	NALC	NRLCA	AFSCME	AFT	IAFF	NEA	SEIU
Wealth	1981	$17.71	$3.66	$46.74	$33.27	$45.86	$2.99	$12.32	$7.34	$2.77	$14.51	$32.03
	1993	18.93	14.87	21.37	64.89	135.61	21.16	8.77	46.47	32.59	2.90	30.58
Total Income	1981	90.98	64.51	147.20	65.80	203.29	30.29	145.64	74.28	45.35	59.77	52.88
	1993	142.46	88.94	147.19	265.71	281.98	104.81	58.43	109.91	70.17	62.21	48.01
Adjusted Income	1981	84.71	62.36	103.67	65.80	93.16	30.29	46.49	65.06	44.83	54.83	33.19
	1993	108.04	88.94	105.17	108.46	96.29	42.75	55.69	96.56	70.17	61.98	46.23

Notes: [1]Financial measures are divided by union membership data for the relevant years.
[2]Wealth, total income, and adjusted income are measured as defined in text.

Source: Unions' LM-2 financial disclosure forms.

The data also point to several logical extensions of fruitful research. These specific questions seem particularly relevant:

1. How do unions spend their money? What are their functional and programmatic spending priorities?
2. How effectively do unions spend their money? What, for example, is the yield from their organizing expenditures?
3. What organizational and environmental factors influence inter-union variation in financial resources and performances?
4. How are unions structured to manage money and allocate funds? Relatedly, to what extent are financial decisions based on strategic plans and vice versa?
5. To what extent do members participate in the financial management and allocation decision making?

Research on these questions would substantially expand our knowledge of the "black box" mystery of unions *qua* institutions.

NOTES

1. In 1991, the federal executive branch employed 2.1 million GS (white-collar) and WG (blue-collar) employees. The U.S. Postal Service employed approximately 831,000 employees, and 15.4 million were employed at the state and local level.

2. Specifically, the LMRDA requires a union's officers "to hold its money and property solely for the benefit of the organization and its members" (29 U.S.C. 501). Technically, it covers unions operating under the National Labor Relations Act and Railway Labor Act. The Postal Reorganization Act of 1970 and Federal Service Labor-Management Relations Statute extend its coverage to unions in the postal and federal service. The unions in the state and local sector are covered only to the extent they operate under these other legal jurisdictions.

3. These measures may be operationalized in various ways and thus may not be directly comparable across studies.

4. The Department of Labor has issued new regulations effective December 31, 1994, raising the financial floor on filing LM-2s as opposed to abbreviated LM-3s from $100,000 to $200,000 (see Atkin and Masters 1995 for a discussion of the new regulations). See the *Federal Register*1993, p. 67594.

5. In 1983, for example, the AFGE, NFFE, and NTEU reported a total of 1,715 local affiliates (Gifford various years).

6. Many state and local union affiliates operate exclusively within the state and local public sector. The national organizations have affiliates with private sector or executive branch members, thus placing them under the jurisdiction of the LMRDA or FSLMRS.

7. According to Sheflin and Troy (1993, p. 151), "[t]he financial resources of American unions have traditionally been divided between the local unions and the national and international organizations, each with about 45 percent of total assets, with the intermediate and regional organizations accounting for the remainder."

8. AFL-CIO data are from its executive council report published in Gifford (various years). The AFL-CIO executive council reports membership data in the form of two-year averages.

9. The AFT, for example, reported the following data for 1990: 759,741 bargaining unit employees and 637,066 dues-paying members in its units. Thus, its free-riding rate in the units was 16 percent, arguably high but considerably less than the problem plaguing executive branch unions.

10.   See Aaron, Nijita, and Stern (1988) and Lewin, Feuille, Kochan, and Delaney (1988) for reviews of public sector labor relations. In particular, see Schneider (1988) for information on states' public sector bargaining laws.

11.   The FSLMRS not only severely limits the scope of bargaining but mandates an expansive management rights clause. President Bill Clinton, via E.O. 12871, broadened the scope of bargaining to make previously "permissive" negotiable items mandatory. Such items include "the numbers, types, and grades of employees or positions assigned to any organizational subdivision, work project, or tour of duty, and the technology, methods, and means of performing work."

12.   Some unions in the private and public sector collect receipts on behalf of affiliates for subsequent transmittal to them. These are receipts available to the union overall but not the national *per se*, which is acting as a financial conduit. In addition, some receipts may be earmarked for allocation to members based on predesignated instructions (e.g., allocators to charities or benefit accounts). Again, these receipts are not available for the national's general purpose use. Finally, receipts from the sale of assets and investments often reflect one-time transactions which artificially inflate revenues. Invariably, such receipts are matched by comparable levels of disbursements; thus, unions do not derive financial windfalls.

13.   According to Perusek (1989, p. 276), the UAW's "real net worth (1967 dollars) *rose* from $111.9 million to $224.3 million" between 1969 and 1984, notwithstanding the loss of more than 400,000 members.

14.   Definitions of specific LM-2 items are provided in a comprehensive Department of Labor document titled, *LMRDA Reports*.

15.   DOL regulations define receipts on behalf of affiliates for transmittal to them as "the net amount of receipts from dues, fees, fines, assessments, and work permits collected by check off or otherwise on behalf of affiliates for transmittal to them." Receipts from members for disbursement on their behalf are defined as "the total receipts from members which are specifically designated by them for disbursement for other than normal operating expenses."

16.   Unions may improve their finances by raising dues. The LM-2 form requires that unions report various dues information. Such information may be reported in ranges (minimum to maximum) or specific rates. Some unions chose to report dues information or separate attachments. Thus, dues rate information is not strictly comparable across unions. However, several of these unions increased their dues rates between 1979 and 1993, according to information available on the forms: SEIU ($1.80 per month to $5.10 per month), AFGE ($5.65 per month to $11.05 per month), NTEU ($71.50 per year to $186.16 per year), NFFE ($4.50 per month to $6.50 per month), NALC ($42.00 per year to $119 per year), NRLCA ($27 per year to $78 per year); AFT ($34 per year to $97 per year).

REFERENCES

Aaron, B., J. M. Nijita, and J. L. Stern. Eds. 1988. *Public Sector Bargaining*, 2nd ed. Washington, DC: Bureau of National Affairs.

Allison, E. K. 1975. "Financial Analysis of a Local Union." *Industrial Relations* 14: 145-155.

Atkin, R. S., and M. F. Masters. 1995. "Union Democracy, Finances, and the Labor-Management Reporting and Disclosure Act: An Alternative Reform Proposal." *Employee Responsibilities and Rights* 8: 193-208.

Bennett, J. T. 1991. "Private Sector Unions: The Myth of Decline." *Journal of Labor Research* 12: 1-12.

Block, R. N. 1980. "Union Organizing and the Allocation of Union Resources." *Industrial and Labor Relations Review* 34: 101-113.

Bok, D. C., and J. T. Dunlop. 1970. *Labor and the American Community.* New York: Simon & Schuster, Inc.

Brimelow, P., and L. Spencer. 1995. "Comeuppance." *Forbes* (February 13): pp. 121-127.

Clark, P. F., and L. S. Gray. 1991. "Union Administration." Pp. 175-200 in*The State of Unions*, edited by G. Strauss, D. G. Gallagher, and J. Fiorito. Madison, WI: IRRA.

Epstein, E. M. 1976. "Labor and Federal Elections: The New Legal Framework.' *Industrial Relations* 15: 257-274.

_____. 1980. "Business Political Activity: Research Approaches and Analytical Issues." Pp. 1-55 in *Research in Corporate Social Performance and Policy*, Vol. 2, edited by L. E. Preston. Greenwich, CT: JAI Press.

Estey, M. S., P. Taft, and M. Wagner. Eds. 1964. *Regulating Union Governance*. New York: Harper & Row Publishers.

Federal Register. 1993. December 21, p. 67594.

Gifford, C. D. Various yars. *Directory of U.S. Labor Organizations*. Washington, DC: Bureau of National Affairs.

Gore, A. 1993. *From Red Tape to Results: Creating a Government that Works Better and Costs Less*. Washington,·DC: The White House.

Hoxie, R. F. 1921. *Trade Unionism in the United States*. New York: D. Appleton.

Kau, J. B., and P. H. Rubin. 1981. "The Impact of Labor Unions on the Passage of Economic Legislation." *Journal of Labor Research* 2: 133-146.

Lewin, D., P. Feuile, T. A. Kochan, and J. Thomas Delaney. Eds. 1988. *Public Sector Labor Relations: Analysis and Readings*, 3rd ed. Lexington, MA: D.C. Heath and Company.

Loewenberg, J. J. 1980. "The U.S. Postal Service." Pp. 435-486 in *Collective Bargaining: Contemporary American Experience*, edited by G. G. Somers. Madison, WI: IRRA.

Masters, M. F., and R. S. Atkin. 1989. "Bargaining Representation and Union Membership in the Federal Sector: A Free Rider's Paradise." *Public Personnel Management* 18: 311-224.

_____. 1990. "Public Policy, Bargaining Structure and Free-Riding in the Federal Sector." *Journal of Collective Negotiations in the Public Sector* 19: 97-112.

_____. 1993a. "A Financial Analysis of Major Unions: Implications for Financial Reporting Reform under the Labor-Management Reporting and Disclosure Act." *Labor Law Journal* 44: 341-350.

_____. 1993b. "Financial and Bargaining Implications of Free-Riding in the Federal Sector." *Journal of Collective Negotiations in the Public Sector* 22: 327-340.

_____. 1995a. "Bargaining, Financial, and Political Bases of Federal Sector Unions: Implications for Reinventing Government." *Review of Public Personnel Administration* (Winter): 5-23.

_____. 1995b. "The Finances of Major U.S. Unions, 1979-1993." Working paper. University of Pittsburgh, Katz Graduate School of Business.

Masters, M. F., and A. Zardkoohi. 1987. "Labor Unions and the U.S. Congress: PAC Allocations and Legislative Voting." Pp. 79-118 in *Advances in Industrial and Labor Relations*, Vol. 4, edited by D. Lewin, D. B. Lipsky, and D. Sockell. Greenwich, CT: JAI Press, Inc.

National Partnership Council. 1994. *A New Vision for Labor-Management Relations: A Draft Report to the President on Implementing Recommendations of the National Performance Review* Washington, DC: Office of Personnel Management.

Perusek, G. 1989. "The U.S.-Canada Split in the United Automobile Workers." *Proceedings of the Forty-First Annual Meeting of the Industrial Relations Research Association* (December 28-30). Madison, WI: Industrial Relations Research Association.

Sandver, M. H. 1978. "The Financial Resources of Federal Employee Unions." *Monthly Labor Review* 191: 49-50.

Schneider, B.V.H. 1988. "Public Sector Labor Legislation—An Evolutionary Analysis." In Aaron, Nijita, and Stern, *op. cit.*, 189-228.

Sheflin, N., and L. Troy. 1983. "Finances of American Unions in the 1970's." *Journal of Labor Research*, 4: 149-157.

Stein, E. 1964. "Union Finance and LMRDA." iI Estey Taft, and Wagner, *op. cit.*, 130-53.

Troy, L. 1975. "American Unions and Their Wealth." *Industrial Relations* 14: 134-44.

Troy, L., and N. Sheflin. 1985. *Union Sourcebook.* West Orange, NJ: Industrial Relations Data and Information Sources.

U.S. Office of Personnel Management. 1981, 1983, 1985, 1987, 1989, 1991. *Union Recognition in the Federal Government.* Washington, DC: U.S. Office of Personnel Management.

Voos, P. B. 1983. "Union Organizing: Costs and Benefits." *Industrial and Labor Relations Review* 36: 576-591.

_____. 1984. "Trends in Union Organizing Expenditures, 1953-1977." *Industrial and Labor Relations Review* 38: 52-63.

_____. 1987. "Union Organizing Expenditures: Determinants and Their Implications for Union Growth." *Journal of Labor Research*, 8: 19-30.

Weil, D. 1994. *Turning the Tide: Strategic Planning for Labor Unions.* New York: Lexington Books.

Willman, P. 1990. "The Financial Status and Performance of British Trade Unions, 1950-1988." *British Journal of Industrial Relations* 28: 313-327.

Willman, P., and T. Morris. 1995. "Financial Management and Financial Performance in British Trade Unions." *British Journal of Industrial Relations* (33): 289-298.

Willman, P., T. Morris, and B. Aston. 1993. *Union Business: Trade Union Organization and Financial Reform in the Thatcher Years.* Cambridge, UK: Cambridge University Press.

UNIONS, HUMAN RESOURCE INNOVATIONS, AND ORGANIZATIONAL OUTCOMES

John T. Delaney

ABSTRACT

This study uses data on human resource (HR) practices in a sample of 495 large busi-nesses to identify factors related to an organization's adoption of HR innovations. In addition, multivariate analyses are used to identify the relationship between HR innovations and intermediate measures of firm performance (turnover and employee support for change). Results suggest that several factors are significantly associated with the adoption of HR innovations, including unionization, firm size, organiza-tional values, and company strategy. HR innovations are negatively related to turn-over and positively related to employee support for change. The findings confirm recent work suggesting that HR innovations enhance organizational outcomes.

Advances in Industrial and Labor Relations, Volume 7, pages 207-245.
Copyright © 1996 by JAI Press Inc.
All rights of reproduction in any form reserved.
ISBN: 1-55938-925-7

In recent years, American businesses have experimented with a variety of innovations in human resource (HR) management policies and practices. The experimentation is a consequence of several factors, including dramatic economic, social, and demographic changes (Kanter 1986), as well as a belief that the introduction of HR innovations will enhance organizational productivity and performance (Lawler 1986; Peters and Waterman 1982). Although some evidence indicates that businesses have adopted innovative HR policies to reduce the likelihood that employees will unionize (Fiorito, Lowman, and Nelson 1987; Freeman and Kleiner 1990a; Kochan, McKersie, and Chalykoff 1986), HR innovations (or changes in HR policies and practices) appear to be seen generally as a force that will revitalize industry by energizing and empowering workers.

Assertions about the value of HR innovations far outstrip systematic research on the causes and effects of such policies and practices. For example, available studies provide a mixed assessment of the effects of specific HR innovations, such as employee involvement, gainsharing, or information sharing programs (see Delaney, Ichniowski, and Lewin 1989; FitzRoy and Kraft 1987; Katz, Kochan, and Weber 1985; Kleiner and Bouillon 1988; Levine and Tyson 1990; Wagner 1994; Morishima 1991). Furthermore, there is disagreement over the definition and measurement of HR innovations, and little is known about the factors that cause businesses to implement innovative HR policies (see Osterman 1994).

One of the most controversial features of the literature on HR innovations is an ongoing debate about the association between unionization and the so-called "new HR management" (see Ichniowski, Delaney, and Lewin 1989; Lawler and Mohrman 1987). The gist of the debate is over the compatibility of unionization and the operation of innovative HR policies in the work place. Considerable evidence shows that unions affect the managerial policies adopted by firms (Freeman and Medoff 1984; Slichter, Healy, and Livernash 1960). It has been contended that unions resist HR innovations in order to protect their role and autonomy in the firm (Moody 1988; Zellner 1989). Resistance stems in part from evidence that some employers use HR innovations specifically to avoid the need for unions (see Verma and Kochan 1985). Indeed, such evidence may make union leaders naturally resistant to HR innovations (Freeman and Medoff 1984). In contrast, although it is presumed that the association between unionism and HR innovation is negative (Lawler and Mohrman 1987), little systematic evidence is available on how unions affect HR innovations, or how unions and organized employees react to innovative HR policies when they are adopted. For example, from the perspective of agency theory, there may be some circumstances where members pressure union leaders to seek and support HR innovations. Further, some researchers have suggested that innovative HR practices are *more* likely to succeed in unionized work places because of the role that the union can play in convincing workers of the merits of such practices (Eaton and Voos 1992).

To gain insight into the debate, this study examines HR innovations in a sample of large American companies. In addition to examining the occurrence of HR innovations in unionized and nonunion work places, some antecedents and consequences of such innovations are identified. Recent research serves as the basis for a model of innovative HR policies and empirical tests are conducted to examine some common assertions about HR innovations. In general, results suggest that HR innovations are associated with lower employee turnover and greater employee support for organizational change. In addition, there is little evidence supporting assertions that innovative HR practices are adopted solely within nonunion working environments.

Below, important issues connected with HR innovations are discussed, a data base on HR policies and practices is described, and models of the causes and effects of HR innovations are developed. In particular, associations between HR innovations and employee turnover and managerial flexibility are examined. After presenting the empirical results, the findings are discussed and some inferences are drawn about the occurrence of HR innovations in U.S. firms.

WHY ADOPT HR INNOVATIONS?

The interests of employers, employees, and unions all play a role in decisions to adopt or reject HR innovations. In recent years, external pressures on American firms have caused each of these groups to consider the extent to which HR innovations can enhance productivity and thereby protect firms' competitive position and workers' jobs. Typically, each of the parties has had a different primary motivation for the consideration of HR innovations.

Employers' Interest in HR Innovations

Motivating the work force is one of the major tasks of a profit-maximizing firm. It is generally believed that workers will be motivated if they are provided with adequate individual incentives (FitzRoy and Kraft 1987) and convinced that shirking will not be tolerated (see Lazear 1981). Employee motivation is a problem, however, because it is difficult for management to estimate employee effort on many jobs, and it is impossible for supervisors to monitor employee activity at all times. Further, employees have an incentive to shirk where possible because expenditure of effort on their part is costly. As a result, firms have been forced to devote considerable resources to the detection of shirking and employee malfeasance. For example, there is evidence that U.S. firms devote millions of employee hours and billions of dollars annually to deter shirking behavior (Dickens, Katz, Lang, and Summers 1989).

Historically, firms have tried a variety of approaches to control shirking. For example, it has been argued that firms embraced Taylorism partly because of its promise to divide work into tasks that could be measured and evaluated objectively (see Gordon, Edwards, and Reich 1982). It has also been argued that bureaucratic employment systems and internal labor markets were traditionally adopted first by firms in new sectors of the economy and in industries producing outputs that were difficult to measure, such as schools (Baron, Jennings, and Dobbin 1988; Jacoby 1985). History has shown, however, that managerial approaches have not eliminated shirking, and this explains partly why employers have emphasized monitoring activities.

Recently, it has been asserted that firms should modify management practices in ways that reduce employees' incentive to shirk and thus increase productivity. Specifically, various efficiency wage models suggest that it is efficient for employers to pay compensation in excess of market clearing levels (see Akerlof and Katz 1989), to offer long-term benefits, such as pensions or job security arrangements (see Hutchens 1987; Lazear, 1981), or to provide incentive pay schemes (see FitzRoy and Kraft, 1987; Jensen and Murphy 1990). In an ideal economic world, workers would be required to pay a bond to employers that would be confiscated if they were caught shirking (Akerlof and Katz 1989). In reality, such bonding arrangements rarely occur (Dickens, Katz, Lang, and Summers 1989), leading some observers to conclude that programs paying workers in excess of prevailing market compensation in certain circumstances provide a pragmatic way for employers to instill in employees a stronger incentive to work (Akerlof and Katz 1989).

Compensation in excess of market levels increases the cost of being caught shirking for each employee because alternative job opportunities pay less. Thus, high wages may encourage employees to engage in "self-monitoring." The efficiency wage models suggest that firms may be better off spending dollars on forms of self-monitoring (especially if output is not easily observable) than on hiring additional supervisors. In addition, some observers have extended these approaches by suggesting that certain management techniques can also produce desired employee behaviors (see Lawler and Mohrman 1987). Specifically, it has been argued that profit sharing programs, due process guarantees, and employee involvement programs may encourage productive behavior by stimulating employees' self-monitoring practices. That is, some HR practices can promote an environment of "positive peer pressure," encouraging employees to work harder (Kandel and Lazear 1992). Consequently, the adoption of HR innovations may enhance productivity among employees.

Despite its theoretical attractiveness, empirical tests of efficiency wage models have produced inconsistent results (see Cappelli and Chauvin 1991a, 1991b; Leonard, 1987). Moreover, research has suggested that relationships among wages, employment practices, and organizational outcomes are more complex than efficiency wage models presume. For example, although Leonard (1987, pp. S149-S150) reported an inverse relationship between wage levels and turnover in a sample of high-technology firms in one state, he indicated that the turnover reduction did not justify the magnitude of the wage premium as a profit-maximizing act. Similarly, Moore and Newman's (1991) analysis of Houston Metropolitan Transit Workers suggested that an inverse relationship between compensation and turnover did not completely offset the size of the compensation differential. On the other hand, Cappelli and Chauvin (1991b) reported a strong positive relationship between wage premiums and worker performance in one empirical study. They interpreted this result as supporting and extending efficiency wage theory.

In short, employers' interest in new approaches to the management of workers has grown in recent years because of the belief that such approaches can influence the economic performance of firms. It has been argued that American firms can greatly improve the productivity and motivation of workers by simply changing the way in which managers treat the work force (see Huselid 1995; Peters and Waterman 1982). Although these arguments have led several researchers to test empirically the link between specific HR policies and different measures of firm performance (see Kleiner and Bouillon 1988; Morishima 1991), results have been inconsistent across studies. Divergent findings may occur because HR policies differ somewhat across employees or cover only certain subsets of employees (e.g., managers have access to benefits that are not available to other employees) or because firm performance is measured at a different level than HR policies. Construction of aggregate HR policy measures likely masks the extent to which HR policies vary across and within firms, even though empirical studies treat the policy measures as identical. For example, an employee participation program at one firm may be very different than the participation program at another firm. Similarly, the merit pay plan for managers may differ from the merit pay plan for other workers in the same firm.

Management has long searched for organizational structures and rules that increase workers' effort, and it is well known that internal rules vary systematically across firms (Doeringer and Piore 1971). Factors that affect firms' adoption of internal organizational rules or "employment systems" (Osterman 1987, 1994) will affect the adoption of HR innovations. In addition, the adoption of such systems is more likely where employee turnover is relatively costly to firms.

Although the adoption of HR innovations can be explained by a variety of economic models, including efficiency wage models, it is curious that firms seem to have taken so long to discover the value of innovative organizational rules. Traditional HR policies, which offered workers little say in their work and were designed to fit a hierarchical company structure, have been used for most of the twentieth century (Baron, Jennings, and Dobbin 1988; Jacoby 1985). But economic circumstances have changed substantially in recent decades. Markets have become more competitive since World War II and firms have been forced to raise productivity in order to remain competitive. In addition, the relatively high cost of capital in the United States in the 1970s and 1980s created an incentive for American firms to focus on "labor-enhancements" in order to increase productivity (see Piore and Sabel 1984).

Work Force Changes and HR Innovations

Changes in the nature of the American work force have also stimulated the demand for HR innovations. The work force today is older, more highly educated, and made up of an increasing proportion of women. The work force is also becoming more ethnically and racially diverse. In addition, as firms increasingly operate globally, it will be necessary for them to deal explicitly with the multicultural nature of their workers. Workers are making new demands on employers, and the changing demographics of the work force are spurring employers to listen to these demands (Kanter 1986). HR innovations, such as flexible working hours and the provision of day-care benefits, are but two examples of employer responses to such work force changes.

Unions and HR Innovations

Unions can influence the extent to which profit-maximizing firms adopt HR innovations directly and indirectly. Unions can directly approve or reject proposed HR innovations that are subjects of collective bargaining. Employers, therefore, must demonstrate to the union the value of HR innovations that are subject to bargaining or provide a *quid pro quo* to achieve them in negotiations.

Because some HR innovations are outside of the scope of mandatory bargaining (e.g., certain employee involvement programs; Sockell 1984), firms are legally permitted to adopt them unilaterally in some circumstances. Where those innovations threaten the union, however, indirect pressure may be placed on the employer to abort the innovation or to bargain over it. For example, employees may engage in slowdowns or "work to rule" at the request of the union to indicate their disapproval of an HR innovation. These possibilities imply that it is more difficult for employers to adopt HR innovations opposed by workers in unionized operations than in nonunion operations. As unions may approve of certain HR innovations, however, a negative relationship between unionization and the adoption of HR innovations is not foreordained. Moreover, it is possible that HR innovations supported by a union will be more effective than the same innovations in nonunion settings because employees' support for the union may increase support for the innovations (see Eaton, Gordon, and Keefe 1992).

The relationship between unions and HR innovations is made more complex because some employers may desire to use such policies to prevent unionization. It has been argued that American employers' values with respect to unions have changed in recent years (Kochan, Katz, and McKersie 1986). In particular, opposition to unions seems to be a much more acceptable management strategy today than it was in the past (Fiorito and Maranto 1987). Further, there is evidence that employers have used a wide variety of tactics to oppose unions, including deliberate violation of the National Labor Relations Act to defeat union organizing attempts (a union avoidance strategy; Kleiner 1984), movement of capital from unionized to nonunion subsidiary operations (a union replacement strategy; Kochan, Katz, and McKersie 1986), and the implementation of "sophisticated" HR policies, such as complaint resolution systems, that provide a substitute for a union (a union substitution strategy; Kochan 1980).

In short, the motivations of employers, employees, and unions influence the likelihood that HR innovations are adopted in any particular firm. Nevertheless, the implementation of such innovations has risen in recent years for a variety of reasons (see Lawler and Mohrman 1987). An examination of those reasons will permit an assessment of some causes and consequences of HR innovations. Next, I describe a data set that allows such an assessment.

DATA ON HR INNOVATIONS

Attempts to study the causes and consequences of HR innovations have been hindered by the lack of appropriate data. Typically, company data sets with many observations contain little information on HR practices or innovations, and comprehensive data on HR policies are available only for a small number of firms. Further, government agencies and private organizations have made few efforts to collect relevant data sets or have not made relevant data sets available to researchers. In general, the burden of collecting firm-level HR policy data has been left entirely to individual researchers, and this has led to the development of small or narrow data sets (see Ichniowski, Shaw, and Prennushi 1994). Although researchers have conducted many studies of specific HR policies and practices (for overviews, see Cascio 1987; Huselid 1995), few attempts have been made to gather data on a wide range of personnel policies across many firms (for an exception, see Huselid 1995). Such data are needed because it is likely that firms implement a portfolio of HR policies (Huselid 1995; Milgrom and Roberts 1993). That is, policies are not adopted independently; firms construct portfolios of HR policies that consider individual policies and their interactions with other policies. By ignoring other HR policies, studies of individual HR policies overlook these interactions and overstate the effects of the policies on firm performance.

The need for comprehensive information on HR policies provided the impetus to collect the data that are analyzed below (see Delaney, Lewin, and Ichniowski 1989). The data set is one of the most comprehensive surveys of human resource practices in U.S. firms that has been conducted to date. During 1986, a questionnaire to identify and assess the HR policies and practices followed by U.S. firms was designed and tested. This comprehensive, 29-page questionnaire requested information on HR policies covering managers, unionized professional and technical employees, nonunion professional and technical employees, unionized clerical employees, nonunion clerical employees, unionized manufacturing and production employees, and nonunion manufacturing and production employees. The questionnaire also requested information on the extent to which each business unit followed certain HR policies in general.

Using a name and address file maintained by Standard and Poor's COM-PUSTAT services, the questionnaire was distributed to executives in charge of 7,765 U.S. corporate business units. Usable data were received from 495 of these business units (a 6.5% response rate). Although the response rate to the survey is low, it is similar to response rates obtained by researchers who have conducted shorter and less comprehensive surveys of firms' HR practices (see Bemmels 1987; Friedman 1986; Rynes and Boudreau 1986; Tsui and Gomez-Mejia 1988). In addition, the response rate is in line with researchers' estimates of the typical response rate obtained when senior executives are sent survey questionnaires (Gaedeke and Tootelian 1976). To identify potential biases in the sample, COM-PUSTAT data were used to conduct a comparison of respondents and nonrespondents. That examination indicated that the industrial distribution of the respondents is generally similar to the industrial distribution of nonresponding COMPUSTAT business units (Delaney, Lewin, and Ichniowski 1989).[1] Responding businesses, however, are larger than nonresponding business units.

The 495 business units forming the core sample analyzed in this study are not a random sample of American firms. No claim is made that the sample fully reflects the population of American businesses. Still, the data appear to be a representative and reasonable sample of large publicly-held U.S. business units—a population of firms that some researchers have characterized as HR policy "pattern setters" (Baron, Jennings, and Dobbin 1988; Jacoby 1986). As long as the data are interpreted cautiously and with this population in mind, they may shed light on HR policies in large American companies.

The sample is diverse, including business units in most major industrial categories. The data set contains both well-known and relatively unknown firms, including one of the world's largest automobile companies, leading high technology firms, investment banks, airline companies, construction companies, utilities, retailers, and even a firm that operates racetracks and casinos. The responding firms provided information on HR policies, the extent of unionization, and turnover for several occupational groups. As a result, the data permit a systematic analysis of the relationships among unionization, the adoption of HR innovations, organizational turnover, and flexibility.

Measures of HR Innovations

Although the literature contains abundant discussions of innovative HR practices, few authors have provided explicit lists of these practices or definitions of the term "innovative."[2] Thus, studies of HR innovations are difficult to assess and compare. For example, one review suggested that HR innovations are designed to reduce the distinction between employees and managers, enhance employees' commitment to the firm, and promote efficiency (Lawler and Mohrman 1987). Another study defined an HR innovation as "a program, policy, or practice that is both designed to influence employee attitudes and behaviors and perceived to be new by members of the organization" (Kossek 1989, p. 264). A common thread in prior research is that HR innovations are generally assumed to be the antithesis of Tayloristic and hierarchical HR policies that have been the norm in many U.S. businesses (Peters and Waterman 1982). HR innovations are highly regarded because they are assumed to promote "flexibility"—managerial discretion—in the work place, as well as other beneficial results, such as greater productivity (Hoerr 1989; Osterman 1994).

Although HR innovations are defined inconsistently by researchers (Huselid 1995; Osterman 1994; Kochan, McKersie, and Chalykoff 1986; Kanter 1984), certain HR policies, such as employee participation programs, have commonly been regarded as innovations. Moreover, researchers have suggested that HR innovations may be placed into several categories. For example, Kanter categorized innovative policies as (1) "quality of working life programs aimed at improving working conditions," (2) HR programs aimed at "equity assurance" (such as complaint resolution systems); and (3) "programs or practices supportive of working parents" (Kanter 1984, pp. 1-9 - 1-10). Similarly, according to Kochan, McKersie, and Chalykoff, the three general functions of HR innovations are to (1) "provide due process and conflict management or resolution processes," (2) "establish principles or rules governing the organization and modification of work systems," and (3) "communicate with and manage the commitment, trust, and motivation of individual workers and work groups" (1986, p. 492).

This analysis focuses on 10 HR innovations drawn from the HR policies identified by Kanter (1984), Kochan, McKersie, and Chalykoff (1986), and Kossek (1989). The 10 policies, which fit into the categories noted previously, are reported in Table 1. In general, many of the policies are not the norm in American work places (see Eaton and Voos 1992; Ichniowski, Delaney, and Lewin 1989). Although these 10 policies obviously do not constitute the universe of HR innovations, they have been broadly accepted as leading examples of innovative HR pol-

Table 1.   Ten HR Innovations

1.	Flexible Job Designs
2.	Employee Involvement Programs
3.	Profit-Sharing Programs
4.	Grievance Procedure
5.	Information-Sharing Program
6.	Attitude Surveys
7.	Flexible Scheduling
8.	Day-Care Programs
9.	Paternity Leave Programs
10.	Employee Counseling Services

Note: The Appendix provides a list of innovations identified by Kanter (1984).

Table 2. Proportion of Employees Covered by HR Innovations by Occupation and Union Status

Innovative HR Policy	Managers	Professional Employees		Clerical Employees		Production Employees	
		Union	Nonunion	Union	Nonunion	Union	Nonunion
Flexible Job Designs	.405	.286	.395	.244*	.395	.238*	.395
	(482)	(56)	(458)	(86)	(461)	(160)	(324)
Employee Involvement	.318	.423	.342	.476*	.338	.493	.436
	(418)	(52)	(401)	(82)	(420)	(152)	(296)
Profit Sharing	.519	.318*	.496	.200*	.423	.204*	.436
	(412)	(44)	(387)	(70)	(395)	(137)	(273)
Grievance Procedure	.429	.965*	.463	.989*	.479	.989*	.546
	(455)	(57)	(441)	(88)	(461)	(178)	(326)
Information Sharing	.592	.500	.566	.643	.527	.642	.567
	(355)	(44)	(343)	(70)	(353)	(137)	(261)
Attitude Surveys	.401	.529	.408	.500	.394	.449	.394
	(444)	(51)	(426)	(80)	(431)	(156)	(297)
Flexitime	.171	.018*	.147	.043*	.108	.017*	.084
	(440)	(47)	(421)	(72)	(432)	(145)	(300)
Day Care	.111	.074	.113	.063	.113	.050	.092
	(476)	(54)	(453)	(80)	(461)	(161)	(314)
Paternity Leave	.170	.170	.166	.156	.170	.133	.140
	(446)	(53)	(429)	(77)	(432)	(150)	(301)
Employee Counseling	.518	.577	.526	.689*	.514	.600	.529
	(444)	(52)	(420)	(74)	(428)	(150)	(295)

Note: Sample size is in parentheses. Asterisks indicate that union and nonunion means are significantly different at the .05 level.

icies. As such, these policies provide a suitable starting point in an analysis of unionism and HR innovations.[3]

Table 2 presents information on the extent to which the large business units in the sample described later have adopted the 10 HR innovations for their managers, unionized and nonunion professional employees, unionized and nonunion clerical employees, and unionized and nonunion production employees. In addition, Table 2 indicates the instances in which significant differences in HR policy coverage occur across unionized and nonunion workers in each job category. The means reported in Table 2 generally suggest that unionized workers are more likely to be covered by employee involvement programs, employee counseling programs, and grievance procedures than are nonunion workers in the same job categories. Unionized workers are less likely than nonunion workers in the same job categories to be covered by flexible job design programs, flexitime (flexible scheduling), and profit-sharing arrangements. Moreover, these patterns generally hold up in an analysis of HR innovations across job categories in double-breasted firms (i.e., firms that have both unionized and nonunion employees in the same job categories). Curiously, coverage by HR innovations is not universally more likely for managers than for other employees.

There is evidence of union status differences in six of the 10 HR innovation subject areas examined here. In three instances, unionized workers are more likely than nonunion workers to be covered by innovative HR policies. In three instances the reverse is true. Innovations solely for nonunion employees, however, tend to be rare. In each case where nonunion employees are more likely than their unionized counterparts to be covered by an HR innovation, less than half of the nonunion employees are covered by the innovation. In short, these results do not indicate that HR innovations are solely a feature of the nonunion sector. But the Table 2 results do not take into account factors other than unionization that may influence the adoption of HR innovations.

Measures of Organizational Performance

Because data on profitability and productivity were not available at the occupational level within each business unit (my unit of analysis), this study examines two intermediate firm performance measures, namely voluntary employee turnover and employee support for change in organizational HR policies. Turnover is a widely-studied intermediate measure of organizational performance (see Huselid 1995; Leonard 1987; Steers and Mowday 1981). Research has indicated that a portion of the effect of HR policies on a firm's financial performance occurs because those policies reduce turnover (Huselid 1995, p. 658). The amount of employee support for organizational change is a new measure of performance. It provides an indication of how difficult it will be for management to make internal adjustments to changing external conditions. Thus, support for change is a crude measure of the flexibility with which human resources can be managed by a firm (see Delaney and Sockell 1990). For the purpose of this study, it is important to note that both turnover and employees' support for change can be measured at the same level of analysis as HR policies, which will permit a straightforward test of the association between HR innovations and these measures of organizational outcomes.

Given the mixed results of studies examining the link between HR policies and economic measures of firm performance (see Huselid 1995; Ichniowski 1990; Ichniowski, Shaw, and Prennushi 1994), the focus on turnover and flexibility may reveal insights that are not apparent in other work. The literature suggests the hypotheses that HR innovations should be negatively related to turnover and positively related to employees' support for change (see Kanter 1984; Huselid 1995; Delaney and Sockell 1990). In addition, the same general model of HR innovations can be used to explain employee turnover (Steers and Mowday 1981) and employee support for change (Delaney and Sockell 1990). Accordingly, the study turns to an examination of forces influencing the adoption of HR innovations and then to the effects of those innovations on turnover and flexibility. Following, some factors that will affect the adoption of HR innovations are identified. It should be noted that the analysis focuses on the *adoption* of HR innovations rather than on the formulation of such innovations.[4]

A MODEL OF HR INNOVATIONS

What factors affect the adoption of HR innovations in American firms? Although several researchers have offered conceptual frameworks addressing the implementation of specific HR policies, such as planning (Fiorito, Stone, and Greer 1985), training (Holzer 1987), or grievance procedures (Ichniowski and Lewin 1988), there is no general theory of HR policy implementation. Moreover, few studies of HR issues have drawn on the business strategy or economics literatures, despite assertions that HR innovations are adopted to serve strategic or economic purposes (for exceptions, see Brown 1990; Holzer 1987; Huselid 1995; Kochan and Barocci 1985; Lazear and Rosen 1981; Lengnick-Hall and Lengnick-Hall 1988; Miles and Snow 1978; Osterman 1994).

Researchers from a variety of disciplines have suggested that certain external and internal forces, such as company values, environmental characteristics, and unions, influence the HR innovations adopted by firms as well as other organizational outcomes (Dunlop 1958; Dyer and Schwab 1982; Huselid 1995; Kochan McKersie, and Cappelli 1984; Lewin 1987; Osterman 1987, 1994). Research also suggests that management is the primary initiator of HR innovations even though the environment and unions affect those innovations. This is thought to be true not only because management retains discretion over the adoption of HR innovations in nonunion settings but because certain HR innovations involve issues that are not mandatory subjects of collective bargaining (and thus may be implemented at management's discretion in unionized settings). Since management is critical to the adoption of HR innovations, specific management characteristics must be included in an analysis of those innovations. More generally, HR innovations can be viewed as the product of innovation-producing inputs, such as organizational structure, characteristics of the external environment, the nature of workers and work, and unions.

Management and HR Policy Implementation

Management devises and adopts HR policies to organize and control workers and the work place. Because management, in most cases, retains unilateral authority to establish and modify HR policies, existing personnel practices generally reflect management's notion of proper employment rules. Although it is reasonable to assume that management attempts to fashion policies that enhance workers' productivity and operational efficiency, there is no singular set of HR policies that guarantees the attainment of productivity and efficiency goals. It is often the case that specific organizational objectives, such as improving product quality, can be achieved through a variety of HR policies, such as the implementation of more stringent hiring standards or the provision of more extensive training.

Ultimately, management's decision to adopt HR innovations is influenced by a variety of considerations, including the characteristics, strategies, and values of management. Because of the wide range of HR policy choices available to businesses, organizational idiosyncracies have a substantial impact on the selection of personnel policies. Some firms are renowned for treating their workers well. Peters and Waterman's (1982) famous book identified such firms and asserted that the association between positive treatment of employees and the economic performance of these and other firms is not coincidental. Other research corroborates the view that organizational policy choices are influenced by the values of the period in which the firm was founded (Stinchcombe 1965), the commitment of top management to specific policies (Dyer, Shafer, and Regan 1982), and the company's stated philosophy or mission (Kanter 1984).

It is well known that organizations differ in the extent to which the enterprise is seen as a community or family (Osterman 1994, p. 179). Organizations holding a family perspective rather than a stockholder perspective may value human resources more and may be more likely to adopt HR innovations than other firms (Dyer, Shafer, and Regan 1982). Although it is difficult to measure precisely the extent to which a firm values its employees, researchers have argued that HR executives are more involved in the business planning process in firms that value employees than in firms that are less concerned about employees (Lawler 1986; Lewin and Sherer 1993; Osterman 1994; Peters and Waterman 1982).

In this study, the extent to which a firm values human resources is measured by a variable that indicates the involvement of a business unit's HR executive in the firm's strategic planning process. The variable is a rating on a seven-point Likert-type scale that ranges from (1) "never" to (7) "always." In a cross-sectional study, it is not possible to infer causality from the coefficient on this variable, though the direction of its association can be predicted. Because the HR executive is likely to play a larger role in firms that emphasize human resources than in other firms, this variable should be positively associated with the adoption of HR innovations.

Kochan, Katz, and McKersie (1986) emphasized the important role that management strategies play in the development of HR practices. Business strategies influence the adoption of HR innovations by affecting the estimated costs and benefits of those policies. For example, a business decision to divest certain operations reduces the benefits of implementing innovative HR policies in those operations. In general, the business strategy literature suggests that firms following the strategy of growing through mergers and acquisitions (this strategy has been called "acquisitive diversification") are different from firms using other growth strategies (Kerr 1985; Leontiades 1980). In other words, some firms focus on identifying targets of opportunity in other businesses rather than on developing their existing businesses. This measure of firm strategy is captured by including a dummy variable that equals one if a business unit was acquired by its corporate parent *and* it or its corporate parent has acquired other businesses within the last five years. Firms that follow acquisitive or "evolutionary" strategies are less likely than other firms to adopt HR innovations because they tend to focus on short term financial performance, rather than on long-term organizational development (Kerr 1985).

Hofer and Schendel (1978) and Miles and Snow (1978) argued that there is a link between the age of a firm's establishments and products and its organizational practices. It has been suggested that firms follow different HR policies during different stages of the life cycle of their products (Fombrun, Tichy, and Devanna 1984; Kochan and Barocci 1985). Similarly, Stinchcombe (1965) asserted that internal organizational arrangements are affected by the "founding period" of a firm and the industry in which it operates. These views suggest that the age of a firm is associated with the HR policies that it chooses to adopt (Baron, Jennings, and Dobbin 1988; Dimick and Murray 1978). But the association between organizational age and innovative HR policies is unclear. On the one hand, HR innovations are a relatively new phenomenon and as such may be more likely to occur in new or young firms than in old operations. On the other hand, if HR innovations provide the advantages popularly attributed to them (see Peters and Waterman 1982), then older firms may have survived because they paid relatively more attention to the HR needs of their workers. In this study, the age of an organization is measured by a variable that equals the average age of the establishments operated by a business unit.

Technology, Work, and HR Innovations

Osterman's (1987) analysis suggests that characteristics of the firm that reflect technology and the nature of work influence the extent to which an organization adopts HR innovations. At the firm level, factors such as firm size, capital intensity, and the nature of work activities characterize what Osterman called physical and social technologies.[5] Firm size influences HR policy choices because large firms have more frequent and complex human resource needs than small firms (Osterman 1994). It is also likely that the potential variety of work tasks, duties, and technologies is positively related to firm size. These factors make monitoring of employees more difficult in large firms than in small firms. The natural logarithm of the number of employees in a business unit is used to measure firm size in the empirical analysis reported in the following text. Because large firms have more formalized HR functions than small firms (Barron, Jennings, and Dobbin 1988), and because HR innovations may substitute for monitoring (Akerlof and Katz 1989), there should be a positive association between firm size and HR innovations.

The degree of capital intensity in a firm may also influence its HR policy choices. Firms employing capital-intensive production technologies have different HR needs than firms employing labor-intensive production technologies. The marginal product of labor rises with capital intensity, and the cost of "down time" is substantial in capital-intensive firms because overhead costs are high. This increases the likelihood that capital-intensive employers will emphasize HR innovations in an attempt to encourage labor force productivity. Although the role of employees is relatively more important in labor-intensive businesses than in capital-intensive businesses, labor-intensive employers can often monitor or replace employees effectively, lessening the need for HR innovations (Brown 1990). The natural log of a business unit's assets per employee is used in the empirical models as a measure of capital intensity; it should be positively related to the adoption of HR innovations.

The nature of work influences the need for HR innovations (Osterman 1987). Because of work force skill and education differences, firms that have a larger proportion of managerial and professional employees may adopt different internal rules than firms that employ relatively fewer managers and professionals. Differences in work tasks are indirectly captured in the empirical models by including a variable that measures the percentage of total firm employment comprised by managers and professional and technical employees. The influence of this measure on HR innovations is not clear. On the one hand, the conceptual framework suggests that variation in work tasks is positively related to the incidence of innovative HR policies. On the other hand, efficiency wage models suggest that "self-monitoring" and "supervisory monitoring" approaches are substitutes, which suggests a negative relationship between the percent of managers and professionals and the adoption of HR innovations.

Market forces may make the adoption of HR innovations more affordable in some firms than in others. Theory predicts a negative relationship between wage levels and HR innovations. Firms paying high wages may not need to offer HR innovations to workers, while firms paying low wages may offer HR innovations as a less costly way to increase workers' efforts. This prediction is confounded, however, by the facts that high wages may be a substitute for monitoring and firms that can afford high wages may turn out to be the same firms that can afford to adopt HR innovations. On balance, average wage levels for workers in a firm's three-digit industry group should be inversely related to the adoption of HR innovations.

The Work Force, Government Regulation, and HR Innovations

Industry dummy variables are included in the model to control for industry differences in HR practices. Note that such differences may be due in part to different levels of government regulation across industries (Long and Link 1983). In addition, both market structure and production processes vary across industries. Thus, the nature of a business unit's primary industry may influence its use of HR innovations. Data presented by Peters and Waterman (1982) indicated that firms rated as "excellent" in their HR strategies are not evenly distributed across industries. To capture these differences, three industry dummy variables, covering manufacturing, retail and wholesale trade, and service industries, are included in the equations. Firms in the agriculture, finance, and transportation, communications, and utilities industries comprise the excluded category for the industry comparisons.

Workers' characteristics and values also influence firms' decisions to adopt HR innovations. In particular, the demand for innovative HR policies may differ across employee groups. For example, a variable measuring the percentage of male workers in an industry captures both potential differences in the preferences of men and women for various workplace arrangements and the possible impact of antidiscrimination laws on those arrangements. Some HR innovations provide benefits, such as flexible work hours, that have traditionally been more important to women than to men. If men and women have different preferences and equal employment opportunity laws forbid discrimination on the basis of gender, then firms in industries with a high percentage of male employees may have a different likelihood of adopting HR innovations than firms in industries with a lower percentage of male workers. Two dummy variables are also included in the analysis to capture differences in the adoption of HR innovations across occupations. One variable equals 1 for manufacturing and production workers and zero otherwise, and the other equals 1 for clerical employees and zero otherwise. Professional and technical employees comprise the excluded occupational category.

Unions and HR Innovations

As noted earlier, unions affect the enactment of HR innovations in organizations. The union effect is both direct, through collective bargaining, and indirect, through communications with management regarding the needs and preferences of workers. In addition, if firms adopt HR innovations to avoid unionization, then a union threat effect also exists. That is, employers' fear of unionization independently raises the likelihood that HR innovations will be adopted by nonunion firms.

The traditional economic view of unions as labor market monopolies suggests that organized labor focuses on wages and employment levels rather than on innovative HR policies in negotiations (Freeman and Medoff 1984). Similarly, the view that unions are bureaucratic organizations that serve the interests of union leaders rather than union members suggests that unions impose barriers to the implementation of HR innovations in order to protect the power of the entrenched leadership and to ensure that workers and employers are divided (see Heldman and Knight 1980). But there exists substantial evidence that unions have supported HR innovations, albeit reluctantly in some cases, in order to preserve jobs (Chamberlain 1948; Kochan, Katz, and McKersie 1986). HR innovations are often the subject of internal union debate because such policies may be used to supersede the role of unions in the work place (Moody 1988; Zellner 1989). These debates have led some unions to support and other unions to oppose HR innovations (Sockell 1984).

In short, unions have access to channels that influence the adoption of HR innovations. Because of a threat effect, unions may affect the extent to which employers adopt HR innovations covering nonunion employees. While unions can theoretically influence the institution of HR innovations, internal politics, leadership preferences, and union characteristics constrain unions' influence on such policies. Moreover, labor law stipulates the subjects that firms and their unionized employees must bargain about; "wages, hours, and other terms and conditions of employment" [29 U.S.C. § 159(a)] constitute the scope of management's mandatory bargaining obligation. Employers and unions may voluntarily choose to bargain over legal subjects that fall outside of the domain of mandatory issues. Evidence suggests, however, that few non-mandatory subjects of bargaining appear in union contracts (Delaney and Sockell 1989).

For this reason, unions are much more likely to influence HR policies covering issues subject to mandatory bargaining than issues outside of the scope of bargaining. Therefore, if HR policies deemed to be innovative by researchers cover non-mandatory bargaining subjects, then unions may have little influence on management's efforts to adopt such policies. Unions could do little directly to force management to implement non-mandatory HR policies and would be unable to prevent firms from unilaterally adopting them. In these cases, unions must rely on indirect methods of affecting employers' decisions to adopt HR innovations, such as insisting on a mandatory issue (e.g., compensation) to gain a concession on the HR innovation. Although the indirect methods may not be as effective as direct negotiations, they still provide an incentive to employers to address union concerns about HR innovations or to abandon the innovations.

Consequently, several measures of unionization are used in this analysis. First, to capture the threat effect of unions, the model includes a variable that equals the percentage of workers in a business unit's primary industry that are covered by collective bargaining agreements (Freeman and Medoff 1979). The coefficient on this variable will be positive if a threat effect leads nonunion employers to adopt HR innovations. Second, a variable is included that equals the percentage of a business unit's non-managerial employees who are unionized. Holding industry unionization constant, the sign on this variable is unclear. Kochan, McKersie, and Chalykoff (1986) suggested that the percentage unionized in a firm will be positively related to the adoption of HR innovations covering the firm's unionized employees and negatively related to the adoption of HR innovations covering the firm's nonunion employees. To test this possibility, some analyses will be conducted using samples of unionized workers in double-breasted firms, nonunion workers in double-breasted firms, and nonunion workers in nonunion firms.[6] In addition, two dummy variables are included in aggregate equations to capture differences due to union status. One variable equals 1 for unionized employees in double-breasted firms and zero otherwise; the other variable equals 1 for nonunion employees in double-breasted firms and zero otherwise. Nonunion employees in nonunion firms comprise the comparison category for each of these variables. For the reasons noted previously, alternate measures of unionization may have different effects on HR innovations.

Finally, a variable measuring each business unit's opposition to unions is included in the analysis to capture the extent to which the desire to avoid unions affects the adoption of HR innovations when other innovation-producing inputs are held constant. This variable is constructed from responses to two survey questions. For each nonunion occupation, the variable equals a business unit's rating of how important it is to keep that employee group nonunion using a scale that ranged from (1) "not important" to (5) "very important." For each unionized occupation, the variable equals a business unit's rating of the extent to which it emphasizes "phasing out unionized operations" for that occupational group using a scale that ranged from (1) "not emphasized" to (5) "heavily emphasized." If opposition to unions leads employers to adopt HR innovations, then this variable should have a positive coefficient in the full sample. In the sample of unionized workers in double-breasted firms, however, opposition to unions will likely be inversely related to the adoption of HR innovations (see Kochan, McKersie, and Chalykoff, 1986).

EMPIRICAL ANALYSES AND RESULTS

Measures and Empirical Procedures

Three dependent variables are used to study the determinants and consequences of HR innovations. One dependent variable is the total number of HR innovations (out of the 10 listed in Table 1) that have been adopted in each business unit for the relevant occupational group. Another dependent variable is the average monthly turnover (in percent) for each occupation within each business unit. The final dependent variable is a measure of organizational flexibility. Specifically, it is a measure of the extent to which different employee groups support changes in HR policies, as perceived by the business unit's HR executive. Support for change was measured using a Likert-type scale that ranged from (1) "strong opposition" to (5) "strong support" for each of the employee groups. The equations to be estimated are recursive, as HR innovations are assumed to influence turnover and organizational flexibility. Ordinary least squares (OLS) is used to estimate the reduced-form HR innovation equation, and two-stage least squares (2SLS) is used to estimate the turnover and flexibility equations.[7] Results will provide insight into the pervasiveness and magnitude of union effects on HR innovations generally, as well as the effect of those innovations on outcomes.

To take advantage of the occupational data gathered in the survey, the sample is constructed so that *an occupation within a business unit is the unit of observation.* A business unit can have a maximum of seven observations, but the average number of observations per company is four, and policies covering managers are excluded from the analysis. It is useful to arrange the data in this way because the survey indicated the existence of systematic differences in HR policies across occupational groups (Delaney, Lewin, and Ichniowski 1989).

Empirical Results: Determinants of HR Innovations

Results of OLS estimation of the reduced-form HR innovation equations are presented in Table 3. The overall models were significant in each equation. Although the results are selectively summarized later, coefficients on many of the independent variables were statistically significant and in the expected directions in the equations. For example, coefficients on the industry dummy variables suggest that HR innovations vary across industry, and the percentage of male employees in an industry is negatively related with the HR innovations dependent variable.[8]

Union Status and HR Innovations

Coefficients on the union status variables in Table 3 present an interesting pattern. The extent to which a firm is opposed to unionization is negatively associated with HR innovations. Furthermore, both unionized and nonunion workers in double-breasted firms are covered by significantly fewer HR innovations than are nonunion workers in nonunion firms. Other things equal, neither the percent unionized in a company nor the percent unionized in its industry is significantly associated with the HR innovation dependent variable. Recall, however, that conflicting forces may be operating within firms that have both unionized and nonunion employees, and those forces may influence the findings reported in Table 3. Consequently, the data were divided into subsamples of unionized employees in

Table 3. Determinants Of HR Innovations

Independent Variables	Dependent Variable: Number of HR Innovations	
	(1)	(2)
Union Opposition	−.084*	—
	(.044)	
Company Percent Union	—	.000 1
		(.003)
Industry Percent Union	.005	.002
	(.003)	(.003)
Union Workers in Double-Breasted Firm	−1.070***	−.868***
	(.205)	(.225)
Nonunion Workers in Double-Breasted Firm	−.891***	−.823***
	(.170)	(.200)
log Size	.507***	.521***
	(.037)	(.025)
log Capital Intensity	.037	.050
	(.045)	(.041)
HR Values	.199***	.210***
	(.030)	(.029)
Company Strategy	−.600***	−.564***
	(.177)	(.162)
Establishment Age	−.007	−.002
	(.007)	(.007)
Percent Managers and Professionals	.007**	.007**
	(.003)	(.003)
Occupation Variables		
Production Workers	−.022	−.057
	(.143)	(.135)
Clerical Workers	−.061	−.023
	(.133)	(.126)
Percent Male	−.010**	−.007*
	(.005)	(.004)
log Industry Wage	.376	.353
	(.342)	(.338)
Industry Variables		
Manufacturing	.0002	−.015
	(.144)	(.136)
Trade	−.750***	−.865***
	(.279)	(.264)

(continued)

Table 3. (Continued)

Independent Variables	Dependent Variable: Number of HR Innovations	
	(1)	(2)
Service	−.747***	−.783***
	(.240)	(.226)
Intercept	−.923	−1.666**
	(.732)	(.675)
F Statistic	22.9***	24.4***
R Square	.296	.289
Sample Size	944	1036

Notes: Standard errors are in parentheses.
    ***Significant at the .01 level.
    **Significant at the .05 level.
    *Significant at the .10 level.
    Two-tailed tests for coefficients.

double-breasted firms, nonunion employees in double-breasted firms, and nonunion employees in nonunion firms. The Table 3 equations were then reestimated using the subsample data, and these findings are reported in Table 4.

The Table 4 results confirm that the extent of unionization within a firm is associated with the adoption of HR innovations. Specifically, double-breasted firms appear to treat their unionized and nonunion employees differently with respect to HR innovations. In those firms, innovations in HR policies are positively related to the percent unionized in the equation for unionized workers but negatively associated with the percent unionized in the nonunion employee equation. The findings suggest that the negative association between firms' opposition to unions and HR innovations reported in Table 3 is most pronounced for unionized employees in double-breasted firms. Still, the results suggest that HR innovations are not solely a product of the nonunion sector. Moreover, union strength (as measured by the percent organized) appears to be strongly related to the adoption of HR innovations. Interestingly, despite the pattern of results in Table 3, there is virtually no difference in the mean number of HR innovations adopted across union-status categories examined in Table 4 (3.3 for unionized employees in double-breasted firms, 3.3 for nonunion employees in double-breasted firms, and 3.2 for nonunion employees in nonunion firms).

Organizational Characteristics and HR Innovations

Results reported in Tables 3 and 4 suggest interesting relationships between selected organizational factors and the adoption of HR innovations. Organizational size displays a consistent positive association with the dependent variable.

Table 4. Determinants of HR Innovations in Double-breasted and Nonunion Firms

Independent Variables	Union Employees in Double-Breasted Firms	Nonunion Employees in Double-Breasted Firms	Nonunion Employees in Nonunion Firms
Union Opposition	-.154* (.089)	-.058 (.066)	-.150 (.106)
Company Percent Union	.009* (.005)	-.008* (.005)	—
Industry Percent Union	.010 (.008)	.005 (.006)	.007 (.005)
log Size	.367*** (.087)	.688*** (.074)	.543*** (.052)
log Capital Intensity	.032 (.098)	.254*** (.086)	.202** (.085)
HR Values	.062 (.073)	.052 (.062)	.320*** (.041)
Company Strategy	-.607* (.344)	-.538** (.274)	-.192 (.400)
Establishment Age	.021 (.017)	-.024 (.015)	-.023** (.010)
Percent Managers and Professionals	.017** (.008)	.018** (.007)	-.004 (.005)
Occupation Variables			
Production Workers	.439 (.326)	-.169 (.274)	-.097 (.197)

	(1)	(2)	(3)	(4)	(5)
Clerical Workers	.214	.256	.029	.111	-.133
	(.347)	(.350)	(.230)	(.211)	(.196)
Percent Male	-.016*	-.011	-.005	-.007	-.011
	(.009)	(.010)	(.008)	(.007)	(.007)
log Industry Wage	.636	.265	-.902	-.264	.003
	(.724)	(.767)	(.637)	(.617)	(.583)
Industry Variables					
Manufacturing	-.099	-.0002	-.287	-.302	.517**
	(.299)	(.306)	(.259)	(.240)	(.245)
Trade	-1.242*	-1.289*	-1.220**	-.833*	-.474
	(.656)	(.670)	(.540)	(.505)	(.427)
Service	-1.450**	-1.287**	-1.266**	-1.513***	-.265
	(.583)	(.620)	(.522)	(.501)	(.397)
Intercept	-1.465	-2.510	-.941	-1.548	-.931
	(1.676)	(1.664)	(1.415)	(1.288)	(1.262)
F Statistic	7.0***	6.6***	9.3***	9.8***	16.2***
R Square	.360	.344	.337	.320	.408
Sample Size	204	206	290	328	369

Notes: Standard errors are in parentheses.
***Significant at the .01 level.
**Significant at the .05 level.
*Significant at the .10 level.
Two-tailed tests for coefficients.

229

This finding is consistent with my prediction but conflicts with the results of Osterman's (1994) analysis. Although the capital intensity variable is not significantly associated with HR innovations in Table 3, results in Table 4 suggest that capital intensity is positively related to the adoption of HR innovations covering *nonunion* employees. Consistent with my expectation, firms following an acquisitive diversification business strategy implemented fewer HR innovations than other firms. Table 3 results show a positive relationship between the HR values variable and HR innovations, confirming findings reported by other researchers (Osterman 1994). Interestingly, Table 4 suggests that the HR values result is much more pronounced in nonunion firms than in double-breasted firms. As empirical studies have strongly suggested that organizational values influence the adoption of HR innovations, the observation of different effects by union status indicates a need for further research.

Empirical Results: Effect of HR Innovations on Turnover

Although there is much speculation that innovative HR policies reduce turnover, evidence of that association is generally limited; relevant studies have tended to focus on specific HR policies, such as seniority rules (Block 1978). Table 5 presents the results of 2SLS estimates of the equations using average monthly turnover (in percent) as the dependent variable. These results provide strong support for the conventional wisdom. Each increase of one HR innovation is associated with a decline of about 3 percentage points in average monthly turnover, other things equal. This suggests that a firm with the mean number of HR innovations will have monthly turnover that is about 10 percentage points lower than a firm that has no HR innovations. In other words, there is a strong negative association between the adoption of HR innovations and turnover, *ceteris paribus.*

Consistent with earlier studies (see Freeman and Medoff 1984), the Table 5 findings also indicate that unionization is inversely related to turnover within a firm. In addition, two particularly interesting findings emerge from the equations. First, there is some evidence that unionization is negatively related to the average turnover rate of nonunion employees in double-breasted firms. This may be partly a product of the fact that double-breasted firms seem to offer similar types of HR policies to their unionized and nonunion workers. Second, the percent unionized in a firm's three-digit industry is positively associated with turnover. As there are coefficients on the variables measuring unionized and nonunion employees in double-breasted businesses, this finding may imply that, as unionization in an industry grows, the nonunion employees in that industry leave their jobs in efforts to gain more lucrative unionized positions in competing firms.

Although the Table 5 equations focus on only one organizational outcome measure, the confirmation of an inverse relationship between HR innovations and turnover has broader implications. Lower turnover likely has positive consequences for other organizational outcomes, such as productivity, product quality, and finan-

Table 5. Determinants of Turnover

Independent Variables	Dependent Variable: Average Monthly Turnover	
	(1)	(2)
Union Opposition	−.504	—
	(.380)	
Company Percent Union	—	−.044*
		(.025)
Industry Percent Union	.089***	.086***
	(.030)	(.028)
Union Workers in Double-Breasted Firm	−3.787***	−.542
	(2.171)	(2.038)
Nonunion Workers in Double-Breasted Firm	−3.054*	−.362
	(1.851)	(1.774)
log Size	2.185***	2.211***
	(.724)	(.688)
log Capital Intensity	.063	.162
	(.387)	(.348)
Innovative HR Policies	−3.224***	−3.085***
	(1.130)	(1.043)
Establishment Age	−.281***	−.244***
	(.063)	(.058)
Percent Managers and Professionals	.167***	.164***
	(.029)	(.028)
Occupation Variables		
Production Workers	.414	.703
	(1.199)	(1.112)
Clerical Workers	−.219	.174
	(1.107)	(1.013)
Percent Male	−.013	.004
	(.037)	(.035)
log Industry Wage	−4.332	−3.494
	(2.926)	(2.805)
Industry Variables		
Manufacturing	−1.794	−1.926
	(1.197)	(1.100)
Trade	14.342***	12.263***
	(2.389)	(2.241)
Service	−5.633***	−5.341***
	(2.158)	(2.006)

(continued)

Table 5.   (Continued)

Independent Variables	Dependent Variable: Average Monthly Turnover	
	(1)	(2)
Intercept	7.184	.301
	(6.330)	(5.934)
F Statistic	9.4***	9.4***
Sample Size	771	835

Notes: .Standard errors are in parentheses.
 ***Significant at the .01 level.
 **Significant at the .05 level.
 *Significant at the .10 level.
 Two-tailed tests for coefficients.

cial performance (Huselid 1995; MacDuffie 1995). To test this possibility further, an examination of the relationship between HR innovations and employees' support for change in the organization is conducted below. Because support for change is essential for the maintenance of flexibility in an organization, the analysis provides another suggestive indicator of the effects of HR innovations.

Empirical Results: Effect of HR Innovations on Support for Change

Table 6 presents results of 2SLS analyses that regress perceived support for change (or flexibility) on a variety of independent variables, including HR innovations. Results indicate a strong positive association between HR innovations and perceived support for change in organizations. Across the two equations, the initiation of each additional HR innovation raises the perceived support for change index by about 5 percent. In combination with the Table 5 results, the findings indicate that organizations benefit in a variety of ways from the introduction of HR innovations and that innovative policies seem to have potentially large effects on organizational outcomes.

Other interesting patterns exist in the results reported in Table 6. The percent unionized in a firm is positively related to perceived support for change, though the magnitude of the effect is small (each 10% increase in percent unionized is associated with a 1.5% increase in the support for change index). Moreover, *ceteris paribus*, unionized employees in double-breasted firms have the lowest average perceived support ratings. Nonunion employees in double-breasted firms have the highest average perceived support ratings, and nonunion employees in nonunion businesses have average perceived support ratings between the other groups. Although the pattern of results may seem surprising at first glance, its implications are consistent with conventional wisdom. Specifically, unionized

Table 6. Determinants of Employee Support for Change (Flexibility)

Independent Variables	Dependent Variable: Employee Support for Change	
	(1)	(2)
Union Opposition	.033	—
	(.024)	
Company Percent Union	—	−.005***
		(.001)
Industry Percent Union	−.002	−.002
	(.002)	(.002)
Union Workers in Double-Breasted Firm	−.233*	−.588***
	(.125)	(.114)
Nonunion Workers in Double-Breasted Firm	.336***	.088
	(.103)	(.100)
log Size	−.137***	−.121***
	(.043)	(.038)
log Capital Intensity	−.053**	−.061***
	(.023)	(.020)
Innovative HR Policies	.176**	.137***
	(.069)	(.059)
Establishment Age	.004	.002
	(.004)	(.003)
Percent Managers and Professionals	.003*	.0034**
	(.0018)	(.0017)
Occupation Variables		
Production Workers	−.226***	−.240***
	(.074)	(.066)
Clerical Workers	−.141**	−.149**
	(.068)	(.061)
Percent Male	.002	.003
	(.002)	(.002)
log Industry Wage	−.345**	−.389**
	(.176)	(.163)
Industry Variables		
Manufacturing	−.154**	−.086
	(.073)	(.065)
Trade	−.014	−.064
	(.150)	(.136)
Service	−.158	−.150
	(.131)	(.118)

(continued)

Table 6. (Continued)

	Dependent Variable: Employee Support for Change	
Independent Variables	*(1)*	*(2)*
Intercept	4.404***	4.618***
	(.376)	(.337)
F Statistic	8.1***	10.2***
Sample Size	857	941

Notes: Standard errors are in parentheses.
***Significant at the .01 level.
**Significant at the .05 level.
*Significant at the .10 level.
Two-tailed tests for coefficients.

employees on average are perceived to be less supportive of change than nonunion employees in nonunion firms or nonunion employees in firms with some unionized workers. Within unionized firms, however, the percent of workers unionized is positively associated with perceived support for change.

Consistent with the literature, perceived support for change is inversely related to firm size and capital intensity. In addition, support for change increases as the job level of employees increases from production workers to clerical workers to professional workers. And, industry wage levels are negatively associated with perceived support for change. In combination, these results suggest that workers in large firms, who are relatively better paid, and work in lower-level jobs are perceived to be more resistant to change than workers in smaller firms, who are less well paid, and employed in higher-level positions. This supports speculation that factors that threaten workers or alienate them make them more resistant to change.

Overall, the findings in Table 6 provide support for the notion that firms can achieve beneficial organizational outcomes (increased support for change) by adopting innovative HR policies. Those beneficial outcomes can occur in any setting—union or nonunion, large or small firm, high or low wage industry. To the extent that evidence of these links is confirmed by other research, it appears that U.S. industry as a whole can benefit from a greater use of HR innovations.

DISCUSSION

The analyses presented in this study have wide-ranging implications. Results suggest systematic associations between a variety of organizational characteristics and the existence of HR innovations in a sample of large publicly-held businesses. The results confirm other studies (Osterman 1994) and support conventional wisdom that HR innovations are associated with improved organizational performance. Although the cross-sectional nature of the data precludes definitive statements about causality, the findings are instructive. Moreover, the results may shed light on a paradox of efficiency wage theory. Specifically, research has indicated that payment of wages above market levels produces some positive organizational results, but that the magnitude of the results is not enough to show that the high wage strategy is a profit maximizing strategy (Leonard 1987). It may be that the benefits of a high wage strategy or an HR innovation strategy are spread across multiple organizational outcomes. Although results may not justify the strategy as profit maximizing for a single outcome, they may pay off across a series of outcomes (e.g., decreased turnover, more managerial flexibility, and perhaps more productivity). Put differently, short-term gains from HR innovations across multiple measures of performance may foster long-term profitability improvements. At a minimum, results of this analysis suggest that research attention should be given to the range of potential benefits that may be produced by a portfolio of HR innovations. Beyond these general implications, the results suggest certain conclusions about innovative HR policies.

Unions, Management Opposition, and HR Innovations

In general, my results do not confirm conventional management views that unions systematically impede the adoption of innovative HR policies. To the extent that this sample is representative of U.S. firms generally, the results place in a favorable light those scholarly arguments that HR innovations may be more effective in unionized organizations (Mitchell 1987). Some researchers have argued that union involvement in various HR innovations will overcome asymmetric information and monitoring cost problems that arise when individual employees work under innovative HR policies. For example, profit sharing plans have been advocated as an HR innovation that can improve workers' productivity and firm performance (Hoerr 1989; Kruse 1994; Weitzman 1984). While workers are assigned a share of profits by some formula under such plans, it is widely known that profit figures may be manipulated by management. Individual workers may not have enough information on corporate performance or understand company accounting practices sufficiently to ensure compliance with the profit-sharing arrangement. Union involvement and monitoring provide insurance that workers are treated fairly and equitably under such plans (Eaton and Voos 1992; Mitchell 1987). Unions can also play a valuable role in the oversight of other HR innovations.

American managers have long been obsessed with a desire to avoid unions (Harris 1982; Kochan, Katz, and McKersie 1986), even though the importance of maintaining a nonunion work force differs across industries and depends on the extent of unionization within firms. It is not surprising then that some researchers have asserted that unions hinder the adoption of HR innovations that could make U.S. firms more competitive in world markets (Weitzman 1984). Although substantial evidence challenges these assertions, the assertions persist partly because of the pervasiveness of antiunion attitudes among U.S. managers (Wolters 1981). In recent years, it has been documented that management opposition to unions is substantial (Freeman and Kleiner 1990a, 1990b; Freeman 1986). NLRB records of employer unfair labor practices (Weiler 1983), employers' desire to provoke strikes and permanently replace strikers (Fiorito and Maranto 1987), and concession bargaining demands by employers (Becker 1987; Cappelli 1985) underscore management's dominant preference to eliminate unions. The extent to which management opposition to unions varies across firms or industries is not clear, however. Interindustry differences in unionization rates (Kokkelenberg and Sockell 1985) indirectly suggest that there are differences in employers' views in this regard. Available direct evidence, compiled from case studies and a few empirical analyses, seems to corroborate this indirect evidence (Kochan, Katz, and McKersie 1986).

For example, Verma and Kochan (1985) described the approach taken by one conglomerate to shift investment gradually from its unionized operations to its nonunion ones. Kochan, Katz, and McKersie (1986, p. 71) documented similar trends in case studies of other firms. Using surveys conducted by the Conference Board in 1977 and 1983, Cappelli and Chalykoff (1986) illustrated that unionization, a single plant bargaining structure, and business expansion were significantly associated with management opposition to unions. Furthermore, examinations of the outcomes of union representation elections demonstrate that management opposition to unions is negatively associated with union election victories (Dickens 1983; Lawler and West 1985; Seeber and Cooke 1983). It has been inferred from these studies that strong management opposition to unions may be responsible for a substantial proportion of the decline in the unionized sector (Cappelli 1984). In essence, this may indicate that the adoption of HR innovations may have little to do with managers' opinion of the intrinsic value of these policies. To explore this issue further, it is useful to examine the extent to which HR innovations are implemented for managerial and non-managerial employees. The results of such an analysis are briefly discussed next.

Occupational Level and HR Innovations

Because managers have no legally protected right to unionize, it is not necessary for firms to adopt HR innovations covering managers as a means of union avoidance. Thus, insight into firms' motivations regarding HR innovations may be inferred from the extent to which companies provide innovative HR policies to their managers. For example, if corporate America believes that HR innovations are valuable and if unions truly hinder the ability of firms to adopt such policies, then evidence may show that HR innovations covering managers are widespread. After all, managers are arguably a firm's most important employees.

The results presented in Table 2, however, do not generally indicate that managers are more likely to be covered by HR innovations. Instead, the findings indicate a general similarity in the extent to which HR innovations are offered across occupations. Although managers are more likely than non-managerial employees to be covered by profit-sharing plans, they are much less likely to have access to a complaint resolution procedure. In essence, Table 2 shows that HR innovations are not the norm for managers and that HR innovations, where adopted, tend to cover managers and other workers equally. While these results could be interpreted to indicate that businesses do not place a high value on HR innovations (given that managers are not regularly covered by them) or that the absence of a unionization threat reduces all employees' (including managers') likelihood of being covered by innovative HR policies, the findings basically show that occupational differences do not alter the results reported earlier.

Societal Changes, Unions, and HR Innovations

Over the past 40 years, society and workers have changed in ways that may have potentially large effects on U.S. businesses. The labor force of the 1990s is very different from the labor force of the 1940s or 1950s. Specifically, the labor force is aging, more women are working, more two-earner couples exist today than existed in the past, unionization rates have plummeted, and questions have arisen about the work ethic of young workers. The global economy and Third World development have made product markets much more competitive today than they were 10 years ago. It has been argued that U.S. firms need to treat workers differently and "better" in order to remain competitive in the global marketplace (Kanter 1984; Peters and Waterman 1982; Pfeffer 1994). Although there has been a call for the implementation of innovative HR policies, evidence presented here and elsewhere indicates that U.S. businesses have not widely adopted HR innovations (see Osterman 1994).

For example, HR innovations aiding working parents, such as flexible work schedules, paternity leave, and day-care benefits, are not common in American businesses. Not only do relatively few firms offer these arrangements to their employees, the business lobby in Washington has actively opposed bills that would require firms to provide some of these benefits (Delaney and Schwochau 1993). Given the inevitability of labor force demographic changes, it is difficult to understand firms' resistance to HR innovations—especially since the benefits seem to outweigh the costs of many innovative HR policies (see Huselid 1995).

The pattern of union-nonunion differences reported in this study may be partly explained by the legal framework governing unionization and collective bargaining. HR innovations that cover mandatory bargaining subjects, such as grievance procedures, exist because unions can and do insist on including them in negotiations. Innovations that involve permissive bargaining subjects, such as certain information-sharing or employee involvement initiatives, may not be widespread, in part because management can lawfully refuse to bargain over them. While the pattern of results reported above shows that unions do not always insist on HR innovations covering mandatory subjects, the absence of innovative HR policies for managers suggests fundamentally that firms have not accepted such policies as necessary or valuable.

If the desire by management to implement HR innovations is motivated by a fear of unions, then the decline of organized labor in the United States could lead to a decline in the incidence of those HR policies. This scenario would be paradoxical, however, given the evidence that HR innovations reduce turnover and increase managerial flexibility. In addition, this scenario would be unfortunate because many HR innovations give workers a voice in their jobs and recognize the importance of their family obligations. Thus, the absence of many kinds of HR innovations in American businesses may indicate both a neglect of workers and a potential lost opportunity to increase organizational performance.

HR Innovations and Economic Performance of the Firm

As noted earlier, one reason for the recent increase in interest in HR innovations is a belief that such policies will enhance the economic performance of firms (Kanter 1984). The belief is based on anecdotes about the accomplishments of specific firms (Peters and Waterman 1982) and by the results of recent empirical research (Huselid 1995; Ichniowski, Shaw, and Prennushi 1994; MacDuffie 1995). Although the empirical evidence is mixed, the results are promising. In the final analysis, the results presented here confirm that HR innovations should be encouraged. At the least, adoption of such innovations ensures that nonunion employees (who comprise a great majority of the labor force) have some voice in their organizations (e.g., through employee involvement programs) and some protection from unfair treatment (e.g., through grievance procedure coverage). In addition, these innovations offer large potential benefits to firms; HR innovations appear to reduce turnover and increase employees' support for organizational change (flexibility).

Additional research on HR innovations is needed. Researchers need to discover why some HR innovations have been more successful in unionized settings than in nonunion ones (see Eaton and Voos 1992; Mitchell 1987). It is necessary to understand the mechanisms through which HR innovations motivate employees to work harder or enable them to work smarter. In addition, standardized measures of HR innovations must be identified so that research results can be compared appropriately and acknowledged more generally. Finally, it would be especially useful for researchers to devote their energies to the analysis of HR innovations, especially the interactive effects of individual HR policies and systems of HR policies.

HR innovations offer an opportunity for American firms to increase productivity and protect employees' work place interests at the same time. Because employers and employees seem to benefit from such policies, it is an appropriate time to encourage firms to adopt HR innovations.

APPENDIX

HR Innovations Identified by Kanter (1984) and HR Innovations Examined in This Study

HR Policies Classified as "Innovative" by Kanter (1984)	HR Policies Analyzed in This Study
1. Job Enrichment	
2. Job Rotation	1. Flexible Job
3. Project Teams	Designs
4. Quality Circles	
5. Labor-Management Committees	
6. Semi-Autonomous Work Groups	2. Employee
7. Works Councils	Involvement
8. Formal Training in Employee Involvement	Programs
9. Career Development Workshops	
10. Career Planning	
11. Special Development Programs	
12. Mentor/Sponsor Programs	
13. Line Management Monitoring Programs	
14. EEO Awareness	
15. Matrix Organization	
16. Cross-Training	
17. Group Training	
18. Nontraditional Career Paths	3. Profit
19. Broad-Based Education	Sharing
20. Tenure (No Layoffs) Policies	
21. Job Posting	
22. Compensation Linked to Development	
23. Gain-Sharing Systems	
24. Scanlon Plan	4. Grievance
25. Pay for Skills	Procedure
26. Internal Dispute Resolution Systems	
27. Nontraditional Information-Sharing Programs	5. Information Sharing
28. Flexitime	6. Attitude
29. Part-Time Jobs	Surveys
30. Job Sharing	7. Flexitime
31. Work-at-Home	
32. Child Care	8. Day Care
33. Paternity Leave	9. Paternity
34. Employee Assistance Programs	Leave
35. Internal Venture Funds	10. Employee
36. Transition at Retirement	Counseling
37. Parallel Organization	
38. Health Facilities	
39. Nontraditional Management Design	
40. Nontraditional Performance Appraisal	

ACKNOWLEDGMENT

The data analyzed in this study were collected as a part of a project that was supported by faculty research grants from the Columbia University Graduate School of Business. I am grateful to Ann Bartel, Casey Ichniowski, Bruce Kaufman, Marianne Koch, David Lewin, Susan Schwochau, Donna Sockell, and seminar participants at Georgia State University for helpful comments on earlier drafts.

NOTES

1. Examination suggested that gas and electric utilities are somewhat overrepresented in the data set (Delaney, Lewin, and Ichniowski 1989, pp. 11-13). A multivariate analysis of respondents and non-respondents indicated differences across two-digit SIC industries (firms in the transportation, communications, and utilities industry category were more likely to respond than firms in other industries). In addition, firm size was positively related with the probability of responding to the survey, and unionization in a firm's two-digit industry was negatively related to responding. Profitability and capital expenditures were not significantly associated with the probability of response.

2. For discussions of innovative HR policies, see Lawler and Mohrman (1987), Kanter (1984, 1986), Pfeffer (1994), and Peters and Waterman (1982). In addition, while the unit of analysis in this study is the corporate business unit, I use the terms "business unit," "firm," and "business" interchangeably.

3. The innovative HR policies analyzed in this study were chosen to cover each of the general policy areas outlined by Kochan, McKersie, and Chalykoff (1986) and Kanter (1984). Some discretion was used in the selection process, in part because some of the HR policies deemed to be innovative by Kanter could be questioned (such as seniority systems), and some of the policies noted by Kochan and his associates are so broad as to cover many management decisions traditionally outside of the realm of HR (such as rules governing the modification of work systems). It is assumed that, by excluding policies that may or may not be HR innovations, the resulting empirical estimations will be more truly reflective of the causes and effects of innovative HR policies in American firms. It should be recognized, however, that this approach may lead to conservative estimates of the effects of HR innovations. The appendix identifies the HR policies that Kanter (1984) saw as innovative.

4. This study does not address the extent to which these HR policies reflect the strategic goals and objectives management intended at the time the policies were implemented. Instead, the paper focuses solely on the factors associated with the adoption of selected innovative HR policies.

5. Osterman's (1987) discussion focused on skill, risk, and configuration of technologies. In this study, I focus on aggregate measures of technologies, however, given the nature of the data available for analysis.

6. Because managers are not covered by the National Labor Relations Act, the empirical analysis initially focuses on non-managerial employees.

7. The turnover and flexibility equations are identified by excluding the HR values and company strategy variables from the 2SLS equations and by including the establishment age and industry wage variables in the 2SLS equations.

8. I considered survey response bias in several unreported empirical models. The existence of response bias implies that unobserved factors related to an organization's decision to respond to the survey are associated with HR innovations, turnover, and flexibility. I formally tested this possibility using a procedure suggested by Heckman (1979). Specifically, selectivity bias variables were calculated and included as independent variables in the OLS and 2SLS regression models. Inclusion of these variables were calculated and included as independent variables in the OLS and 2SLS regression models. Inclusion of these variables had little effect on the regression results and did not alter the conclu-

sions based on the models presented in the paper. The selectivity bias variables are always positive and are statistically significant in about half of the regressions.

REFERENCES

Akerlof, G. A., and L. F. Katz. 1989. "Workers' Trust Funds and the Logic of Wage Profiles." *Quarterly Journal of Economics* 104 (August): 525-536.

Baron, J. N., P. D. Jennings, and F. R. Dobbin. 1988. "Mission Control? The Development of Personnel Systems in U.S. Industry." *American Sociological Review* 53 (August): 497-514.

Becker, B. E. 1987. "Concession Bargaining: The Impact on Shareholders' Equity." *Industrial and Labor Relations Review* 40 (January): 268-279.

Bemmcls, B. 1987. "How Unions Affect Productivity in Manufacturing Plants." *Industrial and Labor Relations Review* 40 (January): 241-253.

Block, R. N. 1978. "The Impact of Seniority Provisions on the Manufacturing Quit Rate." *Industrial and Labor Relations Review* 31 (July): 474-488.

Brown, C. 1990. "Firm's Choice of Method of Pay." *Industrial and Labor Relations Review* 43 (February): S165-S182.

Cappelli, P. 1984. "Union Gains Under Concession Bargaining." Pp. 297-305 in *Proceedings of the Thirty-Sixth Annual Meeting*. Madison, WI: Industrial Relations Research Association.

_____. 1985. "Plant-Level Concession Bargaining." *Industrial and Labor Relations Review* 39 (October): 90-104.

Cappelli, P., and J. Chalykoff. 1986. "The Effects of Management Industrial Relations Strategy: Results of a Recent Survey." Pp. 171-178 in *Proceedings of the Thirty-Eighth Annual Meeting*. Madison, WI: Industrial Relations Research Association.

Cappelli, P., and K. Chauvin. 1991a. "A Test of an Efficiency Model of Grievance Activity." *Industrial and Labor Relations Review* 45 (October): 3-14.

_____. 1991b. "An Interplant Test of the Efficiency Wage Hypothesis." *Quarterly Journal of Economics* 106 (August): 769-787.

Cascio, W. F. 1987. *Applied Psychology in Personnel Management*, 3rd ed. Englewood Cliffs, NJ: Prentice-Hall.

Chamberlain, N. W. 1948. *The Union Challenge to Management Control*. New York: McGraw-Hill.

Delaney, J. T., C. Ichniowski, and D. Lewin. 1989. "Employee Involvement Programs and Firm Performance." Pp. 148-158 in *Proceedings of the Forty-First Annual Meeting*. Madison, WI: IRRA.

Delaney, J. T., D. Lewin, and C. Ichniowski. 1989. *Human Resource Policies and Practices in American Firms*. Washington, D.: Bureau of Labor-Management Relations and Cooperative Programs, U.S. Department of Labor.

Delaney, J. T., and S. Schwochau. 1993. "Employee Representation Through the Political Process." Pp. 265-304 in *Employee Representation: Alternatives and Future Directions*, edited by B. Kaufman and M. M. Kleiner. Madison, WI: Industrial Relations Research Association.

Delaney, J. T., and D. Sockell. 1989. "The Mandatory-Permissive Distinction and Collective Bargaining Outcomes." *Industrial and Labor Relations Review* 42 (July): 566-83.

_____. 1990. "Employee Involvement Programs, Unionization, and Organizational Flexibility." Pp. 264-268 in *Academy of Management Best Papers Proceedings*, edited by L. Jauch and J. L. Wall. Ada, OH: Academy of Management.

Dickens, W. T. 1983. "The Effect of Company Campaigns on Certification Elections: Law and Reality Once Again." *Industrial and Labor Relations Review* 36 (July): 560-575.

Dickens, W. T., L. F. Katz, K. Lang, and L. H. Summers. 1989. "Employee Crime and the Monitoring Puzzle." *Journal of Labor Economics* 7: 331-347.

Dimick, D. E., and V. V. Murray. 1978. "Correlates of Substantive Policy Decisions in Organizations: The Case of Human Resource Management." *Academy of Management Journal* 21 (December): 611-623.

Doeringer, P. B., and M. J. Piore. 1971. *Internal Labor Markets and Manpower Analysis.* Lexington, MA: D.C. Heath.

Dunlop, J. T. 1958. *Industrial Relations Systems.* New York: Holt.

Dyer, L., and D. P. Schwab. 1982. "Personnel/Human Resource Management Research." Pp. 187-220 in *Industrial Relations Research in the 1970s: Review and Appraisal,* edited by T. A. Kochan, D. J.B. Mitchell, and L. Dyer. Madison, Wis.: Industrial Relations Research Association.

Dyer, L., R. A. Shafer, and P. J. Regan. 1982. "Human Resource Planning at Corning Glass Works: A Field Study." *Human Resource Planning* 5: 1-45.

Eaton, A.E., M. E. Gordon, and J. H. Keefe. 1992. "The Impact of Quality of Work Life Programs and Grievance System Effectiveness on Union Commitment." *Industrial and Labor Relations Review* 45 (April): 591-604.

Eaton, A. E., and P. B. Voos. 1992. "Unions and Contemporary Innovations in Work Organization, Compensation, and Employee Participation." Pp. 173-215 in *Unions and Economic Competitiveness,* edited by P. Voos and L. Mishel. Armonk, NY: M.E. Sharpe.

Fiorito, J., C. Lowman, and F. D. Nelson. 1987. "The Impact of Human Resource Policies on Union Organizing." *Industrial Relations* 26 (Spring): 113-126.

Fiorito, J., and C. L. Maranto. 1987. "The Contemporary Decline of Union Strength." *Contemporary Policy Issues* 5 (October): 12-27.

Fiorito, J., T. H. Stone, and C. R. Greer. 1985. "Factors Affecting Choice of Human Resource Forecasting Techniques." *Human Resource Planning* 8: 1-17.

FitzRoy, F. R., and K. Kraft. 1987. "Cooperation, Productivity, and Profit Sharing." *Quarterly Journal of Economics* 102 (February): 23-35.

Fombrun, C. J., N. M. Tichy, and M. A. Devanna. Eds. 1984. *Strategic Human Resource Management.* New York: Wiley.

Freeman, R. B. 1986. "The Effect of the Union Wage Differential on Management Opposition and Union Organizing Success." *American Economic Review* 76 (May): 92-96.

Freeman, R. B., and M. M. Kleiner. 1990a. "Employer Behavior in the Face of Union Organizing Drives." *Industrial and Labor Relations Review* 43 (April): 351-365.

———. 1990b. "The Impact of New Unionization on Wages and Working Conditions: A Longitudinal Study of Establishments." *Journal of Labor Economics* 8 (January): S8-S25.

Freeman, R. B., and J. L. Medoff. 1984. *What Do Unions Do?* New York: Basic Books.

Freeman, R. B., and J. L. Medoff. 1979. "New Estimates of Private Sector Unionism in the United States." *Industrial and Labor Relations Review* 32: 143-174.

Friedman, S. D. 1986. "Succession Systems in Large Corporations: Characteristics and Correlates of Performance." *Human Resource Management* 25 (Summer): 191-212.

Gaedeke, R.M., and D.H. Tootelian. 1976. "The Fortune '500' List—An Endangered Species for Academic Research." *Journal of Business Research* 4: 283-288.

Gordon, D., R. Edwards, and M. Reich. 1982. *Segmented Work, Divided Workers.* New York: Cambridge University Press.

Harris, H. J. 1982. *The Right to Manage.* Madison, WI: University of Wisconsin Press.

Heckman, J. J. 1979. "Sample Selection Bias as a Specification Error." *Econometrica* 47 (January): 153-161.

Heldman, D. C., and D. L. Knight. 1980. *Unions and Lobbying: The Representation Function.* Arlington, VA: Foundation for the Advancement of the Public Trust.

Hoerr, J. 1989. "The Payoff From Teamwork." *Business Week* (July 10), pp. 56-62.

Hofer, C. W., and D. E. Schendel. 1978. *Strategy Formulation: Analytical Concepts.* St. Paul, MN: West.

Holzer, H. J. 1987. "Hiring Procedures in the Firm: Their Economic Determinants and Outcomes." Pp. 243-274 in *Human Resources and the Performance of the Firm*, edited by M. M. Kleiner, R. N. Block, M. Roomkin, and S. W. Salsburg. Madison, WI: Industrial Relations Research Association.

Huselid, M. A. 1995. "The Impact of Human Resource Management Practices on Turnover, Productivity, and Corporate Financial Performance." *Academy of Management Journal*, 38 (June): 635-672.

Hutchens, R. M. 1987. "A Test of Lazear's Theory of Delayed Payment Contracts." *Journal of Labor Economics* 5 (October, Part 2): S153-S170.

Ichniowski, C. 1990. "Human Resource Management Systems and the Performance of U.S. Manufacturing Businesses." National Bureau of Economic Research Working Paper No. 3449.

Ichniowski, C., J. T. Delaney, and D. Lewin. 1989. "The New Human Resource Management in U.S. Workplaces: Is It Really New and Is It Only Nonunion?" *Relations Industrielles* 44: 97-119.

Ichniowski, C., and D. Lewin. 1988. "Characteristics of Grievance Procedures: Evidence From Nonunion, Union, and Double-Breasted Businesses." Pp. 415-424 in *Proceedings of the Fortieth Annual Meeting*. Madison, WI: Industrial Relations Research Association.

Ichniowski, C., K. Shaw, and G. Prennushi. 1994. "The Effects of Human Resource Management Practices on Productivity." Unpublished manuscript, Columbia University.

Jacoby, S. M. 1985. *Employing Bureaucracy: Managers, Unions, and the Transformation of Work in American Industry, 1900-1945*. New York: Columbia University Press.

———. 1986. "Progressive Discipline in American Industry: Its Origins, Development, and Consequences." Pp. 213-260 in *Advances in Industrial and Labor Relations*, Vol. 3, edited by D. B. Lipsky and D. Lewin. Greenwich, CT: JAI Press.

Jensen, M. C., and K. J. Murphy. 1990. "Performance Pay and Top-Management Incentives." *Journal of Political Economy* 98 (April): 225-264.

Kandel, E., and E. P. Lazear. 1992. "Peer Pressure and Partnerships." *Journal of Political Economy* 100 (August): 801-817.

Kanter, R. M. 1984. "The Roots of Corporate Progressivism: How and Why Corporations Respond to Changing Societal Needs and Expectations." Report submitted to the Russell Sage Foundation.

———. 1986. "The New Workforce Meets the Changing Workplace: Strains, Dilemmas, and Contradictions in Attempts to Implement Participative and Entrepreneurial Management." *Human Resource Management* 25 (Winter): 515-537.

Katz, H. C., T. A. Kochan, and M. R. Weber. 1985. "Assessing the Effects of Industrial Relations Systems and Efforts to Improve the Quality of Working Life on Organizational Effectiveness." *Academy of Management Journal* 28 (September): 509-526.

Kerr, J. L. 1985. "Diversification Strategies and Managerial Rewards: An Empirical Study." *Academy of Management Journal* 28 (March): 155-179.

Kleiner, M. M. 1984. "Unionism and Employer Discrimination: Analysis of 8(a)(3) Violations." *Industrial Relations* 23 (Spring): 234-243.

Kleiner, M. M., and M. L. Bouillon. 1988. "Providing Business Information to Production Workers: Correlates of Compensation and Profitability." *Industrial and Labor Relations Review* 41 (July): 605-617.

Kochan, T. A. 1980. *Collective Bargaining and Industrial Relations*. Homewood, IL: Irwin.

Kochan, T. A., and T. A. Barocci. 1985. *Human Resource Management and Industrial Relations*. Boston: Little, Brown and Company.

Kochan, T. A., H. C. Katz, and R. B. McKersie. 1986. *The Transformation of American Industrial Relations*. New York: Basic Books.

Kochan, T. A., R. B. McKersie, and P. Cappelli. 1984. "Strategic Choice and Industrial Relations Theory." *Industrial Relations* 23 (Winter): 16-39.

Kochan, T. A., R. B. McKersie, and J. Chalykoff. 1986. "The Effects of Corporate Strategy and Workplace Innovations on Union Representation." *Industrial and Labor Relations Review* 39 (July): 487-501.

Kokkelenberg, E. C., and D. R. Sockell. 1985. "Union Membership in the United States, 1973-1981." *Industrial and Labor Relations Review* 38 (July): 497-543.

Kossek, E. E. 1989. "The Acceptance of Human Resource Innovation by Multiple Constituencies." *Personnel Psychology* 42 (Summer): 263-282.

Kruse, D. L. 1994. *Profit Sharing: Does It Make a Difference?* Kalamazoo, MI: Upjohn.

Lawler, E. E., III. 1986. *High-Involvement Management*. San Francisco: Jossey Bass.

Lawler, E. E., III, and S. A. Mohrman. 1987. "Unions and the New Management." *Academy of Management Executive* 1 (November): 293-300.

Lawler, J. J., and R. West. 1985. "Attorneys, Consultants and Union Avoidance Strategies in Representation Elections." *Industrial Relations* 24 (Fall): 406-420.

Lazear, E. P. 1981. "Agency, Earnings Profiles, and Hours Restrictions." *American Economic Review* 71 (September): 606-620.

Lazear, E. P., and S. Rosen. 1981. "Rank-Order Tournaments as Optimum Labor Contracts." *Journal of Political Economy* 89 (October): 841-64.

Lengnick-Hall, C. A., and M. L. Lengnick-Hall. 1988. "Strategic Human Resources Management: A Review of the Literature and a Proposed Typology." *Academy of Management Review* 13 (July): 454-470.

Leonard, J. S. 1987. "Carrots and Sticks: Pay, Supervision, and Turnover." *Journal of Labor Economics* 5 (October, Part 2): S136-S152.

Leontiades, M. 1980. *Strategies for Diversification and Change*. Boston: Little, Brown and Company.

Levine, D. I., and L. D. Tyson. 1990. "Participation, Productivity, and the Firm's Environment." Pp. 183-244 in *Paying for Productivity*, edited by A. S. Blinder. Washington, D.C.: Brookings Institution.

Lewin, D. 1987. "Industrial Relations as a Strategic Variable." Pp. 1-41 in *Human Resources and the Performance of the Firm*, edited by M. M. Kleiner, R. N. Block, M. Roomkin, and S. W. Salsburg. Madison, WI: Industrial Relations Research Association.

Lewin, D, and P. D. Sherer. 1993. "Does Strategic Choice Explain Senior Executives' Preferences on Employee Voice and Representation." Pp. 235-263 in *Employee Representation: Alternatives and Future Directions*, edited by B. Kaufman and M. M. Kleiner. Madison, WI: Industrial Relations Research Association.

Long, J. E., and A. N. Link. 1983. "The Impact of Market Structure on Wages, Fringe Benefits, and Turnover." *Industrial and Labor Relations Review* 36 (January): 239-50.

MacDuffie, J. P. 1995. "Human Resource Bundles and Manufacturing Performance: Organizational Logic and Flexible Production Systems in the World Auto Industry." *Industrial and Labor Relations Review* 48 (January): 197-221.

Miles, R. E., and C. C. Snow. 1978. *Organizational Strategy, Structure, and Process*. New York: McGraw-Hill.

Milgrom, P., and J. Roberts. 1993. "Complementarities and Fit: Strategy, Structure, and Organizational Change." Unpublished manuscript, Stanford University.

Mitchell, D. J. B. 1987. "The Share Economy and Industrial Relations." *Industrial Relations* 26 (Winter): 1-17.

Moody, K. 1988. *An Injury to All: The Decline of American Unionism*. New York: Verso.

Moore, W. J., and R. J. Newman. 1991. "Government Wage Differentials in a Municipal Labor Market: The Case of Houston Metropolitan Transit Workers." *Industrial and Labor Relations Review* 45 (October): 145-153.

Morishima, M. 1991. "Information Sharing and Firm Performance in Japan. *Industrial Relations* 30 (Winter): 37-61.

Osterman, P. 1987. "Choice of Employment Systems in Internal Labor Markets." *Industrial Relations* 26 (Winter): 46-67.

_____. 1994. "How Common is Workplace Transformation and Who Adopts It?" *Industrial and Labor Relations Review* 47 (January): 173-188.

Peters, T. J., and R. H. Waterman, Jr. 1982. *In Search of Excellence*. New York: Harper and Row.

Pfeffer, J. 1994. *Competitive Advantage Through People*. Boston: Harvard Business School Press.

Piore, M. J., and C. F. Sabel. 1984. *The Second Industrial Divide*. New York: Basic Books.

Rynes, S. L., and J. W. Boudreau. 1986. "College Recruiting in Large Organizations: Practice, Evaluation, and Research Implications." *Personnel Psychology* 39 (Winter): 729-757.

Seeber, R. L., and W. N. Cooke. 1983. "The Decline of Union Success in NLRB Representation Elections." *Industrial Relations* 22 (Winter): 34-44.

Slichter, S. H., J. J. Healy, and E. R. Livernash. 1960. *The Impact of Collective Bargaining on Management*. Washington, DC: Brookings Institution.

Sockell, D. 1984. "The Legality of Employee-Participation Programs in Unionized Firms." *Industrial and Labor Relations Review* 37 (July): 541-556.

Steers, R. M., and R. T. Mowday. 1981. "Employee Turnover and Post Decision Accommodation Processes." Pp. 235-281 in *Research in Organizational Behavior*, Vol. 3, edited by L.L. Cummings and B. M. Staw. Greenwich, CT: JAI Press.

Stinchcombe, A. 1965. "Social Structure and Organizations." Pp. 142-193 in *Handbook of Organizations*, edited by J. March. Chicago: Rand-McNally.

Tsui, A., and L. Gomez-Mejia. 1988. "Evaluating HR Effectiveness." Pp. 1-187-1-227 in *Human Resources Management: Evolving Roles and Responsibilities*, edited by L. Dyer. Washington, D.C.: Bureau of National Affairs.

Verma, A., and T. A. Kochan. 1985. "The Growth and Nature of the Nonunion Sector Within a Firm." Pp. 89-117 in *Challenges and Choices Facing American Labor*, edited by T. A. Kochan. Cambridge, MA: MIT Press.

Wagner, J. A. 1994. "Participation's Effect on Performance and Satisfaction: A Reconsideration of Research Evidence." *Academy of Management Review* 19 (April): 312-330.

Weiler, P. 1983. "Promises to Keep: Securing Workers' Rights to Self- Organization Under the NLRA." *Harvard Law Review* 96 (June): 1769-1827.

Weitzman, M. L. 1984. *The Share Economy: Conquering Stagflation*. Cambridge, MA: Harvard University Press.

Wolters, R. S. 1981. "Union-Management Ideological Frames of Reference in Bargaining." Pp. 211-218 in *Proceedings of the Thirty-Third Annual Meeting*. Madison, WI: Industrial Relations Research Association.

Zellner, W. 1989. "The UAW Rebels Teaming up Against Teamwork." *Business Week* (March 27), pp. 110-114.

REGULATING THE WORKPLACE:
THE VEXING PROBLEM OF IMPLEMENTATION

David Weil

ABSTRACT

Labor market policies in the United States implicitly or explicitly require that workers play a role in policy implementation through exercise of designated employee rights. Optimal individual exercise of rights, however, is dependent on the presence of a collective workplace agent, such as a labor union. The article empirically tests this insight and provides evidence of systematically higher levels of labor policy implementation in unionized workplaces than in comparable non-union workplaces. Given this finding, the paper examines how labor policy implementation might be improved to deal with an increasingly nonunion workplace environment.

The late 1980s and early 1990s witnessed the passage of a number of major new labor policies including the Worker Adjustment, Retraining, and Notification Act of 1988, the American with Disabilities Act of 1990, and the Family and Medical Leave Act of 1993. As in the case of previous labor policy initiatives, each policy

Advances in Industrial and Labor Relations, Volume 7, pages 247-286.
Copyright © 1996 by JAI Press Inc.
All rights of reproduction in any form reserved.
ISBN: 1-55938-925-7

engendered intense debates concerning their desirability from the perspective of workers, businesses, and the society as a whole.

These debates proceeded (as had previous discussions of such laws as the Fair Labor Standards Act and the Occupational Safety and Health Act) on the assumption that the laws as established on paper would be fully enforced and implemented in practice. Thus, congressional debate concerned the anticipated benefits and costs of the labor policy once implemented but seldom if ever on the determinants of successful implementation itself.

In fact, implementation varies dramatically across and within industries for any given labor policy. Implementation depends on a complex set of factors such as the characteristics of the specific labor policy, the government enforcement strategy, and the nature of the industry or industries under regulation. As a result, while some employers face strong pressures to comply with government standards related to minimum wages, health and safety, or pension investment, others operate in an essentially unregulated labor market.

One determinant of implementation cuts across the majority of labor policies. Labor market policies implicitly or explicitly require that workers play a role in ensuring that the objectives of the law are achieved. U.S. labor laws regulating hours and working conditions, safety and health, plant closing, and hiring and promotion practices create clear employee rights that affect the enforcement and administration of laws. While employee participation has been the subject of a great deal of attention in regards to its connection to labor relations outcomes, job satisfaction, and most recently firm performance, relatively little attention has been paid to its relation to labor policy implementation.

Constrained government enforcement resources make employee participation a necessary condition for carrying out many U.S. labor policies as currently structured. The conditions under which employees exercise their rights therefore affects achievement of policy goals in the workplace. Conceptually, a worker chooses to exercise a right granted by labor legislation if the benefits to the individual worker (arising from the regulation) are greater than the costs associated with exercising that right. However, because of both positive externalities and significant fixed costs associated with exercise of rights, optimal exercise of rights is dependent on the presence of some type of collective workplace agent. For a variety of reasons, labor unions play this role in unionized workplaces. Given this, systematic differences in labor policy implementation should exist between unionized and otherwise comparable nonunionized workplaces arising from the differential use of employee rights. This insight raises questions concerning the efficacy of labor market regulations dependent on exercise of employee rights given the declining percentage of workers represented by labor unions.

This article examines the relationship between labor policy implementation, employee participation and unionization. The article begins by relating employee rights to the implementation of labor market policies. It then examines how a system reliant on individual exercise of rights may lead to underutilization of those rights, and the role of a workplace agent like a labor union in dealing with this utilization problem. Based on the insights from this model on the potential role of unions in implementation, the article surveys empirical literature on a diverse set of labor market regulations. This survey reveals that labor unions play an important role as workplace agents of employee participation under most major labor policies. Given this finding, the article concludes with an examination of how labor policies might be implemented in an increasingly nonunion workplace.

EMPLOYEE RIGHTS AND THE IMPLEMENTATION OF LABOR POLICIES

Many government labor policies attempt to assure that employees work under conditions deemed desirable by that legislation, such as in workplaces free of significant safety or health risks, discriminatory human resource policies, or hours and wage levels not meeting certain standards. Implementation—the means used to achieve legislative objectives—occurs through ensuring employer compliance with the policy prescriptions through government enforcement activities.

This type of labor policy typically creates governmental agencies vested with the authority to enforce standards. Thus, the Occupational Safety and Health Act established the Occupational Safety and Health Administration (OSHA) within the Department of Labor to ensure employer compliance with health and safety standards. The Wage and Hour Division within the Department of Labor ensures enforcement of minimum wage, overtime, and other provisions of the Fair Labor Standards Act (FLSA). The Equal Employment Opportunity Commission (EEOC) was created to enforce Title VII of the Civil Rights Act of 1964.

The regulatory mandates shouldered by these agencies are enormous relative to the size of those agencies. The Department of Labor relies upon 800 inspectors to enforce all labor standard regulations covered by the FLSA. As a result, in 1993 the Wage and Hour Division was able to handle 2,295 cases in comparison to the 46,121 complaints received (Commission on the Future of Worker-Management Relations 1994a; Holmes 1991). OSHA's inspection force has never exceeded 1,500 and currently hovers around 1,200 (Siskind 1993), despite the fact that its mandate covers 6.2 million establishments and 93 million employees (OSHA 1994). In 1993, the EEOC received a total of 87,942 complaints. In that year, the commission filed a mere 481 lawsuits (Commission on the Future of Worker-Management Relations 1994a).

The ability of government agencies to fulfill their legislative mandates therefore relies upon an agency's ability to deploy very constrained resources in an effective manner. For example, government agencies rely partly on "deterrence" pressure to induce voluntary compliance among regulated employers by increasing the cost of noncompliance (e.g., through high penalties, high profile inspections, and strategic targeting of inspections) (see Becker 1968; Kambhu 1989;

Stigler 1970; Viscusi and Zeckhauser 1979 for discussions of enforcement and compliance).

Reliance on government acting as the regulatory agent is not the only means of labor policy implementation. In addition to creating these agencies, federal and state policies vest employees with rights and / or responsibilities directly related to implementation. Several examples are illustrative. The Occupational Safety and Health Act and the Mine Health and Safety Act establish employee rights related to all aspects of enforcement activities, including the right to initiate, participate in, and review the results of workplace inspections.[1] In a related vein, the Fair Labor Standards Act provides for employee-initiated claims concerning nonpayment of overtime or minimum wages. Enforcement of job discrimination provisions of Title VII has similarly become highly dependent upon employee-initiated claims. Most strikingly, the Worker Adjustment and Retraining Notification Act (WARN) did not create a governmental enforcement agent but instead relies solely upon suits brought by affected workers or communities for implementation (Ehrenberg and Jakobson 1990).

In a somewhat different vein, labor policies such as unemployment insurance and workers compensation provide eligible workers with a safety net in the event of unexpected employment loss or disability. Under these programs, implementation occurs when eligible recipients take the administrative steps necessary to receive the benefits to which they are entitled. This type of labor policy also implicitly requires employee involvement for implementation. Workers compensation systems rely upon injured employees filing claims with state workers compensation boards. Similarly unemployment insurance claims are filed by workers who must satisfy a set of eligibility requirements. Thus, implementation of both programs depends on whether workers who are eligible for benefits actually apply for them.

Given the problem of limited government inspection resources, these employee rights profoundly affect the achievement of labor policy objectives. If employees actively draw upon their rights, they can play a crucial role in fulfilling those objectives. Alternatively, if employees do not utilize these rights, implementation of labor laws becomes almost solely dependent on the constrained resources of the government. The determinants of employee exercise of rights therefore becomes critical to an analysis of labor policy implementation.

Exercise of Rights: A Benefit / Cost Approach

There is little reason to believe that workers uniformly exercise rights granted them under various labor policies. Studies in several different areas indicate that the propensity to exercise rights varies along systematic lines across different groups. A number of empirical studies have shown different propensities for individuals to litigate civil claims (see, e.g., Hoyman and Stallworth 1981; Shavell 1987). Other studies have documented factors affecting workers' use of grievance procedures in union and nonunion workplaces (see Peterson 1992 for a review of the union literature, Chachere and Feuille 1993; Feuille and Delaney 1992; Boroff 1991 on use of grievance procedures in nonunion workplaces). This literature suggests that factors related to the individual (sex, education, background), the workplace environment (size, degree of conflict, management, and union policies), and the specific grievance or civil problem involved affect under what circumstances individuals use their rights.

The degree to which individual employees exercise their rights under labor laws can be expected to depend on the perceived benefits versus costs of exercising rights from the perspective of an individual worker. The benefits of exercising a right are a function of the impact of a given piece of labor legislation on the outcome of concern to the worker. For example, initiating an OSHA inspection potentially improves working conditions for the worker by diminishing or removing the risk of an injury or illness. More generally, the benefits received by a worker increase as a function of both the severity of the problem subject to regulation and faced by the worker and the potential relief offered by the labor legislation to that problem. Thus, the perceived benefit of exercising a right are increased by the degree that current conditions differ from those proscribed by labor statutes. Increasing the stringency of a given labor standard increases the potential benefit to a worker, all else equal. Similarly, employer efforts to improve working conditions diminish the benefits arising from exercising a right. As a result, the benefit of exercising a right will vary across different labor standards (depending on their stringency) and for a given standard across employers (given the degree of noncompliance with statutes among employers).

In order to ascertain the magnitude of these benefits, workers must acquire information on the *current* and legally *permissible* level of a regulated outcome. The cost of exercising rights are primarily a function of the costs of gathering this information. These are composed of the costs associated with (a) obtaining information regarding the existence of their basic rights under applicable labor laws (e.g., overtime limitations) or benefit (e.g., unemployment insurance benefits) and what their rights are in the event that their employers violate the standard or law[2], and (b) gathering information on the particular labor market problem giving rise to the labor policy. This is particularly true in the case of safety and health laws where occupational risks might not be fully perceived or appreciated (Viscusi 1983; Viscusi and O'Connor 1984); (c) learning about the specific details of how the law is administered. This may include the procedures to initiate a complaint inspection under OSHA or FLSA. Alternatively, it may involve knowledge of how to file a disability claim under workers compensation or how to apply for unemployment benefits.

In addition to information-related costs, workers face costs arising from potential employer retaliation. This cost may arise from the psychic costs associated with fear of retribution at the job site.[3] More profoundly, the cost may be in the form of reassignment to a less desirable or remunerative job or, in the extreme, being fired.

Different attributes of the workplace will influence the costs associated with gathering information as well as the probability and severity of employer retaliation. For example, employees in large workplaces would seem to face lower costs than those in small workplaces all else equal, both because large firms are more likely to provide information on employee rights as part of formalized human resource policies (Foulkes 1980; Dunlop 1988), and because "whistleblowers" are less likely to be detected in a large workplace.

To illustrate this framework, imagine an individual facing the decision whether or not to make a claim for back-pay under FLSA. In making the claim, the worker can obtain benefits (in the form of back wages and potential change in future behavior by the employer) which are proportional to the amount of back pay owed the worker.[4] On the other hand, the individual faces substantial costs in filing such a claim, related to the factors described above. First he must gather information on basic rights and administrative procedures under FLSA. Second, he must prepare materials to provide evidence for the claim (and make an assessment of the probability that the claim will be found meritorious). Third, he must face the cost that the employer will retaliate against him as a result of the action in terms of treatment, future opportunities for overtime, or at worst termination.[5]

Prevailing workplace conditions, stringency of regulatory standards, costs of information acquisition, and the costs of retaliation together determine the degree statutory rights are exercised across different firms in a given industry and across different types of labor legislation more generally. This, in turn, will affect the implementation of labor policies to the extent that they are reliant on the exercise of employee rights.

Individual Rights, Collective Agents, and Labor Unions

There is reason to believe that workers will systematically underutilize their rights if decisions are made on an individual basis as a result of both the structure of benefits and costs related to exercise of rights. Employee exercise of workplace rights displays positive externalities on the benefit side. If an individual only perceives the benefits accruing directly to them from filing such a claim, they will "under-invest" in exercise of rights because the collective (workplace) benefits arising from their action are not factored into the individual decision. For example, single violations of labor standards like overtime provisions of FLSA are usually associated with a larger pattern of violation across a group of employees. An individual claim for back pay may cause an investigation into the employer's overtime pay practice which in turn may lead to workplace-wide compliance with FLSA from that point forward. Because an individual does not directly perceive these workplace-wide benefits, employee rights will be underutilized.

The divergence between costs on an individual versus collective level may also lead to underutilization of rights. The information requirements of pursuing a case have significant fixed cost elements arising from the requisite time to learn the law and procedures on the one hand and to gather evidence and make a case on the other. The cost of mishandling a case are also significant since a worker's understanding of the strength of his or her case is limited. While workers can (and do) use outside counsel as a means of making these assessments, the use of lawyers also entails significant fixed costs. These information costs imply that the cost of pursuing a case are relatively high for an individual worker but much lower for a group of workers who can all benefit from the same investment in basic information acquisition (although workers may face individual information acquisition costs related to the specifics of their own case).

As a result of the existence of positive externalities in regard to benefits and the structure of information costs, a system of workplace rights relying on individual exercise of those rights will result in use of rights far below what is optimal for the workplace as a whole.[6]

A collective workplace agent can potentially solve the problem described above. It can do so first by internalizing the positive externality to workers arising from a claim as a representative of all workers in the unit. A workplace agent can also gather and disseminate information thereby lowering the cost of information acquisition faced by individuals. The specific elements required of such an agent are straightforward:

- Interests allied with those of the individual work—specifically an interest in the implementation of labor market regulations consistent with those of covered workers (this may imply institutional independence from the employer).
- A means of efficiently gathering and disseminating information on rights, administrative procedures, and the nature of workplace risks.
- A method of providing some type of protection against employer discrimination against individual workers for their exercise of rights.

While a number of different arrangements can potentially satisfy these conditions, labor unions potentially fulfill many of them through their basic agency functions.[7] Specifically, unions act as purveyors of workplace-based public goods regarding labor policies both by internalizing the benefits relating to worker exercise of rights across workers in the unit and by lowering the costs of information acquisition and by providing independent protection against employer discrimination.

As the elected representative of workers, a union is well positioned and has incentives to act on behalf of the collective interests of members in the bargaining unit. This means that a union will base its assessment of benefits arising under workplace regulations based on inframarginal worker preferences. In facing this allocation problem, a union can vertically aggregate preferences for the "public goods" represented by workplace regulations, following the model of public goods described in Samuelson (1955).[8]

Unions can efficiently gather and disseminate information on the existence of workplace laws and rights created by those laws. Unions provide this information formally through educational programs, in apprenticeship training, or through supplying educational materials.[9] Informally, union leaders (e.g., stewards, local officers) or staff (business agents, international representatives) alert members of their rights where a problem or issue arises. Unions also provide information on the existence of specific underlying problems, particularly in the area of safety and health (see Viscusi 1983). As stated previously, this information may be collected and disseminated through formal programs or channels or informally via the union structure or fellow workers.

Unions can also offer individual workers assistance in the actual exercise of their rights. This may result from the operation of committees established under collective bargaining, as is common in safety and health. Union leaders or staff also assist workers in the exercise of rights by triggering OSHA inspections or overseeing the performance of pension fund investments. Unions in industries facing frequent employment downturns assist their members in the mechanics of filing unemployment claims (or provide similar assistance in the case of workers compensation).

Unions also can substantially reduce the costs associated with potential employer discrimination by helping affected employees to use anti-discrimination provisions of the labor policies. More importantly, they provide this protection via collective bargaining agreements regulating dismissals. The formal protection offered by a collective agreement provides security unavailable in the vast majority of nonunion workplaces, even where a grievance procedure exists (Feuille and Delaney 1992).

Thus, if unions act on behalf of the collective preferences of the workers in the bargaining unit, they can be expected to induce greater usage of rights. In this sense, exercise of *individually-based* rights still requires an agent operating in the *collective interest*. More specifically, the connection between employee rights and implementation on one hand and unionization and the exercise of employee rights on the other, sets up a testable empirical hypothesis: *Government labor market policies should be more fully implemented in unionized workplaces than in otherwise comparable nonunion workplaces.* This hypothesis can be tested by examining a wide range of empirical studies of labor market regulations that have measured union / nonunion differences in different aspects of implementation.

The following section reviews major areas of labor market regulation dealing with hours of work, safety and health, pension benefits, discrimination, advanced notice of plant closing, compensation for injury, and compensation for unemployment. Each section briefly describes the determinants of policy implementation under the law. It then examines the role unions can play in their role as workplace agents. Empirical studies of each policy are then reviewed to provide evidence of the predicted union effect on implementation.[10]

GOVERNMENT AND LABOR AT THE WORKPLACE: AN EMPIRICAL REVIEW

Regulation of Overtime

The Fair Labor Standards Act (FLSA) of 1938 creates minimum standards of pay and maximum hours of work for the U.S. labor force.[11] Specifically, in regard to overtime, the FLSA requires employers to pay workers time-a-one-half of their hourly rate for work in excess of 40 hours per week. The two major justifications for overtime regulations are to protect workers from excessive time demands by employers and to promote employment by raising the costs of reliance on overtime in staffing decisions.[12]

FLSA overtime enforcement is relatively simple: government compliance officers initiate investigations on their own or respond to employee complaints concerning nonpayment of overtime wages. Employers found in violation of the law receive one of two penalties: if they are a first-time violator, they must pay affected employees only back payments of the premium pay they have been denied (provided that compliance officers do not find evidence of falsification). A second-time or multiple offender faces fines in addition to back pay.

Resources to enforce overtime pay provisions are very limited. While overtime standards are relatively simple (as opposed to the voluminous and complex standards underlying OSHA and MSHA), compliance officers also enforce standards dealing with minimum wage, equal pay, and child labor provisions. As a result, compliance officers rarely initiate overtime enforcement actions. Instead employee-initiated complaints serve as the principle means of implementing overtime provisions.

The presence of a union at a workplace increases the willingness of workers to initiate overtime complaints for a number of reasons. Union officers and union membership have a direct interest in FLSA enforcement. Enforcement of overtime provisions ensures fair treatment for members but also potentially provides for an expanded workforce (and membership base). In this sense, overtime improves the position of present members of a union and expands the potential number of union members in the long term.

Collective bargaining agreements provide recourse to union members who fail to receive premium pay for overtime. Virtually all collective bargaining agreements include provisions requiring premium pay for overtime work.[13] In 1992, the overtime standard embodied in FLSA was incorporated in 99 percent of manufacturing agreements and 93 percent of non-manufacturing contracts.[14] Hence, through enforcement of the contract (i.e., via contract administration) legal overtime standards are effectively enforced. As a result of this contract administration effect, the probability of an employee initiating a Department of Labor action when a unionized employer fails to provide premium pay is extremely high. Unions therefore provide a strong institutional mechanism to promote FLSA overtime enforcement.

Empirical Evidence: An extensive empirical analysis by Ehrenberg and Schumann (1981, 1982) of the overtime provisions of the Fair Labor Standards Act supports the hypothesized union effect on employer compliance. Drawing on data from the May 1978 Current Population Survey, the authors find that unions lower the level of *noncompliance* relative to comparable nonunion cases of otherwise similar individuals.[15] Specifically, noncompliance with FLSA overtime standards occurs in 18.1 percent of unionized cases versus almost 24.5 percent of nonunion cases, all other factors held constant.[16] In this regard, Ehrenberg and Schumann note, "Both data bases indicate quite clearly that noncompliance rates are significantly lower in firms in which unions are present than they are in nonunion firms" (1982, p.80). A more recent study by Trejo (1991) corroborates the Ehrenberg and Schumann findings that unions on average considerably raise the rate of overtime pay compliance. As a result, Trejo concludes that "…unions can be interpreted as policing organizations which increase the likelihood that noncompliance is recognized and reported to enforcement agencies" (p.730).

Enforcement of collective bargaining contracts is synonymous with enforcement of FLSA. In this sense, the enforcement of FLSA has been virtually "privatized" by labor unions. The counter case can also be made: enforcement in nonunion workplaces must rely predominately upon the threat posed by the Department of Labor in independently initiating actions or the threat of individually initiated employee actions.

Safety and Health Policy: OSHA and MSHA

The passage of the Mine Safety and Health Act of 1969 (MSHA) and the Occupational Safety and Health Act of 1970 (OSHA) marked the beginning of major federal intervention in the improvement of safety and health at the workplace. The purpose of both acts is to improve prevailing conditions at the workplace by encouraging employers to adopt specific safety and health standards (for general background, see Ashford 1976; Mintz 1985; a review of OSHA research can be found in Smith 1992). OSHA and MSHA implementation is premised upon the active enforcement of detailed safety and health standards in the nation's workplaces. Enforcement, in turn, is achieved by workplace inspections which monitor employer compliance with standards.

Employee exercise of OSHA and MSHA rights before inspection, during an inspection, and after an inspection are critical to achieving the quality of enforcement envisioned under the acts.[17] These rights include the right to initiate inspections, the right of employees to participate in pre- and post-inspection meetings between the inspectors and employers as well as actively participate in the inspection itself, the right to participate in any employer attempt to appeal a decision on penalties, violations, or abatement plans handed down by an inspector, and the right to all information dealing with employer compliance or noncompliance with health and safety standards.

Labor unions devote substantial resources to monitoring and improving safety and health conditions at the local and national level. Activities of national departments include sponsoring original research on health risks, creating training materials and programs concerning workplace health and safety, and keeping abreast of changes both in health and safety technologies and laws. Local union safety and health committees engage in workplace inspections, process employee complaints, provide information to members, and act as the designated workplace representative in OSHA or MSHA proceedings.

As a result of these union activities, unionized workers should be more likely to have information concerning the nature of health and safety risks in their workplaces, since on-the-job risk education is a common component of union health and safety programs. Thus, unionized workers should be better equipped to identify potential risks requiring OSHA or MSHA attention.

Empirical Evidence: Data based on 1985 OSHA inspection records in the manufacturing sector allow comparison of union versus nonunion enforcement activity along a number of dimensions (Weil 1991). The comparisons reveal pronounced union impacts on all aspects of OSHA enforcement.

Unionized workplaces are far more likely to be inspected than nonunion workplaces. For example, unionized workplaces with 250-499 workers have a 50 percent chance of being inspected in a given year, while a comparably sized nonunion firm faces only a 19 percent chance. For very large workplaces, unionized employers can virtually be assured of at least one inspection each year, while the probability is barely above 15 percent for a similarly-sized nonunion employer.

Once an inspection has been initiated, union / nonunion differences remain pronounced. Unionized establishments receive far longer and more intense inspections than comparable nonunion establishments. OSHA inspections in larger union workplaces (with more than 100 employees) detect 1.4 to 5.3 more violations per 100 employees than in *comparable* nonunion establishments. In addition, unionized employers are forced to pay higher penalties per violation than nonunion counterparts. This effect is most dramatic for the largest workplaces, where unionized employers pay $67.48 more per violation than their nonunion counterparts. An analysis of the impact of unions in the construction industries reveals similar trends (Weil 1992a).

The United Mine Workers of America (UMWA) has had comparable effects on the enforcement of MSHA in underground coal mines. MSHA's presence in mining is more pronounced than OSHA's in industries generally, owing to greater stringency in the law (e.g., all mines are required to be inspected at least four times per year) and the smaller number of establishments under its purview. Nonetheless, the UMWA has a dramatic impact on enforcement, particularly among the smallest mining operations.

Union mines are inspected more often than nonunion mines—in fact, in 1982 MSHA annually inspected small union mines twice as often as nonunion small mines (21 vs. 11 times). Activities of UMWA health and safety committees reduce the amount of time between when violations are issued and the time they are ultimately corrected, particularly in small mines. Finally, the penalties incurred by small union employers who violate MSHA are far higher than those incurred for comparable violations in nonunion mines (Weil 1990).

The Enforcement of ERISA

Pensions are contracts made between employers and employees that provide income to the employee following retirement. As such, pension benefits represent a form of deferred compensation determined by a set of eligibility guidelines created under the pension plan. The growth of pension benefits for private sector workers has been dramatic since the end of World War II (see Andrews 1985). As a result of the rapid growth of the private pension system, the Employee Retirement Income Security Act of 1974 (ERISA) was passed.

The intent of ERISA is not to require or even promote the adoption of pension benefits by employers.[18] Instead, it seeks to provide guarantees to those workers covered by private pension plans that they will receive agreed upon benefits upon retirement. ERISA increases the likelihood of workers receiving their pension benefits by requiring employers who have established pensions to comply with a set of minimum standards related to eligibility, vesting procedures, financial practices, and fund management.

The presence of a union supports enforcement of ERISA provisions regarding compliance with vesting and reporting requirements and adherence to established actuarial principles by pension administrators. To the extent that collective bargaining agreement provisions overlap with ERISA guidelines, contract enforcement will also serve to enforce ERISA (as was the case with FLSA). Union institutional resources (e.g., international staff expertise) may also assist in monitoring annual pension information provided to beneficiaries and the Department of Labor.

Empirical Evidence: Several studies provide information pertaining to the union impact on ERISA enforcement.

Eligibility Requirements

Unions require pension plans to include vesting provisions that adhere to the strict letter of the ERISA law. Freeman (1985) has found that unions lower the likelihood that pensions will incorporate vesting requirements *more liberal* than required by ERISA, other things equal. In other words, eligibility for pension benefits is easier to achieve under a nonunion than under a union pension plan.

In a related vein, union pensions are more likely to have provisions governing age and service requirements than nonunion cases. Freeman finds that employees in unionized workplaces must work on the average 70 hours longer to qualify for full pension benefits than in the nonunion case. This evidence suggests that unions require employers to adhere more closely to the letter of ERISA in regard to eligibility than might be the case in nonunion workplaces.[19]

Financial Standards

Union plans are more likely to stipulate that employer contributions be related strictly to actuarial principles than in nonunion cases. Conversely, union plans are far less likely than comparable nonunion counterparts to base employer contributions on the basis of profits. Further, unions also decrease the likelihood that a pension plan will allow for voluntary employee contributions. Thus, like its effect on eligibility standards, the evidence suggests that unions require employers to structure their pension plans more in keeping with the strict standards of ERISA.

Fund Management

Despite union investment of some pension funds for social or strategic purposes, the investment portfolios of union and nonunion funds look relatively similar to one another (Dorsey and Turner 1990). If the purpose of ERISA is to ensure that workers receive the benefits they are entitled to upon retirement, one should ultimately be concerned about overall performance of pension fund monies—that is, the rate of return in pension fund investments. Dorsey and Turner's analysis of comparative rates of return on pension funds indicates that the performance of union funds was virtually the same as that of nonunion funds during the 1977-1986 period.

Ippolito (1985) however, found that unionized firms and their pension funds are far more likely to be underfunded than nonunion plans.[20] As a result, union pension funds are more likely to become insolvent, resulting in Pension Benefit Guarantee Corporation (PBGC) bailouts. Citing PBGC data, Ippolito notes that almost 95 percent of the monies transferred through the pension insurance system (arising from the PBGC bailouts) has been claimed by union participants. Thus, the net impact of unions on fund management seems mixed at best.

Anti-Discrimination Policies and Comparable Worth

Anti-discrimination policy for the labor market is primarily based on three major federal statutes: the Equal Pay Act of 1963, Title VII of the Civil Rights Act of 1964, and Executive Order 11246 which draws on the federal government's role as a major purchaser of goods and services as a means of ensuring that contractors abide by existing anti-discrimination laws and promote hiring, training, and promotion of minorities and women. Taken together, the statutes are intended to protect workers from labor market discrimination arising from race, sex, age, religion, national origin, and handicap.

Among all areas of industrial relations / human resource public policy regulation, anti-discrimination policy represents the one case where the actions of unions have contradicted those of government regulatory efforts.[21] Unions in the construction sector have frequently been the targets of anti-discrimination suits. While construction unions have demonstrated the most egregious opposition to hiring women and minorities, disputes between unions and the government over anti-discrimination policies have occurred in other private industries as well as in the public sector (Ashenfelter 1972; Fallon and Weiler 1985).

There are very few studies of anti-discrimination policy enforcement.[22] Leonard (1985) provides some evidence of the union impact on contract compliance activity under Executive Order 11246. In a study of changing patterns of hiring of women and minorities from 1974-1980, Leonard reports that "...unionized plants are not any more likely to undergo a compliance review, the chief affirmative action enforcement procedure. Although the federal government in the 1960s directed especially strong enforcement efforts at the construction unions...our sample suggests that it has recently given equal attention to union and nonunion sectors in manufacturing." Thus, there seems to be little relationship between enforcement of Executive Order 11246 and unionization.

Comparable worth offers a second area to examine the impact of unions on anti-discrimination policy. Comparable worth seeks to reduce the male / female pay gap by increasing compensation for jobs that are dominated by women that in all other senses are "comparable" to jobs where men dominate.[23] Legislation requiring comparable worth settlements as a means of redressing sex-based earnings disparities is currently limited to state or local government employees.[24] Thus, comparable worth differs from other areas of anti-discrimination regulation since it does not yet represent a widely-adopted standard for the private sector.

A comparable worth claim requires analysis of the existing system of job evaluation and compensation. The purpose of the analysis is to determine whether or not female-dominated jobs with characteristics (e.g., stress level, problem-solving demands, autonomy) comparable to those dominated by men receive comparable compensation. If the study finds disparities, methods of altering existing compensation systems are agreed upon in order to narrow male/female earning disparities. Implementing a comparable worth settlement therefore has the effect of raising average womens' earnings relative to those of men.

In unionized work environments, this will be accomplished through collective bargaining, thereby putting unions in the center of comparable worth implementation. The ability and interest of a union pursuing comparable worth adjustments that may benefit female members at the expense of male members will in part depend on the overall percentage of women in a given union.

Empirical Evidence: Orazem and Mattila (1990) and Orazem, Mattila, and Weikum (1992) evaluate the impact of unions on implementing comparable worth settlement. Those studies indicate that in states where public sector settlements have been agreed upon, unions tend to diminish the impact of final settlements on pay disparities. This arises from union opposition to comparable worth recommendations requiring that pay increases for female-dominated jobs be accompanied by *pay reductions* for certain male-dominated job groupings.

The result of these interventions by unions in the case of a comparable worth settlement in Iowa is striking. Orazem and Mattila (1990) report that female / male earnings ratio prior to the initiation of a comparable worth settlement equalled .787. Compensation changes proposed under an initial pay equity study conducted by Arthur Young for the state would have increased the ratio to 0.880. However, modifications of the Young proposals by a joint labor / management steering committee lowered the ratio to 0.870. The ratio fell further to 0.829 subsequent to collective bargaining implementation of the proposals.[25] Orazem, Mattila, and Weikum (1992) found that unions have had similar impacts on pay equity settlements elsewhere, based on an empirical study of 23 states.

The comparable worth evidence suggests that, even in cases where unions have a significant percentage of women members, their activities tend to reduce the impact of pay equity policies. While unions have often taken the lead role in *initiating* comparable worth settlements (Smith 1988), the empirical studies suggest that their role may become less supportive in subsequent stages when comparable worth implementation requires advancing the interests of one membership group at the expense of another.

Worker Adjustment and Retraining Notification Act

The Worker Adjustment and Retraining Notification Act of 1988 (WARN) requires employers with 100 or more full-time workers to give their workers as well as state and local officials 60 days notice before closing a facility. It also requires 60 days advanced notice in the case of a layoff that affects 50 or more workers who represent one-third or more of the workforce or any layoff involving more than 500 workers (see Bureau of National Affairs 1988 for a background on WARN).

The underlying rationale for the legislation is to provide workers sufficient advance notice to allow them to look for other jobs, enter training programs, or otherwise prepare for job loss. Similarly, advanced notification provides communities with time to prepare for revenue loss, economic dislocation, as well as an opportunity for state or local governments to find alternatives to avert the closing.

In contrast to the legislation described previously, the WARN Act does not establish a separate agency or vest an existing agency with enforcement authority.

Instead, WARN relies solely upon civil suits brought by workers, unions, or affected communities in federal district courts as the sole method of enforcement of advanced notice requirements. Employers who do not give the required notice are liable for monetary damages to workers who would have been notified if their employer had obeyed the law. Allowable damages are one day's pay plus the value of benefits for each day up to 60 that advance notice should have been given.[26]

The law contains a complex set of exemptions related to the cause of the closure, its relative size, and certain actions of employers prior to closure (such as efforts to secure capital to remain in operation). Knowledge of the existence and requirements of the law is therefore critical to enforcement.

Implementation is by no means ensured given information on WARN's provisions, however. Since the act relies on suits brought in federal court for enforcement, the cost to an individual worker of bringing an action are potentially very high. Attorneys who have filed suits on behalf of workers note that workers are often hesitant to use WARN because of the expenses of hiring lawyers (GAO 1993).

Finally, since an enforcement action by definition occurs after a closure has occurred, it is more difficult for an individual to pursue a WARN suit than for a workplace institution like a labor union which persists even after the closing. These factors taken together suggest that unions should have a positive impact on enforcement actions brought under WARN.

Empirical Evidence

There have not been comprehensive studies concerning the implementation of WARN.[27] A 1993 General Accounting Office study evaluating WARN's impact on advanced notification of closings (GAO 1993) provides some data, however, which constitute a preliminary test of the hypothesized impact of unions on implementation.

Because of its structure, enforcement of WARN arises from suits filed by workers or communities not adequately notified about an impending closing or mass layoff. The GAO report presents complete data on all suits filed under WARN from its inception to the end of 1992 (see GAO 1993, app. B). From 1988 to 1992, only 66 suits were filed in federal court. Of the 66 suits, labor unions filed on behalf of workers in 26 cases (39%) brought under the act. This compares with 30 suits brought by individuals,[28] two suits brought by state governments, and eight suits brought by other groups.

Given the small number of suits filed under WARN and the limited information on characteristics of those filing, it is not possible to control for potentially confounding factors which might also be associated with the propensity to file suits. Nonetheless, the relatively large proportion of suits filed under WARN by unions is indicative of their important role as an enforcement agent, given WARN's reliance on federal courts. (It is also interesting to note the virtual absence of state and local government as regulatory agents in this area.)

Workers Compensation

State-level workers compensation systems were created as a means to protect workers from earning losses incurred from injuries and illness arising at the job. Employers are required to carry "no-fault" insurance which covers employees against work-related injuries in exchange for employee agreement to forego the right to sue employers as a result of these injuries.

When injured, a person covered under the workers compensation system must file a claim indicating the cause of his or her injury. Once filed, the state workers' compensation bureau determines whether the person qualifies for benefits, for what period of time, and at what level. Finally, most states have appeals procedures to allow workers to appeal denials or challenge allowed levels of benefits.

Implementation of workers compensation differs from the enforcement-based nature of the regulations examined above. While OSHA or ERISA attempt to change employer behavior in order to achieve policy objectives, the workers compensation system provides workers a viable safety net in the case of employment loss resulting from workplace injury. Thus, in analyzing worker compensation, one must explore whether or not workers who are injured on the job receive the benefits to which they are entitled.

Unions should promote use of worker compensation for eligible members. Unions demonstrate their concern over these safety net problems in bargaining for such things as hazardous job wage premiums (injury) and supplemental unemployment benefits (job loss).[29] Union structures are also complementary to the system of administration within workers compensation. Primarily, this arises from unionized workers access to union staff members (such as business agents in the construction industry) who can actively assist in initial claims processing and, if necessary, in subsequent appeals.[30]

As a result of the above, unions workers (1) should be more likely to receive workers compensation benefits than *similarly qualified* nonunion workers and (2) should receive higher levels of benefits *for a given type of workplace injury* for a given industry and occupational group.

Empirical Evidence

Unionized workers are more likely to file claims under state workers compensation systems than nonunion workers. According to a study by Butler and Worrall (1983), a 10 percent increase in the proportion of unions in an industry results in a 10 percent increase in the number of workers compensation claims filed, other factors held constant.

Krueger and Burton (1990), in a study of workers' compensation cost determinants, find similar evidence of a union effect on compensation claims. The study indicates a positive relation between unionization and workers compensation costs *after controlling for injury and benefit rates*. In other words, unions raise compensation costs above nonunion costs beyond what would be accounted for by either higher injury rates or benefit levels in those workplaces. This evidence can be seen as strongly in support of the Butler and Worrall evidence that unions facilitate the filing of claims.

Gleason and Roberts (1993) also report higher utilization of workers compensation system by unionized workers, based on a survey of Michigan workers injured on the job in 1984-1985 who filed a workers' compensation claim. Their results also suggest higher post-accident household income among union workers than nonunion workers, which is consistent with a union impact on benefit levels. The study, however, does not control for possible confounding factors that might account for these differences.

Unemployment Insurance

Unemployment insurance (UI) was brought about nationally via the Social Security Act of 1935 and creation of the Federal Unemployment Tax Act (FUTA).[31] Unemployment insurance is administered at the state level and provides qualified workers who have lost their jobs with benefits to compensate them as a result of these losses.

In order to qualify for unemployment benefits, an unemployed worker must satisfy three sets of eligibility requirements: (1) the person must have lost a job due to layoff in an industry or sector covered by the UI system and be currently available for and actively searching for work; (2) the individual must have been unemployed for a period of time greater than a minimum waiting period (usually one week) and less than a maximum duration; and (3) the individual must have earned a minimum level of earnings and/or worked a minimum number of weeks or hours in the 12-month "base period" prior to the start of the spell of unemployment. Given that a person has satisfied these restrictions, UI benefits are then determined as a percentage of the individual's previous full time earnings.

Implementation under the UI system (as in the case of workers compensation) depends on whether or not those covered and eligible for benefits actually receive them. Specifically, implementation is dependent on (1) whether those who are covered and eligible actually receive benefits and (2) whether those covered receive the level of benefits to which they are entitled.

Unions should positively affect members' use of the unemployment insurance system for reasons similar to those cited in the case of workers compensation. Many local unions in the manufacturing sector experiencing large job losses have established outreach programs for laid-off workers which provide support services, including assistance with filing for and receiving unemployment insurance.[32] As a result, unionized workers should be more likely to receive unemployment insurance benefits than *similarly qualified* nonunion workers.

Empirical Evidence

A study by Blank and Card (1989) on long-term trends in unemployment insurance benefits sheds light on whether or not unions affect unemployment insurance usage as predicted. Using samples of unemployed workers from the Current Population Survey, the authors compare the number of workers *potentially* eligible for unemployment insurance benefits with the number of workers who *actually* receive those benefits (which the authors label the "take-up" rate). Based on the difference between eligible and actual unemployment beneficiaries, the authors studied the determinants of this "take-up" rate. Blank and Card find that the fraction of unionized employees in the state has a strong positive effect on the estimated "take-up rate" of unemployment insurance. In other words, union workers who are qualified to receive unemployment insurance benefits are more likely to receive those benefits than similarly qualified nonunion workers.

Budd and McCall (1994) also find strong evidence that unions increase the use of unemployment insurance for their members. Using National Longitudinal Survey of Youth data from 1979-1990, the authors find that eligible blue collar workers who are union members are 17 percent to 25 percent more likely than comparable nonunion workers to received unemployment insurance benefits.[33] On the basis of their robust results, Budd and McCall conclude, "We believe that the statistically significant and sizable union effect represents an important avenue in which labor unions are helping workers exercise their statutory rights" (p.16).

Labor Unions and Implementation

Table 1 summarizes the evidence presented in this survey of research. With the exception of certain enforcement outcomes under ERISA and the case of comparable worth, empirical studies of labor market enforcement indicate that unions act as agents that assist employee exercise of rights thereby playing a complementary role in public policy implementation. This consistent body of empirical evidence confirms that unions improve the de facto implementation of labor laws.[34]

Absent profound changes in the fortunes of the U.S. labor movement, the workplace of the next decade will be predominately nonunion. Many have commented on the social costs arising from the decline of the labor movement and collective bargaining over the past decade (see, e.g., Freeman and Medoff 1984; Weiler 1990; Kochan, Katz, and McKersie 1986; Heckscher 1988).

This empirical review adds an additional social issue arising from the decline of collective bargaining and unions: the loss of an important workplace-based agent that fosters this type of participation. As such, future considerations of labor law reform (from easing the criteria for union recognition to raising penalties associ-

Table 1.   Union Impacts on Labor Policy Enforcement

Labor Market Policy	Enforcement Outcomes	Observed Impact of Unions	Empirical Studies
FLSA—Overtime Provisions	Adoption of standards	Inclusion in most collective agreements	BNA 1992
	Compliance	Increase Compliance	Ehrenberg and Schumann 1981, 1982 Trejo 1991
OSHA, MSHA	Inspection Probability	Increase	Weil 1990, 1991, 1992a
	Inspection Intensity	Increase	Weil 1990, 1991, 1992a
	Abatement Duration	Decrease	Weil 1990, 1991, 1992a
	Penalties	Increase	Weil 1990, 1991, 1992a
ERISA	Eligibility	More Strict	Freeman, 1985
	Financial	More Strict Standards	Freeman, 1990
	Financial Management	Neutral	Dorsey and Turner 1990
		Increase Underfunding	Ippolito 1986
Affirmative Action (E.O. 11271)	Federal Contract Compliance Inspections	Neutral	Leonard 1985
Comparable Worth (Public Sector)	Implementation of Settlements	Decrease Size of Settlments	Orazem and Mattila 1990 Orazem, Mattila, and Weikum 1992
WARN	Filing suits	Increase probability of filing suits	GAO 1993
Workers Compensation	Filing Claims	Increase Use	Butler and Worrall 1983
			Krueger and Burton 1990
Unemployment Insurance	Take-Up Rate	Increase Use	Blank and Card 1989 Budd and McCall 1994

ated with anti-union tactics) should consider the connection—and growing lack of connection—between unionization and implementation of labor policies as currently structured.

What do these results imply for reform of existing labor laws and the drafting of new laws? One important lesson that can be taken away from this empirical review is that unions in their role as agents of collective interest foster the implementation of laws. To the extent that those attributes of unions can be emulated more broadly, the nation's labor policies will be more successfully put into operation. The following section explores these lessons in order to find avenues to improve labor policy implementation.

IMPROVING LABOR POLICY IMPLEMENTATION

Recent labor policy initiatives continue to rely on employee rights for policy implementation. Despite the widespread reliance on this model of labor policy enforcement, unionization in the private sector continues to decline. One must therefore question whether or not the United States can continue to depend on the enforcement model implied by the majority of our labor laws if it hopes to achieve chosen objectives in practice. That is, continued reliance on employee rights appears to require finding new methods of enhancing worker exercise of rights in a workplace devoid of unions.

Improving performance of labor laws requires finding alternative methods for encouraging exercise of rights and / or drawing on other workplace agents to assist in implementation. The following section provides a detailed evaluation of a spectrum of policy alternatives. It begins by considering how labor policy implementation can be improved *absent* active participation by employees, yet given continued government resource constraints. This involves greater reliance on existing public and private regulatory institutions to serve as a substitute for employee exercise of rights. Second, it considers a number of policies to improve the exercise of individual employee rights, assuming the absence of unions. Finally, it considers the creation of new workplace agents in the form of employee councils to play the role historically played by unions as employee agents.

Drawing on Existing Regulatory Mechanisms

A first set of policy alternatives recognizes the limitations inherent in relying on employee rights for implementation in a world of declining unionization. As a result, the burden of implementation can be entirely shifted to other public and private sector agents. The obvious solution is to increase the enforcement budgets of the Department of Labor. This is an unlikely solution to the problem—even during highly supportive presidential administrations, the ratio of enforcement resources relative to regulatory mandates remained low. Absent the resources to do so (and, given recent national political trends, *decreasing* resources for enforcement) public sector regulators must look to other means related to refocusing regulatory methods. Private sector actors (employers and other institutions), can also potentially serve as agents in certain respects. This section examines the efficacy of enhancing these public and private sector roles as alternative agents of regulatory implementation.

Refocusing Public Sector Regulatory Agents

Most private sector firms fall under the regulatory prescriptions of multiple labor policies and are therefore potentially subject to the enforcement actions of many different arms of the Department of Labor (or similar state agencies).[35] Private sector firms are also covered by regulations arising in areas unconnected to their workforce, such as environmental or product safety laws. Improved coordination among these public sector authorities could enhance the current regulatory role of the government in both union and nonunion workplaces.

Attempting to rationalize the inspection efforts of different agencies linked to federal and / or state labor laws could improve the efficacy of overall enforcement activity. Problems that might fall under the purview of one part of the Department of Labor might be connected to those regulated by another department. Both problems, in turn, might arise from a third, separate area of labor regulation. Take, for example, the problems of safety revealed by the tragedy in a Hamlet, North Carolina, chicken processing plant. In 1991, 25 people at the Imperial Food Products plant died as a result of a fire in the facility. The fire raised awareness of the widespread workplace dangers present in the industry, including poor enforcement of fire code standards and high rates of serious job injuries.[36] An integrated approach to labor policy enforcement would seek to find patterns of violations. For example, the high level of injuries might arise from a pattern of labor law violations: First, the industry may be in violation of key safety standards (as was the case in the Hamlet facility where a number of fire escape doors were blocked). It is also possible, however, that the high industry injury rates are also associated with the use of an inexperienced workforce (possibly in violation of child labor regulations) or the abuse of overtime (in violation of FLSA).

Workplace injuries might also result from violation of other important standards related to worker safety that fall under the domain of other governmental bodies. For example, violation of Food and Drug Administration regulations affecting inspection might allow processing operations to exceed the optimal pace for production lines. Failure to comply with fire code standards governed by state and local building codes was a contributing factor in Hamlet, where a number of fire escape doors were physically blocked (Smother 1991).

In this light, government inspection efforts would become multi-pronged where tenable, directed at analyzing compliance with a *system* of labor market policies. Regulatory efforts would examine whether a workplace was in compliance with clusters of interrelated labor market policies, thereby requiring employers to bring *human resource systems* into compliance with public policy standards.[37] Not only would a systems approach to enforcement improve implementation, it could also lead to achieving overall labor regulatory ends in a more cost effective manner.

Child labor laws have drawn upon other regulatory agents in the past. Most notably, many states in the early part of the century relied upon local school boards to help enforce child labor laws. Describing the interaction of school boards and labor agencies, Commons and Andrews (1927) noted:

> Cooperation between the child labor inspectors and the schools is necessary that both may discharge their responsibility to the best advantage of the child. A careful issuance of employment certificates and thorough enforcement of the compulsory education law make the work of the labor inspector much easier. It is desirable, furthermore, that truant officers have the power to inspect establishments, where children are employed, and they should be the local representatives of the state child labor inspectors, reporting to them all violations and aiding them in getting evidence to bring prosecutions(p. 381).

School boards in several northeastern states began education campaigns in response to the Department of Labor crackdown on child labor violations (in 1989-1990).

Government agencies that regulate product quality and/or safety can act as labor policy enforcement agents. As mentioned earlier, the regulations of the Food and Drug Administration and the U.S. Department of Agriculture impact production issues in meat-packing and other food processing industries (e.g., production line speeds or hygiene conditions in work rooms). Since the enforcement of USDA or FDA guidelines also affect issues of worker safety and health, workers compensation claims, overtime, and other labor standards, their activities could be more explicitly tied into labor policy enforcement.[38]

In a related vein, there is overlap between the regulatory mandate of transportation safety agencies governing trucking, airline, and railroad industries and labor standards in those industries. Enforcement of standards relating to public safety can have spill-over effects on working conditions in those industries.[39]

A final area of regulatory overlap potentially arises between environmental and workplace health regulation. The passage of "Right-to-Know" laws in the majority of U.S. states creates shared interests between workers at facilities using or producing toxic substances and residents in the surrounding communities. By connecting residents' concern with potential exposure to toxic substances to how materials are handled *within* the facility, environmental agencies can act as agents of labor policy in the area of worker health.[40]

Harnessing Private Sector Agents

Businesses in the private sector frequently have an interest in assuring regulatory compliance by other firms both in the case of competitors and in the case of firms with which they do business (e.g., key suppliers). Firms that currently comply with labor legislation have an incentive to ensure that competitor firms also comply with those laws in order to ensure a "level playing field" in the industry. Disparities in compliance behavior can mean that those firms that comply with labor regulations face a competitive disadvantage relative to non compliers. This is a frequent problem among union and nonunion competitors in such industries as trucking (Wyckoff 1979), mining (Main 1991), and construction (Allen 1994). Competitive impacts of differential compliance is also an issue in terms of small versus large firms (Brown, Hamilton, and Medoff 1990; Dunlop 1988).

While firms are unlikely to directly police competitors, industry associations or trade groups can be effective forums for influencing member firms to comply drawing on the enlightened self-interest of complying members. For example, industries with predominately small employers sometimes pool resources in order to share training costs arising from compliance with complex safety and health regulations. Similarly, in construction where safety and health regulations apply to individual contractors and subcontractors but often involve practices that cut across the project as a whole, cross-company arrangements for safety and health are often created (these are often found as part of formal "project agreements" in unionized construction projects).

Private sector firms from one industry can also exert influence as regulatory agents on firms in other industries through their role as buyers and / or suppliers. This might be particularly applicable in cases where large, stable firms in one industry buy from numerous, small firms in another industry. One example of this phenomena can be found in the tripartite industrial agreement between the Campbell Soup Company, the Farm Labor Organizing Committee (an agricultural union), and small tomato farmers in Ohio. Under the agreement, the Campbell Soup Company provides assurances of tomato purchases to small farmers in exchange of those farmers' compliance with wage, benefit, and working condition provisions of the agreement with FLOC. By taking labor costs out of competition between signatory farms while assuring them a market for their products, the agreement creates an economic model in which all participating farmers have an economic incentive to comply with labor statutes.[41]

The Labor Department is attempting to draw on buyer / supplier relations as a regulatory tool in the apparel industry (U.S. Department of Labor, 1996). Minimum wage, overtime, and child labor violations are common among the small contractors and subcontractors operating in the apparel industry. Given their small size, the high level of firm turnover, and the reluctance of workers in those operations (often recent immigrants) to take actions against their employers, enforcement of standards is difficult.

In 1992, the U.S. Department of Labor announced a "nationwide education and enforcement initiative" to alert major apparel manufacturers and retailers of possible violations of the Fair Labor Standards Act among their contractors and suppliers. In addition to an educational component, the initiative warned manufacturers and retailers that they could be liable for FLSA noncompliance among industry jobbers, contractors, and subcontractors. Specifically, under

FLSA's "hot cargo" provision, the Department of Labor is able to seek an injunction to prevent the shipment, delivery, or sale of goods produced by employees employed in violation of the act (Bureau of National Affairs 1992b). Thus, economic incentives are placed on a limited number of major private sector players who in turn can place much greater direct pressure on a large number of small firms.

Encouraging Worker Exercise of Rights

The second method to address the problem of labor policy implementation is to find methods for improving nonunion worker exercise of rights. Following the benefit / cost framework described previously, improving implementation by relying on individual workers requires lowering the cost of information acquisition concerning laws and procedures as well as on workplace risks. It also requires finding methods to enhance protection from employer discrimination / retaliation which impose the highest potential costs on individual workers.

Improve Worker Access to Information

Unions provide a public good in the form of workplace information on legislation, job risks, and administrative procedures. They also provide resources to further encourage exercise of these rights. Absent such a workplace agent, other methods must be secured to provide this role. While knowledge about such legislation as OSHA, overtime, minimum wage, and discrimination is probably widespread due to their long existence, knowledge about specific rights under these laws is not. Individuals may know about the existence of workers compensation yet be unaware of how to file for benefits, follow claims through administrative channels, or appeal final benefit decisions. Similarly, information about the existence of OSHA does not mean that a worker knows how the agency may be able to address a problem related to, say, repetitive motion trauma.

Creating policies to improve access to information is relatively straightforward.[42] Policies can mandate the provision of educational materials within the workplace (e.g., through information posting requirements or workplace-based meetings with government agencies). The government can also attempt to educate workers outside of the workplace (via television, newspapers, etc.).

The government may also encourage other public, private, or nonprofit institutions to provide information on labor laws. For example, federal or state agencies could provide resources to nonprofit groups that have arisen to assist workers in learning about their rights, particularly in the area of safety and health.[43] Local school boards could provide students with information on minimum wage, child labor, and overtime laws. One might even propose providing incentives to insurance companies concerned with rising workers compensation cost to provide information on OSHA rights to covered workers (as is currently done on a voluntary basis by some insurers).

The decline in the take-up rate of unemployment insurance provides an example of the potential benefit of improving information concerning administrative procedures. The overall number of unemployed workers who receive unemployment insurance has steadily declined since 1975 (Rosenbaum 1991; Vroman 1990, 1991). Blank and Card (1989) have found that a major cause of this decline arises from the growing number of *eligible* workers who do not take advantage of unemployment benefits rather than a reduction in the number of workers eligible for benefits.

Presumably, the number of eligible unemployed workers who receive benefits could be raised through substantial educational efforts on procedures for filing claims. State employment agencies with responsibilities for administering unemployment insurance could target informational efforts toward communities with particularly high rates of unemployment. Those agencies could also find methods of streamlining administrative procedures.

Efforts to better inform eligible recipients of their right to file for disability benefits under the Social Security system provides evidence of the success of this type of informational effort. Increased eligibility information was cited as a major factor in an upsurge in Social Security disability claims for the fiscal year ending in September 1993 (*Wall Street Journal* 1993).

Yet, information provision efforts can only go so far in improving nonunion employee exercise of their rights. Particularly in the realm of complex labor policies, providing meaningful information is difficult absent a workplace agent. Indicative are the difficulties encountered in implementing OSHA's Hazard Communication standard. The standard requires that employees receive information and training concerning chemical hazards in their workplaces. A 1991 study by the General Accounting Office found widespread noncompliance with the standard in general, and particularly high levels of noncompliance among small businesses where the absence of a workplace agent is particularly acute (GAO 1991).

Strengthen Protection Against Discrimination

Even with information, fear of discrimination and employer retaliation can thwart the exercise of rights by a well-informed worker. Most labor polices provide some protection against employer discrimination related to exercise of rights. Yet, fears of retaliation persist (Steiber and Blackburn 1983, Boroff 1991). The experience of OSHA is particularly indicative. Despite the existence of an anti-discrimination clause in OSHA, its application has been limited. A study of 249 workers in Wisconsin who were fired for job-safety protests between 1981 and 1986 found that only 6 percent ultimately won reinstatement (based on a study conducted by Joan McManus, Director of Wisconsin Committee on Occupational Safety and Health and reported in Moberg 1990). This suggests that, at the very least, existing anti-discrimination provisions must be beefed up considerably.[44]

The problem of employer discrimination raises the larger issue of protection against the arbitrary or illegal termination of nonunion workers—one of the most controversial areas of labor law over the last 20 years. The changing status of "at-will" employment presumptions are at the heart of this controversy (this section draws on Perritt 1988a).

More than three-fourths of U.S. states have abandoned the Employment-at-Will rule (Perritt 1988a, sec. 1.12). In the past decade, a number of states have passed legislation protecting workers against unjust dismissal (for an interesting discussion of the emergence of unjust dismissal legislation, see Krueger 1991). The National Conference of Commissioners on Uniform State Laws released a "Employment Termination Act" as a model for considering unjust dismissal legislation.[45] Enactment of statutes based on this model could provide considerable protection from employer discrimination against workers who file claims under the aforementioned public policy statutes.

The model law would work in the following manner. Civil suits for unjust dismissal would no longer be permitted in the majority of cases. Instead, workers would be given a right to file a complaint in the event of a dismissal and have a right to appear before an arbitrator. If the arbitrator upheld the employer's position, the firing would stand. On the other hand, if the arbitrator held for the employee, he or she would be reinstated or receive up to three years' severance payments.

The use of arbitrators would presumably make recourse under the law relatively swift. Under existing termination law, evidence of employer discrimination as an underlying cause of dismissal is grounds for a public policy tort claim. By expediting such claims of retaliation in arbitration proceedings, and providing for quick reinstatement or maximum severance payments, a far more effective protective net for nonunion workers could be created than under current practice.

The most promising avenue of helping to make nonunion workers act more like union counterparts may therefore be the passage of effective termination statutes with expedited procedures specifically regarding discrimination linked to exercise of rights guaranteed under other labor policies. This, in concert with better information policies, may build a more aware and "aggressive" nonunion workforce.

The Plaintiff Bar

One can argue that individual employee exercise of rights can also be augmented through the plaintiff bar. In one sense, the typical economic arrangements between lawyers and their clients (i.e., payment of the lawyer contingent on winning the suit) create principal / agent relationships conducive to increased exercise of individual workers. The role of the plaintiff bar in regard to workers compensation claims is indicative (American Trial Lawyers Association 1991).

Reliance on the plaintiff bar, however, suffers from a number of serious drawbacks. First, information on the existence of rights under different laws remains a central problem. If the onus of seeking counsel resides with the worker, lack of information on rights and / or risks will deter implementation in some cases. Second, access to competent legal representation is by no means assured, even where legal fees are paid on a contingency basis. Third, reliance on the already highly overburdened courts to assure employee redress under the labor law inevitably leads to uneven patterns of labor law compliance since "enforcement" becomes a function of individual prosecution of claims rather than enforcement of workplace-wide policies.[46] In short, utilization of the plaintiff bar as agents of regulatory implementation will be limited by essentially the same factors regarding individual versus collective benefits and costs that limit use of rights under the status quo.

Creating New Agents

Seeking to create alternative workplace agents addresses the underutilization of workplace rights by both reducing the costs associated with exercise (similar to the policies described in the previous section) and by providing an agent that internalizes the collective benefit arising from the exercise of rights for the workplace as a whole. A number of academics have called for the creation of government encouraged or mandated employee committees, councils, and other workplace structures for employee representation (Freeman and Lazear 1992; Freeman and Rogers 1993; Weiler 1990, 1991, 1993). This issue was most recently addressed by the Dunlop Commission in its Report and Recommendations concerning the future of worker-management relations (Commission of the Future of Worker-Management Relations 1994). Specifically, the commission recommended "...encouraging experimentation with workplace self-regulation procedures in general and with specific reference to workplace safety and health" (p. xviii).[47]

Weiler (a member of the Dunlop Commission) has elaborated elsewhere on the merits of employee councils, modeled on the West German "works councils," as a partial answer to weaknesses in U.S. labor policy, including those discussed in this essay.

> [West German works councils] offer a workable and attractive alternative model. They have legal responsibility not just for carrying out collective bargaining agreements and enforcing employment regulations. The councils also influence, even co-determine, a host of personnel policies...A North American counterpart could require that every workplace above a certain size (say twenty-five employees) have an employee participation committee (EPC)...EPC's would deal with a broad expanse of employment issues...[and] would be entitled to be consulted before management could make changes in such workplaces conditions. In addition, the committee would play the front-line role in administering health and safety rules and other regulatory programs (Weiler 1990).

Thus, in addition to a broader, quasi-union set of functions, EPCs would play a role as the regulatory agent similar to that found in union workplaces today. Specifically they would fulfill the preconditions for employee exercise of rights in regards to labor policies.

While EPCs in theory could internalize workplace-wide benefits and lower the marginal costs of using rights, the proposal also raises a number of questions. First, the political difficulties in passing such legislation are considerable.[48] It is especially difficult to imagine a political consensus emerging around the concept of requiring employee councils coterminous with a larger labor policy shift toward individually-focused rights. Even if a political consensus emerges, however, such legislation would paradoxically face a problem akin to the central issue posed in this essay: ensuring the law's implementation. Mandating EPCs and securing the establishment of active and effective committees is hardly synonymous.[49]

As in other areas of labor policy, the government would need to ensure that workers were informed about their rights to form EPCs. Also, the government would need to regulate the process of EPC formation if, as Weiler argues, these committees would be composed of rank and file employees elected by a secret ballot of fellow workers.

Finally and most problematic, government would need to ensure that EPCs operated "effectively" and were capable of undertaking their regulatory and consultative role in the workplace. The voluminous labor law arising under the Labor Management Relations Act vividly illustrates the complexity of enforcing labor laws rooted in contractual labor / management relations. A non-contractually based system of workplace regulation raises even more difficulties.

These problems with the employee council concept can be seen in analyzing their application to safety and health regulation. The Comprehensive Occupational Safety and Health Reform Act (COSHRA) introduced by Sen. Edward Kennedy in August 1991 embodied many of the proposals discussed here. Among other provisions, it would have created stronger rights to refuse hazardous work, strengthen anti-discrimination provisions, and enhance worker rights to initiate inspections.[50] The feature of COSHRA, however, that received greatest attention was the one that mandated all employers with 11 or more workers to establish management / employee safety and health committees.

The committees would be vested with the authority to review employer safety and health programs, investigate fatalities, injuries and illnesses, conduct inspections once every three months, and make recommendations to employers. Thus, by mandating safety and health committees in all workplaces, risks would be addressed in an ongoing fashion even absent OSHA intervention.

The stumbling block to this proposal again lies in the problem of implementation. Mandating the formation of committees does not ensure the creation of active and effective safety and health committees. Nonunion workers are reluctant to exercise their rights under the circumscribed set of rights currently granted them by OSHA. The probability that these workers will exercise more extensive rights in committee settings seems highly questionable, particularly in small nonunion workplaces.

This problem is reflected in the experience of the state of Oregon which imposed labor-management committee requirements similar to those in COSHRA in 1991 (Weil 1994b). Much like COSHRA, the intent of the legislation was to encourage internal regulation of safety and health conditions in both union and nonunion workplaces. Nonetheless, union / nonunion differentials in a wide range of OSHA enforcement outcomes *grew* substantially between 1989-1990 (previous to passage of the committee requirements) and 1992-1993 (the first two full years of operations). This suggests that safety and health committee mandates have *augmented* the impact of unions as workplace agents while having little overall effect in nonunion workplaces. Evidence from the longer-term Canadian experience with mandated safety and health committees reveals similar disparities in implementation and effects of mandated committees (DeMatteo 1991; Tuohy and Simard 1993). Success in establishing safety and health committees in the majority of the nonunion sector will therefore only occur if attention is paid to providing incentives, information, and resources for establishing these efforts. Similar conclusions hold for the more general application of mandated employee councils as a method of fostering employee involvement in policy implementation.

Labor policy implementation could be augmented by refocusing and better utilizing private and public regulatory institutions, finding new means of increasing employee exercise of rights, and by creating new workplace agents. For example, OSHA implementation could be improved by simultaneously increasing worker training concerning job risks and safety rights, beefing up anti-discrimination enforcement, providing more comprehensive, cross-agency inspections, and possibly mandating safety and health committees (at least in risky workplaces) (Weil 1992b provides a detailed application of these principles of reform to the case of OSHA).

Yet each of these policies suffers from their own distinct limitations. That there is no single panacea, however, should not be completely surprising: No single policy can adequately deal with the fact that U.S. labor law was not fashioned with a uniform notion of how laws on paper might be optimally implemented in fact.

CONCLUSION

A critical, but neglected, facet of employee participation involves workers acting as agents of public policies. This notion implies that, quite apart from the potential impact of employee participation on performance (e.g., Ichniowski 1992; Kleiner, Block, Roomkin, and Salsburg 1987), such participation is an important element in securing implementation of our complex body of labor policies. Absent this aspect of employee participation, there will continue to be a major gap between the de jure and de facto impact of labor regulations.

The importance of employee participation to policy implementation highlights an emerging irony in U.S. labor law: labor policy implementation increasingly relies on individually- rather than collectively-based rights in the workplace.[51] Yet, the use of these individual rights appears to be highly reliant on the presence of a *collective* agent. Nowhere is this irony more apparent than under WARN: a collectively-based workplace problem (plant closings and major layoffs) are dealt with through suits brought by individual workers.[52]

Debates on labor policy have always focused on the relative merits of interventions in the labor market. Relatively little attention has been paid to the question of whether the labor policy, once enacted, can be realistically implemented. Yet implementation is increasingly problematic: studies of such recent pieces of legislation, such as WARN, the Hazard Communication Standard under OSHA, and the Americans with Disabilities Act, all indicate low or at best moderate levels of compliance among covered employers (GAO 1991, 1993).

The implication of this enquiry is that questions of implementation must also be central to future labor policy debates.[53] Should we worry about the merits of extending unemployment insurance benefits when half of eligible workers do not ultimately receive them? Should safety and health debates focus on reducing permissible chemical exposure limits when a majority of workplaces are out of compliance with present limits? Should we believe that communities are protected from major employment dislocations arising from plant closings if workers in those communities are unaware of federal legislation pertaining to advance notice? Is it realistic to extend discrimination protection to the disabled if few will actually have recourse to such protection in practice? These and related questions testify to the importance of reexamining the conceptual and implementation foundations of the laws regulating U.S. workplaces.

ACKNOWLEDGMENTS

I am grateful to John Delaney, Peter Doeringer, John T. Dunlop, Shulamit Kahn, David Lewin, Ronald Mitchell, Donna Sockell, participants in the 1993 Industrial Relations Research Association panel on employee rights, and members of the MIT Industrial Relations Seminars for comments on earlier drafts of this article.

NOTES

1. The acknowledged importance of workers to implementation of OSHA is revealed throughout House and Senate committee hearings related to the Occupational Safety and Health Act. For example, "The Committee recognizes that accomplishment of the purposes of this bill cannot be totally achieved without the fullest cooperation of affected employees. In this connection, section 5(b) expressly places upon each employee the obligation to comply with standards and other applicable requirements under the Act." See U.S. Senate (1970, p.10).

2. This is a recurring problem under a number of labor laws. For example, a comprehensive survey of OSHA compliance officers by the General Accounting Office (GAO) concluded that "...many OSHA inspectors believe workers' participation [in OSHA] is limited by their lack of knowledge about their rights and lack of protection from employer reprisal" (GAO 1989).

3. Fear of such retaliation has been shown to have a dampening effect on use of grievance procedures in both union and especially nonunion environments (Feuille and Delaney 1992).

4.   Under FLSA, workers are entitled to back pay unless punitive damages are sought. In the latter case, in addition to criminal prosecution of the employer, workers can receive double back pay.

5.   The FLSA provides protection against employer discrimination arising from exercise of rights. Nonetheless, undertaking such a claim still carries with it costs if those antidiscrimination provisions are imperfectly enforced.

6.   It is a separate and more difficult question to determine the socially optimal level of workplace exercise of rights. This requires determination of the overall benefits of the labor policy per se and the comparative costs. However, if one believes that government resources must be augmented through the worker exercise of rights, the individual-based solution can be viewed as suboptimal.

7.   Williamson (1985, p. 254) points out, "[u]nions can both serve as a source of information regarding employee needs and preferences..." In addition to Williamson, the role of unions in providing basic agency functions is discussed in Freeman and Medoff (1984), particularly in regard to personnel practices and benefits.

8.   Union and worker interests may also diverge for a number of reasons. Median voter models of union behavior predict that union leadership tend to pursue policies reflective of more senior members of the unit whose use of rights might not be equivalent with the public goods solution to benefit valuation. Alternatively, principal / agent problems may lead away from optimal behaviors from the perspective of collective worker interests. For example, the union may have incentives to "overuse" certain rights for strategic reasons unrelated to the workplace regulation (e.g., as a source of pressure in collective bargaining or strikes). However, these principal / agent divergences in behavior may be moderated both through electoral processes and by worker recourse via duty of fair representation claims which tend to induce unions to pursue activities consonant with the preferences of represented workers.

9.   Indicative is a small handbook issued by the AFL-CIO Civil Rights Department in 1992 titled "The Americans with Disabilities Act of 1990: Unions Fighting for a Better Life for All People." The pamphlet was disseminated to AFL-CIO affiliate unions for membership distribution.

10.   This article does *not* address the separate question of whether implementation results in the labor market *outcomes* of concern to public policy makers. That is, it does not directly answer questions such as, does OSHA ultimately lead to a reduction in workplace injuries? There are several reasons for this approach. Our inability to adequately understand the characteristics of regulatory enforcement limits the adequacy of studies that have attempted to gauge more global questions of policy effectiveness. If we do not know whether or not laws are being implemented as structured (an area we do not seem to know much about), how can we interpret study results that indicate "no policy effectiveness"? These results may arise from the failure to implement policies or from the failure of the policy as a whole.

For example, from its inception analyses of OSHA have attempted to link OSHA activity to injury outcomes. Those studies have found evidence of only minimal impacts of OSHA on injury rates. Analysts have been quick to conclude that these results stem from the inferior quality of a "command and control" regulatory strategy. Yet few have questioned whether or not the law as formally structured is actually carried out in practice. Since OSHA has not been implemented as envisioned in the law, this leap in logic may be too large or even invalid.

11.   The Fair Labor Standards Act also sets the minimum wage. There is reason to believe that unions have an impact on minimum wage enforcement (see Ashenfelter and Smith 1979). However, the vast majority of union collective bargaining agreements provide for base wages in excess of the minimum wage. Of future research interest is the level of compliance with minimum wage provisions in union workplaces where contract wages are equal or slightly above the minimum wage and the comparable compliance rate of nonunion establishments.

12.   Employer coverage under FLSA varies both in terms of industry and occupational group. For example, Section 13(a)(1) exempts employees who work in executive or administrative positions while Section 7 exempts a variety of industries including agriculture, federal fire protection, tobacco handling, and the self-employed. As a result of these exemptions, only about 60 percent of wage and salary workers are currently covered by FLSA overtime provisions.

13. The inclusion of the overtime standard itself in collective bargaining contracts contrasts with the case of OSHA and MSHA where one does not find OSHA *standards* imbedded in the contract (although OSHA rights sometimes are).

14. Daily overtime premiums are spelled out in 92 percent of agreements (92% of these specify 8 hours as the "magic number," 5 percent require less than eight hours). Further 99 percent of contracts that included overtime provisions include the FLSA standard of time and half for premium pay (Bureau of National Affairs 1992a, pp.49-50).

15. Noncompliance is defined as failing to provide employees who work overtime with premium pay for additional hours worked.

16. These estimates are based on Ehrenberg and Schumann's (1982) Table 5.5 (p. 88) estimates of noncompliance, model 2, and Appendix Table D.5, "Implied Partial Derivatives, OLS Noncompliance Results" (p. 160).

17. The Labor Management Relations Act and subsequent interpretations of it by the National Labor Relations Board also enumerates a set of worker rights germane to safety and health but are not dealt with here. For an overview of these rights, see Ashford and Katz (1977) and Bokat and Thompson (1988, chap. 17).

18. Empirical evidence indicates that unions have played a dramatic role in promoting the adoption of pension plans in the private sector. This effect of unions became particularly pronounced following the Supreme Court decision in the 1949 *Inland Steel* case (336 U.S. 960. 24 LRRM 2019) where the Supreme Court ruled that pensions were a mandatory subject of collective bargaining. Allen and Clark (1987) demonstrate that workers covered by union contracts are 26.3 percent more likely to be covered by a pension than nonunion workers, holding constant the impact of establishment and company size, wages, industry, and other variables. However, since the intent of ERISA is not pension *promotion*, this union effect cannot be cited as comparable to the effects examined in this paper.

19. As the results indicate, however, stricter adherence can actually make it more difficult for a given worker to qualify for pension benefits.

20. Ippolito (1985) makes a different argument resulting in the same prediction. Ippolito hypothesizes that unionized firms have an incentive to underfund defined benefit plans as insurance against union attempts to increase wages when those firms begin to receive returns on long-term investments in human capital. By underfunding, the senior union members risk losing pension benefits not guaranteed by the Pension Benefit Guarantee Corporation, thereby lowering the incentives for "holdups" by the union. The absence of such bargaining games in the nonunion case leads to Ippolito's prediction of greater underfunding in the union sector, other things equal.

21. Unions have been shown to reduce overall pay inequitites relative to comparable nonunion workplaces (Freeman and Medoff 1984). Our focus here, as in the rest of the paper, however, concerns impact on enforcement activity per se.

22. No studies are currently available on the impact of unions on filing of suits under the various anti-discrimination laws. While anecdotal evidence suggests that unions have helped workers in certain industries bring anti-discrimination suits, the author is currently attempting to estimate the impact of unions on the filing of complaint suits under Title VII of the Civil Rights Act.

23. As in other areas of this paper, I do not attempt to evaluate the efficacy of the specific public policy initiative. Whether or not it makes sense to pursue a larger policy of comparable worth in the workplace is not at issue here. For an introductory discussion, see Hill and Killingsworth (1989).

24. As of 1992, eight states implemented comparable worth provisions for state employees, although more than half of all states have established comparable worth task forces to study the issue (see Orazem, Mattila, and Weikum 1992).

25. Based on Orazem and Mattila (1990, Table 3, p.144). The reduction in the female / male earning ratio from collective bargaining resulted from an agreement between the state and the American Federation of State County and Municipal Employees that reduced the size of comparable worth pay increases in exchange for no pay cuts to any employee group in the unit.

26.   Employers are also liable to the local community for damages of up to $500 a day for each day that notice was not given. While a federal court may require payment of damages, it does not have authority to enjoin the plant closing or layoff.

27.   Several studies have examined the impact of advance notice on employment outcomes (see, e.g., Addison and Portugal 1992; Swaim and Podgursky 1990). These studies, however, do not evaluate enforcement or compliance, per se.

28.   The union status of individuals who brought suit cannot be determined from the information provided in the GAO study. To the extent that some of the individuals were assisted by unions, the number of suits involving unions cited in the text is a lower bound estimate.

29.   Under workers compensation, however, there is also a possibility that contradictory objectives might exist between government and union objectives in the case that unions promote worker compensation use in excess of that which is desirable from the public perspective (that is for non-meritorious claims for benefits). While union officers might be adverse to pursuing such claims, since it causes their employers to bear higher worker compensation costs in the long run, political pressures might force unions to pursue such claims where they might not be pursued in nonunion settings.

30.   In terms of financing, the structure of unions are also complementary to that of the workers compensation agency: It is in the interest of the union to ensure that employers correctly represent the true composition of their workforce, which partially determines the contribution an employer must pay in a given year to the workers compesation system.

31.   Several states had created forms of unemployment compensation prior to 1935. For a history of early unemployment insurance laws, see Malisoff (1939) and Peterson (1935).

32.   Unions in many industries also affect the total benefits received by members experiencing job loss as a result of collective bargaining provisions providing for supplemental unemployment insurance benefits (SUB). While only 20 percent of all manufacturing collective bargaining agreements in manufacturing industries contain SUB language, 48 percent of agreements in primary metal, and 44 percent in motor vehicle industries contain such provisions (Bureau of National Affairs 1992a, pp.42-47).

33.   The union effect remains even after controlling for expected duration of unemployment which are longer among union workers (and presumably raise the benefits relative to costs of filing for unemployment insurance benefits).

34.   The results do not allow us to conclude whether the degree of enforcement represents the optimal level of enforcement. For example, one may argue that unions lead to a misallocation of limited inspection resources to large union establishments under OSHA. As a result, small workplaces in the nonunion sector have become virtually untouched by safety and health enforcement activity. Ultimately, such questions can only be answered by returning to the question of the relationship between regulatory inputs (described here) and labor market policy outcomes of interest.

35.   "The amount of federal workplace regulation facing a particular employer varies...depending on the employer's number of employees and industry and whether it is a federal contractor. Of the 26 statutes and one executive order, 16 apply to employers across all industries, with the remainder applying only to employers who are federal contractors or only operating in particular industries" (GAO 1994).

36.   The injury and illness rate for the poultry slaughtering and processing industry in 1989 was 22.8 injuries per 100 workers. The comparative rate for the manufacturing sector as a whole was 13.1 (U.S. Department of Labor, Bureau of Labor Statistics, 1993).

37.   A potential model can be found in recent pilot projects in environmental regulation. The Blackstone Project of Massachusetts involves replacing historic "end of pipe" approaches to pollution reduction (i.e., separate standard for air, water, and toxic waster pollutants) with cross-media enforcement efforts to reduce all pollutants in the production process (Roy and Dillard 1990). In the project, two Massachusetts state environmental agencies are coordinating regulatory and technical assistance activity to increase overall compliance with air, water, hazardous waste, and Right-to-Know require-

ments. An early analysis of the program concluded that it provides a more efficient means of ensuring compliance with environmental standards than traditional "end-of-pipe" inspections.

38. In the aftermath of the Hamlet fire, the U.S. Department of Agriculture (USDA) agreed to train its inspectors to recognize a subset of workplace safety hazards. Under the proposed system, USDA inspectors on their normal rounds (which often include daily plant visits) would inform OSHA if they found evidence of safety violations. The training program, however, has been stalled within the USDA since 1991.

39. The complementary relation of unionization and transportation standards deserves mention. A study of the trucking industry conducted in the late 1970s found that unionized trucking companies were far more likely to comply with trucking industry safety standards (e.g., vehicle maintenance, adherence to speed limits, following weight restrictions) than nonunion truckers with comparable characteristics (Wyckoff 1979, chap. 4, 10, 11).

40. Improving cross-agency coordination is particularly important in one of the most difficult public and worker safety and health issues currently being tackled: the clean-up and disposal of radioactive waste. This approach is emerging in the current efforts of the Environmental Protection Agency, OSHA, and the Department of Energy to coordinate the clean-up of facilities like the Rocky Flats Weapon plant in Golden, Colorado.

41. Campbell was originally induced to enter this agreement as a result of a protracted corporate campaign conducted by FLOC over a decade. For a description of this contract and its evolution, see Weil (1994a). This type of industry agreement has historical roots in the industry agreements reached in coal industry in the 1870s which dealt with both coal prices and wage rates (see Brody 1993).

42. Ensuring understanding about the underlying labor market problems is less straightforward than informing workers about their rights. This is particularly true in regard to teaching people about job-related risks regulated under OSHA and MSHA. The general difficulty of perceiving low levels of risks and the particularly vexing problem of educating workers about long-term occupationally related problems is well documented (e.g., Fischhoff 1981).

43. Many states have "COSH" (Committees on Safety and Health) groups which attempt to educate workers on their rights as well as provide more general information on safety and health issues. The Occupational Safety and Health Law Center similarly grew out of a desire to improve nonunion miners' understanding of the operation and role of MSHA. For an example of material created by the latter group, see McAteer and Bethell (1985).

44. The Mine Safety and Health Act provides far more extensive discrimination provisions than OSHA (see Federal Mine Safety and Health Act of 1977, 30 U.S.C., Sections 801-962, Section 105[c].) The Comprehensive Occupational Safety and Health Act Reform legislation originally introduced in Congress in 1991 contained improved anti-discrimination language patterned after MSHA as well as strong clauses contained in the Surface Transportation Act.

45. National Conference of Commissioners on Uniform State Laws, "Uniform Law Commissioners' Model Employment Termination Act," approved and recommended at the Annual Conference Meeting, August 1991.

46. Early labor scholars of this century saw the rise of labor unions and the emergence of collective bargaining as a progressive step in workplace regulation. The "self-regulation" arising from collective bargaining, this view argued, was more efficient and socially desirable than that arising from direct government regulation, which in turn was more desirable than attempting to regulate through individual pursuit of complaints through the judicial system (see, e.g., Commons and Andrews (1927).

47. More specifically, the commission recommends, "Encouraging individual regulatory agencies (e.g., OSHA, Wage and Hour Division, EEOC, etc.) to develop guidelines for internal responsibility systems in which parties at the workplace are allowed to apply regulations to their circumstances" (Commission of the Future of Worker-Management Relations 1994 p. xix).

48. Businesses have been skeptical of such legislation in that it could be a "Trojan Horse" for incipient unions. Labor unions, on the other hand, are even more skeptical of the proposal's reminiscence to "company unionism" of the 1920s (see Nelson 1993 for a history of company unions). Since

that period, the AFL (and later AFL-CIO) has been on record in opposition to any policy of employee councils outside of those established for collective bargaining. However, recent AFL-CIO support of OSHA reform legislation requiring mandatory safety and health committees indicates a shift in organized labor's long-standing skepticism toward worker council arrangements in the context of specific programs.

49.   Freeman and Lazear (1992) and Freeman and Rogers (1993) advocate the use of government incentives to encourage the formation of EPCs on a voluntary basis. The problem of ensuring that such voluntary councils fulfill the objectives of public policy remains, however.

50.   For the text of COSHRA, see *Congressional Record—Senate*, pp. S11833-S11845. Despite Clinton administration support, the legislation was ultimately tabled because of Senate opposition in 1994.

51.   An early article describing this movement appeared in *Business Week* in 1985 under the title, "Beyond Unions: A Revolution in Employee Rights is in the Making" (July 8, 1985, pp.72-77). Perritt (1988b) and Weiler (1990) offer insightful discussions of this trend and its implications for labor policy.

52.   Bognanno and Kleiner (1992) raise a second irony emerging under U.S. labor policy. "...On balance, do labor market regulations, such as WARN or proposed 'termination for cause' legislation, substitute for collectively bargained benefits? If large union wage premiums are responsible for managements' resistance to unions, then public policy interventions should reduce these premiums and, therefore, employers' resistance to unions. There are two effects at work here. On the one hand, legislation may reduce workers' demand for union representation, and, on the other hand, it may reduce employers' resistance to unionization. Which of these two effects is dominant?" (p. 11)

53.   With respect to this observation, it would be wise to consider the admonishment of Dunlop (1976): "Ensuring compliance with a regulation is far more difficult than promulgating it...."

REFERENCES

Addison, J. and P. Portugal. 1992. "Advance Notice and Unemployment: New Evidence From the 1988 Displaced Worker Survey." *Industrial and Labor Relations Review* 45(4): 645-664.

Allen, S. 1994. "Construction." Pp. 411-445 in *Contemporary Collective Bargaining in the Private Sector*, edited by Paula Voos. Madison, WI: Industrial Relations Research Association.

Allen, S., and R. Clark. 1987. "Pensions and Firm Performance." Pp. 195-242 in *Human Resources and the Performance of the Firm*, edited by M. Kleiner, R. Block, M. Roomkin, and S. Salsburg. Madison, WI: Industrial Relations Research Association.

American Trial Lawyers Association. 1991. *Safe Work: Preventing Injury and Disease in the Workplace*. Washington, D.C.: Author.

Andrews, E. 1985. *The Changing Profile of Pensions in America*. Washington, DC: Employee Benefit Research Institute.

Ashenfelter, O. 1972. "Racial Discrimination and Trade Unionism." *Journal of Political Economy* 80(3): 435-464.

Ashenfelter, O., and R. Smith. 1979. "Compliance with the Minimum Wage Law." *Journal of Political Economy* 87(2): 333-350.

Ashford, N. 1976. *Crisis in the Workplace*. Cambridge, MA: MIT Press.

Ashford, N., and J. Katz. 1977. "Unsafe Working Conditions: Employee Rights Under the Labor Management Relations Act and the Occupational Safety and Health Act." *Notre Dame Lawyer* 70 (June): 802-837.

Becker, G. 1968. "Crime and Punishment: An Economic Analysis." *Journal of Political Economy*, 76: 169-217.

Blank, R., and D. Card. 1989. "Recent Trends in Insured and Uninsured Employment: Is There an Explanation?" *National Bureau of Economic Research* Working Paper No. 2871.

Bognanno, M., and M. Kleiner. 1992. "Introduction: Labor Market Institutions and the Future Role of Unions." *Industrial Relations* 31(1): 1-12.

Bokat, S., and H. Thompson, III. 1988. *Occupational Safety and Health Law.* Washington, DC: Bureau of National Affairs.

Boroff, K. 1991. "Measuring the Perceptions of the Effectiveness of a Workplace Complaint Procedure." Pp. 207-233 in *Advances in Industrial and Labor Relations* edited by D. Lewin, D. Sockell, and D. Lipsky. Greenwich, CT: JAI Press Inc.

Brody, D. 1993. "Labor's Crisis in Historical Perspective." Pp. 277-311 in *The State of the Unions,* edited by G. Strauss, D. Gallagher, and J. Fiorito. Madison, WI: Industrial Relations Research Association.

Brown, C., J. Hamilton, and J. Medoff. 1990. *Employers Large and Small.* Cambridge, MA: Harvard University Press.

Budd, J., and B. McCall. 1994. "The Effect of Unions on the Receipt of Unemployment Insurance Benefits." Working paper, University of Minnesota Industrial Relations Center.

Bureau of National Affairs. 1988. *Plant Closings: The Complete Resource Guide.* Washington, DC: Bureau of National Affairs.

Bureau of National Affairs. 1992a. *Basic Patterns in Union Contracts,* 11th edition. Washington DC: Bureau of National Affairs.

Bureau of National Affairs. 1992b. "Department of Labor Urges Garment Manufacturers to Comply With Fair Labor Standards Act." *Daily Labor Report* (March 24), pp. A10-A11.

Butler, R. J., and J. D. Worrall. 1983. "Workers' Compensation and Injury Claims Rates in the Seventies." *The Review of Economics and Statistics* 60 (November): 580-590.

Chachere, D., and P. Feuille. 1993. "Grievance Procedures and Due Process in Nonunion Workplaces." Pp. 446-455 in *Proceedings of the Forty-Fifth Annual Meeting.* Madison, WI: Industrial Relations Research Association.

Commission on the Future of Worker-Management Relations. 1994a. *Fact Finding Report.* Washington, DC: Author.

Commission on the Future of Worker-Management Relations. 1994b. *Report and Recommendations.* Washington, DC: Author.

Commons, J. R., and J. Andrews. 1927. *Principles of Labor Legislation,* rev. ed. New York: Harper Brothers Publishing.

Delaney, J., and P. Feuille. 1992. "The Determinants of Nonunion Grievance and Arbitration Procedures." Pp. 529-538 in *Proceedings of the Forty-Fourth Annual Meeting.* Madison, WI: Industrial Relations Research Association.

DeMatteo, B. 1991. "Health and Safety Committees: The Canadian Experience." *New Solutions* 1(4): 11-15.

Dorsey, S., and J. Turner. 1990. "Union-Nonunion Differences in Pension Fund Investments and Earnings." *Industrial and Labor Relations Review* 43(5): 542-555.

Dunlop, J. T. 1976. "The Limits of Legal Compulsion." *Labor Law Journal* 27(1): 67-74.

_____. 1988. "Proceedings of the Twenty-Second Annual Symposium on Labor Law: Should American Labor Law be Applied to Small Business?" *Villanova Law Review* 33(6): 1123-1139.

Ehrenberg, R., and G. Jakubson. 1990. "Why WARN? Plant Closing Legislation." *Cato Review of Business and Government* (Summer): 39-42.

Ehrenberg, R., and P. Schumann. 1981. "The Overtime Provisions of the Fair Labor Standards Act." Pp. 264-286 in *The Economics of Legal Minimum Wages,* edited by S. Rottenberg. Washington, DC: American Enterprise Institute.

_____. 1982. *Longer Hours or More Jobs? An Investigation of Amending Hours Legislation to Create Employment.* Ithaca, NY: ILR Press.

Fallon, R., and P. Weiler. 1985. "Firefighters v. Stotts: Conflicting Models of Racial Justice." *The Supreme Court Review* 1(1): 1-68.

Feuille, P., and J. Delaney. 1992. "The Individual Pursuit of Organizational Justice: Grievance Procedures in Nonunion Workplaces." *Research in Personnel and Human Resources Management* 10: 187-232.

Fischhoff, B. 1981. *Acceptable Risk*. Cambridge, U.K.: Cambridge University Press.

Foulkes, F. 1980. *Human Resource Policies in Large Nonunion Firms*. Cambridge, MA: Harvard Business School Press.

Freeman, R. 1985. "Unions, Pensions, and Union Pension Funds." Pp. 89-118 in *Pensions, Labor and Individual Choice*, edited by D. Wise. Chicago: University of Chicago Press.

Freeman, R., and E. Lazear. 1992. "An Economic Analysis of Works Councils." Unpublished manuscript. Harvard University.

Freeman, R., and J. Medoff. 1984. *What Do Unions Do?* New York: Basic Books.

Freeman, R., and J. Rogers. 1993. "Who Speaks for Us? Employee Representation in a Nonunion Labor Market." Pp. 13-79 in *Employee Representation: Alternatives and Future Directions*, edited by B. Kaufman and M. Kleiner. Madison, WI: Industrial Relations Research Association.

General Accounting Office. 1989. *How Well Does OSHA Protect Workers from Reprisal: Inspector Opinions*. GAO, T-HRD-90-8. Washington, DC: Author.

General Accounting Office. 1991. *OSHA Action Needed to Improve Compliance With Hazard Communication Standard*. GAO, HRD-92-8, Washington, DC: Author.

General Accounting Office. 1993. *Dislocated Workers: Worker Adjustment and Retraining Notification Act Not Meeting Its Goals*. GAO, HRD-93-18. Washington, DC: Author.

General Accounting Office. 1994. *Workplace Regulation: Information on Selected Employer and Union Experiences*, Vol. 1. GAO/HEHS-94-138. Washington, DC: Author.

Gleason, S., and K. Roberts. 1993. "Worker Perceptions of Procedural Justice in Workers' Compensation Claims: Do Unions Make a Difference?" *Journal of Labor Studies* 14(1): 45-58.

Heckscher, C. 1988. *The New Unionism: Employee Involvement in the Changing Corporation*. New York: Basic Books.

Hill, M. A., and M. Killingsworth. 1989. "Empirical Consequences of Comparable Worth." Pp. 90-106 in *Comparable Worth: Analysis and Evidence*, edited by M. Hill and D. Killingsworth. Ithaca, NY: ILR Press.

Holmes, S. 1991. "Workers Find It Tough Going Filing Lawsuits Over Job Bias." *New York Times* (July 24), pp. A1, A17.

Hoyman, M., and L. Stallworth. 1981. "Who Files Suits and Why: An Empirical Portrait of the Litigious Worker." *University of Illinois Law Review* 198(1):115-159.

Ichniowski, C. 1992. "Human Resource Practices and Productive Labor-Management Relations." Pp. 239-272 in *Research Frontiers in Industrial Relations and Human Resources*, edited by D. Lewin, O. Mitchell, and P. Sherer. Madison, WI: Industrial Relations Research Association.

Ippolito, R. 1985. "The Economic Function of Underfunded Pension Plans." *Journal of Law and Economics* 28 (October): 611-651.

————. 1986. "A Study of the Regulatory Impact of ERISA." Unpublished manuscript.

Kambhu, J. 1989. "Regulatory Standards, Noncompliance and Enforcement." *Journal of Regulatory Economics* 1: 103-114.

Kleiner, M., R. Block, M. Roomkin, S. Salsburg. 1987. *Human Resources and the Performance of the Firm*. Madison, WI: Industrial Relations Research Association.

Kochan, T., H. Katz and R. McKersie. 1986. *The Transformation of American Industrial Relations*. New York: Basic Books.

Krueger, A. 1991. "The Evolution of Unjust-Dismissal Legislation in the United States." *Industrial and Labor Relations Review* 44(4): 644-660.

Krueger, A. B., and J. F. Burton, Jr. 1990. "The Employers' Cost of Workers' Compensation Insurance: Magnitudes, Determinants, and Public Policy." *The Review of Economics and Statistics* 72(2): 228-240.

Leonard, J. 1985. "The Effect of Unions on the Employment of Blacks, Hispanics, and Women." *Industrial and Labor Relations Review* 39(1): 115-132.

Main, J. 1991. "Regulating Small Mines." Unpublished manuscript. United Mine Wrokers of America.

Malisoff, H. 1939. "The Emergence of Unemployment Compensation." *Political Science Quarterly* 54(2, 3, 4): 237-258, 391-420, 577-599.

McAteer, J.D., and T. Bethell. 1985. *Miner's Manual: A Complete Guide to Health and Safety Protection on the Job*, 3rd ed. Washington, DC: Crossroads Press.

Mintz, B. 1985. *OSHA: History, Law, and Policy.* Washington, DC: Bureau of National Affairs.

Moberg, D. 1990. "Weak Workplace Safety Law Needs Strength to Do It's Job." *In These Times* (May 23 - June 5), pp. 32-35.

Nelson, D. 1993. "Employee Representation in Historical Perspective." Pp. 371-390 in *Employee Representation: Alternatives and Future Directions*, edited by B. Kaufman and M. Kleiner. Madison, WI: Industrial Relations Research Association.

Occupational Safety and Health Administration. 1994. "A Study of the Effects of the Comprehensive Occupational Safety and Health Act." Washington, D.C.: Author.

Orazem, P., and J. P. Mattila. 1990. "The Implementation Process of Comparable Worth." *Journal of Political Economy* 98 (February): 134-152.

Orazem, P., J. P. Mattila, and S. Weikum. 1992. "Comparable Worth and Factor Point Pay Analysis in State Government." *Industrial Relations* 31(1): 195-215.

Perritt, H., Jr. 1988a. *Employee Dismissal Law and Practices.* New York: Wiley Law Publications.

_____. 1988b. "The Future of Labor Law: A Discussion Paper." Prepared for the Deputy Assistant Secretary of Labor for Policy. Washinton, D.C.: U.S. Department of Labor.

Peterson, F. 1935. "Unemployment Relief." Pp. 218-258 in *History of Labor in the United States*, edited by D.D. Lescohier and E. Brandeis. New York: Macmillan.

Peterson, R. 1992. "The Union and Nonunion Grievance System." Pp. 131-162 in *Research Frontiers in Industrial Relations and Human Resources*, edited by D. Lewin, O. Mitchell and P. Sherer. Madison, WI: Industrial Relations Research Association.

Rosenbaum, D. 1991. "Unemployment Insurance Aiding Fewer Workers." *New York Times* (December 2), pp. 1, 38.

Roy, M., and L. A. Dillard. 1990. "Toxics Use Reduction in Massachusetts: The Blackstone Project." *Journal of the Air & Waste Management Association* 40(10): 1368-1371.

Samuelson, P. 1955. "Diagrammatic Exposition of a Theory of Public Expenditure." *Review of Economics and Statistics* 37: 350-356.

Shavell, S. 1987. *Economic Analysis of Accident Law.* Cambridge, MA: Harvard University Press.

Siskind, F. 1993. *Twenty Years of OSHA Federal Enforcement Data: A Review and Explanation of the Major Trends.* Washington, DC: U.S. Department of Labor.

Smith, R. 1988. "Comparable Worth: Limited Coverage and the Exacerbation of Inequality." *Industrial and Labor Relations Review* 41(2): 227-239.

_____. 1992. "Have OSHA and Workers' Compensation Made the Workplace Safer?" Pp. 557-586 in *Research Frontiers in Industrial Relations and Human Resources*, edited by D. Lewin, O. Mitchell, and P. Sherer. Madison, WI: Industrial Relation Research Association.

Smother, R. 1991. "North Carolina Examines Inspection Lapses in Fire." *New York Times* (September 5,) p.D25.

Steiber, J., and J. Blackburn. 1983. *Protecting Unorganized Employees Against Unjust Discharge.* East Lansing, MI: Michigan State University, School of Labor and Industrial Relations.

Stigler, G. 1970. "The Optimum Enforcement of Laws." *Journal of Political Economy* 78: 526-536.

Swaim, P., and M. Podgursky. 1990. "Advance Notice and Job Search: The Value of an Early Start." *Journal of Human Resources* 25(2): 147-178.

Trejo, S. 1991. "The Effects of Overtime Pay Regulation on Worker Compensation." *American Economic Review* 81(4): 719-740.

Tuohy, C., and M. Simard. 1993. "The Impact of Joint Health and Safety Committees in Ontario and Quebec." Study prepared for the Canadian Association of Administrators of Labour Law.

U.S. Department of Labor, Bureau of Labor Statistics. 1993. *Occupational Injuries and Illnesses in the United States, 1991*. Washington, DC: Government Printing Office.

U.S. Department of Labor, Wage and Hour Divison. 1996. Augmented Compliance Program Agreement. Washington, DC: Author.

U.S. Senate, 1970. "Occupational Safety and Health Act of 1991," Senate Report No. 91-1282. 91st Congress, 2nd Sestion.

Viscusi, W. K. 1983. *Risk by Choice: Regulating Health and Safety in the Workplace*. Cambridge, MA: Harvard University Press.

Viscusi, W. K., and C. O'Connor. 1984. "Adaptive Responses to Chemical Labeling: Are Workers Bayesian Decision Makers?" *American Economic Review* 74(5): 942-956.

Viscusi, W. K., and R. Zeckhauser. 1979. "Optimal Standards With Incomplete Enforcement." *Public Policy* 27: 437-456.

Vroman, W. 1990. *Unemployment Insurance Trust Fund Adequacy in the 1990s*. Kalamazoo, MI: W.E. Upjohn Institute for Employment Research.

_____. 1991. "Why the Decline in Unemployment Insurance Claims?" *Challenge* 34(5):55-58.

Wall Street Journal. 1993. "Rising Disability Claims Swell Social Security." (September 7), p. A1.

Weil, D. 1990. "Government and Labor at the Mine Face." Unpublished manuscript. Boston University.

_____. 1991. "Enforcing OSHA: The Role of Labor Unions." *Industrial Relations* 30(1): 20-36.

_____. 1992a. "Building Safety: The Role of Construction Unions in the Enforcement of OSHA." *Journal of Labor Research* 13(1): 121-132.

_____. 1992b. "Reforming OSHA: Modest Proposals for Major Change." *New Solutions: Journal of Environmental and Occupational Health Policy* 2(4): 26-36.

_____. 1994a. *Turning the Tide: Strategic Planning for Labor Unions*. New York: Lexington Books / Macmillan Inc.

_____. 1994b. "The Impact of Safety and Health Committees on OSHA Enforcement: Lessons from Oregon." Working Paper No. 112. Economic Policy Institute, Washington, DC.

Weiler, P. 1990. "Who Will Represent Labor Now?" *The American Prospect* (Summer): 78-87.

_____. 1991. *Governing the Workplace*. Cambridge, MA: Harvard University Press.

_____. 1993. "Governing the Workplace: Employee Representation in the Eyes of the Law." Pp. 81-104 in *Employee Representation: Alternatives and Future Directions*, edited by B. Kaufman and M. Kleiner. Madison, WI: Industrial Relations Research Association.

Williamson, O. 1985. *The Economic Institutions of Capitalism*. New York: The Free Press.

Wyckoff, D.D. 1979. *Truck Drivers in America*. Lexington, MA: Lexington Books.

Advances in Industrial and Labor Relations

Edited by **David Lewin,** *University of California, Los Angeles,* **Donna Sockell,** *Rutgers University* and **Bruce Kaufman,** *Georgia State University*

Volume 6, 1994, 236 pp. $73.25
ISBN 1-55938-488-3

Edited by **David Lewin,** *University of California, Los Angeles* and **Donna Sockell,** *Rutgers University*

CONTENTS: Introduction, *David Lewin and Donna Sockell.* Beyond Empiricism: Towards a Reconstruction of IR Theory and Research, *John Godard.* The System Perspective in Labor Relations: Toward a New Model, *Arie Shirom.* Industrial Relations in Canada and the United States: From Uniformity to Divergence, *Pradeep Kumar.* Productivity-Enhancing Innovations in Work Organization, Compensation, and Employee Participation in the Union Versus the Nonunion Sectors, *Adrienne E. Eaton and Paula B. Voos.* Industrial Relations and Technological Change in the Workplace: Lessons from a Field Study, *Mario F. Bognanno and Robert A. Kearney.* A Multi-Method Analysis of Surviivors Reactions to Seniority-Based Layoffs, *Joel Brockner, Casey Ichniowski, Rochelle Cooper and Jeanette Davy.* An Exploratory Study of Employee Perceptions of Lump-Sum Payments, *James E. Martin and Thomas D. Heetderks.* Lump Sum Bonuses in Union Contracts, *Christopher L. Erickson and Andrea C. Ichino.* The Publishing Performance of Industrial Relations Academics, *Ahlburg and Michael B. Lee.*

Also Available:
Volumes 1-5 (1983-1991)
  + Supplement 1 (1990) $73.25 each

JAI PRESS INC.
55 Old Post Road No. 2 - P.O. Box 1678
Greenwich, Connecticut 06836-1678
Tel: (203) 661- 7602   Fax: (203) 661-0792

J A I P R E S S

J A I   P R E S S

Advances in the Economic Analysis of Participatory and Labor-Managed Firms

Edited by **Derek C. Jones,** *Department of Economics, Hamilton College and* **Jan Svejnar,** *Department of Economics, University of Pittsburgh, and Cerge,Charles University, Prague*

Volume 5, 1995, 232 pp. $73.25
ISBN 1-55938-586-3

CONTENTS: Foreword, *D.C. Jones and J. Svejnar.* Acknowledgments. PART I. EMPIRICAL ADVANCES. Workers Participation, Employee Ownership, and Productivity: Results from French Producer Cooperatives, *Saul Estrin and Derek C. Jones.* The Use of Hired Labor in Israeli Worker Cooperatives: 1933-1989, *Raymond Russell and Robert Hanneman.* Employee Ownership and Worker Participation: Effects on Absenteeism and Quit Rates, *Patrick Michael Rooney.* The Pepper Report: Profit Sharing and Employee Share Ownership in the European Community, *Milica Uvalic.* PART II. THEORETICAL ADVANCES. Allocative Efficiency and Discrimination in the Labor Managed Firm, *Ottorino Chillemi.* Transfer Uncertainty and Organizational Choice, *Thomas J. Miceli and Alanson P. Minkler.* The Optimum Size of Brigades, *Hans Aage.* An Overlapping Generations Model of Investment in Labor Managed Firms, *Michael A. Conte and Meng-Hua Ye.* The Size of the Executive Board of Labor-Managed Firms, *Nava Kahana and Jacob Paroush.* Altruism and Cooperative Survival: Is Altriusm Essential for the Survival of the Kibbutz?, *Yehuda Don.* Equality and Efficiency in the Moshav, *David Bigman.*

Also Available:
Volumes 1-4 (1985-1992) $73.25 each

JAI PRESS INC.
55 Old Post Road No. 2 - P.O. Box 1678
Greenwich, Connecticut 06836-1678
Tel: (203) 661- 7602   Fax: (203) 661-0792

Current Topics in Management

Edited by **M. Afzalur Rahim,** *Western Kentucky University,* **Robert T. Golembiewski,** *University of Georgia,* and **Craig C. Lundberg,** *Cornell University*

Volume 1, 1996, 260 pp. $73.25
ISBN 0-7623-0150-3

J
A
I

P
R
E
S
S

Advances in Interdisciplinary Studies of Work Teams

Edited by **Michael M. Beyerlein**, *Director, Center for the Study of Work Teams and Department of Psychology, University of North Texas*

Volume 3, 1996, 320 pp. $73.25
ISBN 0-7623-0006-X

Edited by **Michael M. Beyerlein** and **Douglas A. Johnson,** *Center For The Study of Work Teams, Department of Psychology, University of North Texas* and **Susan T. Beyerlein**, *Center for Public Management, University of North Texas.*

CONTENTS: Introduction, *Michael M. Beyerlein, Douglas A. Johnson, and Susan T. Beyerlein.* Foreword, *David Rawles.* Acknowledgements. Leadership and Team Citizenship Behavior: A Model and Measures, *Jonathan F. Cox and Henry P. Sims, Jr..* Self-leaders within Self-leading Teams: Toward an Optimal Equilibrium, *Christopher P. Neck, Greg L. Stewart and Charles C. Manz.* Leadership of Work Teams: Factors Influencing Team Outcomes, *Ren Nygren and Edward L. Levine.* Communal-Rational Authority as the Basis of Leadership for Self-managing Teams, *James R. Braker.* Creating an Environment for Personal Growth: The Challenge of Leading Teams, *Alok Baveja and Gayle Porter.* Better Leadership through Chemistry: Toward a Model of Emergent Shared Team Leadership, *Anson Seers.* Building Highly Developed Teams: Focusing on Shared Leadership Process, Efficacy, Trust, and Performance, *Bruce J. Avolio, Dong I. Jung, William Murry, and Naga Sivasubramaniam.* Leadership Teams and Culture Change: Changing Processing Structures and Dynamics, *Robert G. Lord and Elaine M. Engle.* The Roles of a Facilitator in Top Management Team Decision Making: Promoting Strategic Group Consensus and Information Use, *William P. Anthony and Don D. Daake.* Team Leadership and Development: Theory, Principles, and Guidelines for Training Leaders and Teams, *Steve W. Kozlowski, Stanley M. Gully, Eduardo Salas, and Janis A. Cannon-Bowers.*

Also Available:
Volumes 1-2 (1994-1995) $73.25 each

J A I P R E S S

New Approaches to Employee Management

Edited by **David M. Saunders**,
Faculty of Management, McGill University

Volume 3, Employee Management in Developing Countries
1995, 255 pp. $73.25
ISBN 1-55938-930-3

Edited by **Rabindra N. Kanungo**,
Faculty of Management, McGill University

CONTENTS: Preface, *Rabindra N. Kanungo and David M. Saunders.* Going Beyond Traditional HRM Scholarship, *Nancy J. Adler and Nakiye Boyacigiller.* Transnational Corporations, Human Resource Development and Economic Growth: Directions for Future Research, *Susan Bartholomew.* Restructuring Public Enterprise in East Africa: The Human Resource Management Dimension, *Jan Jorgensen.* Social and Labor Issues of Privatization in South Asia: A Comparative Study, *C.S. Venkata Ratnam.* The Culture of Collectivism and Human Resource Management in Developing Countries, *Rabi S. Bhagat and Ben L. Kedia.* Performance Management Systems Designed for Total Quality: A Comparison Between Developed and Developing Countries, *David A. Waldman and Helena Addae.* State Policies and Career Structure and Strategies in an Asian Nie: The Singapore Case, *Ern-Ser Tan and Irene K.H. Chew.* Cultural Diversity in Managing The Employee Selection Event, *Peter B. Smith, Mark F. Peterson, and Zulfiqhuar Gilani.* Modal Orientations in Leadership Research and Their Implications for Developing Countries, *Rabindra N. Kanungo and Jay A. Conger.* Prospects of Participative Management in Developing Countries: The Role of Socio-Cultural Environment, *Miriam Erez.* Organization Development for National Development: A Review of Evidence, *Kalburgi M. Srinivas.* Impact of Management Practices on Employee Effectiveness in South Asia, *Zafar Iqbal Qureshi.* A Review of Human Resource Management Successes in Developing Countries, *Alfred M. Jaeger, Rabindra N. Kanungo, and Nidhi Srinivas.*

Also Available:
Volumes 1-2 (1992-1994) $73.25 each

JAI PRESS INC.
55 Old Post Road No. 2 - P.O. Box 1678
Greenwich, Connecticut 06836-1678
Tel: (203) 661- 7602   Fax: (203) 661-0792